Barry O'Halloran has worked as an ... with the Irish state broadcaster, RTE. ... mother falsely accused of murdering ... *Innocence: the Inside Story of the Kerry Babies Mystery*. He later founded a digital communications company working in real-time financial information services with Reuters, Dow Jones Telerate and Thompson Financial. He has degrees in Economics and Politics, and in French and Renaissance Studies. More recently (2017), he was awarded a Ph.D. in Classics at Trinity College Dublin. His book, *The Political Economy of Classical Athens: a naval perspective*, was published by Brill in 2019. For the past two years he has been a Visiting Research Fellow at Trinity College. Barry lives in Dublin.

www.100dayscoronavirus.com

'The menace to understanding was not so much ignorance as the illusion of knowledge'

Daniel F. Boorstin.

Introduction to Edward Gibbons' *Decline and Fall of the Roman Empire.*

100 Days That Changed the World: the coronavirus wars

by Barry O'Halloran

First published by Raytown Press in 2021.

ISBN: 978-1-5272-8293-3

Printed and bound in the UK by Clays Ltd, Elcograf S.p.A.

www.100dayscoronavirus.com

This book is dedicated to the thousands of journalists around the world who covered all aspects of the Covid-19 pandemic. I have relied heavily on their professional reports as my principal source in writing this book. They are far too numerous to name individually, but I have credited their work with citations throughout, where practicable. However, for reasons that will be immediately obvious, I have made one exception to this naming rule.

Gao Yu has already spent over 7 years in jail. In 1989 she was locked up for 15 months as part of the Tiananmen Square crackdown, and in 1993 she was given a further 6 years under a catch-all charge of leaking state secrets – widely used in China to jail journalists.

Last year she received a further 7-year sentence. Her 'crime' on this occasion was reporting on a secret Party document that ordered CCP members to confront the seven subversive influences on society, which included, 'Western constitutional democracy' and 'universal values' such as human rights and free speech. Speaking truth to power has become a cliché in the west, in Xi Jinping's China it carries severe penalties which the regime demands be paid in person by journalists who dare to do their job.

Just before her arrest last year Gao said, 'You can change mountains and rivers but not a person's nature – seven years in jail did nothing to dampen my enthusiasm for news.' In November, she was allowed to serve her sentence outside of prison because of deteriorating health.

CREDIT: EPA

Gao Yu, Veteran Chinese Journalist (76)

Acknowledgements

Writing and publishing a book about the pandemic during the pandemic brough its own challenges. Doing so in a relatively short period of nine months has meant that, even more than is normally the case, I have relied on the generosity of many friends. When called upon, they have given unstintingly of their time and considerable expertise. The collective effect of this has been to add immeasurably to the book's readability. Those who have read the manuscript in its various drafts, either in whole or in part, and have offered astute comments and observations include; Brendan Barrington, Peter Barry, Hugh Barry, Ismay Ferguson, Andrew Lownie, Yvonne Murray, Suzanna O'Driscoll, Carolyn Ryan, and Declan Sugrue.

Though it happened by default, the indefatigable editorial support provided by David Blake Knox has been indispensable to the production of this book. David's detailed editing skills and thoughtful editorial guidance have been an invaluable corrective to the slips and lapses that are an inescapable aspect of the solitary business of writing a lengthy manuscript. It goes without saying, however, that David, and his fellow stars mentioned above, bear no responsibility for any of the remaining faults; those, dear reader, lie solely with me.

Producing a book to the highest standard of technical specification is well beyond my meagre electronic publishing skills. Luckily, as on previous occasions, I have been able to draw on the formidable professional talents of Florin and Dana Stroiescu. Their efforts have turned my often vague and ill-defined concepts into the pleasing publishing creation that you hold in your hands.

Marketing a book when the retail bookshop network was all but shut down meant relying like never before on online sales and distribution. As a social media neophyte, I realised that I needed to up my game considerably on that front. Those formidable challenges were eased enormously by the consummate professional advice and assistance of the up-and-coming public relations specialist, Catie Barry. James Barry, a software specialist, played a starring role in developing the website; www.100dayscoronavirus.com. It stands as a testament to his superb professional skills.

As already mentioned, this book was written during the Great Pandemic of 2020 and, like everyone else in the world, I experienced various phases of lockdown. The first lockdown was in Crete where my long-standing friends, Suzanna and Nektarious Koutoulakis, afforded me the kind hospitality of their home during my initial stay in Chania. Likewise, in Dublin, Mary and Declan Sugrue were equally accommodating in making my sojourn there a memorable and joyful experience.

Dublin, January 2021.

Contents

Introduction

We're just 20 years into the new century, and already we've been struck by two pandemics. SARS was the first in 2002-3, and its close relative, SARS-CoV-2, caused the second pandemic of the 21st century. At an average of one every ten years so far, the evidence of this book would suggest that the Great Pandemic of 2020 is most unlikely to be the last of the microbial assaults on humanity that we shall experience this century. The first pandemic could not have been foreseen, but that is certainly not true of the second. The response of most governments to the threat posed by Covid-19 may have been breath-taking in its ineptitude. But it has also been the product of a degree of negligence that borders on criminality.

A so-called 'black swan' event is an extremely rare and wholly unpredictable occurrence that results in severely adverse consequences. It has often been claimed that the Great Pandemic of 2020 was such an occurrence. It was not. The spillover event that caused this pandemic was not only predictable: it had been predicted many times over many years. In books and journals, virologists, epidemiologists and various scientific specialists, had not just warned that it was likely, but had insisted that it was inevitable. The precise date of the pandemic might have been uncertain, but there was a scientific consensus that it *would* happen. And there were very good reasons for that consensus. Infectious respiratory diseases had crossed from animals to humans - in Asia, in general, and in China, in particular - many times in the recent past. Scientists knew that the environmental conditions that had produced those spillover episodes still existed. For that reason, they continued to warn that similar outbreaks were bound to happen again. Their warnings were comprehensively ignored. As a result, most countries were not prepared for the onslaught of Covid -19. Will we be better prepared the next time? That depends.

From the start of the outbreak, most governments were staring at the unfolding disaster in China with a mixture of horror and fascination. Yet, astonishingly, they seemed oblivious to its instructive – and destructive – potential. Instead, the attention they paid amounted to a form of virus-disaster rubber necking. It seems only to have been China's closest neighbours who moved with speed and resolution at this stage. Inexplicably, most other countries failed to take any concerted action by way of preparation. The consequence of this delayed reaction was that the disease was able to establish itself endemically before they could do anything to stop it.

All advanced health care systems are impeccably well designed to handle discrete disasters like car crashes, explosions, building fires, and mass shootings. Their staff are likewise trained to deal with such events with the utmost degree of professional competence. Pandemics, however, are a very different matter. Despite hubristic claims by politicians that their health care systems and infrastructures were well-prepared to cope with the rapidly evolving pandemic crisis, their rhetoric was confounded by the reality in most cases.

Claims that they are merely "following the science" seem to have an irresistible allure for politicians – since it appears to absolve them from of any direct responsibility. An appeal to scientific authority also comes with the incomparable benefit of not having to justify, or perhaps not even to explain, their policy choices: if it's science, it's self-evidently good. This has the regrettable, and often intentional, effect of shutting down any further debate. However, these over-blown claims by political leaders to be on the side of the scientific angels works against the founding principles of science itself. Such an approach is specifically cautioned against by scientists themselves, most notably by the Royal Society of London (1660). Its motto, *Nullius in verba*, though often mistranslated, actually means 'take nothing on authority': advice that many of our political leaders should have been well-advised to follow.

At the start of 2020, the concept of "social distancing", and words like "coronavirus" were completely unknown to us. The emergence in Wuhan, in central China, of a 'pneumonia of unknown etiology' at the end of 2019 caused the worst global health crisis in 100 years. Not only that, it brought the most technologically sophisticated societies on earth to their knees in a matter of a few months. These were, indeed, the 100 days, in China and later in many other countries, that changed the world. But, like most black comedy, the control of an incipient disease epidemic is all about timing. There is a very narrow window at the start of an outbreak in which failure to take decisive action can lead, very quickly, to an outright catastrophe. Understanding exactly what happened in China during the first couple of months of the outbreak of Covid-19 is therefore crucial. That astonishing story is told here for the first time, using both Western and Chinese sources.

China's initial and calculated failure to sound the alarm about the coronavirus was compounded by the slow and indecisive responses of most other countries' governments. There were some exceptions – notably, China's close neighbour, Taiwan – but most of the world's countries have been besieged by a rapacious microbe for well over a year. Across the western world, lockdowns have fallen like a pall over our cities, and their bustling life has been silenced. Not knowing how or when this siege would be lifted – and for how long - added to a widespread and debilitating sense of helplessness. In a matter of weeks, a microscopic virus had ruthlessly exposed our collective vulnerabilities like never before.

We live in an age of mass communications, social media, and 24-hour news cycles. That means, when major stories break, the public is presented with a welter of undifferentiated detail whose real significance is often difficult to decipher. For people with busy lives, separating the signal from the noise in real time is a luxury few can afford. All the various news media, electronic and print, are in intense competition and scramble to be the first to reveal the latest details of fast-moving events. But this form of obsession with the latest minutiae often conceals as much as it reveals. We can, so to speak, become preoccupied with the individual trees, and fail to see the forest.

This book has been written during an evolving pandemic. Its purpose is to provide the reader with a prompt, comprehensive, and reliable account of a phenomenon that, in one way or another, has now touched the lives of every human being on the planet. There is an obvious need for people to understand what has hit them and why. They need to know why the response of most governments has been haphazard, hapless and largely ineffectual in getting the virus under control. They need to know the costs and consequences of all this. And, above all, they need to know now and not wait for a retrospective understanding to be made available some years down the road.

The account you will read here is not exhaustive – no account can be. It explores how a microscopic organism emerged out of the blue, and caught the world completely unprepared. It offers an extensive analysis of the short-comings and failures – but also the successes – of various governments' responses to that viral threat. In particular, it explains why, almost universally, governments resorted to the sledgehammer strategy of lockdowns to deal with the contagion, and why they have persisted with this strategy for so long – regardless of the damage it was doing to their economies and civil societies.

We have been sustained, indeed inspired, by the mundane heroism of the foot soldiers of our health and social care systems. Without question, when these frontline troops were called upon, they rode to the sound of the guns. But there were limits. And as wave after wave of the contagion swept through communities, those limits were sorely tested.

The coronavirus has cast a high-beam light into one of the darkest corners of the social-care system across the world. A shocking vista has been exposed. To put it simply: the most vulnerable in almost every society on earth were in receipt of the least comprehensive care. They were uniquely vulnerable to the virus, but the plight of these elderly citizens wasn't even recognised – let alone catered for - at the outset of the viral onslaught. There have been many failures by governments across the world, but the care home catastrophe has been without doubt the most calamitous. As a direct result of this wanton neglect by health systems, states, and societies, the elderly residents of care homes have borne the brunt of the pandemic and have died like flies – often in conditions of extreme isolation.

Like an earthquake, the virus seemed to strike suddenly. But the pandemic was no momentary evil: it tormented humanity for well over a year. At its simplest, this book is a guide for those who wish to know how Covid-19 emerged and spread throughout the world in 2020. But more than that, it analyses the significant consequences of this event for thc world economy and for the future of geopolitical relations.

Part 1

The China Syndrome

Chapter 1: The Bat Woman of Wuhan

The Call

On Monday, December 30, 2019, Shi Zhengli had been attending a conference in Shanghai. A small but dynamic woman, Shi was one of China's top virologists who had collaborated extensively with many US virologists over the years. At 7 p.m. that December evening, Shi's mobile phone rang. It was her boss Wang Yanyi, the Director of the Wuhan Institute of Virology. She sounded anxious, and as it turned out, Wang Yanyi had every reason to be concerned.

Just minutes earlier, samples from two Wuhan hospital patients had arrived at the Institute for further analysis. Both patients had been diagnosed with an atypical form of pneumonia of unknown cause. The preliminary investigations on these samples carried out by the Wuhan Centre for Disease Control and Prevention (CDC) had come to a very worrying conclusion: both samples contained a novel coronavirus pathogen.

For everyone involved, this immediately reignited memories of the disastrous SARS outbreak of 2002-3. Could it be happening again? Deeply concerned, the CDC sought the opinion of the Institute's pathogen experts, urgently. On the phone from Wuhan that evening, Shi Zhengli's boss was adamant, 'drop whatever you are doing and deal with it now', she insisted.

Shi arranged to take the next available bullet train back to Wuhan. Later that evening, the train departed Shanghai, China's largest and wealthiest city, and sped due west through almost 1,000 kilometers of urban and industrial landscape. Just a generation previously this had been some of the heartlands of rural China. But Shi was busy on the phone with her colleagues back at the Institute, and was too preoccupied to notice the images of a new modern urban China that were whizzing past her window.

On her mobile, Shi discussed with her laboratory team at the Institute the details of how they were going to set about testing the hospital samples the Wuhan CDC had sent them. A plan was agreed. They would begin work early the next morning. Though the train still had many hours to go before it reached Wuhan, Shi could not relax. Her mind was racing with unanswered questions. She had only started her professional scientific career as a virologist when the SARS pandemic struck China in 2002. Now, almost two decades later, had it re-emerged, she wondered? But how? From where? And why Wuhan in central China?

SARS 2002-3

The first SARS pandemic started in China's southern province of Guangdong in November 2002 where a local farmer became the first known case to be infected with the disease: so-called patient 'zero'. It quickly spread throughout much of the world, eventually infecting 30 countries. The pandemic's final tally was 8,096 recorded cases and 774 fatalities, with the vast majority of both infections and fatalities occurring in Asia.

Apart from China, the other Asian countries where the terrifying effects of SARS were felt most acutely were Hong Kong, Taiwan, and Singapore. The SARS pandemic created deep psychological scars which were to prove far more enduring than the disease itself. Even a decade and a half after the threat from the disease had dissipated, many people across Asia still continued to wear face masks in public.

Facemasks became the outward public symbols of the visceral fear and psychological trauma that SARS had inflicted, and a signal that coronaviruses had become a new preoccupation for humanity. At the start of the 21st century we had little inkling of the scale of the threat that these invisible microbes posed to human health and psychological well-being. Pandemic, a concept that in our modern complacency we thought we had put behind us, soon became part of everyday conversation. Even for those of us far removed from the epicentre of what was taking place in China, the possibility of a pandemic had very disquieting undertones. What we didn't and couldn't appreciate then was how viscerally unnerving it would soon become.

The Perfect Host

Scientists were aware that the SARS coronavirus strain had originated in animals, but they did not know which ones, or how the pathogen could make the jump to humans. There was a long-standing suspicion that bats were the principal culprits. These flying mammals were well known in scientific circles to be a major reservoir for many of the viruses that were extremely pathogenic to humans. A peculiarity of this phenomenon is that though the bats play host to these viral pathogens and can be heavily infected with them, the bats themselves show no overt sign of the disease. Technically, to use a term with which we were soon to become very familiar, the bats are asymptomatic.

There is no obvious explanation why there should be a relatively benign relationship between these hosts and the virus. However, from the extensive scientific investigations carried out in recent years, there is compelling evidence that bats are far and away the most prolific source of emerging viral threats to humanity.

In fact, scientists believe that because of a unique genetic quirk, bats can tolerate far more viruses than other mammals.[1] Not only do bats play host to a large variety of coronaviruses but, in the right circumstances, they can infect humans. One of the principal reasons why these zoonotic (capable of animal to human transmission) viruses are especially dangerous is that, having incubated in animals, humans have no natural immunity – we are, as it were, immunologically naked and exposed.

The Virus Hunter

The SARS pandemic of 2002 also had a dramatic impact on the career of a young Chinese scientist based in Wuhan. In many ways, Shi Zhengli was typical of the generation that had benefited from the opening up and subsequent transformation of China that Deng Xiaoping's 1978 reforms had started. Shi was bright, ambitions, outward-looking, and proud to play her part in the new China. Having studied at Wuhan University and gained a Masters from the Wuhan Institute of Virology, Shi received her Ph.D. from Montpellier University, France. In 2000, having completed her Doctoral studies in France, she returned to Wuhan to work at the Institute. As a direct consequence of the SARS pandemic and the subsequent international scientific quest to discover its origins, Shi became a professional virus hunter.

CREDIT: Shuyi Zhan

Bat Woman in Action

From a professional point of view, Shi Zhengli proved to be in the right place at the right time. The critical first step in the scientific detective work of investigating pandemics is to identify the origins of the virus and the channels through which it can be propagated. As the US-based disease ecologist, Peter Daszak puts it, 'it's incredibly important to pinpoint the source of the infection and the chain of cross-species transmission.'[2] The young Wuhan virologist was soon catapulted into the forefront of a major international scientific effort to discover the source of the SARS virus.

In 2006, Shi spent three months as a visiting scientist at the Australian Centre for Disease Preparedness high-containment laboratory in Geelong, south-west of Melbourne. The placement, which was funded jointly by the Australian and Chinese governments, allowed her to study viruses in Australian bats. Her collaboration with international scientists, including those from Australia and the US, continued successfully throughout the subsequent years. It culminated in 2013 with the publication in the prestigious scientific journal *Nature* of a paper by an international research team led by Shi Zhengli in which for the first time a live bat virus was successfully isolated. The paper confirmed that bats were the origin of SARS-like virus, and drew attention to the fact that that Chinese Horseshoe bats were a prodigious reservoir of SARS viruses.[3]

Given the virus's clear association with bats and the fact that the SARS pandemic began there, the subtropical provinces of southern China, Guangdong, Guangxi and Yunnan became the focus of the scientific search for the origins of the virus. The mountains of that region are pockmarked with caves which are home to dense colonies of these nocturnal creatures – in a sense, southern China is bat central. As a result, Shi, along with many of the international virology fraternity, have spent much of the last two decades stalking their quarry in the numerous caves of these sub-tropical provinces of southern China

Teams of scientists have spent years roaming the bat caves collecting samples of urine, faeces, and blood from over 10,000 bats. This ongoing research effort is vital. Not only do bats have a greater tolerance for viruses than other mammals, they also carry a higher proportion of zoonotic viruses. On top of all this, the virus reservoir of bats is not confined to coronaviruses, it includes a toxic menu of other viral threats, such as rabies, Ebola and Marburg viruses. By any yardstick, the threat to humanity from bat-virus spillover is enormous.

But bats are elusive. Some of their favourite habitats are the darker recesses of the caves where those seeking them are forced to crawl through narrow crevasses, sometimes on their hands and knees. It is, to say the least, extremely demanding and unpleasant work. The caves are dark and the atmosphere has a pervasive and stomach-turning stench of the bats' urine and faeces. Clearly, it was not for the squeamish or the faint-hearted. But it was what the recently qualified PhD graduate had dedicated her life to – and she was very good at it. Like most virologists, she had been drawn by a curious fascination with the dangerous and fiendish beauty of viruses. Because of these exploits, among her colleagues at the Wuhan Institute of Virology, Shi became affectionately known as 'Bat Woman'

Having trekked across the mountainous terrain and taken bat droppings, blood and saliva from deep inside its caves, Shi has been instrumental in the creation one of the world's most comprehensive database of bat-related viruses. In recognition of these scientific research endeavours, in 2020 Shi was made a member of the US Academy of Virology. In the almost two decades since her graduation in France and her becoming a member of one of America's most prestigious scientific academy's, China, Wuhan and the Wuhan Institute had witnessed dramatic changes.

The Power Couple

As Shi Zhengli returned from France having attained her PhD, Wang Yanyi, the future Director of the Wuhan Institute, was 17 years younger than her and still in high school.

CREDIT:Wiv

Wang Yanyi, Director of Wuhan Institute of Virology

She did her bachelor's degree in Life Sciences at Beijing University. Shortly after graduation she married Shu Hong-Bing, a distinguished Life Sciences professor at the University and 14 years her senior. She then went to the United States where she did a Master's degree in immunology at the University of Colorado School of Medicine in 2006. By then, her husband had been appointed Dean of the School of Life Sciences at Wuhan University where, on her return from the U S, his wife began her post graduate studies.

Wang Yanyi's ambitions went well beyond academia. 2010 was an important one for Wang Yanyi and her husband, Shu Hong-Bing. A combination of politics and the academia were to be the twin launch pads for their combined ascent into the Communist Party's privileged elite. Wang Yanyi and her husband were clearly becoming a 'power couple' in Wuhan society.

Having completed her Ph.D. in that year, she joined an affiliate of the Chinese Communist Party in Wuhan, the Zhi Gong Party, and later became deputy director of the Wuhan Municipal Party Committee. In China, that sort of political grounding is not likely to harm one's career prospects. Within a few months of finishing her Doctorate, Wang Yanyi was made an Associate Professor at the Wuhan University School of Life Sciences. That same year, her husband became a member of the influential National Committee of the Chinese People's Political Consultative Conference (known as the PCC) which acts as an advisory legislative upper house, or national senate.

Then in 2012 Ms. Wang left Wuhan University and started a new career as a researcher at the Wuhan Institute of Virology. Her rise through the Institutes ranks was on a fast track, a progression described by Chinese netizens as 'helicopter-like'. In less than three years, from the modest rank of researcher she was quickly promoted to become, first Assistant Director; then, Deputy Director; and finally, in October 2018, Wang Yanyi became Director of the Institute. During these years, Wang Yanyi wrote a number of scientific papers in collaborations with several other scientists, seven of these articles were published in the acclaimed Proceedings of the National Academy of Sciences (PNAS). Her husband, Hong-Bing Shu was the corresponding author (effectively owner of the research) for six of these papers published between 2009 to 2020.

Shortly after becoming Director of the Wuhan Institute she also became a member of the Wuhan PCC while her husband was promoted to membership of National PCC's standing committee (with deputy ministerial rank). In a society where septuagenarian males seem to rule the roost, Ms. Wang's vertiginous elevation at such a relatively young age was quite remarkable. When the Institute became the subject of popular criticism around the time of the virus outbreak in Wuhan, some Chinese netizens on social media were less than complimentary about Wang Yanyi and her husband: 'A good study is worse than a good marriage'; 'Because they are young, smart and beautiful, they say they rely on their cheeks? In 2000, they were admitted to Peking University by their cheeks?'; 'They are true love😂😂😂😂'; 'Immortal Legend, Chinese Version of the Curie Couple.'

A Baptism of Fire

The Wuhan Institute was at the epicentre of the Chinese coronavirus epidemic in Hubei province in 2019. The newly appointed director of the Institute (2018), the youthful Wang Yanyi, had never experienced anything like this. The pressures from all sides were immense. Now, to add to her difficulties, on the first weekend of February she found herself at the centre of a media firestorm – an unusual occurrence in tightly censored China. What happened next is an illustration of the fact that in China nothing of any significance ever happens without the imprimatur of the Chinese Communist Party and, ultimately, its supreme leader. We will come across many more such examples in this book.

On Friday January 31, 2020, as the Wuhan lockdown was in full swing and the rest of China braced itself for another SARS -like pandemic, the state-controlled news agency *Xinhua* carried sensational news. Two highly respected scientific organisations had just completed research which

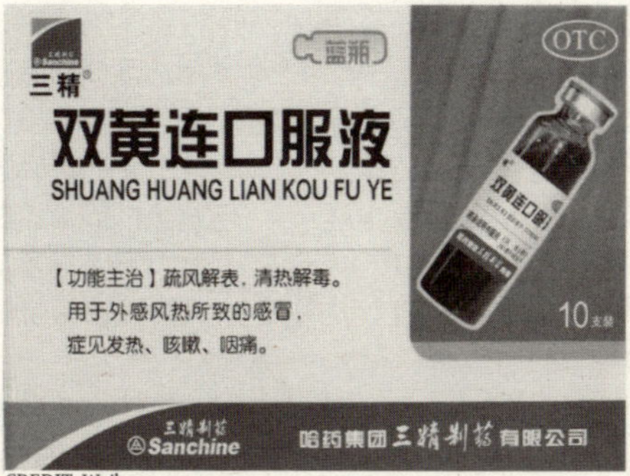

CREDIT: Weibo

Shuang Huang Lian Herbal Remedy

showed that a traditional Chinese herbal medicine, Shuang Huang Lian, had been shown to be effective in containing the novel coronavirus infection. The organisations responsible for the joint research report were constituent parts of the Chinese Academy of Sciences: the Shanghai Institute of Materia Medica and the Wuhan Institute of Virology.

A week before the results of the joint research report on Shuang Huang Lian were released to the media, China's National Health Commission (Ministry of Health) announced that in their treatment of coronavirus patients, medical institutions should 'actively promote the role of traditional Chinese medicine.' This announcement came just two days after a meeting of the Chinese Communist Party's Politburo standing committee (China's supreme ruling authority) in which President Xi Jinping, a long-time proponent of traditional Chinese medicine, called for the 'combination of Chinese and Western medicine' in the treatment of the disease.[4]

Based on the *Xinhua* news agency information, the *People's Daily* reported the news that the popular herbal-based oral liquid, Shuang Huang Lian could be used to 'inhibit' the deadly virus. Weibo, the Chinese Twitter equivalent, lit up as the herbal remedy became its most searched item. Hundreds of posts appeared on Chinese social media showing photographs of long queues outside pharmacies across China as citizens frantically tried to purchase what they had been led to believe was a miracle coronavirus cure. Long into the cold winter night, people queued, and those who failed to get supplies of Shuang Huang Lian returned early the next morning. That was because the product had also sold out overnight on Chinese e-commerce platforms. As stocks of the herbal remedy dwindled rapidly, authorities feared there might be social unrest and quickly began to backtrack.

The following day, the *People's Daily* carried some important clarifications with regard to the Shuang Huang Lian herbal remedy. It warned that 'inhibiting does not equal preventing and treating,' The newspaper went on to state that 'so far, the finding is still under preliminary study, and a large number of experiments is needed to test if it is effective on patients', before finally urging people not to rush out to purchase the medicine.

The later speculation by foreign governments and the international media that the Wuhan Institute of Virology was a possible source for the origin of the coronavirus could easily be dismissed as 'malicious rumours spread by foreign anti-China forces'. However, internal criticisms by

Chinese citizens – of both the Institute and its director – were an entirely different matter. The response of the Chinese media – which are, of course, controlled by the Communist Party – are particularly revealing.

In the aftermath of the speedy puncturing of the Shuang Huang Lian herbal remedy bubble, Chinese netizens took to social media to criticise the role played by the Institute in the unfolding health crisis. In that process, some openly questioned the competence of director Wang. *The Global Times*, the international mouthpiece of the Chinese Communist Party began to echo these criticisms in its coverage, saying, 'Some experts and netizens expressed their disappointment with the institute on its performance in handling the epidemic.'

Even more ominously, the article went on to state that 'Netizens also questioned how Wang Yanyi, who is the director general of the institute, can have an important position without what some perceive as enough qualifications.' And the *Global Times* article was clear about what had caused the dark shadow of criticism to fall on the Institute and its director: 'Doubts about Wang mounted after the *Xinhua* News Agency on January 31 reported Chinese patent medicine, Shuanghuanglian oral liquid, containing three herbal ingredients, is effective in containing the novel coronavirus infection.'[5] We shall see later that as the virus extended its grip over Wuhan and other parts of China, Wang Yanyi was to play a significant role. That was not because she played a significant part in containing the virus, but because she played a critical role in promulgating the Chinese Communist Party's narrative about dealing with the virus.

The Wuhan Institute of Virology, and particularly its P4 lab, has played a central role in the unfolding story of the virus that caused the Great Pandemic of 2020. To understand how all this happened, we need to have a better understanding of the unusual circumstances through which the P4 lab at Wuhan came into being.

Chapter 2: Pandora's Box

Biosecurity Level 4 laboratories (P4) are designed for researchers to work with highly pathogenic microbes that pose a significant risk of transmission to humans, are frequently fatal, and have no reliable cure. Following the 2002-3 SARS outbreak, the Chinese government decided to build a P4 lab in Wuhan, but critically, it lacked the technical know-how. In the spirit of the ongoing international endeavour to bring China in from its self-imposed exile in communist outer darkness, there was no shortage of Western countries anxious to assist in making up the glaring shortfall in China's scientific and technological capabilities.

CREDIT: Getty

P 4 Lab at the Wuhan Institute of Virology

P4 facilities are high-containment laboratories which essentially consist of a box within a box: a sealed environment within a larger building. Entering and leaving a P4 lab is a security-intense process governed by strict rules. In the laboratory itself where researchers are at most risk, all personnel wear full-body positive-pressure "space suits" that are connected by a tether-hose to a common air supply. The exit procedures from the lab take about 30 minutes as it includes a chemical shower to decontaminate the surface of the suit which is then followed by a body shower after the suit is removed. As sophisticated biocontainment facilities designed for conducting research on some of the most pathogenic viruses known to humanity, P4 labs are technically complex, expensive to build, and very costly to run. So, if China was going to join the elite club of worldwide operational P4 facilities it could not do so on its own.[1]

China may have made staggering economic and technical progress in the opening years of the present century. But China still lacked the scientific know-how or technological competence to build and sustain a complex and sophisticated facility such as a high-security P4 biolab. The one at the Wuhan Institute of Virology could not have come into existence without the active participation of Western scientists and expertise, accompanied by substantial finance from Western governments. These critical components were being made available to China under the aegis of the prevailing globalist orthodoxy. Lady luck had smiled on the Chinese Communist Party, and China found itself pushing open doors in the West.

This whole political project was founded on the belief that these types of benevolent gesture on the part of the West would eventually wean the Chinese Communist Party away from its authoritarian ways and gradually chaperone it onto the path of democratic righteousness. Communist China had, after all, enthusiastically embraced a robust form of capitalism. It was thus, the argument went, just another short step before democracy itself would take root and flourish on Chinese soil.

For the Chinese Communist Party, a P4 laboratory was seen as a further manifestation of China's rapid progression on the road to technological sophistication and by implication, a vindication of its strategy of 'socialism with Chinese characteristics'. For the West, and the US in particular, what was being attempted through the barrel of a gun in the Middle East was being done in China through a form of 'soft' power – with more than half an eye to the world's fastest growing consumer market of over one billion people. This policy of scientific-hands-around-the-world ticked most, if not all, the globalist boxes.

On the P4 project, countries were falling over themselves to be seen to cooperate with the new rising power in the East. This apparent altruism, however, was leavened with considerable self-interest. As we have seen, south China's horseshoe bat population was well recognised a posing a considerable health and economic risk to the rest of the world. Anything that could mitigate that risk had to be positive; and a P4 laboratory in the heart of the contagion zone was top of the list. But there were other incentives. The size of the Chinese market had escaped no one's notice. There were well over a billion commercial reasons to be first in the queue to help China with its aspirations to become a fully-fledged member of that vaunted but ill-defined club, the international community. As we shall see, considerable largesse, an enormous investment of advanced technological know-who and a persistent high-level Gallic charm offensive gave the prize to France.

In 2004 a contract was signed with France through which the new Chinese P4 lab, modelled on the P4 Jean Mérieux-Inserm Laboratory in Lyon, was built in Wuhan, the capital of China's central province of Hubei. But the French were not the only ones who were instrumental in its construction. During the Obama Presidency, according to Forbes magazine, 'the U.S. government helped build and fund the Wuhan virology lab.'[2] . The EU also played an active role. The lab became part of European Virus Archive through funding from the European Commission's Horizon 2020 Programme, an €80 billion fund described by the EU as 'a Europe 2020 flagship initiative aimed at securing Europe's global competitiveness.'

The French Connection

China's P4 lab in Wuhan may have been conceived in controversy and, following a difficult birth, it also had a rancorous upbringing. In order to understand the ways in which the Chinese government responded to the Covid-19 virus, it is necessary to explore the preceding years, and the relationships that had developed between China and the West.

This was not a relationship that displayed much evidence of trust on either side. There is compelling evidence to suggest that the Chinese government was consistently less than honest and transparent in its dealings with the West, but the West may also have been politically naïve in its relationship with the People's Republic. Mao Zedong's interpretation of Marxism had been grimly deterministic. He believed that a proletarian revolution was inevitable and there was no human action that could resist the "Great Wheel of History". The West, on the other hand, seems to have viewed liberal democracy as the inevitable product of China's growing economic prosperity. In their own ways, both views reflected a mechanistic and deterministic view of history – and both proved to be equally illusory.

At a meeting in Paris in 2003, the powerful Chinese Academy of Sciences announced its desire to acquire a top level P4 biosecurity laboratory for China. Beijing's request, however, did not meet with universal approval within the French state apparatus. France's equivalent of the CIA or MI6, the DGSE, had strong suspicions that China was secretly pursuing an active biological weapons programme and so feared that French technological know-how would be diverted towards the production of biological weapons.

Following a visit to Beijing at the height of the SARS epidemic in April 2003, the French Prime Minister, Jean-Pierre Raffarin, returned to Paris with assurances he had been given regarding the concerns raised by DGSE about biological weaponry being developed by the Chinese. In the light of those assurances, he recommended that the project be given the green light.

It was described in innocuous language as an 'intergovernmental agreement on emerging diseases', but in reality the deal covered not only the building of the P4 laboratory but also committed the French government to supply 4 mobile P3 laboratories 'exclusively intended for screening, identification and research of pathogenic agents', and the establishment of a Pasteur Institute in Shanghai.[3] The then French President, Jacques Chirac and his Chinese counterpart, Jiang Zemin met in Shanghai and signed off on the accord. Following the Heads of State meeting, the agreement was finally signed in September 2005 by the then French Foreign Minister, Michel Barnier – who subsequently became the EU's somewhat intransigent Brexit negotiator.

Despite the support of Barnier and the French Cabinet, things began to fall apart at an early stage. To begin with, French intelligence soon discovered that the Chinese construction company given the contract to build the laboratory was part of the China National Equipment of Machinery Corporation (CNEMC). This was an entity that was controlled directly by the People's Liberation Army. The PLA is an army with an explicitly political role that is not comparable to any in the West.

On top of this came a range of technical, legal and political difficulties. In 2007, Technip, the French engineering company that was supposed to certify that the building complied with international safety standards refused to do so and decided to withdraw from the project altogether. French concerns were compounded by what seemed to be dissembling and deliberate obfuscation by China about what had happened to the mobile P3 labs donated by France. In 2008, when the then French President Sarkozy met the Dalai lama in Poland, the project again ran into the sand when the Chinese warned that, if they expressed any continuing interest in the position of Tibet in the People's Republic, then 'bilateral trade relations could suffer.'

Finally, in 2015, Alain Mérieux resigned his co-chairmanship of the Joint Commission which had supervised the P4 project. He stated that 'I am giving up the co-chairmanship of P4 which is a very Chinese tool. It belongs to them, even if it was developed with technical assistance from France.'[4] This effectively put an end to French involvement in the Wuhan P4 laboratory project. A total lack of candour on the part of China had frustrated the French throughout their involvement. They could, for example, cite a firm commitment they received from the Chinese that they had no other P4 lab and had no intention of building one. However, about eight months after the Wuhan P4 lab was commissioned, another P4 lab also commenced operations in Harbin, the capital of Heilongjiang Province.[5]

As a result of France abandoning the project, according to *Le Figaro* and the state broadcaster *France Inter*, the 50 senior French scientists who were meant to move to Wuhan to work there during its first five years of operation never arrived. Though the P4 lab at Wuhan was built to accommodate 250 scientific researchers, it still does not have the international accreditation for this number of people and so continues to function with only a skeleton staff from the Institute.[6] This may well explain a number of cables sent by US diplomatic staff in early 2018. These were sent following a number of visits to the Wuhan Institute, and raised concerns about basic safety and management shortcomings. According to *The Washington Post*, one of the cables dated Jan 19, 2018 highlighted 'a serious shortage of appropriately trained technicians and investigators needed to safely operate this high-containment laboratory'.[7]

Biocontainment

There are very good reasons for the inordinate security measures at P4 laboratories across the world – since the risks involved if such measures are lacking are enormous. Under its 'Safety' section (now deleted) the website of the new P4 facility at Wuhan did not mince its words in highlighting the inherent dangers of the activities being carried out within its precincts: 'because the P4 lab researches highly pathogenic microorganisms ... once the virus test tubes have been opened, it's like opening Pandora's box.'[8] Though graphic, the Institute's now disappeared description is not just a reflection of the concerns of many regarding these laboratories but, more importantly, of their far from unblemished track record with regard to biosafety.

These facilities are designed to such high levels of biosecurity to ensure that they don't become the source of the very contagions that their scientists seek to prevent. But, ultimately, because they are operated by human beings, 100% security all of the time cannot be guaranteed – mistakes happen. The risks associated with biosafety at laboratories, including to the researchers and to the surrounding communities, can be greatly minimized, but they can never be eliminated entirely.

Though laboratory acquired infections are rare, they do happen. International data on the incidence of laboratory acquired infections is of limited value because there is no systematic reporting system in place so the data acquired relies solely on voluntary reporting. However, from the limited data that is available the most common threat to laboratory staff is from airborne infections (87%) while the remainder result from skin punctures due to needles, animal bites or scratches. Unsurprisingly, the investigators also concluded that 78% of these laboratory-acquired infections were due to human error. In the US between 2006 and 2013, according to CDC reports, fifteen people contracted laboratory-acquired infections and there were three unintended infections of animals. All of this merely highlights the fact that high quality training and personal behaviour are the best guarantees of biosafety, irrespective of the expensive hardware involved.

Yet, potentially fatal lapses have occurred even at one of the world's most renowned infectious disease research facilities. In July 2014 concerns about biosecurity were reignited in the US when highly pathogenic microbes were mishandled by federal laboratories. In the wake of those incidents, the US CDC closed two laboratories. One involved the shipment of live anthrax, another smallpox, and the third was a CDC shipment of a dangerous influenza strain to another laboratory.[9] The anthrax case potentially exposed up to 75 CDC employees when the samples that were thought to be inert turned out to be live. For Marc Lipsitch, a professor of epidemiology at Harvard University, 'What the CDC incidents showed us ... is that the very best labs are not perfectly safe ... if it can happen there, it certainly can happen anywhere.'[10]

There is one type of research carried out in these laboratories, however, which has caused considerable controversy in the past and on which the scientific community itself is divided. Technically, this activity is known by the innocuously sounding term, 'gain of function' – but this means the artificial creation of mutant viruses. The purpose of this controversial experimental research has admirable aims: it is to get a deeper understand how organisms cause disease, and, in the process, learn how we can better protect ourselves against them. But this involves purposely engineering active strains of deadly viruses, such as SARS, to make them either more transmissible or give them greater lethality than those found in nature.

Chinese laboratories have been involved in this mutant virus research for many years. In 2013, researchers at the Harbin Veterinary Research Institute[11] crossed two strains of avian flu virus (H5N1 and H1N1) to create one that could be transmitted through the air, something that had not happened in nature. When published in the journal *Science*, it caused uproar.[12] Lord May of Oxford, the former UK government chief scientist denounced the study saying, 'The record of containment in labs like this is not reassuring. They are taking it upon themselves to create human-to-human transmission of very dangerous viruses. It's appallingly irresponsible.'

It was precisely the risk of accidentally releasing viruses with pandemic potential that prompted the US government in October 2014 to suspend the funding of studies that make viruses more dangerous, pending a safety assessment. In particular, the halt was called particularly on research work involving making viruses such as SARS either more dangerous or more transmissible.[13] Because of growing concerns about this type of research, scientists had themselves imposed a voluntary moratorium two years earlier on research involving these mutant viruses. However, in 2017 the government funding ban was lifted and research resumed.

One of the experiments that initially fell victim to the US government's decision was a joint collaboration between the University of North Carolina at Chapel Hill, and the Wuhan Institute of Virology which was investigating a particular virus found in Chinese horseshoe bats. The researchers created a chimeric SARS virus which could be grown in mice in order to mimic human disease. Because the study had been underway before the moratorium took effect and was not considered overly risky, the National Institutes of Health (NIH) allowed the research to continue. But given the accidents that had occurred, as an editorial in *Nature* points out, 'the idea of an accidental release of a potentially pandemic flu virus cannot be completely written off.'[14]

All of the above is well known to professional virologists throughout the world. As the train from Shanghai hurtled towards Wuhan that December evening, in 2019, Shi Zhengli, the "Bat Woman of Wuhan", could not help but consider the implications of the dramatic news that the Institute's Director had just told her. Could the whole thing be a mistake? 'I wondered if [the CDC] got it wrong', she recalled later.

But there was one other very disturbing thought that kept re-occurring. Shi had spent most of her professional life chasing the source of the coronavirus pathogens 1,000 kilometers away in South China, so the news from her Director was very puzzling: 'I had never expected this kind of thing to happen in Wuhan, in central China.' It didn't really make sense. So where did the coronavirus pathogens come from? As she continued to grapple with the conundrum, a shocking thought struck her, 'Could they have come from our lab?' The train got in to Wuhan station late that night, but Shi was unable to sleep. Later, it transpired that the Wuhan Virology Institute's extensive database of viral genomes was accessed that evening, whether remotely or from withing the Institute itself, remains unclear.

The first task for Shi and her team was to identify the source of the contagion. They did test after test and re-checked the results several times. Samples were also sent to another laboratory to do a full genome sequence of the virus. Within a week they were able to show that the pneumonia illness of the Wuhan hospital patients was caused by the novel coronavirus that later become known as SARS-CoV-2. But the real relief only came for Shi when the genome sequence from the outside laboratory arrived. Her nightmare ended when the results indicated that none of the genetic sequences matched those of the bat viruses that she had collected over the years from the caves of south China. As she told *Scientific American*, 'That really took a load off my mind. I had not slept a wink for days.'[15]

Although Shi Zhengli had satisfied herself that the Wuhan P4 lab was not the source of the virus, many around the world were not so easily convinced. The Chinese government continued to claim that the Wuhan wet market was the source of the virus, but offered no convincing evidence to back up the claim. Even worse, the market had been closed down on December 31 and the whole place chemically cleaned – thus effectively eliminating the possibility of ever finding evidence to support the government's contention. Governments around the world demanded that a team of international scientists be allowed carry out a thorough investigation to identify the source of the contagion that was decimating their countries. The CCP rejected the suggestion point blank. The WHO had been negotiating for many months to get an international scientific inspection team – but to no avail. One year later, the CCP was still refusing to relent until finally, in January, following exasperated public statements by the WHO, a deal was reached. But for over a year, in the absence of any reliable information, speculation filled the vacuum, with some suggesting that the reason for the secrecy was that the virus had been part of a bioweapons programme that had gone terribly wrong.

Security concerns about what could go on at the Wuhan Institute were long standing. As we have already seen, even before the P4 lab had been given the go-ahead, French security services had argued strongly against the project, but they were overruled. As the French became increasingly disenchanted with the behaviour of the CCP, they finally abandoned their oversight role which the whole P4 project had been predicated upon. With no French scientists present on the ground in Wuhan as planned, worries about the security of the operational aspects of this complex facility multiplied in the West. As was the norm during this era of globalisation, the US under President Obama, was prepared to step into the breach.

Chapter 3: Global Collaboration

From the outset, international scientists were also heavily involved in enhancing the operational capabilities of the highly specialised Wuhan P4 laboratory. As early as 2013, while construction work on the new lab was still in progress, some of the Institute's research personnel were being trained in the highest level of bioresearch security in the United States at the Galveston National Laboratory (GNL) in Texas.[1] Two postdoctoral researchers from the Institute were also hosted at Galveston for a year where they received intense biosecurity training. According to Galveston's Director, James LeDuc, they returned to the Wuhan Institute 'where they were instrumental in establishing their biosafety and biosecurity training programme for the new BSL-4 laboratory and where they continue their independent research in the new facility.'[2] LeDuc told the *Houston Chronicle* 'We did our best to share best practices so that they knew how to drive it and keep it safe. But it would be foolish to say there's no risk, because there's risk in everything.'[3]

The cooperation between the Galveston and Wuhan laboratories has been ongoing and close. In an article in *Science* jointly authored by LeDuc and senior Wuhan director, Zhiming Yuan, they confirm that 'We succeeded in transferring proven best practices to the new Wuhan facility. Both labs recently signed formal cooperative agreements that will streamline future scientific and operational collaborations on dangerous pathogens.'[4]

New York-based EcoHealth Alliance has been studying bat coronaviruses for more than 15 years. In this time, it has established deep scientific links in China: working closely, in particular, with the Wuhan Institute of Virology. A joint 6-year research project with the Institute into bat-borne coronaviruses was funded by the US Government through a grant of $3.4m from the National Institutes of Health (NIH). As the Chief Executive of EcoHealth Alliance, Peter Daszak, has confirmed 'our collaboration with Wuhan was preapproved by NIH.' At the height of the controversy between the Trump administration and China over the precise origins of the Covid-19 virus, the grant was cancelled.

Australia Fair

The support given to Chinese research was not confined to the northern hemisphere. In 2006, the Institute's up-and-coming ace virologist, Shi Zhengli, spent three months as a visiting scientist at Australia's high-containment P4 facility based at the Centre for Disease Preparedness laboratory in Geelong, south-west of Melbourne. It is Australia's top-level animal health laboratory. While there, she continued her research on links between the SARS virus and bats. Five years later, in 2011, her protégé, Peng Zhou, did his Doctoral studies there before returning to the Institute in 2014 where he later became Director of the Bat Virus Infection and Immunity Project. Both placements were jointly funded by the Australian and Chinese governments.

But Australian academic traffic wasn't all one way. There was substantial research collaboration between Australian university scientists in China. Two important academic papers, for instance, on the likely animal source of the SARS-CoV-2 virus were written by the highly regarded University of Sydney virologist and evolutionary biologist, Prof Edward Holmes, in collaboration with a group of Chinese scientists. Indeed, Prof Holmes played a key role at the outset of the current pandemic in China: he was a member of the consortium of the Shanghai Public Health Clinical Centre that carried out the critically important first genetic sequencing of the Covid-19 virus. Even more significantly, on January 10, this genetic sequencing was uploaded onto an open access international genome site where researchers across the world could use it for a variety of scientific purposes, including developing vaccines and other possible therapeutic remedies for the virus. The GenBank database is run by the US National Institutes for Health (NIH) and provides open access within the scientific community to the most up-to-date and comprehensive DNA sequence information.[5]

In the acknowledgements of that article that was published in *Nature*, as is usual, individuals and organisations are thanked for their assistance and cooperation. The first on the list of those thanked 'for their substantial contributions to this study, including co-ordinating among research parties' was Prof. Wu-Chun Cao and the Beijing Institute of Microbiology and Epidemiology. The Beijing Institute of Microbiology and Epidemiology is a constituent part of the Academy of Military Medical Sciences, the highest-level research institute of the People's Liberation Army (PLA).

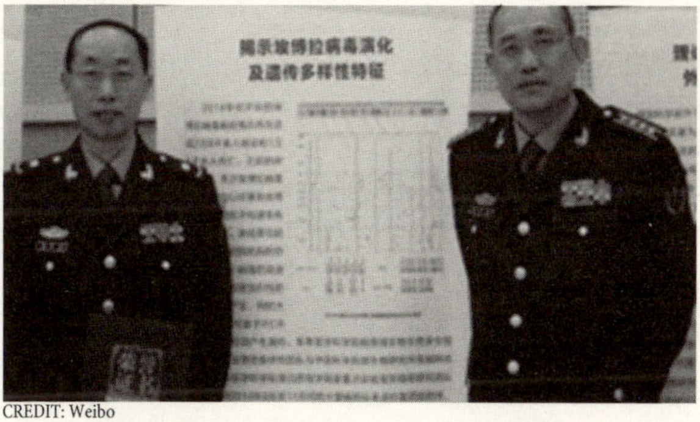

CREDIT: Weibo

Yi-Gang Tong (L) and Wu-Chan Cao (R), of China's PLA

As his biography on the official website confirms, Prof. Cao has another title, the rank of colonel in the PLA and is 'the Director of the Institute of Microbiology and epidemiology, Military Medical Science Academy of the PLA.' The web site then adds that 'Colonel Cao also sits on the board for the Wuhan Institute of Virology's Scientific Advisory Committee of Centre for Emerging Infectious Diseases.' Lest there be any doubt as the significance of Professor Cao's military standing, this information is accompanied by a photograph of him in his colonel's military uniform.

Needless to say, when news of these connections was broken in Australia by Sharri Markson of the *Daily Telegraph*, there was a degree of consternation. The University of Sydney was especially keen to distance itself from any taint of being seen to be working with the Chinese PLA – an army that has been used by the Chinese Communist Party to suppress any dissident voices within the People's Republic, and which was directly responsible for the massacre of pro-democracy protesters on Tiananmen Square in 1989. A University spokeswoman said Professor Holmes' work was "academically independent". The spokeswoman went on to stress that 'Prof Holmes has no link with the Academy of Military Science. Their involvement with the research was declared in the acknowledgments, as is standard practice. Dr Cao co-ordinated the laboratory work before Prof Holmes' involvement. He did not direct or supervise the work of Prof Holmes which was undertaken independently.'[6]

A Cure for Covid-19?

What also became clear at this time were the manoeuvrings of the Chinese government to position itself to gain the maximum commercial benefits from any new vaccine. On January 31, the *New England Journal of Medicine* (NEJM) published a case study of the first recorded US patient with coronavirus who, on compassionate grounds, was treated with intravenous Remdesivir. The clinicians noted that 'no adverse events were observed in association with the infusion' and that on the following day 'the patient's clinical condition improved.' The article went on to stress, however, that 'randomized controlled trials are needed to determine the safety and efficacy of Remdesivir.'[7]

Gilead is a biopharmaceutical company that specialises in anti-viral drugs and holds the patent rights to the chemical formula for Remdesivir. (It is also the name chosen by Margaret Attwood for the totalitarian Republic in her dystopian novel, *The Handmaid's Tale.)* There has been considerable market speculation about the suitability of Remdesivir as a possible treatment for coronavirus. However, the drug had not yet been given approval for use in humans, except on compassionate grounds. But the Remdesivir had shown promising results in some laboratory studies, and as a consequence, Gilead's share price had increased by 25% since January.

On the same day that the *NEJM* article was published, California-based Gilead Sciences, the developer of Remdesivir, announced that 'Gilead is working with health authorities in China to establish a randomized, controlled trial to determine whether Remdesivir can safely and effectively be used to treat 2019-nCoV.' Three days later, China announced that it would immediately begin clinical trials of Remdesivir in an attempt to find an effective treatment for the disease. The trial was to be conducted on 270 novel coronavirus patients beginning on February 3 in Wuhan. But two weeks before the Wuhan trial was due to start, something interesting happened.

On February 4, 2020 the Wuhan Institute of Virology announced that it had filed for a Chinese patent for the experimental antiviral drug Remdesivir for the treatment of Covid-19.[8] The Institute had recently conducted extensive research on a selection of potential coronavirus antidotes, and the ones that showed the most promise were, hydroxychloroquine (an anti-malarial drug also favoured by President Trump) and the antiviral drug, Remdesivir. According to the research, Remdesivir looked like being, literally, a lifesaver on an unimaginable scale.[9] As the Institute's website confirms, the research was done jointly with 'the Military Medical Research Institute of the Military Academy of Sciences' – in other words, the PLA was, once again, centrally involved in this process. Given that Covid-19 was then ravishing the 11 million inhabitants of one of central China's principal cities, Wuhan, and was threatening to bring the whole of Chinese society to its knees, this should have been an occasion for enormous celebration. However, there was a fundamental problem, Remdesivir had been developed by Gilead Sciences, which held the worldwide patent rights its chemical formula, including those for China.

The Institute's scientific research of both drugs was conducted, like many before and since, *in vitro*. In other words, the experiments were conducted on samples in a laboratory, their efficacy for the treatment of coronavirus in humans was still unproven. However, their conclusions were emphatic: 'Our findings reveal that remdesivir and chloroquine are highly effective in the control of 2019-nCoV infection in vitro.'[10]

As China's foremost virology institution situated at the epicentre of the coronavirus outbreak, many Chinese netizens complained bitterly that the Wuhan Institute should have devoted its resources to containing the virus that was killing their fellow citizens rather than spending time and resources patenting drugs which it neither owned nor developed. The Wuhan Institute responded to these complaints by arguing that it had only sought a patent in the national interest and would forego its patent rights if, in this instance, Gilead were to cooperate with China in confronting a pandemic.

This is an entirely spurious argument as existing international patent law already allows for the creation of compulsory licences in the event of a public health national emergency. If the Institute's usage patent licence were approved, then Gilead could find itself unable to market or sell its own drug in China without the Institute's agreement. What the Institute did in this instance is legally admissible under patent regulations but, in ethical terms, is highly questionable. In the longer term, it may erode the confidence of Western pharmaceutical companies in collaborating with Chinese state entities on public health initiatives and revive longstanding and justified concerns about China's respect for intellectual property rights.

But before we go any further in our story of the particular circumstances of the origins of Covid-19, we need to get a better appreciation of the origins and evolution of the microbial organism that has precipitated the global devastation. In any war, knowledge of the enemy is always useful.

Chapter 4: In the Beginning was … the Virus

Viral Ubiquity

Viruses have been around since the dawn of life on earth. In evolutionary terms, they are one of the most successful organisms on the planet. Their story began over 3.5 billion years ago, yet their existence only came to light a little over a century ago, in 1892.[1] Because they were there, almost from the beginning, viruses are the most ubiquitous (and prolific) biological organisms on earth. They are everywhere. There is not a single living species that does not contain viruses.

Viruses are at the heart of the origin of life, and yet as organisms they remain something of a biological enigma and difficult to classify. Although both viruses and bacteria are microbes and originated in the same cellular life form, they should not be confused. Bacteria followed a fundamentally different evolutionary path to viruses. Bacteria and human beings went down the road of increasing complexity, but viruses have evolved in the opposite direction and have become simpler. In that sense, viruses could be regarded as one of the first organisms on earth to have adopted the so-called KISS principle – Keep It Simple Stupid.

While we have only gradually and recently gained a better understanding of them, viruses have been on intimate terms with human beings for millennia. And, despite their capacity for mischief and potential lethality, it is an inescapable - if counterintuitive - fact of biological life that without viruses humanity would not exist – or at least in its present form. Without our knowing it, they have been our constant companions throughout our existence. In fact, viruses and ourselves have been exchanging 'contact details' for such a long time that viral gene sequences have become an integral part of our genome. By some estimates, they account for up to 8% of the human genome. To put it slightly more technically, viruses and ourselves are in a classic symbiotic or co-dependent relationship.

Given the misery and havoc that some of them have caused us throughout human history, it is difficult to accept that viruses have no malevolent intent. But, like ourselves, and all other products of evolution, they are simply trying to get on with the business of surviving and multiplying. From the viruses' point of view, the fact that they can cause us incredible harm and even kill us, is neither here nor there. Their behaviour is, perhaps, somewhat similar to the distinction that is drawn between murder and many types of manslaughter – it is all about the intention of the perpetrator even though for the victim, the end result is the same. For the virus this is not personal, just business.

They exist throughout the environment, including the oceans.[2] It has been estimated that there are over 100 million types of viruses on the earth's surface. But with the ongoing discovery of hundreds of thousands of new species, it is also likely that this number is probably a vast underestimation and that what has become known as the virosphere is unimaginably large. Fortunately, out of this vast viral universe only about 250 have targeted us humans to act as their host.

One of the most unusual aspects of viruses is that, in scientific parlance, they are not metabolically independent entities – they need a host to survive. In a strict sense, viruses aren't even alive. In biology, the technical distinction between living and non-living entities is usually based on an organism's ability to synthesize proteins and replicate autonomously. It is because of their inability to do the latter that most scientists do not consider viruses to be alive.

Friend or Foe

However, the modern reputation of viruses as primarily disease-causing pathogens is not entirely deserved. Only a minority of viruses are pathogens – and most of them do not cause diseases. Strange as it may seem, viruses are actually more of a friend than a foe to humanity. The reputational damage suffered by viruses is principally down to modern medicine. Medicine's centuries-long focus on combating the many diseases caused by some viruses has, more than anything else, framed the public's lopsided perception of them as the microbial villains of the piece. This has, of course, also been fuelled by a host of Hollywood movies in which viruses are sometimes endowed with what approaches sentient characteristics. Given the scale of their notoriety, is worth repeating that most viruses pose no fundamental threat to their hosts.

Nonetheless, the devastation caused to humanity by a minority of viruses has been on such a scale that our visceral fear is understandable. Much of it is down to the fact that many of the diseases caused by the malevolent few have proved to be incurable – and quite a few still are. One has only to think of AIDS or Ebola, which have been around for many decades. Despite enormous well-funded scientific efforts, no vaccines have as yet been developed for AIDS. This disease has already killed up to 40 million people, with an estimated further three-quarters of a million dying each year. One of the few bright spots on this otherwise very bleak AIDS horizon has been the development of antiretroviral therapeutics which have helped to extend and improve the quality of life for millions of victims of this virus.

It is salutary to think that, regardless of modern advances in science and medicine, the only viral disease to have been completely eradicated to date is smallpox. It was once mankind's greatest killer, and, during the European conquest of the New World, it changed the course of history. It is the sole exception that proves the rule: other viruses have been humbling and tormenting humanity for centuries. Specific viral scourges such as measles, small pox, polio, rabies and influenza, for example, have relentlessly exposed humanity's fundamental vulnerability and impotence in the face of these microbial threats. Some of them have brought down empires, determined the outcome of wars, depopulated cities, destroyed cultures, and brought proud nations to their knees. And all of this is still a work in progress.

More recently, however, viruses have been given a bit of a reputational makeover: at least in the eyes of virologists. Modern science has been looking increasingly on the credit side of the viral balance sheet. It has concluded that, despite the aggressive infectious diseases which many of them cause, viruses are not all bad. An unexpected discovery has been that viruses have played an essential role in the evolution of life. They perform an important function as gene modulators. As transmitters of genetic material, they are important agents of innovation, and this includes the human genome where up to 45% consists of sequences related to retroviruses.[3] This realisation that viruses have bestowed positive benefits on humans is a relatively recent revelation, and for the non-specialist, a quite remarkable one.

In the last few decades, there has been dramatic progress on one front: viruses that were historically the leaders of the pathological pack and our greatest killers, have been dramatically re-purposed to tackle one of humankind's most prolific killers, cancer.[4] Our greatly enhanced knowledge of viruses and the counter-intuitive idea that they can be a cure as well as a curse has come about because of a single new technology, genome sequencing. As we shall see, the genetic revolution has also played a starring role in the story of the Covid-19 pandemic.

Spillover

Infectious disease pandemics caused by viral pathogens raise important questions for which there are no simple or straightforward answers. Are these outbreaks of pathogenic viruses something that just happen, for unknown reasons? Are they what would once be referred to as arbitrary acts of God? Mother nature having a tantrum? Or, are they something which we have caused to happen? Is humankind's behaviour contributing, directly or indirectly to viral pandemics which have increased in frequency in recent decades? As the recent pandemic has made abundantly clear, these are questions which we fail to address, literally, at our peril.

If these pathogenic outbreaks are just random events like earthquakes, tsunamis, or hurricanes then in a general sense they can be anticipated and we can prepare for them: we can improve our early warning systems and take appropriate steps to mitigate the consequences before, during, and after disaster strikes. But fundamentally there is little we can do to prevent them. If, however, it is human activity that is either causing or amplifying these contagions, then we face a different set of issues.

If the cause-and-effect analysis can be shown to lead back to us then, hypothetically, we can take action to tackle them directly. I say 'hypothetically' for two reasons. First, establishing unambiguous evidential linkages between cause and effect for complex occurrences in nature is easier said than done. Secondly, effective solutions indubitably require collective action on a global scale: something for which, to put it charitably, we have shown little appetite even in the face of our current viral travails.

In advance of even attempting to come up with a solution, we need to define the problem. Put simply, what we are facing in the current epidemic is the disastrous consequences of viral spillover. Spillover is a term used by virologist and disease ecologists to denote an event in which a pathogen jumps from one species to another. To avoid confusion, we need to distinguish spillover from another word we will come across in this story, emergence. In common usage both words are similar and sometimes interchangeable. Epidemiologists, however, draw an important distinction between the two: spillover is an event, while emergence is a process. Once a spillover event has occurred and an alien virus infects some members of a new host species and then begins to proliferate throughout that host population, the infectious disease is said to have emerged.[5] In the case of Covid-19, for instance, the virus had reposed undisturbed among the cave-dwelling bat population of South China until, for reasons yet unknown, it suddenly jumped species and onto the pages of human history.

Hop Skip and Jump

SARS-CoV-2 is the third pathogenic coronavirus to jump species in the past two decades. Because these viruses originated in other animals our human immune system has no experience of them and so is poorly equipped to fight them – just as the indigenous peoples of the Americas had no natural resistance to the viruses that European colonists brought to their shores. Though they vary in lethality and infectiousness, all of these new coronaviruses have caused a serious form of atypical pneumonia among the populations they infected. The first emerged in China in 2002 and caused SARS. The second happened a decade later in the Middle East and is referred to as MERS-CoV. The third and latest also emerged in China and has been by far the most devastating to date. All three seem to have originated in bats and spread to humans via, it is presumed, other intermediate animals. Three in two decades also represents a worrying trend. As the eponymous villain in Ian Fleming's *Goldfinger* pointed out to 007: 'Mr Bond, they have a saying in Chicago: 'Once is happenstance. Twice is coincidence. The third time it's enemy action.' We need to sit up and take notice.

These so-called zoonotic spillover events where viruses jump from other species to humans are nothing new. One of the most common viral infections to which we have all succumbed at one time or another, is influenza. This virus also has its origins in animal reservoirs; in this case, waterfowl such as ducks, geese and related species. Sometimes these avian viruses can jump from birds to humans but then fail to transmit between humans and so they die out. But one avian virus that successfully jumped the species barrier to humans and then proved highly infectious among humans was the H1N1 virus that caused the Spanish flu pandemic in 1918.

For a variety of reasons bats are the primary animal reservoir for many viral spillover occurrences. They pose enormous challenges for researchers trying to identify the most likely source for the next pandemic. One of the foremost difficulties facing scientists is that they know that bat viruses can jump to humans but they also know that they don't always do it. The riddle as to what makes a particular bat virus become a bad actor is now the focus of much scientific attention. The answer, however, lies in a complex mixture of stochastic factors which, among other things, include physical environment, ecology, viral molecular evolution, and human immunity.

As scientific researchers pursue their quest to discover the next viral villain, there is at least some good news. Though they have the capability to jump the species barrier, most viruses never do that; and for a good reason – that transition is extremely difficult to make. A lot of things need to be in alignment for the virus to execute this demanding manoeuvre successfully. First, humans need to get up close and personal with whatever species acts as the reservoir for the virus, bats for example. Secondly, quantity plays a role, so the encounter needs to happen when the animal is in the process of shedding significant amounts of the virus. Thirdly, the virus needs to be already equipped with the particular molecular machinery to latch on to human cells and gain access while at the same time, evading the defences of the human immune system. Finally, having found the right molecular key to pick the human cellular lock, the virus needs to be able to replicate and infect lots of other cells. Mastering this sequence of events is not a slam dunk for any virus, but as we know to our cost, some can do it. And as we'll see next, they've been doing it for some time.

Chapter 5: Contagion Rules

Since the mid-20th century, the prevailing orthodoxy among experts was that the final victory over infectious diseases was in sight. The optimistic buzzword of the period was 'eradication' which quickly came to replace the by then outdated objective of 'control'. Books with titles such as *World Eradication of Infectious Diseases*, and *The Evolution and Eradication of Infectious Diseases* were being written by world-renowned epidemiologists. They were soon consigning the whole category of communicable diseases to the dustbin of history. In 1963, one of a number of incorrigible optimists wrote 'it seems reasonable to anticipate that within some measurable time, such as 100 years, all the major infections will have disappeared'.[1]

The progress of science had been such that it was widely assumed that soon, all that would remain of these diseases would be 'their memories in textbooks, and some specimens in museums.', The Australian virologist and Nobel laureate, Frank Macfarlane Burnet went even further, proclaiming that a disease-free world had already been created as there was a 'virtual absence of serious infectious disease today'.[2] The WHO reflected the prevailing optimism as its 1979 World Health Assembly adopted a new international public health objective with the upbeat title, 'Health for All, 2000'.[3]

It has to be said that this optimism, though vastly overstated, was not entirely groundless – at least in the West. With improvements in sanitation, food hygiene, the development of vaccines and antibiotics, mortality and morbidity from infectious diseases had decreased dramatically since the latter half of the 19th century. Contagions that had, literally, plagued humanity for centuries were being severely curtailed. The paradigmatic example was smallpox, which in 1979 was the first such disease to have been eradicated through concerted human agency. Scientific progress was indeed giving us considerable mastery over numerous familiar infectious pathologies, but, as is often the case in human affairs, real danger lurks in the unfamiliar: what have been termed the unknown unknowns.

As an explanation for the emergence of life on earth, Darwin's theory of evolution through natural selection is unsurpassed. In this process, when mutations occur the beneficial ones that aid survival of an organism get passed on while the rest get discarded. The abiding impression among the public, and up to a few decades ago within the scientific community, is that evolutionary change is an inexorably slow, smooth and continuous process. This belief in the sedentary and agonisingly gradual nature of evolution has informed the predominant view that the microbial world was also virtually static, with movement being imperceptibly glacial. It led to the inevitably complacent conclusion that the risk of something new, nasty, and deadly emerging suddenly out of the viral woodwork was negligible.

Virologists and epidemiologists tend to be over-influenced by immediately prior events and just like generals, they always seem to be fighting the last war. In Europe alone, during the last half millennium the fourth horseman of the apocalypse had made regular and devastating appearances: bubonic plague (1347), syphilis (1490) cholera (1830), and Spanish flu (1918) were just the principal ones. The idea that what had happened in the past was a sufficient guide to the contagious diseases that we needed to guard against in the future was even baked into the WHO's strategic thinking.

In 1969, the three diseases which member states were mandated to immediately notify the WHO about, in the event of an outbreak were; plague, yellow fever, and cholera: in other words, the microbial killers of the previous century.[4] It was only in 2005, almost 35 years later, that the WHO finally amended its rules and replaced specific disease names with the more generic and open-ended notification requirement of a 'public health emergency of international concern.' Though vaguely constructed, this at least allowed for unknown pathogens and emerging infections to be part of the notification process.

In the 70s and 80s, global public health experts had been arguing that during the 20th century the burden of human diseases had undergone a dramatic transition from naturally occurring diseases to man-made degenerative ones. This meant that diseases of poverty were being replaced by diseases of affluence.[5] The hubristic optimism that was then in fashion is best illustrated by the US Surgeon General who, in 1969, told Congress that 'It is time to close the book on infectious diseases, and declare the war against pestilence won.'[6]

Unfortunately, nature's capacity to harbour lethal infectious diseases had not been exhausted. What many experts had previously thought to be unthinkable, actually happened. During the early 80s, two new three-letter acronyms, HIV/AIDS struck mortal fear into the heart of gay communities, haemophiliacs, and other receiving blood transfusions. This was experienced initially in the West but then around the globe. By the end of the decade, AIDS had spread to the general population, especially in Africa, where it was being transmitted through heterosexual sex and was affecting women more than men. From the commencement of the epidemic, the HIV virus has infected 75 million people globally, of whom 32 million have died. Unprecedented amounts of money and resources have been invested in the search for a cure for AIDS yet, after almost 40 years, there is still no vaccine. As wake-up calls go, they don't get much louder.

Come Fly with Me

Throughout history, one of the most important vectors for the transmission of infectious diseases has been the migration of people. But the unimaginable scale of the modern travel phenomenon is without parallel. According to IATA, the International Air Transport Association, there were 4.4 billion airline trips taken by people in 2018 alone. What this means in practice is that an infectious disease breaking out on the far side of the world can be on your doorstep by the following morning. This is a dark side of globalisation and one that is rarely even spoken about.

For those who were willing and able to take note, it was becoming very evident that humanity was facing an array of infectious diseases that were growing at an unprecedented and unpredictable rate. Even more significantly, the invisible microbe had transitioned from being primarily a threat to human health to one that threatened national security, and the stability of the global order. Pathogens were becoming political.

There is an increasing recognition that the threat posed by direct military action to many states, so-called kinetic warfare, has decreased considerably in recent decades. At the same time, there has been a corresponding increase in security threats arising from non-traditional forms of attack such as terrorism, cyber warfare, information warfare and, more recently, the profoundly destabilising effects of infectious disease pandemics.

Though few realised it at the time, the SARS 2002-3 outbreak was a game changer. The pathogen that caused the disease was completely unknown at the time, and so we had neither diagnostic tests nor effective treatments to hand. The nature of the disease exposed key vulnerabilities within the globalised system. SARS was a respiratory disease that spread easily from person to person, but its more insidious features included: an asymptomatic incubation period of at least a week; symptoms that were very similar to other common infectious diseases; it spread rapidly on aircraft; had a high death toll among healthcare workers; and it had a very high fatality rate for the elderly – sounds familiar?

In many respects, SARS was also a great leveller. It didn't respect borders, nor did it discriminate between rich and poor – wealth alone could not offer failsafe protection. The application of advanced technological and medical know-how was able to rapidly identify the hitherto unknown causative agent in a remarkably short two weeks. The newly identified virus was christened SARS-CoV.

At the end of eight months, in July 2003, the WHO declared that the SARS virus had been contained. It is sobering to realise that this had been achieved, largely through public health strategies that were first devised in the 17th century to contain the bubonic plague. These elementary strategies which were later to serve as the foundational basis for the 19th-century discipline of epidemiology included: isolation, quarantine, case tracking, cancellation of mass gatherings, improved personal hygiene, and extensive use of masks, gowns, gloves and eye protection.

Throughout those centuries, the frontline people dealing with these pandemics were not data driven, evidence-based, or following the science; the science of infectious diseases was virtually non-existent. At best, it was rudimentary, and consequently very hit and miss. Doctors observed what was happening and drew common-sense conclusions based on what did and didn't work. The paradigmatic example of this was John Snow, the English physician, now considered a founder of modern epidemiology. As the 1854 cholera epidemic raged through Soho in London, by painstaking empirical work he was able to identify a major source of the outbreak – the water supply. By the simple act of removing the handle of the most popular water pump in the area, he succeeded in ameliorated the progress of the disease. His hunch that the cholera was being spread through contaminated waters proved decisive.

In the immediate aftermath of the SARS 2002-3 pandemic, significant investment was made in augmenting our capacity to combat future infectious disease pandemics successfully. But little has been done to analyse the particular aspects of modern society that have increased our vulnerability to such attacks. In particular, scant attention has been paid to how we might go about alleviating any such underlying conditions. Population growth and urbanisation are two of the most important factors in this regard.

And the debate between optimists, pessimists and realists on the dangers posed to humanity by biothreats continued. In his bestselling book *Enlightenment Now*, the evolutionary psychologist, Steven Pinker claimed, in effect, that the era of pandemics was over. 'Disease outbreaks don't become pandemics' any more, he argued. This is because 'advances in biology ... make it easier for the good guys (and there are many more of them) to identify pathogens, invent antibiotics that overcome antibiotic resistance, and rapidly develop vaccines.'

His optimism was not shared by the renowned astrophysicist, Martin Rees, who publicly offered a bet in 2002 that 'A bioterror or bioerror will lead to one million casualties in a single event within a six-month period starting no later than Dec 31 2020.' The bet was for $400 and the challenge was taken up by Steven Pinker. As a consequence of SARS CoV-2, the Astronomer Royal, Martin Rees won his bet.[7]

No Sex Please, We're Viruses

At their simplest, viruses are infectious microbes that invade cells and cause disease. They are incredibly small, smaller for instance than many other microbes, such as bacteria. They are not capable of surviving on their own and so these microscopic biological agents have to invade the cells of living hosts in order to replicate. That is why most biologists do not even consider viruses to be alive. But viruses have evolved one really clever evolutionary ability: they can subvert the host cell's metabolic machinery to their own survival and replication purposes.

Despite their microscopic size, and their inability to replicate or survive on their own, RNA viruses can multiply on an astounding scale. But unlike humans and most other life forms, viruses do not reproduce sexually since they are asexual. Unburdened in this way by the enormous evolutionary and other 'costs' associated with sexual reproduction, viruses seem to be able to replicate almost at will.

Unlike virtually every other living organism, viruses can undergo phenomenally fast rates of development. RNA viruses could well be a classic example of evolutionary punctuated equilibrium as they possess the potential for rapid evolution at the molecular level.[8] Conventional evolutionary theory posits that changes to organisms, including humans, evolve slowly and gradually over millennia. But in the early 70s, two Harvard paleobiologists, Stephen Jay Gould and Niles Eldredge put forward a revised hypothesis.[9] Based on their analysis of the fossil record they concluded that evolution progressed through very prolonged periods in which nothing much happened, followed by short periods in which rapid change occurred. For a Marxist like Gould, it was a happy reflection of a supposed observation by V.I. Lenin on human affairs: 'There are decades where nothing happens; and there are weeks where decades happen.'[10]

During periods of crisis and extreme stress, living organisms undergo significant evolutionary change in short bursts of time: so-called non-equilibrium conditions. Unlike slower-replicating organisms such as hominids, RNA viruses can replicate a million times faster than us and, critically, they also have the ability to mutate rapidly. When they are confronted by the challenges of new environmental conditions, they employ these skills to adapt quickly, and so can survive and thrive in their new circumstances.

The new theory developed by Gould and Eldredge was a modified form of gradualism that incorporated the notion of fits and starts. While it was fossil record evidence that inspired punctuated equilibrium, more recently, molecular evidence from viruses also offers support for the theory. In particular, there is evidence that viral genomes have undergone dramatic and rapid change which has given rise to new strains of virus with the capacity to infect different hosts.

It is this capacity for rapid evolution that makes viruses extremely 'efficient'. When viruses enter a new ecological niche, they continue to evolve and adapt until the variant that best suits that particular niche becomes dominant. If the environmental conditions remain stable and there are no further selective pressures, then there is viral stasis as there is no need for the virus to continue evolving. Viruses thus evolve unevenly and depend on changes in their ecological environment. It has been estimated that 50 years of virus evolution is the equivalent of 50 million years of DNA evolution.[11]

The rate of evolutionary change in RNA viruses is so fast that it can happen in a matter of months or even weeks. These are extremely high rates of spontaneous mutation with enormous consequences for human health. These remarkably high mutation rates are a defining characteristic of RNA viruses. It gives them an extraordinary adaptability which is the reason why they have become the principal cause of emerging infectious diseases. And once they have jumped the species barrier and infected humans, their speedy mutational capacity makes RNA viruses extremely difficult to control, if allowed to survive and proliferate in their new host species for a sustained period. This is precisely what happened in Britain and other countries when a new, more infectious, variant of Covid-19 was found to have become widespread by December.

This is proof, if proof were necessary, that RNA viruses pose a singular threat to the health of humanity. The human ecological framework has changed dramatically in recent decades, with rapid urbanisation and increased patterns of global travel offering vastly expanded the opportunities for viral proliferation. In the case of SARS, for instance, changes in the proximity of human recipients and populations of animal hosts have resulted in the creation of sustained networks of transmission increased that have elevated our exposure to the burdens of these infectious diseases.

In this ongoing microbial 'arms race' we are not, of course, completely defenceless. The human immune system is also adaptive and so can develop resistance to some pathogens through the creation of antibodies. But pathogens in turn can also adapt to either evade or suppress these antibodies. This becomes a constant struggle for supremacy between man and microbe. The virulence of a pathogen is simply the amount of morbidity and mortality caused by a pathogen to its host. But the pathogen also has to strike a fine balance. Too much virulence is obviously bad for the pathogen as it kills the host upon which its very survival depends. This may well be one reason why SARS died out so quickly.

The Cold Wars

A significant misconception has developed regarding coronaviruses. The impression has been created that science and medicine were unfamiliar with these viruses and that they have had little impact on the health of the public at large until recent decades. This is not quite the case. Common respiratory coronaviruses have been part of a palette of pathogens that have menaced humanity for quite a while. According to some molecular clock analysis, coronaviruses have been around for over 10,000 years.[12] As microbes go, that's actually quite young. Coronaviruses which were known to cause respiratory and intestinal infections were never thought of as benign, but neither were they considered an inordinate threat to human health. That all changed in 2002.

Coronaviruses comprise a large family of viruses which can infect both humans and a number of animal species. They circulate widely throughout the globe. In humans, coronaviruses are responsible for a wide spectrum of illnesses which include the common cold and influenza. The flu and the common cold are similar, but they not the same. They are similar in that they both can cause upper respiratory tract infections but they differ in speed of onset and duration. For most people, these infections result in a mild to moderate illness with unpleasant, often debilitating and, thankfully, transient consequences of the type with which we are all only too familiar. For a variety of reasons, we have developed an easy familiarity with influenza and an acceptance of its consequences. The flu has become a familiar foe.

Influenza even has its own 'season'. Such is its constancy that the arrival of the annual influenza outbreak can be predicted with considerable accuracy by epidemiologists. The pendular regularity of influenza's arrival, combined with its relatively low mutation rate have helped us in the arms race against this particular strain of the coronavirus. In particular, this has allowed scientists to developed curative vaccines to combat the pathogen. In tandem, pharmaceutical companies have also been able to develop a well-honed production system that can deliver these vaccines in quantity, and virtually on demand.

The annual influenza visitations are recorded in considerable detail by the relevant health authorities in most countries. In Europe, for example, during the winter months, seasonal influenza can infect up to 20% of the population. But even a cursory review of the available figures shows that, in terms of morbidity and mortality, the consequences of these coronavirus-derived infections are not trivial.

Yet, despite their relative significance, the annual influenza numbers rarely hit the headlines. Such public nonchalance is not warranted by the statistics themselves. According to a 2015 joint study by the United States Centers for Disease Control and Prevention (CDC) and the World Health Organization, 650,000 people die of respiratory diseases linked to seasonal flu every year. In the US alone, and depending on the virulence of a particular year's virus, the CDC has estimated that influenza has caused between 12,000 and 61,000 deaths annually since 2010.[13] These are very stark numbers. Yet for the SARS 2002-3 outbreak, according to the figures released by the WHO, there were 8,096 cases and a total of 774 deaths over a nine-month period, a high case fatality ratio of 9.6%.[14] But that's only an average of 86 deaths per month, globally.

Despite the SARS figures being incongruously low, compared to the annual flu statistics, the SARS pandemic really commanded the world's attention. For the first few months of 2003, the world looked on with increasing trepidation as the various national and international public health authorities grappled with the virus. It affected Asia, in particular, and it was there that facemasks became the public symbol of the visceral fear that the fast-spreading contagion had triggered. Despite SARS comparatively low mortality rate, the shock of an unknown highly contagious viral attack that came completely out of the blue delivered a very considerable jolt to a complacent world. As we shall see, it was the first battle in what turned out to be a protracted coronavirus war from which lessons were learnt by some, but, unfortunately, not by most.

Chapter 6: Dress Rehearsal

Whatever You Say, Say Nothing

From an early stage in the SARS outbreak, the questions of how the virus had emerged preoccupied virologists, epidemiologists and international health officials. Though the finger of suspicion pointed towards an animal to human transmission occurrence, there was little by way of definitive evidence. In fact, conclusive scientific evidence for the zoonotic origin of SARS wasn't finally assembled for another 15 years. In the short-term, however, the geographical location of this particular species-jumping pathogen was quickly identified as Guangdong, a province in southern China.

The identification of southern China as the source of the SARS virus came as little surprise to international contagious disease experts. South China possesses a myriad of so-called wet markets where a bewildering variety of exotic wild animals are sold and butchered alongside farmed animals. In traditional Chinese cuisine, many of these species are considered culinary delicacies. As locations where people and wild animals circulate freely in close proximity, Western epidemiologists have long considered these markets to be potent petri dishes for the incubation of microbial pathogens that pose considerable dangers to humans.

There had already been some warnings about this: one in particular stood out. In 1997 there were disquieting suspicions that the H5N1 avian influenza outbreak, so-called 'bird flu', had been transmitted to humans in a Hong Kong wet market. As luck would have it, that particular virus did not develop efficient human-to-human transmission mechanisms so its impact on human health was limited. However, scientific experts needed little further evidence that a novel source of a potentially lethal viral threat to humanity had emerged. Five years later, in 2002, the rest of the world witnessed that potential become reality.

Within a few months of the SARS outbreak, Chinese authorities carried out an investigation into the growing number of atypical pneumonia cases that were happening in Guangzhou city, Guangdong. Not only did China not share this report with the WHO, it didn't even inform the organisation that there had been an infectious disease outbreak, though it was obliged to under the WHO's international regulations. Even more egregiously, the report and any information about the escalating health crisis was declared 'top secret' by the CCP. This made any discussion or sharing of information about the report a violation of China's strict state secrecy laws, which carried severe penalties.

But the CCP's compulsive desires to keep any kind of bad news secret were dashed by modern communications technology. Sometime in early February, the following text message was sent from a mobile phone: 'There is a fatal flu in Guangzhou'. Over each the subsequent three days that text was resent 40 million, 41 million, and 45 million times, respectively. On February 10, the WHO received an alarming e-mail from the son of a former WHO employee in China: 'Am wondering if you have information on the strange contagious disease . . . which has already left more than 100 people dead. The outbreak is not allowed to be made known to the public . . . but people are already aware . . . and there is a "panic" attitude'. That same day the WHO made its first formal approach to the Chinese government seeking information.

Recognising that the jig was up, on February 11 China notified the WHO 'of an outbreak of acute respiratory syndrome with 300 cases and five deaths in Guangdong Province'. Despite being forced to acknowledge the existence of an infectious disease outbreak within its territory, the CCP continued to cover up the true scale of the epidemic. In subsequent communications, China declined the WHO's offers to send technical experts to help contain the epidemic. It insisted that the disease was under control and that the number of cases was declining, while also falsely claiming that the disease had not spread beyond Guangdong Province. To maintain this fiction, the CCP ordered a complete news blackout on reporting of the disease outbreak by domestic Chinese media. Two weeks later, the Chinese Ministry of Health, informed the WHO that the cause of the outbreak in Guangdong was *Chlamydia pneumoniae*, a bacterial infection more commonly known as 'walking pneumonia'. Throughout February, the Chinese Communist Party persisted with its strategy of orchestrated deception by variously denying, dissembling, or downplaying the crisis. But towards the end of February, events began to spin out of the Party's control and the strategy unravelled.

SARS Takes Off

The fact that the SARS outbreak became a global event can be traced to one man who spent one night in a Hong Kong hotel in February 2003. Dr Liu Jianlun, a 64-year-old medical doctor had been treating atypical pneumonia patients in a hospital in Guangdong, the epicentre of the outbreak. A few days before he was due to go to Hong Kong to attend his nephew's wedding, he felt a bit feverish. He dosed himself with antibiotics and had a chest X-ray taken. The X-ray showed his lungs were clear and he thought himself well enough to make the three-hour bus journey to Hong Kong. On 21 February, he checked into the Metropole Hotel, a 487-room, three-star hotel located in Hong Kong's Kowloon district. One day after arriving in Hong Kong, Dr Liu fell ill and was admitted to Kwong Wah Hospital suffering from severe pneumonia. Two weeks later he was dead.

During his one-night stay in room 911 of the Metropole Hotel, Dr Liu had infected up to 16 other people, including foreigners with whom he had shared the same ninth floor of the hotel. Over the following days, these people fanned out to various other international destinations. Unaware that they were carriers, the disease spread with them. Within a few days, there were 150 new suspected cases of atypical pneumonia in countries as far apart as Canada, Indonesia, the Philippines, Singapore, Vietnam, Ireland, and, of course, Hong Kong itself.

In a highly mobile globalised world, SARS had become the first infectious disease epidemic of the 21st century. It turned out that Dr Liu had been what was subsequently known as a 'super spreader', and the Metropole Hotel in Hong Kong had become the ground-zero of the SARS outbreak. Of the over 8,000 people infected by SARS globally, the WHO estimates that more than 4,000 of them can be traced back to Dr Liu's stay at the Metropole Hotel. Even after two decades, and though there are lots of hypotheses, it still remains a mystery how exactly so many of Dr Liu's fellow guests on the ninth floor of the Metropole Hotel became infected by him.

In hospital, X-rays confirmed that Dr Liu had the deadly disease and as his condition deteriorated, he was put on a respirator and heavily sedated – he never regained consciousness.[1] Unsurprisingly, the unfortunate Dr Liu also had a devasting impact on the other people he came into contact with during his brief stay in Hong Kong. As a result, Hong Kong had the second highest number of SARS infections in the world. Only mainland China's infection rate was greater.

The speed with which SARS spread was unprecedented and took epidemiologists completely by surprise. This, combined with its almost 10% lethality had a chilling effect on people worldwide. HIV/AIDS, for example, took over two decades to spread around the world. Ebola made people too sick to travel, while two other new Asian diseases, Nipah and Hendra did not transmit efficiently between people.

SARS was different – it had the potential to change the world. The triumphalist optimism of the 1950s, 60s and 70s disease experts that humanity had conquered infectious diseases was entirely misplaced. SARS inaugurated a new and deadly phase of the war between man and microbe. It also put an abrupt end to the lingering conceit that had prevailed since the mid-20th century, that humanity's struggle with infectious diseases was at an end.

By now it was abundantly clear that a major international disease outbreak was under way and, worryingly, the cause of the disease had still not been identified. On March 12, the WHO issued a carefully worded global infectious disease alert involving cases of atypical pneumonia. With the limited evidence available to it, the WHO issued a politically sensitive emergency travel advisory notice with potentially enormous consequences for international air travel and tourist businesses. In was in this travel alert issued by WHO Director-General Dr Gro Harlem Brundtland that the new disease was first given a name, Severe Acute Respiratory Syndrome, or SARS, which she stressed. 'is now a worldwide health threat.'

As health officials, scientists, and medical personnel in multiple countries began working on the disease the epidemiological profile of SARS started to become clearer. It was becoming increasingly evident that SARS was caused by a virus, probably of the coronavirus family. Yet the CCP continued to insist that the cause of the disease was bacterial while understating the real number of infections and deaths. On top of this, China was refusing to allow the WHO personnel working in China to visit Guangdong. Meanwhile, both the infection and mortality rates were increasing internationally. By April, international scientists had established beyond doubt that the causative agent of SARS was a coronavirus and not a bacterium as the CCP was claiming. Though its 'story' was falling apart, the CCP still refused to play ball with the WHO. The WHO's frustrations with China were mounting.

With just a few months to go before the end of her five-year term as Director General of the WHO, it was clear to Dr Brundtland that her patient behind-the-scenes pressure on China had failed to bear fruit: the CCP had not significantly modified its behaviour. Normally the WHO refrains from publicly criticising its member states. Its long-standing preference is to abide by the niceties of international diplomacy in the expectation that, eventually, recalcitrants would see the error of their ways and change their behaviour. In China, the evidence for such benign optimism was non-existent; actually, the reverse was the case. It was becoming crystal clear that 'business as usual' with China was no longer an option for the WHO.

Dr Brundtland's WHO changed tack. The head of the organisation's Beijing office was uncharacteristically blunt in addressing himself to Chinese officials; 'We have very clearly said you have an international community over here that does not trust your figures.' The WHO had little choice at this stage as the Communist Party's obfuscation and lies were undermining the organisation's core objective of protecting the health and well-being of the rest of the world. The WHO's uncharacteristic candidness towards China brought immediate benefits, some of which were entirely unexpected.

On April 3, the Minister for Health appeared on national television where he persevered with the four-month-old fiction that the outbreak in China was under control. But then suddenly, China's unified authoritarian facade began to crack. Within 24 hours there was a further unexpected and unprecedented announcement. For a regime that had never previously acknowledged its mistakes, China's Centre for Disease Control issued a startling public apology 'for failing to inform the public about a sometime fatal respiratory illness that has infected more than 2,000 people worldwide.'

For seasoned China-watchers, this sudden change of direction was a clear indication that there was a power struggle going on among factions within the Party's top echelons. The Party was no longer speaking with one voice. Within days, the Chinese Communist Party's recidivist authoritarian tendencies soon reasserted themselves, at least in the capital. The Beijing city leadership continued to report case figures that were unbelievably low. The extent of the underreporting prompted dissent from within. Jiang Yanyong, a Chinese doctor and Communist Party member, publicly accused the city government of covering up the extent of the SARS outbreak in Beijing. Soon other doctors followed suit and their statements were carried extensively throughout Western media.

As only authoritarian regimes can do without suffering any adverse political consequences, the Chinese Communist Party did a complete *volte face*. Things began to move quickly. The CCP declared a national war on the SARS virus and ordered its officials to refrain from further cover-ups and report openly on the epidemic that was continuing to ravage the country. As a token of its new-found earnestness, on April 20, the CCP stripped both the Minister of Health and the mayor of Beijing of their party positions.

In a tacit acknowledgement of its previous mendacity, the government announced that the number of cases in Beijing was 346 and not 34 as originally claimed. At the same time, the Secretary of Beijing's Communist Party issued an apology for the mishandling of the epidemic up to that point. Very late in the day, the Chinese Communist Party had, apparently, seen the light. But not before the SARS epidemic had caused extensive suffering and death around the world, much of which would have been avoided if the CCP had not been so duplicitous from the outset, and then persisted with it for so long.

Initially, economists had difficulties calculating the economic costs of SARS and were largely unperturbed about its macroeconomic consequences, concluding that its effects would be negligible. The speed with which events on the ground unfolded, in particular the immediate impact it had on travel, tourism and other parts of the services sector, soon put paid to this complacency. Core aspects of the economy such as retail and manufacturing were soon being affected, especially in China. Uncertainty about the disease, combined with intense media attention, stoked widespread public fear which quickly exacerbated the economic fallout. The Asian Development Bank warned that East Asia alone would suffer a $US 28 billion drop in income as a consequence of SARS.

Fallout

In China, the worst affected country, the reverberations of SARS were not confined to public health and the economy. The initial cover-up and the subsequent back-pedalling intensified the political rivalries between the factions of Hu Jintao and Jiang Zemin. In the ensuing struggle for power Jiang, who had initially downplayed SARS, lost out to Hu. Eventually, President Hu publicly acknowledged the seriousness of the threat posed by SARS and began to ease the authoritarian iron-grip with which, up to then, the Chinese media had been restrained. The public signalling of the regime's political about-face came when the Minister of Health who had overseen the crisis, a Jiang loyalist, was fired.

Meanwhile, throughout the developed world there were the usual pious political pronouncements that 'lessons would have to be learnt'. In the US, at least, there was some action. The CDC assembled a group of international disease experts to analyse the SARS pandemic. Their findings were published in 2004 in a report titled *Learning from SARS: Preparing for the Next Disease Outbreak*. Among the critical questions to which the specialists sought answers were: 'Will SARS re-emerge, and with greater virulence? Can we contain a more widely disseminated epidemic? Will we have preventive or therapeutic countermeasures? Can the necessary global cooperation and resources for containment be sustained? In the light of what happened to the world in 2020, those turned out to be prescient questions.

The report contained a number of particularly pertinent conclusions. First, 'most emerging infections other than influenza will represent a truly novel threat for which the world is inadequately prepared.' Secondly, with respect to China's flagrantly covering up and lying about the extent of the SARS outbreak, the report states rather coyly that "China missed an opportunity to show the world its considerable intellectual and scientific potential … it remains to be seen whether China will show leadership in proactively addressing the problem.'[2] At the height of the globalist appeasement of the CCP, this was a genuflection to Chinese sensibilities in the hope of reducing future recidivist behaviour.

The WHO representatives' contribution to the report is of particular note, given the organisation's centrality in dealing with infectious diseases with international potential: 'The first and most compelling lesson concerns the need to report, promptly and openly, cases of any disease with the potential for international spread. Attempts to conceal cases of an infectious disease, for fear of social and economic consequences, must be recognized as a short-term stop-gap measure that carries a very high price.'[3] Though the WHO's point is absolutely valid, because of the international rules of the game it was, and still is, devoid of any power to compel member states to report incidences of infectious diseases.

Apart from in times of war, states rarely adopt such a hyper-invasive role in the lives of ordinary citizens other than when trying to combat communicable diseases. Historically, all sorts of intrusive state actions have been tolerated by the citizenry of most countries in the name of controlling infectious disease outbreaks. To the extent that such outbreaks were highly localised they had considerable merit, and often worked. However, infectious diseases are no respecters of national borders, and as people crossed them so too did the infection.

Controlling these silent, highly infectious, international interlopers was seen as the task of each individual state according to the rules of the international order – and therein lies the dilemma. What were once thought of as localised, and therefore distant threats, became imminent ones of urgent worldwide concern in an era of globalisation. If a state, especially one where the disease had originated, was unwilling to cooperate with international efforts to control an incipient pandemic, or worse denied or downplayed the outbreak, there was little that anyone could do about it. Though the attitude and efficacy of domestic responses had important global ramifications, what happened inside the sacrosanct perimeters of a state was a matter solely for those who ruled that state: a state of affairs that had been sanctified by international law since 1648 and is known as the Westphalian Settlement.

In that year, the Thirty Years War, the long-running dispute between the Pope, the Emperor and the German barons over their respective sovereignty rights to rule, was brought to an end by the Treaty of Westphalia. That Treaty has provided the legal basis for international relations between states ever since. The two essential principles of the Westphalian settlement are the inviolability of borders and non-interference in the internal affairs of sovereign states. Stemming from this, it became a bedrock principle of international law that for a state to be bound by any global governance rules it had first to give its consent.[4]

The dilemmas posed by the Westphalian system rules to the operational capacity of the WHO to do its work were well recognised by Dr Brundtland: 'Globalization of disease and threats to health mean globalization of the fight against them. SARS has been a wake-up call. But the lessons we have learned have implications that go way beyond the fight against this public health threat ... The events of the last few weeks also prompt us to look closely at the instruments of national and international law. Are they keeping up with our rapidly changing world?'[5]

The international rules which all the member states of the WHO are obliged to follow are detailed in its International Health Regulations (IHR). Under them, the principal obligation of the WHO's member states is to notify it immediately if an infectious disease with international potential breaks out within its territory. The rules are classically Westphalian in that they are consent-based and restricted solely to the international aspects of infectious diseases – the WHO has no role in individual states health systems.

But even with these severely delimited governance rules, the WHO had been routinely ignored by its members – when it suited them. In 2002, with limited authority and a tendency for member states to buck the rules, the WHO found itself facing an unprecedented infectious disease epidemic with potentially disastrous international consequences. To make matters worse, the epicentre of the SARS disease was also the world's largest Communist-controlled country, and one that jealously guarded its Westphalian rights and privileges. The Chinese Communist Party's unrivalled record of dictatorial rule over the world's most populous country had emboldened it to treat the WHO with insolent disdain during the critical first three months of the outbreak. That was until the WHO's first female Director General let it be known that such behaviour was no longer acceptable.

Dr Gro Harlem Brundtland was a passionate trailblazer. A trained physician with a Master's in Public Health from Harvard, the mother of four worked as a doctor in Norway's public-school health system before she entered politics and became Norway's youngest Prime Minister. Dr Brundtland has chalked up some impressive landmark achievements. The first woman Prime Minister of her country (serving three times), the first woman to be elected to lead a major UN commission, and in 1998 she became the first woman Director General of the WHO.

She was under no illusions about the challenges she faced her in her new role: 'WHO was seen as unfocused, even corrupt, and overrun by middle-level management ... The state of affairs, however irreparable, actually stimulated me to step forward. But it would not be an easy job.'[6] At the outset of taking up her global health responsibilities, she could not have possibly realised the unprecedented disaster-management challenges that her new job would eventually bring forth.

In the immediate aftermath of the SARS outbreak, the WHO had played a reasonably good game, considering the very weak hand it had been dealt at the start of the outbreak by the CCP. In a July 2003 press release, the Director General of the WHO announced that the worldwide SARS pandemic had been contained. Dr Brundtland, the tough, no-nonsense, three-time Prime Minister of Norway, ended her statement with an astute, if understated, warning for the world's political leaders: 'SARS is teaching us many lessons. Now we must translate those lessons into action. We may have very little time, and we must use it wisely.'

The primary reason for the rapid spread of SARS was that people had no immunity to the coronavirus pathogen that caused the disease. It also became evident from an early stage that healthcare workers and close family members of those infected had a disproportionately high incidence of the disease. People were also being infected through contact with inanimate objects where the disease could linger for a time. But the single most important lesson from the 2002-3 SARS epidemic was that the disease's most devastating impact was on the elderly and those with underlying health conditions. In May 2003, the WHO reported that for those aged 65 and over, the death rate was a staggering 55%.

At a WHO global meeting on SARS in Kuala Lumpur, June 17, 2003, Dr Brundtland announced that in the 100 days since the WHO had first sounded the global alarm bells on the disease on March 12, 2003 'we have seen SARS stopped dead in its tracks in some of the worst affected areas.' She went on to spell out graphically for her audience what the world had just experienced: 'We are dealing with a new disease, striking a globalized society. We have seen its rapid international spread. We have seen stock markets move up or down according to the latest success or setback in the SARS situation. We have seen bustling transportation hubs go quiet. We have seen SARS on the front pages and on our TV screens. We have seen the closure of hospitals, schools, and borders. We have witnessed the economic impact, population movements from affected cities, and unwarranted discrimination.' Two decades later, the world would experience it all again – this time on an even more unimaginable scale.

It is entirely a matter of speculation as to how many lives could have been saved and economic damage avoided if the Chinese Communist Party had been forthcoming much earlier about the scale of the SARS 2002-3 outbreak. Right on its doorstep in Hong Kong, China had a shining example of how openness and the timely sharing of information with the WHO and the international community could help to alleviate the worst effects of an infectious disease outbreak. Just about the time that it was reverting to Chinese rule in mid-1997, Hong Kong was struck by an epidemic of avian flu. But having reached out early, local and international health experts were able to mitigate the worst effects of the bird flu epidemic.

It was a signal example that the CCP chose to ignore during SARS. Even two decades later, the Party was still parading its slow-learning capacity. When a similar infectious disease emerged in Wuhan in late 2019, it became apparent very quickly that, like Talleyrand's Bourbons, the Chinese Communist Party 'had learnt nothing and forgotten nothing'.

Chapter 7: Censoring the Outbreak

At both national and local levels, the Chinese Communist Party officials were slow to react to the disease outbreak in Wuhan. They then compounded their initial dilatory response to the fast-moving crisis by first trying to suppress information, and then by intimidating and punishing those who had tried to raise the alarm, including scientists and doctors. Their reflexive instincts were to deny and then censor anything that might pose a threat to the party's hegemonic political control.

Many of the patterns of behaviour indulged in by the CCP during the SARS pandemic of 2002-3 resurfaced during the SARS-CoV-2 outbreak in 2020. Attempts by scientists to map the pattern of the early transmission of Covid-19 were severely hampered by the failure of the Chinese Communist authorities to be open and transparent about what they knew and when they knew it. Access to this early-stage information on such a major infectious outbreak was essential if epidemiologists were going to be able to quantify the scale of the looming threat. During the initial phase, there was really only broad agreement on one thing; that the disease had emerged in the central Chinese city of Wuhan in 2019. Critically, what remained unclear was when precisely this happened, how many were being infected, and how the disease was being transmitted.

In subsequent months, blatantly, the CCP tried retrospectively to control the narrative of how China initially dealt with the outbreak. For example, though they were circumscribed, belated and sought to downplay the severity and scale of the epidemic when they were first issued, all traces of any early official statements on the outbreak issued by the Wuhan authorities about what was happening in the city have been erased from government sites. This calculated effort to excise incriminating evidence of the Communist authority's disastrous reaction during the initial phase of the epidemic was ultimately futile, as contemporaneous reports of the relevant parts of all these statements were carried extensively in Western media. In Xi's autocratic China, the compulsion to censor is so ingrained that it has become reflexive – even when futile and self-defeating. In this atmosphere, state media has, once again, risen to the challenge of being a mouth-piece for the Communist Party. It's a state of affairs that did not come about by accident.

A central aspect of Xi Jinping's new authoritarianism is his subordination of all the principal Chinese media to the will of the

Communist Party. There was nothing clandestine, coy or subtle about his announcement in 2016 that the role of China's media was to serve as a propaganda tool for the Party and, by extension, the party leader. In Xi Jinping's own words, according to the state news agency, *Xinhua*, 'All news media run by the party must work to speak for the party's will and its propositions, and protect the party's authority and unity.'[1]

As an indication of the new authoritarian control of news media in China, in order to renew their press cards, journalists are required to take a test in order that they can 'uphold the Marxist journalistic ideals more consciously.' In such an atmosphere, it is little wonder that transparency in pandemic reporting also played second fiddle to the propaganda needs of the Party. The detailed manner in which the CCP went about censoring and manipulating information about the infectious disease that was menacing the Chinese people and clearly posed an existential threat to people around the world is worth looking at in some detail.

A New Year Message from China

At the dawning of the third decade of the 21st century, while the rest of the world was celebrating New Year's Eve, the Chinese authorities are supposed to have sent a statement to the WHO in Geneva on December 31, 2019 informing it of a viral pneumonia outbreak then underway in Wuhan. With Geneva, like the rest of Europe in the midst of the New Year holidays, it wasn't until four days later, Saturday January 4, that the WHO alerted the world to the unfolding situation in China – by tweet.

In its tweet of January 4, the WHO stated that 'China has reported to WHO a cluster of pneumonia cases – with no deaths – in Wuhan, Hubei Province.' The following day, January 5, in its first lengthy statement on the epidemic in China, the WHO stated that 'a total of 44 patients with pneumonia of unknown etiology have been reported to the WHO by the national authorities in China.' There were no deaths, but 11 patients were severely ill and the other 33 were stable. In this, the organisation's much discussed first detailed communication on the disease outbreak in China, the WHO claimed that its 'China Country Office was informed of cases of pneumonia of unknown etiology (unknown cause) detected in Wuhan City'. The statement said there was 'no evidence of significant human-to-human transmission and no health care worker infections have been reported.'

The key aspect of this quotation from the WHO statement is its use of the word 'significant'. That adjectival qualification was, in reality, a clear admission by the WHO that in early January it had a pretty good idea that there was human-to-human transmission of the virus in Wuhan. By continuing to use the weasel-word 'significant' in the statement, the WHO may have been trying to have it both ways. On the one hand, it did not want to be seen to be reality-deniers by acquiescing completely in the Chinese narrative while, on the other, trying desperately not to offend China either. As events were to unfold over the ensuing months, this attitude of what many considered to be undue deference and public appeasement towards China, became an ingrained feature of the WHO's behaviour – at least in public.

From the beginning, there was widespread scepticism regarding the credibility of China's disease statistics. Most commentators believed that the numbers were contrived and had substantially understated both the case numbers and fatalities. These dubious numbers have been faithfully reported by the WHO, even when, on occasion, they were internally contradictory.

On January 12, a week after its first lengthy statement, a further WHO release said 'among the 41 confirmed cases, there has been one death.' It went on to say that this 'cluster was initially reported on 31 December 2019, when the WHO China Country Office was informed.' There is no explanation as to why the number of reported cases (41) was actually three fewer than the previous week's statement (44). Nor should the figures be taken as separate totals for each week because, as the statement confirms, 'no additional cases have been detected since 3 January 2020.' This WHO statement threw one other interesting piece of light on these Covid-19 cases when it stated that the symptom onset of the 41 patients occurred between December 8, 2019 and January 2, 2020.

So, if we are to take these official Chinese figures as reported by the WHO at face value, then between December 8 and January 12 there were a total of 41 (44) cases of infection and one death. This was a 6-week period during which a highly infectious disease was spreading through a densely populated city of 11 million people, at a time when no mitigation measures of any kind had either been announced or implemented. During a similar 6-week timeframe at the outset of the outbreak in Italy, from January 31 to March 9, there were 9,172 cases of infection and 463 deaths, at a time when a severe lockdown had been in place in the worst affected areas of Lombardia for three weeks.[2]

In summary, what China was claiming through the WHO was: first, the total number of confirmed cases for most of the month of December and into January was 44/41; secondly, there had been one fatality; thirdly, the first confirmed Covid-19 case in China was on December 8 (*The Lancet* paper says December 1. See below); fourthly, though the average number of cases per day for December was 1.5, for the nine days between January 3 and January 12, there were none. This last figure is really astonishing when one considers that there had been no official announcement that a SARS-like epidemic was under way in Wuhan and that no mitigation measures had been instituted.

Lies, Damn Lies, and Statistics

According to government data seen by Hong Kong's *South China Morning Post* (SCMP), a 55-year-old from Hubei province could have been the first person to have contracted Covid-19 as early as November 17. According to the numbers reported by the *SCMP*, by mid-December the total number of infections stood at 27, with the first double-digit daily rise reported on December 17. By December 20, the total number of confirmed cases had reached 60. In the 24 hours between the last day of 2019 and the first day of 2020 the number of confirmed cases increased from 266 to 381. While these government figures have not been released to the public, the *SCMP*'s report of them is an invaluable indication about what was really happening with the disease in Wuhan during the early days of the outbreak.[3] This *SCMP* report also confirms that the Chinese Government knew exactly what was going on in Wuhan at a very early stage of the infectious disease outbreak in December.

One of the most salient and authoritative pieces of evidence we have for this important early phase of the outbreak in Wuhan is a report published in medical journal *The Lancet* by Chinese doctors. Published online on January 24, the paper analysed the first group of the viral pneumonia cases who had been admitted to the dedicated infectious disease hospital in Wuhan, Jinyintan Hospital, up to January 2. One of the principal authors of this report is Dr Huang Chaolin, vice-president of Wuhan Jinyintan Hospital, who had treated severe patients with the new corona pneumonia. The epidemiological research carried out by these Chinese specialists on the first 41 cases who were treated throughout December established an unambiguous link between the outbreak and the local Wuhan seafood market. Of the 41 laboratory-confirmed infectious patients the team analysed, 27 (66%) had a history of exposure to the local seafood market.[4]

These doctors also put the date for the first known infectious case in Wuhan as December 1, while the WHO's website states that the first confirmed Covid-19 case was on December 8, as reported to it by China. The significance of the confirmation by *The Lancet* paper that the first patient to be medically attested as infected occurred on December 1 is that, with an incubation period of between 5 and 14 days, the disease was spreading in Wuhan from November – corroboration of the veracity of the *SCMP* story quoted above.

There is a further very important detail about this first recorded infection case that The *Lancet* article did not make clear: had this first infected patient acquired his infection at the Wuhan seafood market? If he did not, then Covid-19 had been spreading in central China since November and, most importantly, had originated from a source separate from the Wuhan market. It would place a major question mark over the CCP's claim that the origin of the virus was the Wuhan seafood market.

A little over three weeks after *The Lancet* article was published, one of its authors Dr. Wu Wenjuan, director of the Intensive Care Unit (ICU) of Jinyintan Hospital gave an interview to the BBC's China service. Dr Wu gave some critically important new evidence regarding the patient who became ill on December 1. She confirmed that the December 1 date for his symptom onset had been ascertained through extensive interviews with his family carried out as part of an epidemiological survey.

The patient was an elderly man in his 70s who had had a stroke and suffered from dementia. Dr Wu explained that 'he was in very bad condition when he was sent here. He lives four or five stations (stops) away from the seafood market. And because he is ill, he basically doesn't go out.' The BBC interviewer asked the next obvious question: 'Is there any other channel of infection? But Dr Wu did not respond directly, 'What you asked is the direction of our next research.'[5]

This unnamed elderly patient is the closest we have come to identifying so-called 'patient zero' for Covid-19. It was also clear that he did not contract the disease in the seafood market. A further three patients were admitted to Jinyintan Hospital with the Covid-19 virus on December 10, only two of them had exposure to the seafood market. This evidence casts serious doubt on the seafood market as the origin of the virus. Within a week of *The Lancet* paper's publication its lead author, Dr Huang Chaolin gave an interview to the reputable Chinese business publication *Caixin* in which he said 'from the point of view of the overall incidence, the seafood market is no longer the only source of exposure ... It is multi-sourced.'[6]

Apart from the numbers, an important aspect of the statements issued by the WHO right up to mid-January was their repeated insistence that 'there has been no suggestion of human-to-human transmission'. This was usually accompanied by a further amplification that 'there have been no infections reported among health care workers'. This latter point, as some of the WHO statements themselves make clear, is a leading indicator for the existence of person-to-person transmission. Remember, this was a novel disease about which little was known definitively.

One of the most significant aspects of this knowledge gap was the exact transmission dynamics of the virus. If the disease could pass efficiently from person-to-person then that changed everything. It was critical therefore to ascertain any evidence for person-to-person transmission as rapidly as possible. On January 16, a WHO statement said 'not enough is known about 2019-nCoV to draw definitive conclusions about how it is transmitted.' Despite these ongoing denials by the WHO, based on information supplied to it by the communist authorities in China, there were unambiguous indications of person-to-person transmission from a very early stage.

The Lancet article by the Chinese medical specialists contained one such important piece of evidence. The state news agency *Xinhua* had earlier confirmed that the first death from the disease in Wuhan occurred on January 9.[7] According to *The Lancet,* the man had had continuous exposure to the Wuhan seafood market. However, about a week before he died, his 53-year-old wife 'who had no known history of exposure to the market, also presented with pneumonia and was hospitalised in the isolation ward.'[8] Clearly, the most likely explanation was that she had been infected by her husband, a clear indication of person-to-person transmission in early January.

While *The Lancet* article stressed the fact that 27 (66%) of the patients had direct exposure to the seafood market, it raised the obvious question: how did the other 14 (34%) get infected? The article provides no answer. There were also numerous reports circulating in December in Wuhan that medical staff were being infected. Lu Xiaohong, director of the Department of Gastroenterology in a Wuhan hospital heard that medical staff in two other hospitals in Wuhan were suspected of being infected with unexplained viral pneumonia and had been quarantined.[9]

Just five days after *The Lancet* paper was published, on January 29, the *New England Journal of Medicine* (*NEJM*) also published a paper by a different group of Chinese medical specialists on the epidemiological characteristics of a group of Wuhan infected patients that was 10 times larger than *The Lancet* cohort. Of this first group of 425 infected patients, the majority (55%) were linked to the Wuhan seafood market and, critically, had become infected prior to January 1. The corollary of course was that 45% had been infected elsewhere. Of this latter group, the paper states 'there was an exponential increase in the number of nonlinked [to the seafood market] cases beginning in late December.' The *NEJM* paper therefore concluded, 'on the basis of this information, there is evidence that human to human transmission has occurred among close contacts since the middle of December 2019.'[10]

In response to the *NEJM* article Professor Wang Liming of the College of Life Sciences at Zhejiang University messaged on Weibo, the Chinese Twitter, 'To say that I am furious is to fall short. I have no words. From this article, the National Centers for Disease Control and Prevention has already had clear evidence of human-to-human transmission of the virus as early as the first few days of January. This is the first solid proof that it was intentionally concealed that there were infections among humans. Then the news [question] is at which step was it covered up?' (This Weibo message has been deleted).

By the end of January, Chinese scientists and medical researchers had published no fewer than six papers of a high academic standard in a combination of *The Lancet* and the *New England Journal of Medicine*; two of the West's most prestigious medical journals. For a Party that likes to control its media with an iron grip, these articles in foreign publications over which they had no say, were an indication that things were getting out of hand and had to be reined in. On January 30, the Ministry of Science and Technology issued a notice which spelled out that the CCP expected of these medical researchers to apply themselves to epidemic research and control; 'scientific researchers must first adhere to the interests of the nation and the people... They should not focus on publishing their papers.'

Despite the preponderance of evidence for person-to-person transmission that was available to it, on December 31 the Wuhan Municipal Health Commission released a statement (now deleted) on its website stating that 'The investigation so far has not found any obvious human-to-human transmission and no medical staff infection.' Four days later the Commission released another statement (also deleted) repeating the same assurances that there was no person-to-person transmission and no medical staff infections.

Meanwhile, government censors in China were hard at work silencing any 'rumours' regarding the outbreak. On China's most popular social media platform, Weibo, the censors blocked the hashtag #WuhanSARS. But Chinese citizens continued to voice their outrage, anger and frustration at the censorship and ongoing coverup. One citizen posted the type of rhetorical questions for which an authoritarian state has no sensible answer; 'I don't have the right to speak and I don't even know the truth. Don't I have the right to panic and save myself?'[11]

On December 30, the same night that the Wuhan Institute's most experienced virologist, Shi Zhengli, was on the high-speed train back to Wuhan from Shanghai on her boss' instructions, a young ophthalmic surgeon, Dr Li Wenliang, had just finished a long shift at Wuhan Central Hospital. Earlier that day the Wuhan CDC had sent an 'Urgent notice on the treatment of pneumonia of unknown cause' to all hospitals in the city warning them to 'strengthen the multidisciplinary expertise of respiratory, infectious diseases, and intensive care medicine in a targeted manner'. Some of the details of this 'urgent notice' were carried in a report in *The Beijing News Express* which also reported that the National Health Commission (Ministry of Health) based in Beijing had sent experts to Wuhan to investigate that same day.[12]

Just before he left work that eventing to return home to his child and pregnant wife, Dr Li had received an internal medical report from a colleague about a patient who was suspected of having SARS. On foot of the report, Dr Li sent a message to doctor friends of his in other hospitals telling them about the SARS-like outbreak and warning them to take precautions to protect themselves from the disease. Within days of sending the tweet to his fellow medics, Dr Li found himself helping the Wuhan police with their enquiries, as he and seven other doctor colleagues were accused of spreading 'rumours'. What happened next turned into one of the most controversial episodes of the epidemic in Wuhan and is covered in detail in chapter 9.

While all of this was going on, in Wuhan during the first few days of January, there was mounting and incontrovertible evidence that a potentially disastrous infectious disease outbreak was gripping the city.[13] The figures in the *New England Journal of Medicine*, as quoted above, indicate that hundreds of people were becoming infected, with the numbers 'doubling in size approximately every 7.4 days in Wuhan at this stage.'[14] It was blindingly obvious that the disease was spreading through human-to-human transmission and medical staff were being infected.

Yet, for at least another two-week period, up to and including its statement of January 17, the WHO claimed 'there is no reported infection among healthcare workers, in China ... No additional cases have been reported since 3 January in China.' It continued, 'Additional investigations are needed to determine how the patients were infected, whether human-to-human transmission has been observed …' Even the international media were being recruited to promote the non-transmission between humans fallacy. In its second report on the Wuhan outbreak, the *New York Times* stated 'There is no evidence that the new virus is readily spread by humans, which would make it particularly dangerous, and it has not been tied to any deaths.'[15]

Whatever myths and falsehoods the CCP and the organisations it controlled wished to pedal, the one group that knew what was really happening were the healthcare workers and medical personnel who were facing the disease on the frontline every day. Official claims that medical personnel were not succumbing to the disease were confounded by their daily experience.

On or about February 4, at an internal Chinese CDC meeting a chart was shown which, for the first time, gave the true figures of how many medical staff in Wuhan hospitals were being affected by the highly infectious disease. For the period from the start of the outbreak up to January 20, across Wuhan's 13 hospitals, the actual figures displayed on the screen showed that 501 medical personnel had been diagnosed with Covid-19, and a further 600 were suspected of having it.

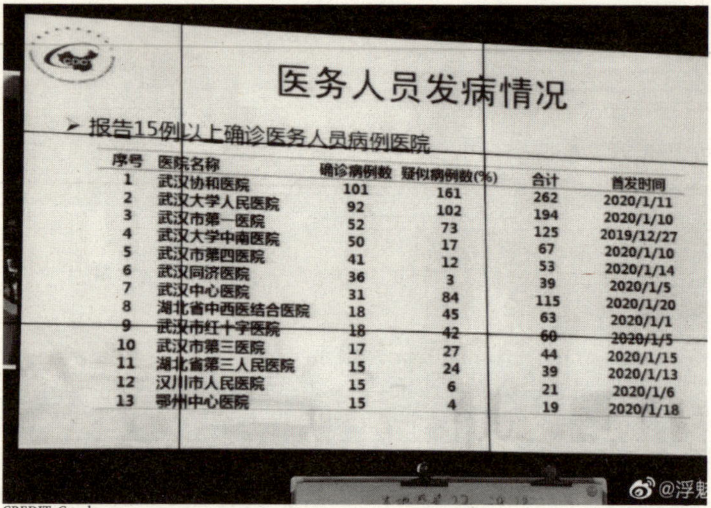

医务人员发病情况

➢ 报告15例以上确诊医务人员病例医院

序号	医院名称	确诊病例数	疑似病例数(%)	合计	首发时间
1	武汉协和医院	101	161	262	2020/1/11
2	武汉大学人民医院	92	102	194	2020/1/10
3	武汉市第一医院	52	73	125	2019/12/27
4	武汉大学中南医院	50	17	67	2020/1/10
5	武汉市第四医院	41	12	53	2020/1/14
6	武汉同济医院	36	3	39	2020/1/5
7	武汉中心医院	31	84	115	2020/1/20
8	湖北省中西医结合医院	18	45	63	2020/1/1
9	武汉市红十字医院	18	42	60	2020/1/5
10	武汉市第三医院	17	27	44	2020/1/15
11	湖北省第三人民医院	15	24	39	2020/1/13
12	汉川市人民医院	15	6	21	2020/1/6
13	鄂州中心医院	15	4	19	2020/1/18

CREDIT: Google

CDC Figures for Medical Staff Infections in Wuhan up to January 20

Photos of this screen were leaked on social media by two separate sources. Yet, despite the Communist health authorities knowing full well the true scale of the number of medical personnel that had been infected up to January 20, the following day, January 21, the Wuhan Health Commission announced that a total of 15 Wuhan health workers had been infected and there was one suspected case. They were lying, the real figures were 34 times greater for infections, and 600 times greater for suspected infections.

Just as troubling, these deliberate deceptions and suppression of critically important information about the epidemic were not confined to the frontline medical staff in hospitals. It was a blanket attempt at information suppression that extended throughout China's scientific network as well.

Chapter 8: The Silence of the Labs

Like the other Asian countries that had been badly affected by the SARS outbreak, China also had learnt an expensive lesson – it needed a streamlined infectious disease reporting system. The online reporting system that was developed covered the whole of China and any information put into the system went directly to Beijing. Hospitals were legally obliged to report incidences of infectious diseases through the new online system. Because of the SARS scare, the law on the Prevention and Treatment of Infectious Disease was amended on December 1, 2004 to specifically include 'infectious atypical pneumonia'.

If more than five cases of atypical pneumonia were reported from any location, the system automatically triggered a verification process in which the CDC carried out an epidemiological investigation that included interviewing patients and collecting samples. To make assurances doubly sure, the newly amended law required that any 'sudden outbreak of an unidentifiable infectious diseases must be reported to higher authorities.'

In a command-and-control political system like China, that meant only one thing; reporting to Zhongnanhai, the CCP's headquarters in the Forbidden City, Beijing, which also houses the State Council (the central government). In line with the CCP's pathological preoccupation with controlling information, the law also stipulated that 'the health administrative department [the Ministry of Health] under the State Council shall be responsible for announcing information about the infectious disease when there is an outbreak and an epidemic.'

Despite being fed into the online system by hospitals in Wuhan in December and early January the information failed to elicit any response from central authorities that would have warned the Chinese public about what was going on and prepared the Wuhan hospital system for an infectious disease onslaught. As the *Caixin* business magazine put it 'health officials missed opportunities to control the virus in the initial stages of the outbreak, as questions mount about who knew what and when, and what, if any, actions helped the disease to spread.'

By the second week of December, it was clear to medical staff at several Wuhan hospitals that the virus was spreading through human-to-human contact. On December 25, medical staff at two Wuhan hospitals had developed viral pneumonia symptoms themselves and were quarantined. On December 26, the head of the respiratory department at Hubei Xinhua

Hospital in Wuhan, Zhang Jixian, had also noted an increasing number of acute pneumonia patients coming from the local Wuhan seafood market. Concerned, and as required by law, he reported this information to the city and provincial health authorities. In the last week of December, the hospitals of Wuhan continued to experience exponential increases in the number of cases, many of which, unlike the initial cases, had no connection with the seafood wholesale market.

It is important to emphasise that the constant references to the Wuhan seafood market, the fact that some wild animals were sold there, and that many of the initial infection cases were associated with this wet market, is an evidentiary non-sequitur when it comes to tracing the original source of the pathogen. Despite the proliferation of assertions by Chinese authorities, the WHO, and most media reports, there was absolutely no direct scientific evidence that the Covid-19 virus jumped from animals to humans in the Wuhan seafood market. By the same token, neither is there any direct scientific evidence (not publicly available at any rate) that it escaped from a Wuhan laboratory either. These are two competing hypotheses that are fervently invoked by their respective champions with an ardour that is inversely proportional to their basis in fact.

The Communist authorities could no longer ignore the mounting evidence that a serious infectious disease epidemic was under way in Wuhan. Yet they still continued to prevaricate about warning the public of the incipient dangers. Instead, on December 30, the Wuhan and Hubei Health Commissions sent an internal memo to senior medical officials within the hospital system alerting them to the pneumonia cases linked to the seafood market and requesting them to monitor the situation carefully.

Very shortly after this internal email notification had been sent, it was leaked on social media. This leak was the first official inkling that the Chinese public had had that a serious infectious disease crisis was unfolding in their midst. The fact that this information was only intended to be seen by a closed circle of hospital managers and administrators caused enormous public disquiet and reawakened memories of the infamous political cover-up that had taken place during the SARS outbreak 20 years previously. There was worse to come.

By the end of the first week in January, there was unambiguous publicly available anecdotal evidence that the virus was passing from person to person, including within hospitals where medical staff were being infected. Yet the Wuhan Municipal Health Commission in a further statement on January 3, persisted with the fiction that there was no human-to-human transmission. This was echoed in a statement by the WHO on January 5 which said that, based on the information it had from Chinese authorities, there was 'no evidence of significant human-to-human transmission and no healthcare worker infections have been reported.'

Fearing they were beginning to lose control of the situation, the CCP pursued two separate courses of action. Externally, they began to open up to the WHO. From early January the WHO claimed that on December 31 China informed it that an unidentified infectious disease had emerged in China. This was not the case, it would be much more accurate to say that the WHO became aware of the disease outbreak on December 31, but not from Chinese authorities: though the WHO persisted with this fiction for months and it has been reported as a 'fact' by global media ever since. Like everything else at this early stage, the CCP only acknowledged critically significant information about the virus when it was forced to by circumstances outside its control. At about the time that China was gingerly opening up to the WHO, the CCP was taking much more decisive action in China.

The Genome Key that Picked the Lock

The growing medical and epidemiological evidence was soon bolstered significantly by the relatively new scientific method of genome sequencing. The enormous advances in genome sequencing technologies and techniques since the mid-1990s were quickly brought to bear on the knotty problem of identifying the virus behind the outbreak. The significance of genome sequencing was that it established beyond doubt that the virus that had caused the outbreak was new to mankind and therefore we had very limited natural immunity to prevent it proliferating rapidly. From an early stage in the outbreak, Chinese laboratories were actively engaged in sequencing the genome of the virus that was causing what was still being referred to as 'atypical pneumonia of unknown origin'. Very quickly, the genome analysis showed that the virus responsible for the fast-spreading infectious disease in Wuhan had alarming similarities with the deadly SARS virus.

The earliest complete genome results came from tests done on a 65-year-old delivery driver who worked at the Wuhan seafood market (see below for details). He had been admitted to the Central Hospital of Wuhan on December 18 with pneumonia. On December 24, fluid samples from his lungs were sent by the doctors to a company in Guangzhou called Vision Medicals. By December 27, the company had completed the genome sequence of the virus and was able to conclude that it was a coronavirus similar to the SARS virus.

Instead of sending the results as per normal, the company recognised the urgency of their findings and, in an unusual move, Vision Medicals immediately phoned the head of respiratory medicine at the hospital to give him the results directly. As Dr Zhao Su recalled later 'they just called and said it was a new coronavirus.' In the meantime, the patient's condition had deteriorated and he was transferred to the Wuhan Jinyintang Hospital where he later died. At the same time that it contacted the medics at the Central Hospital of Wuhan, Vision Medicals also reported its findings to the Chinese health authorities.

While Guangzhou city-based, Vision Medicals, was the first to decode the genetic sequence of the virus, it was also the first to feel the heat of the Communist Party's information clampdown. Having dutifully reported its findings to the appropriate authorities on December 27, the private company received an order from the Hubei Provincial Health Commission on January 1, to cease testing any further samples from Wuhan hospitals and to destroy all existing ones. The company was also ordered not to release any information on test results related to the virus and instead report them directly to the authorities.

Two days later, this regional attempt to censor and control the scientific flow of information was extended nationwide. On January 3, China's principal health authority, the Ministry of Health in Beijing issued a confidential notice that ordered all scientific and medical institutions to desist from publishing any information related to the virus outbreak. On top of that, they instructed all laboratories to transfer any virus samples in their possession to approved institutions, or destroy them on site. In all of this, the public, both in China and around the world was being deliberately deceived by the Chinese Communist health authorities with regard to the severity of the imminent danger posed by the virus.

In the last days of December, as more and more genome lab reports became available, the scientific evidence for a SARS -like outbreak was becoming unassailable. By then, Wuhan hospitals had furnished the industry heavyweight, Beijing Genomics Institute (BGI), with at least 30 samples from pneumonia patients for genome sequencing. The information on the positive results from this batch was sent to the Wuhan Municipal Health Commission on January 1.

The significance of all this genome sequencing was that it established beyond doubt that the virus that had caused the outbreak was new to mankind and therefore people had very limited natural immunity and was therefore likely to be highly contagious. In their early statements, the WHO and the Wuhan health authorities repeatedly claimed that the virus had jumped from animals to humans and that there was no or limited person-to-person transmission.

By early January, when the genome sequences of these and other coronaviruses were compared, the evidence pointed to a single spillover event that occurred in November or December 2019. In addition, the lack of diversity in these genomes was further evidence that all these virus genomes had resulted from the one zoonotic spillover event, the circumstances of which were still to be determined. These conclusions are supported by an analysis of 176 full-length genome sequences that have since been made publicly available. This analysis by the Professor of Molecular Evolution at the University of Edinburgh, Andrew Rambaut, concludes that 'the lack of diversity is indicative of a relatively recent common ancestor for all these viruses.[1]

Following her return from Shanghai on the night of December 30, Shi Zhengli worked flat-out with her colleagues at the Wuhan Institute of Virology to complete the genetic sequence of the patients samples that had been sent over from the Wuhan CDC. Four days later, on January 2 they had competed the genetic sequence of the virus. Meanwhile, samples from infected Wuhan patients continued to be sent to leading genome laboratories across China by anxious Wuhan medical staff trying to identify the disease.

A metal box containing a test tube packed in dry ice was sent from the Wuhan Central Hospital and arrived at the Shanghai Public Health Clinical Centre about lunchtime on January 3. It contained samples from lung fluids taken from a 65-year-old male delivery driver who worked at the Wuhan seafood market and had suffered a severe infection. Working through two straight nights, the laboratory staff had made Herculean efforts and by 2 a.m. on January 5 they had mapped the first complete genome sequence of SARS-CoV-2. It was clear to the clinic's director, Prof Zhang, that the sequence had strong similarities with SARS and was likely to be a highly dangerous pathogen. As a consequence, he immediately reported the findings to the Ministry of Health. In his report Prof Zhang recommended that 'relevant prevention and control measures' be taken in public places immediately.

A few days later, as Prof. Zhang was boarding a plane at Shanghai airport, he received a call on his mobile from Edward Holmes, a renowned virologist at the University of Sydney with whom he had collaborated extensively in the past. Prof Holmes explained that it was important to publish the genome of the virus as soon as possible and he asked for Prof. Zhang's permission to do so. Prof. Zhang asked for a minute to think about it. As he settled into his seat and buckled his seatbelt for the flight to Beijing, he rang Prof. Holmes back and told him to go ahead.

Shortly after their conversation, the full genome of the SARS-CoV-2 which the Shanghai Clinic had sequenced was posted by the Sydney Professor on the open access Virology website and on GenBank, on behalf of Prof Zhang. From the date of the posting, January 10, scientists and medical researchers around the world could now utilise the full genome data sequence of the virus in their efforts to develop vaccines and therapeutics – it was a seminal moment in the scientific fight against the virus. During his two-hour flight to Beijing, Prof Zhang was completely oblivious to the sensational impact the publication of the genome sequence had created. By the time he landed in Beijing, it had become headline news. But the news didn't please everyone.

Within a day of the Shanghai Clinic publishing the newly decoded genome sequence on the Internet, Prof. Zhang received a very surprising notification. On the instructions of the Shanghai Health Commission, the Clinic was ordered to close down for 'rectification'. Despite numerous requests for an explanation for this extreme action, none was forthcoming. The most likely explanation was that Prof. Zhang' Shanghai Clinic with the assistance of Prof. Holmes in Sydney had breached the Ministry of Health's January 3 instruction to all scientific and medical institutions to desist from publishing any information related to the virus. The Clinic was being punished for letting the genome genie out of the bottle, against Party orders.

It also transpired that within a few hours of the public release of the details of the virus genome by the Shanghai Clinical Centre, the Chinese Ministry of Health announced that China would share the genome sequence with the World Health Organisation. It looked like the CCP was making a virtue out of necessity. The organisation that the Ministry of Health designated to send the genome information to the WHO was the Wuhan Institute of Virology.

In compliance with the Ministry of Health's order silencing the laboratories, Yanyi Wang, the Director of the Wuhan Virology Institute, a stalwart of the Communist system, sent a strongly worded email to all staff. In her email she warned that 'inappropriate and inaccurate information was causing general panic.' This part of Wang's email is probably a reference to the taking into custody in Wuhan of Dr Li Wenliang and seven of his fellow medics who were sanctioned by the police for 'rumour mongering' just a day or two earlier. Wang's email went on to stress that the Ministry of Health 'unequivocally requires that any tests, clinical data, test results, and conclusions related to the epidemic shall not be posted on social media platforms, nor shall [it] be disclosed to partner institutions.' At least the Wuhan Institute was insisting on the Party line being adhered to.

WHO officials have praised Beijing for what Dr Tedros calls "its co-operation and transparency" In this context, one of the most egregious statements by Dr. Tedros of the WHO was on January 23 when he said, 'Once again, I would like to thank the Government of the People's Republic of China for its cooperation and transparency. The government has been successful in isolating and sequencing the virus very quickly, and has shared that genetic sequence with WHO and the international community.'[2] Five days later at a meeting with Xi Jinping in Beijing, in widely reported comments, Dr Tedros was in a similar eulogistic state of mind: 'We appreciate the seriousness with which China is taking this outbreak, especially the commitment from top leadership, and the transparency they have demonstrated, including sharing data and genetic sequence of the virus.'

Recall that Shi Zhengli and her colleagues at the Wuhan Institute of Virology had indeed carried out a speedy sequencing of the virus, but then nothing was done with it for almost two weeks. This was in compliance with the Health Ministry's diktat prohibiting the release of any information about the virus, and strictly enforced by the Institute's Director, Wang Yanyi in her email to all staff as detailed above.

In a long statement on its web site dated January 29, the Wuhan Institute of Virology proudly paraded its record of adherence to all Communist Party instructions as it 'resolutely implemented the Party Central Committee's decision, stepped up scientific research, [and] fully supported and participated in the related prevention and control work.'[3] The statement then rehearses a very favourable interpretation of the Institute's role in assisting in the national effort to combat the virus. It highlights, in particular, its early success in sequencing the genome. It claims to have completed the genome of the virus on January 2 which it then lodged in the national virus resource library on January 9. The Institute then states that on January 11 on behalf of the National Health Commission (Ministry of Health) it 'submitted the 2019 new coronavirus genome sequence information to the World Health Organisation', which was then made available publicly on the GISAID platform 'to achieve global sharing.'

In the light of the evidence that I have adduced for the existence of a comprehensive crackdown on information sharing, it looks like the CCP was making a virtue out of necessity by releasing the Wuhan Institute's genome sequence to the WHO on January 12. If Prof. Zhang's Clinic had not published its genome on the Internet just days earlier, it's really anyone's guess when China would have released this critically important scientific information. In the case of the genome, the CCP only acted when it was forced to do so by circumstances outside its control. Despite Dr Tedros' assertions to the contrary, during the first seven weeks of the outbreak the CCP's behaviour was the antithesis of transparency. As we shall see next, it was some of those on the frontline of the fight against disease itself that felt the full force of the crackdown.

Chapter 9: First they Came for the Doctors

One of the most shameful episodes of this period of Chinese cover-up was the Communist authority's treatment of the Wuhan medical whistle-blowers, and in particular Dr Li Wenliang. As much of the foregoing evidence makes clear, the Party's singular focus had been on anything that might undermine its legitimacy by strictly controlling all information pertaining to the epidemic and its causes.

The Whistle Blower

On Monday, December 30, the young ophthalmologist, Dr Li Wenliang was busy seeing patients at the Wuhan Central Hospital where he had worked since his graduation as a specialist eye surgeon in 2014. The hospital is situated close to the banks of the Yangtze River in downtown Wuhan, about 8 kilometres from the Wuhan seafood market. That day, the hospital was abuzz with talk about the viral pneumonia outbreak that was affecting the city. In Dr Li's hospital, seven patients with the disease had just been quarantined in the hospital's emergency department – all had come from the seafood market.

The conversations became really intense when Dr Li and his colleagues got wind of the contents of an internal notification that had just been issued that same day to all senior administrators in medical institutions throughout Wuhan. The "urgent notice" that bore the familiar red logo of the Wuhan Municipal Health Commission warned of "successive cases of unknown pneumonia". It ordered the senior management of the hospitals to "strengthen responsible leadership", and, more ominously, to ensure that nobody "disclose information to the public without authorisation."[1]

Having also just read one of his patient's diagnostic reports which expressed a high confidence in the presence of the SARS virus in the patient, Li's medical instincts needed no further confirmation that a major infectious disease epidemic was under way. At about 5 p.m. he sent a message to some fellow doctors and medical colleagues on a WeChat group warning them to be vigilant and protect themselves. There was nothing sensationalist or alarmist in what he said. In fact, it was largely a sober and accurate medical description of the situation that then pertained in Wuhan: 'It's not entirely accurate to call it SARS', he explained, 'it seems to be a coronavirus. But its specific composition awaits confirmation.'

Finally, he asked them all to keep this information confidential. That didn't happen.

Somebody took a screenshot of his WeChat post which contained the statement 'seven SARS cases confirmed at Huanan seafood market'.* The screenshot proliferated rapidly throughout the Internet. At just about the same time, the "urgent notice" sent earlier that day to the hospitals by the Wuhan Municipal Health Commission was also leaked online. It too went viral. The combined effect of the two simultaneous leaks really set people off. The virus information genie was well and truly out of the bottle.

The Communist-controlled Municipal Health Commission was left with little choice but to respond to the extensive public expressions of concern and disquiet that were sweeping through Chinese social media platforms. On December 31, the Wuhan Health Commission issued a statement, part of which reads 'recently, some medical organisations have diagnosed multiple cases of pneumonia in connection with the Huanan Seafood Market: the total number of cases has reached 27, of which seven of the patients are in critical condition.' The statement continued 'obvious signs of human-to-human transmission have yet to be discovered, and no medical staff are known to have contracted the illness.'

Unnerved by the public's reaction, the Wuhan authorities decided to take a stern hand with those who they considered to be 'spreading rumours.' At 1.30 a.m. on December 31, Dr Li was summoned by phone to come to the Wuhan Health Commission headquarters where he was interrogated by senior managers from his own hospital. Having been severely reprimanded for his behaviour, he was eventually allowed to go home at 4 a.m. Three days later, in a further twist, Dr Li also found himself helping the local police with their enquiries.

Dr Li was summoned to the Wuhan Public Security Bureau where he was forced to sign a document in which he confessed to "spreading rumours". In the document, Dr Li and up to 7 others doctors acknowledged their "crime" and promised not to commit further "unlawful acts". Dr Li later released on social media the reprimand letter he was forced to sign, part of which reads: 'We solemnly warn you that if you stick to your guns and remain impenitent, and continue to engage in illegal activities, you will be punished by law.' In the topsy-turvy world of

* The official name of the market was the Huanan market and Chinese documents refer to it as Huanan. However, international media have consistently referred to it as the Wuhan market. To avoid confusion, I refer to it as Wuhan seafood market.

Communist authoritarianism, having done the right thing by his family, colleagues, and society, Dr Li was forced to sign a humiliating letter in which he "confessed" to misdeeds that "gravely disturbed social order."

In early January, Chinese national state television, CCTV, was prominently touting the Party line. It announced that eight people in Wuhan had been accused of spreading rumours, before adding 'Cyberspace is by no means a lawless frontier, the police has zero tolerance for any illegal acts of fabricating or spreading rumours that disrupt social order.' A few days later, Dr Li was back on duty at the Central Wuhan hospital where, in treating an asymptomatic elderly patient for glaucoma, he contracted Covid-19. It turned out that though she was 82 years of age, she ran a small stall at the seafood market. As his condition deteriorated, Li was soon admitted as a patient in his own hospital.

As he lay in his hospital bed, Dr Li recounted these events in a Weibo post: 'I was feverish on January 11 and was hospitalised the next day. Back then, the government still insisted that there was no human-to-human transmission, and said none of the medical staff had been infected. I was just confused.' A few days before his death, in an interview with the *New York Times*, Dr Li said, 'if officials had disclosed information about the epidemic earlier, I think it would have been a lot better ... There should be more openness and transparency.'

Within weeks Dr Li had died from the very virus he had tried to warn his colleagues about. He is survived by his son and his wife who was pregnant with their second child at the time. His death sparked an unprecedented online revolt on Chinese social media. Liberated by a combination of anger, grief and frustration, Chinese citizens let loose. Communist censors were put to the pin of their collars to control the outpouring of defiant comments on Chinese social media.

Even in death, Dr Li also caused confusion among the Communist-controlled senior management at his hospital. Acutely aware of the public's mood and its outrage at the treatment of Dr Li by officialdom, his death caused the hospital management to react chaotically. On Thursday, February 6, official Chinese media, including *Global Times*, were carrying reports that Dr Li was dead. In a tweet from Geneva, the WHO expressed itself 'deeply saddened by the passing of Dr Li Wenliang'. Yet that same Thursday his own hospital in Wuhan was denying that he was dead, insisting that he was in a 'critical condition'. It was only at around 3am on Friday that the Wuhan Central Hospital finally admitted the truth that the young ophthalmologist was dead.

Online Revolt

The level of public anger directed at the Chinese Communist Party as a result of the Dr Li affair was unprecedented and forced the Party to act. It sent its powerful internal anti-corruption agency known as the Central Discipline Inspection Commission (CDIC) to Wuhan to investigate 'the problems reported by the public concerning Doctor Li Wenliang'. The CDIC operates under the rules of the Party, and not under legal rules. It is, effectively, Xi Jinping's security praetorian guard which he has utilised extensively to purge actual and prospective internal opponents. No one in Wuhan was in any doubt that the Communist Party's equivalent of Torquemada's Spanish Inquisition had arrived in town.

As the enforcer of Xi's interpretation of Communist discipline, the CDIC in its report did not completely exonerate Dr Li. Though it said he was a brave professional and had not disrupted public order, however, he had not verified the information prior to sending it, and the information itself was 'not consistent with the actual situation at the time.' Even in its efforts to mollify the public, the CCP's disciplinarians gave no quarter when it came to upholding orthodoxy. But in the time between the carrying out of the investigation in Wuhan and the issuing of the CDIC report, events had moved apace rapidly.

Then China's leading epidemiologist and the public face of its struggle against the SARS, Dr Zhong Nanshan went on television to say what the majority of Chinese people believed, that Dr Li was a hero of China. In a voice tremulous with emotion, he added, 'I'm so proud of him, he told people the truth at the end of December.' The sprightly 83-year-old disease veteran had undoubtedly grasped the mood of the Chinese people.

By 6 a.m. on the Friday morning of Li's death the Weibo hashtags 'Dr Li Wenliang has passed away' had 670 million views; 'Li Wenliang has passed away' had 230 million views, while the hashtag 'Wuhan government owes Dr Li Wenliang an apology' was viewed some 180 million times before censors deleted it as well. And the much more controversial, 'We want freedom of speech' was viewed 2.86 million times. All were quickly removed by Communist authorities.[2]

That Friday evening as darkness fell over Wuhan, on the stroke of 9 p.m. the citizens of the city turned off the lights of their apartments, opened their windows, turned on the lights of their phones, and began a collective whistle that reverberated throughout the high-rise tower blocks of the city. From the recently locked-down citizenry of Wuhan it was a coordinated act of remembrance and defiance; their final symbolic salute to the memory of their martyr doctor.

The CCP was rattled by this unprecedented show of solidarity with what the public saw as a fallen medical hero. The Chinese people had staged what amounted to an online revolt. The sheer scale of the digital uprising had the Party's censors in overdrive trying to delete millions of expressions of grief for the way the authorities had treated the deceased doctor. It was one of the few occasions in recent Chinese history where everyone could see that there was a clear divide between the Communist Party and the Chinese people.

Within recent memory, dangers to the regime on this magnitude had happened only once before – Tiananmen Square. At all costs the Party strove to avoid another episode of mass public emotion becoming highly politicised. Tanks on the streets of Beijing or Wuhan in 2020 would have completely destroyed the image that the Party had carefully and successfully nurtured in the West for decades. Defusing the public's palpable anger became an immediate and absolute priority for the CCP – whatever it took.

What it took was for the Communist Party to reverse engines completely on the Wuhan medics. It had to accept that the doctor the Party had branded a 'rumour monger' was in fact the hero that the Chinese people had deemed him to be: by acclamation. But in a totalitarian political system to do this directly or openly could be interpreted as a sign of weakness on the part of its authoritarian leader, Xi Jingping.

As life-long practitioners of the dark arts of communist political survival, Xi's elite circle could read the danger signs. They knew that like Hemingway's description of bankruptcy, major political shifts in ostensibly 'frozen' authoritarian systems happen in two ways: 'gradually, then suddenly.' Even a hint of political blood in the water would invite the anti-Xi sharks within the Party to start circling immediately. A major political climbdown like this had to be communicated clearly but subtly through a process of signalling. In this instance, the instrument chosen to communicate the about-turn was an institution under the total control and direction of the Party, but with at least a patina of credibility in the eyes of the people – the Chinese Supreme Court.

On its official WeChat account, China's Supreme People's Court said that the eight Wuhan medics should not have been punished. In a rare occurrence, it rebuked the police and went on to say, 'it might have been a fortunate thing if the public had believed the 'rumours' then, and started to wear masks and carry out sanitisation measures, and avoid the wild animal market.' The Court's statement even had a warning for the ruling Communist Party with regards to how it was handling the crisis: 'To punish any information not totally accurate is neither legally necessary nor technically possible, [it] undermines the credibility of the government and chips away at public support for the Communist Party.'[3]

Freedom of Speech

The Internet eruption came from a wide cross-section of society. It was an unparalleled episode of nationwide soul-searching. All were united in voicing their dismay at the treatment by the communist authorities of what many of them referred to as the 'whistle-blower doctor.'

In their view, the communist authorities had not only botched their initial handling of the outbreak, but having failed in their duty to alert the public, they then made matters worse by trying to cover things up. If there was a common theme to this outpouring of Internet anger it was this: here was an everyman medic who had tried to alert people at an early stage and then, having done the right thing was forced, in effect, to admit to wrongdoing. For the vast majority of Chinese citizens, Dr Li had been doubly wronged. Yet, immediately after his ordeal, he went straight back to work at the frontline in the Wuhan Central Hospital where, a few weeks later, he died in the line of duty of the contagion he had tried to warn his colleagues about.

During the digital revolt prompted by the death of Dr Li, one of the most common messages was 'R.I.P. Our hero. Thank you.' Some even posted videos of the *Les Misérables* revolutionary song 'Do You Hear the People Sing.' The law enforcement agency of Shandong province posted a picture of Dr Li with the words; 'Heroes don't fall from the sky. They're just ordinary people who stepped forward.' The Shanghai Bureau Chief of the Communist Party's *People's Daily* newspaper messaged on WeChat, 'How big a price do we have to pay to make you and your whistling sound louder, to reach every corner of the East?' It may sound a bit cryptic to Western ears but that message was, as it were, clear as a whistle for its Chinese audience.[4]

In an Orwellian twist, despite the fact that freedom of speech is guaranteed by article 35 of the Chinese constitution, what was particularly unnerving for the CCP was the appearance on Weibo (the Chinese Twitter) of the hashtag #wewantfreedomofspeech#. This was created at 2 a.m. on

Friday, February 7, shortly after the death of Dr Li. It survived for five hours until the CCP's censors took it down at 7am. During those few hours it received 5,500 posts and over two million views. In death, Li had not only become the focus of peoples' anger at his treatment and sadness at his death, he was rapidly becoming the public face of growing opposition to an authoritarian regime that brooks no dissent.

None of this was his intention when he sent that confidential WeChat message to his colleagues on the night of December 30 warning them of the dangers of the emerging highly infectious virus in Wuhan. Six weeks later on February 6, as he lay in his sickbed in the hospital where he had worked since his graduation, the handsome 34-year-old ophthalmologist gave an interview to Chinese media in which he said 'I think there should be more than one voice in a healthy society.'[5] These were some of the last words spoken by the accidental hero; within 24 hours he was dead. He left behind his pregnant wife and a son.

None of this is to suggest, far less to argue, that it presages the demise of Communist rule in China. Most Chinese citizens are tremendously proud of the enormous economic progress that China has made in recent decades which, unbidden, many of them ascribe to the political and social stability provided by single-party rule. When these citizens look to the democratic West, they see a cumbersome, inefficient and at times, anarchic political process and a capitalist market system that often delivers both low growth and regular hiccups.

In the Faustian pact that the Chinese citizenry have made with the Communist Party, in return for constant and high economic growth, they have forsworn cardinal liberal values such as unencumbered personal liberty and freedom of expression. As one long-time Hubei dissident Sun Desheng, a 38-year-old truck driver puts it, 'They [the Chinese people] see we've had decades of growth, our clothes are nicer, our sanitation is better' before asking, 'Is our society truly better?'[6] What the short-lived digital uprising inspired by Dr Li's death really amounted to was a sharp and very public reminder to the whole of the Chinese people that the bargain they had made was not without costs: ultimately, that classic liberalism and the rule of law have a value that go beyond mere materialist calculation.

Chapter 10: The Penny Drops

Strategically situated in central China at the intersection of the Han and Yangtze rivers, Wuhan has been an important transportation hub that has featured prominently in the cultural, economic, and political story of China over the centuries. The Yangtze River, which divides the city in two, made Wuhan a prosperous trading centre for over 700 years. With the flow of commerce and the exchange of goods came new thinking and new ideas – sometimes revolutionary ones.

In 1911, what became known as the Wuchang uprising took place in Wuhan. It sparked the nationwide Xinhai revolution which put an end to thousands of years of imperial rule in China as the Qing dynasty fell. As a result, the Republic of China was established in 1912 and lasted until it was replaced by the People's Republic of China in 1949 following the nationalist government's defeat by Mao's Communist forces in the civil war. The defeated Kuomintang nationalist government then retreated to the island of Taiwan where a modern democratic state still operates under the name of the Republic of China – and thereby hangs another tale which we will pick up later.

Wuhan has enjoyed some moments in the limelight of modern Chinese history. One of the economic hubs of central China, it was twice briefly China's capital under the nationalists. In 1966, it was also the scene of a celebrated publicity stunt when Mao Zedong did his famous swim across the Yangtze river at Wuhan.[1] The Great Helmsman's display of vigour signalled the beginning of the Cultural Revolution, one of the most disastrous periods of modern Chinese history in which millions died, tens of millions were persecuted, and the economy was brought to its knees.

Today Wuhan is a modern Chinese megalopolis with a total metropolitan population of 15 million. It has an impressive higher education system with 20 Universities and 100 other institutes of higher learning. As a consequence, the city is home to one of China's largest student populations of almost 1 million. With four scientific and technological development parks, a range of enterprise incubators and research institutes, Wuhan is well on the way to achieving its ambition of becoming one of the leading technology cities of China, and indeed the world. Yet despite all these impressive achievements, and its historical, strategic, and modern economic significance, prior to 2019 few people in the West had ever heard the name Wuhan: by January 2020 it was a name few would ever forget.

In the current political atmosphere of Xi's China, obedience is valued far more than competence, and security always takes precedence over safety. This has incentivised local Communist officials to play down problems, hide negative news and censor dissenting opinions. Under Xi Jinping's authoritarian rule, these tendencies have been greatly amplified. In the crucial early phase of the epidemic in Wuhan they led to gross shirking of responsibilities and inaction by those in power. It helped to create perfect conditions which gave the virus free rein to spread unhindered.

Throughout December, Communist officials repeatedly claimed that there was no human-to-human transmission, or if there was it was limited, despite extensive medical testimony from doctors on the frontline that this was not true. On December 27, for example Zhao Jianping, a pulmonologist at a local Wuhan hospital said that he and his colleagues 'were sure it could spread from human to human.' The doctor went on to confirm that he reported this fact to the Wuhan Centre for Disease Control.

Even more damning of Wuhan Communist officialdom was the incredible absence in official reports of *any* new cases in Wuhan between January 2 and 16. Yet, during this crucial two-week period the national state news agency, *Xinhua* reported that a doctor fell ill with the virus in the city on January 11. While *Caixin* ran a story in which a Wuhan hospital radiologist had identified 50 new cases on January 15. It's simply inconceivable that six weeks into a highly infectious disease epidemic there were no new cases in this critical two-week period of the first half of January.

The official Chinese position is that the outbreak only came to the Communist authorities' attention on December 29 when four workers at the seafood market were admitted to hospital with pneumonia symptoms. A fortuitous outcome to which the WHO's Director General, Dr Tedros attributed to Communist Party foresight and planning: 'it was detected because China had put in place a system specifically to pick up severe lower respiratory infections.'

Having dropped the ball initially, by the end of January the CCP was frantically trying to regain the initiative. The Party's tried and trusted method of achieving this has been to rewrite the history of events to suit its own purposes. In these revisions of history, unsurprisingly, the

Communist Party always emerges as pre-eminently in control of any unfolding crisis, the worst consequences of which are usually averted by the resolute action of the Party, guided by the sagacity of its supreme leader. In addition to its propaganda mouthpieces, these politically-inspired narratives are often promulgated by institutions firmly within the ambit of the Party's control.

The CCP likes to promote the image that it holds absolute power over the Chinese people – it does not, and it knows it. Even in the most authoritarian regimes, absolute power is rare. The citizens of China have, by and large, gone along with the bargain of exchanging political freedoms for material and economic gain. And as long as the economic band keeps playing, the political two-step can proceed, as so-called Western values remain firmly out in the cold, peering in forlornly through the fogged-up windows.

It would, however, be a grave mistake to conclude that the people of China are entirely biddable, all of the time. When their collective interests are threatened, and their lives and the lives of their families placed in mortal danger by the ineptitude of their political masters, then, as we have seen, even the Great Firewall of China is insufficient to contain their anger. No matter how transient, the mass withdrawal of consent by the governed, even for politicians in a democracy, is a deeply worrying development: for authoritarians it is unnerving in the extreme.

Within China, by mid-January it was very apparent that its politically controlled bureaucratic early warning system had failed. A highly critical Chinese analysis goes so far as to argue that 'an epidemic governance system dominated by bureaucratic forces is doomed to failure.'[2] In particular, this assessment identifies the cause of the failure as 'the lack of autonomy of scientific/professional communities – in this case, virologists, physicians, and epidemiologists – as one of the major contributing factors to the malfunction of the early warning system.'[3]

Though it did not implicate the CCP explicitly, in its final conclusions the report did not pull its punches: 'As gatekeepers of the advancement, dissemination, and application of relevant knowledge, scientific/professional communities play a key role in epidemic governance, especially in the early warning stage. If the autonomy of scientific/professional communities is seriously crippled by bureaucratic forces, delayed action is inevitable, which can lead to disastrous consequences.' The report writers describe what had happened in China as 'a vivid example of a public governance system abducted by bureaucratic forces ... [whereby] the resulting political, economic, and social costs turned out to be unprecedentedly large.'[4]

Initially, it was the cack-handed treatment of the whistle blower Dr Li by the Wuhan Communist authorities and police at the turn of the year that provided the catalyst for the digital revolt by the citizenry. The scale and intensity of the internet uprising clearly rattled the CCP. Normally the subject of the first few leading articles of all Communist Party newspapers and the top news stories on China's national television channel, for almost a week in early January, Chairman Xi was nowhere to be seen. Despite appearances, China is not a monolithic society, and a political hiatus like this opens up opportunities for other, normally quiescent, social forces to enter the political arena. This began to happen on the morning of January 20.

That morning events began to move quickly as the Chinese Prime Minister, Li Keqiang called a meeting of the State Council (China's highest government body). As the official account of the Council's meeting states in its opening paragraph, what was unique about this meeting was that 'Two "new faces" appeared on the seats: Academician Zhong Nanshan and academician Li Lanjuan, a famous infectious disease expert.' In phraseology strangely reminiscent of that used by the US President, Prime Minister Li Keqiang expressed his appreciation to the two academics for their advice; 'thank you for the professional advice provided by these two experts' before ending with a Trumpesque non sequitur, 'Very important.'[5]

That evening, Zhong Nanshan, China's pre-eminent health specialist on respiratory diseases and a hero who helped defeat SARS, went on China's national television channel and confirmed that the disease was spreading from person-to-person. Though the rumour machine in Wuhan had been in overdrive for weeks, this was the first time that the Chinese people had been made aware of the seriousness of the epidemic. A few days later, at 10 a.m. on January 23, the Chinese central government imposed a complete lockdown on Wuhan's 11 million residents. This was a monumental task considering that the land area occupied by the city of Wuhan is much larger than that of Greater London, and more than twice the size of Shanghai – it is one of the world's megacities. With a population one third larger than that of New York city, this was the first time in history that a quarantine exercise of this magnitude had been attempted.

Chapter 11: Wuhan Goes Viral

In confronting the epidemic during its early phase, the Communist authorities' highest priorities were maintaining secrecy and public order so as to avoid their corollaries; political embarrassment and public alarm – it was a policy that had deadly consequences. Instead of mustering a concerted public health assault on the virus, the Chinese authorities showed an appalling lack of concern for the health of their fellow citizens. The critical failures occurred during a seven-week period from the detection of the first symptomatic patient on December 1, to the imposition of an unprecedented lockdown of Wuhan and Hubei's population of over 50 million people on January 23.

This critical initial phase of the epidemic was characterised by delay, denial, denouncements, and downright deceit on the part of the Communist authorities. Their inaction permitted the virus to gain a tenacious grip on the city, the province, much of China, and ultimately the rest of the world. The Party and its local cadres had made a crass political calculation to control the narrative rather than the virus. As we have already seen from both *The Lancet* and the *New England Journal of Medicine* articles, there was ample evidence for person-to-person transmission which the authorities ignored.

Party Political Priorities

On January 15, the Wuhan Municipal Health Commission issued a Q & A information leaflet on the outbreak which contained the following: 'no clear evidence of human-to-human transmission has been found, and the possibility of limited human-to-human transmission cannot be ruled out, but the risk of sustained human-to-human transmission is low.' The clear intention of this Jesuitical pronouncement was to assuage the public's growing concerns by downplaying the threat posed by the virus. But there may also have been a more immediate political reason for Wuhan's communist officials persistently seeking to minimise the dangers of the virus.

The first two weeks of January were high points in the regional calendar of the Communist Party. For 12 days, from January 6 to January 17, the annual plenary meetings of the Hubei's People's Political Consultative Conference and Hubei's People's Congress were due to take place in Wuhan. It is what the Party refers to as the 'Two Sessions Time' and within the Chinese Communist system, these annual people's congresses and political consultative conferences are meant to give voice to the 'will of the people' which in turn is supposed to guide the actions of the Party for the subsequent year.[1] Probably for the first time in decades, the packed meetings of the 2,369 delegates from all over Wuhan and Hubei did become the focus of popular will and sentiment, but not in a way the Party expected.

The four local and provincial newspapers, *Hubei Daily*, *Chutian Metropolis Daily*, *Changjiang Daily*, and the *Wuhan Evening Post*, all propaganda mouthpieces controlled by the CCP, carried wall-to-wall coverage of the meetings – 148 pages in total, but nothing about the virus that was playing havoc with the lives of the citizens of Wuhan. Instead, the delegates spoke endlessly and in glowing terms about the CCP's enormous achievements of the past year and about the Party's great hopes for the New Year that was about to dawn. Though the delegates were well aware of the dark shadow of the looming infectious disease crisis that hung over the city, the viral epidemic was not an agenda item for either of these two mass meetings.

At one of the meetings the provincial governor, Wang Xiaodong, demanded that 'the problems that cause the people anxiety must be treated as major issues, be met with real action, and be given full energy, steadily increasing the people's sense of benefit, prosperity and security.' Yet, all the while he studiously ignored the coronavirus elephant in the room. As if to compound these incongruities, at the end of the provincial meeting, Jiang Chaoliang, the Hubei Party Secretary praised 'all delegates for faithfully fulfilling their responsibilities and reflecting the will of the people.' The gap between rhetoric and reality could scarcely be greater. It is hardly unrelated that during most of this 'Two Meetings Time', no new cases of infections were recorded in official statistics. All of which goes to illustrate the extent to which the CCP in Wuhan and Hubei was living in a parallel ideological universe of its own creation.

On reading these newspaper reports, the city's residents took to the Internet to complain bitterly about the CCP delegates' failure to address the issue of the deadly virus in their midst that was threatening their lives. Many highlighted the risks of packing so many delegates together in a confined space for days on end in the middle of an infectious disease epidemic. Even more worryingly, when the meetings ended on January 17, these thousands of delegates dispersed throughout Hubei province many of whom, presumably, were now carriers of the virus.

Celebration Time

Every year for the previous two decades, Wuhan city's Baibuting district had held a special banquet during the week preceding the Lunar New Year. The annual Baibuting banquet is no ordinary affair. It is a mass public event attended by tens of thousands of Wuhanese who see it as a community celebration to mark the beginning of the New Year festivities. For many of the attendees it is a final opportunity to have a collective feast before they headed off to their home districts across China to celebrate the New Year itself in the traditional Chinese manner with their families.

Because it was the 20th anniversary of the shindig, the organisers set themselves a particular goal for this year's event: they wanted to create a new Guinness World Record for the largest number of dishes served at a banquet. According to the *Financial Times*, up to 40,000 families responded to the call and prepared 13,986 platters of food, some labelled with inspiring or otherwise patriotic-sounding names such as "Motherland in My Heart" (cucumber and ham) and "One Belt One Road" (vegetable salad).[2]

Despite the fact that scores of pneumonia cases were already being reported throughout the city, the banquet went ahead on Sunday, January 19. Photographs of this mass banqueting event held in the middle of the infectious disease outbreak show no masks being worn by any of the attendees. For many of these Wuhan residents the writing was already on the wall, but unlike at Belshazzar's feast, there was no Daniel in Baibuting to forewarn the unfortunate citizens of Wuhan.

One Baibuting mother, who because she had two young children to look after could not attend the banquet, commented, 'I feel very lucky I didn't take part in the banquet ... There are now more than 10 infections among my neighbours.' Shortly after that Sunday's banquet, the epidemic began to take its toll as the infection spread throughout the district. Notices in red and black letters soon appeared on 57 apartment blocks around Baibuting bearing the stark words "Fever Block".[3]

As the health consequences of this communal feast began to emerge, anger at the Communist party's management of the outbreak was at first directed at the mayor of Wuhan, Zhou Xianwang, On January 21, he went on Chinese national television to justify the holding of the event. 'The reason why the Baibuting community continued to host the banquet this year was based on the previous judgment that *the spread of the epidemic was limited between humans*, so there was not enough warning.' (italics added).

Action Time

The critical importance of taking action early in an epidemic and the disastrous consequences of these early failures in China were spelled out in a study published in March 2020 by the University of Southampton and carried out in conjunction with researchers in Wuhan. The study concluded that, if concerted action by the authorities had been 'conducted one week, two weeks, or three weeks earlier in China, cases could have been reduced by 66%, 86%, and 95%, respectively.' The study also emphasised that the corollary was equally true; if actions were not taken until 'one week, two weeks, or three weeks later, the number of cases could have shown a 3-fold, 7-fold, and 18-fold increase across China, respectively.'[4]

There is little doubt that city and provincial officials in Wuhan and Hubei actively suppressed information about the extent and severity of the epidemic. The primary purpose of this seems to have been to keep the public in the dark for as long as possible. In this, unfortunately, there were successful. Charitably interpreted this was done to avoid public panic; uncharitably, it was to save their careers by suppressing bad news. The actions of the Wuhan police in punishing the eight doctors for so-called 'rumour-mongering' had a chilling effect on all medical personnel across the Wuhan hospital system. As an exercise in official intimidation, it succeeded in silencing the one group in society which had a legitimate and indeed professional obligation to voice their concerns and warn the public about the pandemic they were witnessing.

But the actions, and the considerable evidence for inaction, by the CCP in Beijing also indicates that the top echelons of the Party and State were equally complicit in these early failures. In early January, the Party sent two expert groups to Wuhan to assess what was happening in the city. The leader of the first group, Xu Jianguo, told the Hong Kong newspaper, *Takungpao*, on January 6 that, 'China has many years of disease control [experience], there is absolutely no chance that this will spread widely because of Spring Festival travel.' Before concluding that the threat from the virus was low, he repeated the usual platitude that there was 'no evidence of human-to-human transmission'.[5]

The second investigation team was led by respiratory disease specialist, Wang Guangfa, and arrived in Wuhan on January 8. On January 10, Prof. Wang said in an interview with national state television that the Wuhan pneumonia was 'under control' and mostly a 'mild condition.'[6] The following day he gave an interview to reporters in which he said that the situation in Wuhan was "preventable and controllable." A week-and-a-half later he had fallen victim to the virus himself, and was being treated in an isolation unit in hospital.[7]

As the leaders at the apex of a rigidly hierarchical political system, the Party elite must carry the lion's share of the culpability for the ongoing information suppression. There is damning evidence that the Communist top brass was fully aware of the details of what was unfolding from early on in January. The evidence comes from internal Communist Party and State apparatus documents obtained by the *Associated Press* which provide a unique insight into what was going on within the Communist elite during this decisive period in early January.

For instance, between January 5 and January 17 internal documents from the national Centre for Disease Control and Prevention (CDC) in Beijing show that there were no new cases of infection registered in China for a full 12 days. Yet this was precisely the time when hundreds of infected patients were turning up on the doorsteps of hospitals across Wuhan. This fact was corroborated by anecdotal evidence from social media of infected people spending days going from hospital to hospital in Wuhan and being turned away because of overcrowding. Many of these postings were accompanied by photographs of queues outside a range of different hospitals. It simply beggars belief that no infections were registered for almost two weeks at local or national level.

Even epidemiological numbers from outside Wuhan were being suppressed at this time. Yuen Kwok-yung, a microbiologist from Shenzhen in southern China found six members of one family who tested positive for the virus. In an interview with the respected Chinese finance magazine *Caixin,* Dr Yuen says he notified all levels of the CDC of his findings on January 12, including Beijing. Yet, these statistics do not appear anywhere in the leaked Beijing CDC documents.

Among these documents there is a revealing memo by Ma Xiaowei, the Director of China's National Health Commission (Ministry of Health) regarding a teleconference on January 14 in which instructions from President Xi Jinping, Premier Li Keqiang, and Vice Premier Sun Chunlan were conveyed to provincial health officials. In the memo, Ma summarises what the highest echelons of the Party knew at this time: 'The epidemic situation is still severe and complex, the most severe challenge since SARS in 2003, and is likely to develop into a major public health event.' In a section headed 'sober understanding of the situation', Ma's memo continues; 'clustered cases suggest that human-to-human transmission is possible ... With the coming of the Spring Festival, many people will be traveling, and the risk of transmission and spread is high.' All participants in these meetings and the recipients of the documents were under strict instructions to keep the discussions secret, with many of the documents clearly marked 'internal', 'not to be spread on the Internet', and 'not to be publicly disclosed.'

Meanwhile, the public was still being fed misinformation. Li Qun, the head of China's CDC went on national state television on January 15 and said 'we have reached the latest understanding that the risk of sustained human-to-human transmission is low'. But, as we have seen above, behind this public façade of official insouciance in the face of the escalating health crisis, the authoritarian behemoth started to move up the gears very quickly. So, what gave rise to this sudden flurry of behind-the-scenes activity by the Beijing government that included; a teleconference on January 14, a confidential memo and top-secret guidance for provincial health authorities and, for the first time, 'instructions' from President Xi? In a word, the answer is Thailand.

The Virus Takes Flight

Just at a time when Communist authorities were claiming that no virus cases were happening in China, the WHO issued a statement on January 13, the opening lines of which read: 'The Ministry of Public health of Thailand reported an imported case of infection caused by the novel coronavirus recently identified in Wuhan, China. The concerned individual is a Chinese national who was found to have fever on arrival at Suvarnabhumi airport on 8th January.'[8] The woman, a 61-year-old Chinese tourist, was hospitalised near Bangkok for a week and once her fever had subsided, she was allowed to return to China. The Communist elite in Beijing realised that the jig was up on any further prevarication. The hastily convened teleconference of January 14 was a concerted effort to focus the minds of Party cadres and the resources of the state on a disease epidemic that had just gone international. Ma's leaked memo confirmed that because there was now authoritative evidence that the virus had spread to Thailand, the situation had 'changed significantly.'

Three days later, the situation had changed even more significantly. On January 16, the WHO issued another statement saying that, 'the Japanese Ministry of Health, Labour and Welfare, today informed the World Health Organisation (WHO) of a confirmed case of a novel coronavirus (2019-nCoV) in a person who travelled to Wuhan, China.'[9] The WHO had been notified on January 15 that a Japanese man had travelled to Wuhan at the end of December, and though he had not visited the Wuhan seafood market, he developed a fever on January 3 and travelled back to Japan on January 6. Within a week of these first announcements, up to 8 other countries announced they had cases of the virus – all were either residents of Wuhan or had been recent visitors to the city.

Across Asia, health officials began scrambling to prevent the spread of the virus. They initiated health crisis emergency measures and began stockpiling protective gear, preparing isolation beds and even boarding trains to individually screen passengers in frantic efforts to contain the virus. In preparation for the influx of Chinese Lunar New Year tourists at the end of January, transport authorities in popular holiday destinations across Asia tightened checks on arriving passengers and instituted temperature screenings.[10]

The internationalisation of the epidemic was undoubtedly a serious blow to the Communist Party's self-image of being master of all it surveyed. But, disappointing and all as that was, it paled into insignificance in comparison with the immediate gargantuan problem that it had to confront on home soil. Just as reports emerged that the Wuhan virus had surfaced in Thailand and Japan, a unique event in world culture was about to kick-off in China. Just as a fast-spreading infectious disease with no cure was proliferating in central China, the world's biggest annual human mass migration event was happening at the same time. Hundreds of millions of Chinese were criss-crossing the county to celebrate Lunar New Year – it was the ultimate nightmare scenario for Chinese Communist authorities.

New Year Lockdown

The Chinese Lunar New Year is the most important holiday in China. New Year's Eve is a special time when all Chinese have their annual family reunion. A population of 1.4 billion and a large migratory workforce means that New Year travel in China constitutes the largest annual human migration in the world. In the few weeks leading up to this Spring Festival, hundreds of millions of people head to every nook and cranny across China in order to make it home for the extended family celebrations.

In 2020, the travel season started early and stretched for 40 days, from January 10 to February 18. During this time, Chinese citizens made over 3 billion journeys, with over 70% of them relying on the recently constructed network of high-speed trains or bullet trains. In Wuhan's case, it wasn't just migrant workers who were on the go, the city's 1 million students had also set out on their travels across China to celebrate New Year at home.[11]

As the Year of the Pig ended and the Year of the Rat approached, the need for millions of Wuhan residents to get out of the city had become more urgent than ever. The numbers were swollen massively by a population acutely anxious to escape the virus-infected city. The dash to get out of the city became even more urgent as rumours of the imminent imposition of travel restrictions began to circulate. Very quickly, the flow of people leaving Wuhan became a flood.

The web of delay, denial, and deception that officialdom in both Wuhan and Beijing had spun throughout December and most of January had the catastrophic effect of facilitating the exodus of some 5 million people from the epicentre of the disease in the weeks immediately preceding the imposition of quarantine on January 22.[12] It was undoubtedly the single most fateful consequence of the Communist authorities' early-stage failures. It was instrumental in spreading the disease not only all over China, but ultimately all over the world.

By Monday, January 20, the pace of developments quickened considerably. There was a dawning realisation within the Communist elite in Beijing that they were going to have to take a firm grip of developments in central China before matters spun completely out of control. Though they would never admit it, the CCP also understood that their initial reflexive politico/bureaucratic response to the pandemic was not just inadequate, it had been completely counter-productive.

Apart from the escalating health crisis and the inevitable economic damage it would inflict, this was the biggest political crisis that the party had to contend with since Tiananmen Square in 1989. To recover lost ground on the pandemic, re-assert centralised authoritarian control, and rebuild its tarnished image with the Chinese public, the Party knew it urgently needed assistance from professional experts in the medical and scientific community.

Zhong Nanshan, the 83-year-old specialist in respiratory diseases who became a national hero in the fight against SARS in 2003, was appointed to spearhead the fight against this coronavirus. On January 20, he went on the national television channel CCTV and confirmed that the virus was spreading from person to person. According to *Xinhua*, China's state news agency, Prof. Zhong confirmed that 'Two people who have contracted the disease didn't go to Wuhan but were infected by family members who did. So, we now have confirmation that the disease is spreading through human-to-human transmission.'

Zhong's team also made an interesting observation on the extent of the threat China was facing in the initial stages of the crisis. Quite simply, they believed it was a race against time at this early stage. Prof. Zhong noted that the actual situation in Hubei in January was far worse than the media had been suggesting as the second expert team that had gone there from Beijing had calculated that 'a five-day delay in controlling the virus would have led to three times as many infections.' An epidemiologist at the University of California, Los Angeles, Zuo-Feng Zhang, agreed with these sentiments: 'If they took action six days earlier, there would have been much fewer patients and medical facilities would have been sufficient. We might have avoided the collapse of Wuhan's medical system.'[13]

In a hierarchical command-and-control political system like that of China, once the authoritarian State-Party structure swings into action it can quickly mobilise impressive amounts of materials and manpower to deal with a problem. On January 23, the Beijing government imposed a complete lockdown on Wuhan. In an action thought inconceivable in a democratic state, Wuhan, the cradle of the coronavirus, was cut off from the rest of the country and its people quarantined en masse.

In a historically unprecedented social experiment, the Chinese government shut down all public transport in and out of the city in an effort to contain the spread of the disease. Nobody was allowed to leave Wuhan without permission from the authorities. Quarantine on this scale was unprecedented in modern times. Within days, the lockdown had been extended to include 15 other major cities in central China.[14] By then up to 60 million people had been placed in quarantine. One Australian who found himself locked down in Wuhan with his Chinese spouse described his predicament; 'I'm hiding from a virus that you can't see and a government that you don't want to muck around with.' Overnight a bustling, vibrant city of over 11 million people was turned into a ghost-town. The normally lively streets, shopping malls, train stations, and other public spaces in the city fell eerily quiet. But the preternatural silence that pervaded Wuhan did not betoken serenity.

A totalitarian communist police state was soon doing what it does best: the lockdown was enforced with an authoritarian iron fist. Police and army personnel began going door to door checking people's temperatures in their homes. Anyone in Wuhan suspected of having a fever was immediately taken away and placed in a government-controlled isolation centre. Videos began appearing on social media of people being dragged screaming from their homes while distraught family members looked on helplessly. One video shows paramilitary police sealing the doors of an apartment block with welding equipment to prohibit people leaving. This type of arbitrary detention was used on an increasingly wide scale. It was a military-style lockdown involving large scale human rights violations that would not be acceptable in the West. As the lights went out across central China, one can't help wondering that if the CCP had reacted differently in the opening stage of the pandemic these extreme measures could most likely have been avoided.

Chapter 12: Dr WHO

Xi Jingping wasn't the only global leader for whom 2020 was turning out to be an unpreceded challenge. Dr Tedros' tenure as the first African and the first non-medical doctor to become Director General of the WHO began in July 2017. He had previously served as Minister for Health (2005-2012) and Minister of Foreign Affairs (2012-2016) in the Ethiopian government. Halfway through his five-year term at the WHO, Dr Tedros found himself playing a central and controversial role in the international maelstrom that resulted from the Covid-19 outbreak in Wuhan.

The Road to Geneva

Ethiopia has a population of 100 million and is Africa's second most populous country after Nigeria. During the last quarter of the 20th century, it had been the focus of intense Cold War superpower attention. For most of this time, the country was ruled by a Soviet-backed military junta. Following the overthrow of this murderous military regime in 1991, the Tigray People's Liberation Front (TPLF) led a coalition of left-wing groups that set about building a revolutionary democracy in Ethiopia.

Fond of quoting Chairman Mao's dictum that 'power grows out of the barrel of a gun', the concept of 'revolutionary democracy' is intrinsically linked to the ultra-leftist stance of the TPLF's leader, Meles Zenawi, who served as President and Prime Minister of Ethiopia for over two decades until his death in 2012. Meles version of Marxism-Leninism was so extreme that even Maoism was considered 'revisionist' and so for a time, the TPLF supported the 'more correct' version of Maoism; that of Enver Hoxha's regime in Albania. The concept of revolutionary democracy was built into the Ethiopian Constitution and has been the guiding ideological light of the government ever since.

The future Director General of the WHO, Tedros Adhanom Ghebreyesus, began his political career with the left-wing TPLF and later became a member of its ruling politburo. As a senior TPLF member and a personal friend of its Marxist-Leninist leader, Meles Zenawi, he served in the Ministry of Health and rose through the ranks to become Minister of Health in 2005. During his tenure, which lasted until 2012, Ethiopia made considerable advances in health, especially in reducing rates of HIV, measles and malaria. As Health Minister, he also increased hospital staffing levels and made enormous improvements in technology use. In

2012, he became Ethiopia's Minister for Foreign Affairs where he was instrumental in building relationships with the Clinton administration and the Bill and Melinda Gates Foundation. Under the prevailing globalist umbrella, money flowed into the Ethiopian government coffers.

But Ethiopia didn't just look to the West for finance and investment. Of all African countries, Ethiopia had ideological and governance structures that were closest to the newly emerging superpower in the East. While priding itself on its revolutionary democratic model of state-building, the Ethiopian government was also committed to modernising its economy. Given these circumstances, it was only natural that it should look to China for large-scale development assistance. The 21st century had seen the emerging superpower, China, take a very keen interest in the country. During the past 15 years, China has deepened its economic relationship with Ethiopia very considerably. This coincided with the period when Dr Tedros was either Minister for Health or Minister for Foreign Affairs in Ethiopia's leftist government.

Ethiopia has become one of the largest recipients of assistance under the so-called Belt and Road Initiative, President Xi Jinping's master project that has become the centrepiece of China's foreign policy. It is the economic complement of geopolitics and hence is referred to as geoeconomics – 'the use of economic tools to advance geopolitical objectives'.[1] Ethiopia has multiple Beijing-financed infrastructural mega-projects, everything from hydropower dams to skyscrapers that are being built by Chinese companies. As a consequence, Ethiopia has become China's largest trading and investment partner in Africa. The massive investment boom led to double-digit economic growth and made Ethiopia Africa's fastest growing economy.

In 2016, Dr Tedros announced that he was running in the election to become Director General of the WHO to replace Dr Margaret Chan of China who had been in charge of the organisation for a decade. In the end, the election came down to a contest between a British doctor, Dr Nabarro, who was backed by mainly Western countries, and Dr Tedros who was supported by a coalition of African and Asian countries within which China exercised a growing influence. Following a lengthy campaign, which got nasty towards the latter stages, Dr Tedros won an overwhelming victory, 133 votes to 50.

Shortly after his election as Director General of the WHO, at a Health Conference in Uruguay in October 2017, Dr Tedros lauded Zimbabwe as 'a country that places universal health coverage and health promotion at the centre of its policies to provide health care to all.' He then went on to nominate the country's 93-year-old despotic leader, Robert Mugabe, as a goodwill ambassador for the WHO. Mugabe's reign of over three decades had been marked by the violent repression of his political opponents and the utter ruination of the Zimbabwean economy which had once been the breadbasket of Africa.

However, as head of the African Union, Mugabe had been instrumental in getting the bloc to endorsed Dr Tedros in his campaign to become Director General of the WHO. Many believed the goodwill ambassadorial appointment was pay-back for that critical support. However, the nomination provoked such international outrage that five days later, Mugabe's appointment was rescinded. If it had been allowed to stand, Mugabe would have joined other illustrious goodwill ambassadors such as the renowned Chinese folk-singer and Major General in the PLA, Peng Liyuan. Ms Peng's other claim to fame is that she is the wife of the CCP's General Secretary, Xi Jinping.

Split Decision

On Wednesday, January 22, the WHO's emergency committee convened in the 'situation room', a high-tech communications facility in the basement of its Geneva headquarters. When a global health emergency strikes, is in this room that some of the world's leading health experts gather to formulate the organisation's response. Those unable to attend in person are beamed in electronically to appear around the room's various screens. Insiders refer to this room by its acronym, SHOC (strategic health operations centre), which probably gives a better sense of type of crisis-laden discussions that it has witnessed over the years. That Wednesday, the members of the committee had an important decision to make.

Just seven weeks earlier, on December 1, the first officially recorded incidence of an unusual pneumonia illness of unknown cause had emerged in Wuhan. By the time the health experts met in their Geneva bunker during the fourth week of January, the virus had spread to a total of 32 provinces and municipalities across China.[2] But of even greater immediate concern to the WHO was the fact that the virus had gone international with multiple other countries becoming infected.

Chairing the meeting of the 15 committee members and their 6 advisers was the WHO's Director General, Dr. Tedros. Under the International Health Regulations 2005 (IHR 2005) of the WHO, the committee members' obligation was to provide advice to Dr. Tedros.[3] In this instance, the issue before the committee was to decide whether or not, on the available information, the escalating international infectious disease crisis constituted 'a public health emergency of international concern' (PHEIC).

All were health experts of international repute and, in technical terms, the health question they had before them was well within their compass. But each member was also acutely aware that the issue they were about to pronounce on had implications far beyond the domain of health – international health was also international politics by other means. The rules were clear, the committee advised but, in the final analysis, it was Dr. Tedros who made the decision.[4]

After intense debate the meeting failed to come to a definitive answer, so the members were asked to reconvene the next day. Maybe, it was hoped that some new information from the fast-developing situation on the ground would become available overnight which might help to break the logjam? The following day the standoff continued and so, having failed to make a decision in two days of extensive discussions, the meeting was adjourned until further notice. Another week would be squandered before the world was officially warned that an international public health emergency was underway.

Why did the WHO procrastinate at this critical juncture? Though the deliberations of the emergency committee's meeting and its voting record are confidential, press reports, which seem to be based on impeccable WHO sources, claim that on the critical issue of whether to declare a PHEIC, 'the emergency committee was split down the middle on the question.' That same article also states that the Chinese representative at the meeting 'argued against declaring an emergency on 22 January.'[5]

Under the legal framework of the WHO (IHR 2005), Dr. Tedros has sole discretion to declare a PHEIC, if he deems that the information warrants it. In this context, an important piece of information was known to Dr Tedros and his fellow committee members at this point: human-to-human transmission of the virus had been confirmed. Though the precise mechanism was unclear at that stage, the fact of human-to-human transmission was incontrovertible and significant.

Ultimately, whether Dr. Tedros was justified in not declaring a PHEIC at this meeting has to be judged against the background of the criteria for such decisions, as defined by IHR 2005. They are set out clearly on the WHO's website. According to IHR 2005, a PHEIC is defined as' "an extraordinary event which is determined to constitute a public health risk to other States through the international spread of disease and to potentially require a coordinated international response". The 'extraordinary event' is further clarified as having three elements:

- serious, sudden, unusual or unexpected;
- carries implications for public health beyond the affected State's national border; and
- may require immediate international action.

By any reasonable assessment, what had been unfolding in the weeks immediately preceding January 22 in China and in many of its neighbouring countries, and as far away the USA, met those criteria handsomely. Yet it wasn't until one week later, on January 30, following a second meeting of the emergency committee, that the WHO declared a Public Health Emergency of International Concern. While the calling of a PHEIC by the WHO is largely symbolic, it does have one important consequence – it allows the Director General to make temporary recommendations regarding trade and travel. At the press conference in Geneva that eventually declared a PHEIC, the WHO did make strong recommendations on travel, it urged member states NOT to restrict travel or trade with China. When asked about travel restrictions on China, Dr Tedros emphasised the WHO's position, 'in fact, we oppose it'. On February, 3 in an interview with Reuters he reiterated the point saying that there was no reason for measures that unnecessarily interfere with travel and trade.'[6]

The week of the PHEIC hiatus in Geneva, from January 22 to January 30, was a tumultuous one in China. As we have already seen, it was only on the CCTV evening news on January 20 that the Chinese people heard for the first time from the epidemiologist, Dr Zhong Nanshan that the disease was spreading from person to person (see Chapter 10). Three days later, Wuhan was placed in an unprecedentedly severe lockdown, and followed within days by many other major cities in central China. It was also this week that Dr Tedros decided to visist Xi Jinping in Beijing. The meeting took place in the resplendent surroundings of the Great Hall of the People on January 28.

According to the WHO statement released after that meeting, 'Stopping the spread of this virus both in China and globally is WHO's highest priority' and to that end an important aspect of the meeting was the fact that, 'The two sides agreed that WHO will send international experts to visit China as soon as possible to work with Chinese counterparts on increasing understanding of the outbreak to guide global response efforts.'[7] Over six months later on July 7, the WHO issued a short two-paragraph statement, the first paragraph of which reads 'WHO experts will travel to China to work together with their Chinese counterparts to prepare scientific plans for identifying the zoonotic source of the SARS-COV-2 virus.'[8] But what this statement does not make explicit is that, despite the 'as soon as possible' commitment by Xi Jinping in January, six months later the two WHO experts were only going to negotiate with the Chinese for permission to start their investigation. Following many more months of negotiations, it was only in December that the CCP finally agreed to allow a WHO-led investigation team into China in January 2021 – so much for 'as soon as possible'. A WHO press official told Reuters, 'We hope the team will be able to travel in January.'[9] For much of January the CCP continued to block the WHO investigation team from travelling to China.

On the other hand, what this statement made absolutely clear was that the WHO inquiry had a very narrowly defined focus: 'identifying the zoonotic source' of the virus. This was missed by most observers at the time, but its critical significance was to become very clear by the end of the year.

To many of those who know him, Dr Tedros is a knowledgeable and committed international public health expert with the requisite skills to run a complex and a highly politicised organisation like the WHO. To his detractors, the epidemic has exposed some fatal flaws in his leadership style; in particular, an obsequious attitude to the Chinese Communist government that has manifested itself in a willingness to kowtow to the authoritarian demands of Xi Jinping. He also stands accused of an over-zealousness in rushing to the defence of Chinese interests and actions.

In an interview with the *Financial Times* in early February, Dr Tedros made a robust defence of his position and reiterated his defence of China. 'Nobody knows for sure if they were hiding [anything]," he said, adding that, 'if they had, the virus would have spread earlier to neighbouring countries. The logic doesn't support the idea [of a cover up]. It's wrong to jump to conclusions.' China, he said, deserved 'tailored and qualified' praise. 'They identified the pathogen and shared the sequence immediately,' he said, helping other countries to quick diagnoses.[10] They quarantined huge cities such as Wuhan, he continued, 'Can't you appreciate that? They should be thanked for hammering the epicentre.

They are actually protecting the rest of the world.' He then continued with the interview by lavishing praise on Xi Jinping: 'I was stunned by the knowledge he had. He was personally living it. That's good leadership.'[11] In defending himself in this manner, the Director General was giving voice to the kind of sentiments that had occasioned the concerns about his attitude to China in the first place. These comments by Dr Tedros were perfectly *ad idem* with those he made following his meeting with Xi Jinping in Beijing two weeks earlier.

Dr Tedros had said on a number of occasions, 'The virus is a common enemy. Let's not play politics here.' But that is exactly what he himself has been accused of, especially by critics in the US government, the WHO's largest single financial backer. In this regard, he didn't do himself any favours in what he said following the meeting with Xi Jinping in Beijing on January 28. Again, lavishing praise on China, according to media reports, Dr Tedros said 'China's speed, China's scale, and China's efficiency ... This is the advantage of China's system.'[12] Even allowing that some of what he said may have been 'lost in translation', there is no combination of those words or phrases that wouldn't have made President Trump and the senior members of his administration, literally, see red. Given its context, this statement in particular, was interpreted by many of his critics as Dr Tedros giving overt support for the CCP's system of authoritarian dictatorship.

The Devil and the Detail

That meeting in Beijing was also notable for other statement, one made by General Secretary, Xi Jinping: 'The virus is a devil. We cannot let the devil hide.' To non-Chinese ears, coming from a secular Marxist it sounded distinctly odd to hear the leader of the CCP talking like a medieval monk about demons and devils and the need to exorcise them. But China has a long tradition of associating devils, demons, and spirits with natural disasters, including epidemics. In this tradition, these natural phenomena are also seen as harbingers of political upheavals.

The instance of this tradition with which most modern Chinese people are particularly familiar is the Manchurian plague of 1910-11. It was an incredibly deadly bacterial pneumonia that was spread from person-to-person through airborne particles. It reputedly had a mortality rate of almost 100% and killed over 60,000 people. Etched into Chinese folk memory are the heroics of a Cambridge-trained military doctor, Wu Lientet, who brought the disease under control through a combination of quarantine and the wearing of face masks. One of the effects of the disease was to further weakened the ruling Qing dynasty. A year later, following the insurrection in Wuhan (see chapter 10) China's lengthy period of imperial rule ended with the establishment of the Republic of China in 1912. It reinforced the association of plague with political change in popular Chinese imagination.

Ever alert to a propaganda opportunity, Mao Zedong also jumped on the plague-solving political bandwagon. In 1958 he celebrated the eradication of snail fever in southern China by writing a poem with which every Chinese schoolchild is familiar, *Farewell to the God of Plague*. In referencing the devil in the way that he did, Xi was evoking these still resonant memories of Wu and Mao's achievements as triumphant battlers against pestilence.[13]

The significance of these historical and cultural allusions in Xi's choice of phrase would not have been lost on his Chinese audience far beyond the precincts of the Great Hall of the People. Fewer still would have missed its political message either: The Party is all-powerful, it can lockdown megacities, enforce draconian quarantines, eschew all foreign offers of assistance, and still vanquish the virus. Xi's words appealed to an authoritarian tradition to deliver an authoritarian message spoken by China's most authoritarian leader of recent decades.

Travel Restrictions

From the SARS outbreak in 2002-3, it was well known that travellers where the primary means of disseminating the disease. Air travel was at the root of the speed with which SARS spread internationally, once the first cases emerged in Hong Kong at the end of February 2003. For epidemiologists ever since, air travel and the rapid spread of the disease were inextricably linked.

Within two weeks of SARS escaping from China, the WHO began issuing an unprecedented series of travel advisories intended to limit the international spread of the disease. Air travel to the areas covered by these advisories dropped off dramatically.[14] These detailed travel alerts continued to be issued by the WHO despite the fact that one month earlier, on February 12, China's state news agency *Xinhua* had announced that the disease had been 'brought under control.' Clearly, the WHO, under Gro

Harlem Brundtland, was far less credulous and did not take China's statements about its handling of the disease at face value.

At the same time, the WHO continued to exert relentless pressure on Chinese officials and this, combined with concerted international diplomacy, resulted in the Chinese CDC issuing the unprecedented public apology for the government's mishandling of the health crisis that we have seen earlier. By mid-April 2003, there was a new government in Beijing. One of its first actions was to fire those senior officials associated with the previous campaign of denials and coverup. Though it wasn't all plain sailing after that, the WHO's first female Director General, Gro Harlem Brundtland's resolute and forthright approach to China had paid off.

At the start of the 2020 Covid-19 outbreak, the issue of travel restrictions to and from affected areas in China also became a contentious issue. In virtually all its statements throughout much of January, the WHO persisted with the same travel advice: 'WHO advises against the application of any travel or trade restrictions on China …' Though China itself effectively ignored this advice by cancelling all flights from the infected areas of central China to the rest of the country, incongruously, it allowed international flights to continue to fly out of Wuhan.

Even in its statement of January 30, in which the WHO finally declared the outbreak a global emergency, it continued with its travel advice that it 'does not recommend any travel or trade restriction based on the current information available.'[15] It was the US Government's imposition of travel restrictions on China the next day, January 31, that garnered the most attention. In an executive order signed by President Trump, all foreigners who had visited China during the previous 14 days were barred from entering the US. On the other hand, US citizens and residents returning from China were directed to 7 specified airports were screening facilities had been set up. Those who tested positive were quarantined for 14 days, while those travelling from Hubei province were subjected to a mandatory 14-day quarantine.

In her criticism of the US travel ban, Chinese Ministry of Foreign Affairs spokeswoman, Hua Chunying was anxious to cite Dr Tedros' benign comments in Beijing three days previously. 'As the WHO Director-General noted, China is setting a new standard for outbreak response.' In the same speech, she referred to Dr Tedros position that the 'WHO continues to have confidence in China's capacity to control the outbreak. There is no reason for measures that unnecessarily interfere with international travel … some countries, the US in particular, have inappropriately overreacted, which certainly runs counter to WHO advice.'[16]

Though there were accusations of racism and xenophobia levelled against him at the time by the media and some politicians, President Trump's China travel ban had the effect of slowing down the spread of the infection. One month later, the *New York Times* science correspondent, Donald G. McNeil Jr. wrote that even subsequent modelling by the WHO had come to a similar conclusion. 'The W.H.O.'s epidemic-modeling teams concluded that travel restrictions had slowed the spread of the virus outside China by two to three weeks. For the United States, the delay was probably far greater. Air-traffic data shows that flights from China to the United States dropped much more than they did to Europe.'[17]

Disaffection in the Ranks

Dr Tedros' public commendations of China throughout January continued to raise eyebrows everywhere, and hackles in the White House. But among senior staff inside the WHO itself, it was a different story – the spirit of Dr Brundtland, it seems, was still alive and very much kicking. While Dr Tedros was describing China's transparency as 'very impressive, and beyond words', according to recordings of internal meetings leaked to the *Associated Press*, senior members of his Geneva-based team were far from complimentary about China's behaviour.

'We're going on very minimal information, it's clearly not enough for you to do proper planning' was the opinion of American epidemiologist Maria Van Kerkhove and technical lead in the WHO's Covid-19 response. The head of the WHO's office in China, Dr Gauden Galea, commented that 'we are currently at the stage where yes, they're giving it to us 15 minutes before it appears on CCTV.' As comments such as these make clear, WHO senior staff believed they were being given the runaround by China.[18]

By the second week of January, tolerance within the WHO for China's continuing prevarication was reaching its limits. Dr Michael Ryan, a long-standing staffer in Geneva, told his colleagues that it was time to 'shift gears' and apply more pressure on China. He explained, 'this is exactly the same scenario [as SARS], endlessly trying to get updates from China about what was going on. WHO barely got out of that one with its neck intact given the issues that arose around transparency in southern China.' Dr Ryan complained that China was not cooperating in the same way that other countries affected by infectious diseases had done in the past. 'This would not happen in Congo and did not happen in Congo and other places. We need to see the data… It's absolutely important at this point.'[19]

Clearly frustrated and annoyed, Ryan was alluding to China's behaviour during the 2002-3 outbreak. During that pandemic, under a very different Director General, WHO staff were not confined to voicing their frustrations in private, they did so in public, repeatedly. Voicing similar frustrations as the current senior WHO members, the then WHO spokesperson in Asia, Peter Cordingley, said in 2003, 'The WHO team doesn't understand how the virus is being spread and has not been given enough data [by China] to join up the dots.' This quotation is from an article in the British Medical Journal, the heading of which was 'China is still not open enough about SARS, says WHO.'[20]

Dissatisfaction with China in 2020 was not confined to the staff at the WHO. A long-time consultant to the WHO and a member of the organisation's emergency committee, Professor John Mackenzie, was highly critical of China's response to the pandemic. In an interview with the *Financial Times*, Prof Mackenzie described China's response as "reprehensible" and that the numbers they were providing defied logic. 'There must have been more cases happening that we weren't being told about. I think they tried to keep the figures quiet for a while because of some major meeting they had in Wuhan but I think there was a period of very poor reporting, or very poor communication,' he said.[21]

The criticism even extended to the senior ranks of China's own health authority. A senior public health expert who works with China's Center for Disease Control and Prevention (CDC) and Ministry of Health said internal politics were partly to blame. Speaking anonymously, he said 'The broader political climate in China definitely slowed the response rate. Because of Xi and the centralisation of his control, the CDC and Health Commission were more cautious to act initially', he added.[22]

Chapter 13: A Smoking Gun?

Like a number of other words and phrases, up to the outbreak of the coronavirus pandemic the public across most of the world remained in blissful lexical ignorance of the term 'wet market' – outside of Chinese Asia at any rate. Then in January 2020, the Wuhan wet market was cast as the villain of the pandemic piece by both China's health authorities and, as a consequence, the WHO. Suddenly, caught in the glare of the international media spotlight, wet markets were revealed to the world in all their inglorious gory details. For most people, what was on display was not a pretty sight. Even a cursory look at what went on in these markets would give any self-respecting health and safety officer a fit of the vapours.

The Free Market

The Wuhan market occupies a significant area of a recently developed part of Wuhan city centre. Incongruously, it is situated in a largely middle-class district just about a kilometre from the city's principal Hankou railway station. It consists of a warren of up to 20 streets lined with hundreds of stalls that not only sell meats, fish, poultry, vegetables, spices, and condiments, but also more exotic fare such as wild animals and birds. Though long noted for its dismal reputation for poor hygiene, ventilation, sanitation, and disease control, the Wuhan seafood market is very popular among Wuhan city-centre shoppers largely because it offers a large selection of produce, and it is cheap.

There were two primary reasons why Communist health officials were adamant that the Wuhan wet market was where the epidemic started. First, the large number of the first group of laboratory-confirmed infected patients had either worked at the market or were otherwise associated with it. Secondly, this outbreak of viral pneumonia looked like a case of history repeating itself. The SARS epidemic in 2002-3 had a trajectory that began in the bat caves of south China and then somehow is thought to have jumped to an intermediate host species in a wet market, in that instance, civet cats. Once in the civet cats, the virus evolved further and multiplied and, as an airborne pathogen, it was eventually passed on to humans in some crowded and unhygienic wet market environment.

The working assumption by Chinese officialdom was that a similar transmission mechanism was at play here and the Wuhan seafood market was the source of the virus. However, no evidence whatsoever has emerged that identifies the seafood market as the location where the virus made the jump to humans. And this has not been for the want of trying. One study, about which there was much scepticism, suggested snakes were the culprits.[1] Another investigated pangolins as the intermediate host species.[2]

Despite the inferences in official Chinese statements that the Wuhan seafood market was a likely source for the origins of the virus, there is formidable evidence against this suggestion. First, the medical and epidemiological evidence makes clear that the very first confirmed cases of the disease had no association with the seafood market. Secondly, bats were not on sale in the Wuhan market and are not part of the culinary repertoire of central China. Thirdly, the particular type of bat that Chinese virologists and others have identified as the host species for the Covid-19 virus has its natural habitat in the caves of China's southern provinces, almost 1000 km away – a very long way for a bat to fly.

The WHO has repeated many times that the virus originated in the Wuhan wet market. As late as February, in a major WHO assessment titled '*Report of the WHO-China Joint Mission on Coronavirus Disease 2019 (COVID-19)*', stated that 'Early cases identified in Wuhan are believed to be have acquired infection (sic) from a zoonotic source as many reported visiting or working in the Huanan Wholesale Seafood Market. As of 25 February, an intermediate animal source host has not yet been identified.'[3]This mirrors what the CCP was also saying, however, neither has provided any evidence for this assertion.

By the end of March, the WHO seemed to be moving away from this unsupported assertion. In a statement on 26 March, it said, 'The virus which causes COVID-19 most probably has its ecological reservoir in bats, and transmission of the virus to humans has likely occurred through an intermediate animal host – a domestic animal, a wild animal or a domesticated wild animal which has not yet been identified.'[4]

This statement is entirely reasonable and avoids mentioning the specific location of the Wuhan seafood market which for animal to human transmission has no corroborating scientific evidence – at least none that has been made publicly available. By not insisting on the seafood market as the location where the zoonotic transition took place, the WHO implicitly, but correctly, accepts that the market may well have been the venue where an extensive initial person-to-person transmission took place. In other words, it allows for the possibility that some already infected person, either a customer or one of the vendors, came to the market and in the normal course of moving around infected many others – just like Dr Liu in the Metropole Hotel in Hong Kong in 2003.

During the busy pre-Lunar New Year period stallholders at the Wuhan seafood market knew that something was seriously amiss. Many of them started coming down with nagging fevers. Soon, some of the vendors started not showing up for work. Word began to spread around the market that the owners of those stalls that remained shuttered were in hospital, and that some had been put in quarantine. The numbers falling ill and the rumours multiplied.

Then suddenly, during the last hours of 2019 a small army of the health officials in hazmat suits, accompanied by paramilitary police, descended on the seafood market. The entire market was cordoned off and notifications were placed at all entrances informing the public and stallholders that the market was closed until further notice, as it was undergoing an environmental and hygienic clean-up because of a pneumonia outbreak. Though everyone in the market had their suspicions, this was the first official confirmation that something was seriously wrong. This happened on December 31, 2019, and the Wuhan seafood market has never re-opened.

Avoiding the End of Days

Biosecurity laboratories are designed to facilitate research into some of the most dangerous pathogens known to humankind. They have biosecurity levels of an inordinately high standard. This is not only to protect the researchers who work there, but also to eliminate, as far as possible, the risk that something highly pathogenic to humans might escape into the community. As the WHO's website warns, 'Perhaps the failure to follow appropriate biosafety and laboratory biosecurity practices may still be the greatest threat for the reappearance of SARS.[5]

However, because it is ultimately reliant on human beings, safety even in the highest standard Level 4 biolabs is not inviolable. Unfortunately, accidents do happen. Luckily, as laboratory-incident reports indicate, the vast majority of these are mishaps as a result of human error.[6] But on occasion, breaches of the high-level biosecurity safety standards have had potentially disastrous consequences. In probability terms, this is not a trivial risk.

In August 2016 the United States Government Accountability Office (GAO) submitted a report to Congress whose title alone left little doubt as the potential dangers involved: *High-Containment Laboratories: Improved Oversight of Dangerous Pathogens Needed to Mitigate Risk*. In its highly commendable non-technical and forthright style, the GAO states why it was asked to undertake its analysis: 'Several incidents involving the shipment of live pathogens, thought to be inactivated, have recently occurred, potentially exposing people to dangerous pathogens that cause infectious diseases such as the bacterium that causes anthrax.'[7]

It is this possibility of accidental escape, no matter how improbable, that has particularly exercised the minds of both regulators and many scientists during the past decade. The focus of these serious concerns relates to one activity in particular; so-called 'gain-of-function' research. This 'gain-of-function' experimental work involves genetically modifying known pathogens in order to create mutant varieties with increased lethality or to otherwise enhance the efficacy of the virus.

Its supporters argue that increasing the transmissibility or virulence of a pathogen under laboratory conditions offers significant potential benefits. In particular, it allows researchers to, as it were, get ahead of the viral curve by better understanding possible disease pathways and thus facilitate the design of therapeutics for the kind of even more lethal viruses that may evolve in the future. But opponents are adamant that second guessing how a virus 'in the wild' will mutate is unrealistic. More importantly, any possible benefits in the future are insufficient to outweighed the risks that undertaking this research poses in the present. Though such experiments are clearly intended to bestow benefits, the worry is that they may inadvertently cause harm. It's a complex debate involving issues of scientific freedom, ethics, and biosecurity.

Viral Politics

In 2014, the Obama administration placed a temporary prohibition on gain-of-function experiments involving influenza, SARS, and MERS viruses in order to assess the risks involved.[8] Worried by a number of serious incidents at several US Federal high-level biolabs, in October 2017 the White House Office of Science and Technology Policy announced a detailed review of so-called gain-of-function research because, 'Gain-of-function studies may entail biosafety and biosecurity risks; therefore, the risks and benefits of gain-of function research must be evaluated.'[9]

Dr Antony Fauci is one of the longest serving public health officials in the US. He has been director of by the National Institutes of Health a body operating under the National Institute of Allergy and Infectious Diseases (NIAID) since 1984. Dr Fauci is a long-time advocate and supporter of gain-of-function virology research and has discussed the merits or otherwise of publishing controversial papers on experiments that 'engineered' the transmissibility of influenza viruses, 'There is always a risk ...But I believe the benefits are greater than the risks.'[10]

In an important contribution to the debate in *Science* written jointly with his colleague, Francis S. Collins they concluded by saying: 'The public, which has a stake in the risks and the benefits of such research, deserves a rational and transparent explanation of how decisions are made ...A social contract among the scientific community, policy-makers, and the general public that builds trust is essential for success of this process.'[11] Five years later in 2017, Dr Fauci breached that 'social contract' in a most flagrant manner. The circumstances and timing are interesting.

The original White House moratorium announcement of 2014, set a deadline for the deliberative process and a further deadline 'for the development, approval, and *publication of the policy*' (emphasis added).[12] But before effect could be given to this laudable aspiration, as is often the case, life threw a curved ball. On December 19, 2016, Donald J. Trump was elected the President of the United States by the electoral College. In the meantime, the incumbent President Obama remained in office until the president-elect's inauguration which was scheduled for January 20, 2017.

On December 19, the same day that Donald Trump was officially elected President, Dr Fauci's NIH announced the lifting of the ban on gain-of-function research.[13] While a new framework for such research was published, the 1,000-page risk-benefit assessment which had been completed as far back as June 2016, along with an ethics white paper, were never published as had been promised by the White House. Why President Obama lifted the ban during Christmas week, a few weeks before he left office, and without publishing the discussion document remains unclear. But what is clear is that by not making public the discussion document behind the last-minute Obama administration decision to lift the ban was an egregious breach of Fauci's self-declared 'social contract'.

Despite the ban on gain-of-function experimentation, similar experiments continued – including ones that involved US laboratories working with scientists at the Wuhan Institute of Virology. A paper published in November 2015 in *Nature*, confirms that scientists from University of North Carolina at Chapel Hill were working in collaboration with the Wuhan Institute of Virology creating mutant SARS viruses. Their research involved using the SARS-CoV reverse genetics system to create a mutant or chimeric virus capable of infecting a mouse – the mouse being the mammalian stand-in. The mutant virus was found to replicate efficiently in primary human airway cells and generate concentrations 'equivalent to epidemic strains of SARS-CoV.' The published results went on to confirm that, 'Additionally, *in vivo* experiments demonstrate replication of the chimeric virus in mouse lung with notable pathogenesis.'[14] In other words, it was potentially an effective killer.

The research indicated that coronaviruses which had the capacity to directly infect humans, rather than requiring an intermediate host species, may be more common in bats than had been previously assumed. Its scientific merits aside, we should remember that this paper was published during the period when 'gain-of-function' experimentation was banned in the United States, a prohibition that did not, of course, extend to work in China.

Though in strict scientific terms, chimeric experimentation did not come within the ambit of the gain-of-function ban, this did not stop many from viewing the collaboration between US virologists and the Wuhan Institute of Virology as simply a means of circumventing the US interdiction. While scientists will argue that the two experimental processes are not the same, for lay people, this amounts to a distinction without a difference. Whether it arose from a gain-of-function or a chimeric process, if the resultant mutant virus escaped from a lab, the consequences would be equally catastrophic.

When published, this experimental research that created a hybrid version of the coronavirus found in horseshoe bats in China sparked scientific controversy. One virologist based at the Pasteur Institute in Paris mused that having created a hybrid virus that grew remarkably well in human cells, worried that 'if the virus escaped, nobody could predict the trajectory.' Another critic expressed misgivings that 'the only impact of this work is the creation, in a lab, of a new, non-natural risk.'[15] Even the authors of the study that reignited the gain-of-function controversy seemed to accept that it has a questionable future: 'scientific review panels may deem similar studies building chimeric viruses based on circulating strains too risky to pursue.'

In 2019, with the support of Dr Fauci's NIAID, the NIH provided $3.7 million of funding for collaborative research between New York-based EcoHealth Alliance and the Wuhan Institute of Virology, some of which involved gain-of-function experimentation. At a press conference in mid-

April 2020, President Trump was asked why the US was still funding research being carried out by the Wuhan Institute of Virology, an organisation about which his administration had expressed public misgivings. The President responded, 'We will end that grant very quickly.' One week later, EcoHealth Alliance received a notification from the NIH saying 'At this time, NIH does not believe that the current project outcomes align with the program goals and agency priorities.' When asked at a Congressional meeting why the grant was terminated, Dr Fauci replied 'I don't know the reason, but we were told to cancel it.' But Peter Daszak, the President of EcoHealth Alliance was under no illusions as to the reason, it was he believed an 'obvious case of political interference.'[16]

The primary worry in all this centres on laboratory acquired infections, especially by those working on airborne transmissible pathogens such as SARS and MERS. Simply put, there is a credible risk of someone walking out of a lab with an infection and unwittingly infecting others. How do we know this? Because it had happened before – in 2004 in China. In separate incidents up to a month apart, two laboratory workers in Beijing's National Institute of Virology new P3 laboratory were exposed to active SARS coronavirus samples and became infected. On exiting the lab, they passed the infection on to others, mainly close family members and the medical staff who cared for them in hospital. There followed a series of infections and one death before the outbreak was brought under control.[17] The one fatality involved the mother of one of the infected lab researchers.

The WHO issued a statement on this outbreak in May 2004, the headline of which speaks for itself: 'China's latest SARS outbreak has been contained, but biosafety concerns remain'. The concerns centred on the National Institute of Virology in Beijing where experiments using live and inactivated SARS coronavirus were being conducted. The WHO statement confirmed that 'investigators have serious concerns about biosafety procedures at the Institute – including how and where procedures using SARS coronavirus were carried out, and how and where SARS coronavirus samples were stored.'[18]

But concerns about the operational safety of Chinese biosecurity laboratories have an even more recent provenance. An exclusive report by Josh Rogin of *The Washington Post*, revealed that US officials voiced similar worries about aspects of the P4 laboratory at the Wuhan Institute of Virology following a number of visits to the facility from January to March 2018. In the wake of their visit, diplomatic staff from the US embassy in Beijing, including the embassy's counsellor for environment, science, technology and health, sent repeated reports back to the State Department in Washington highlighting their safety concerns.

As Rogin's article confirms, the first of these diplomatic dispatches 'warns that the lab's work on bat coronaviruses and their potential human transmission represented a risk of a new SARS-like pandemic.' In particular, the diplomatic cables sent back to Washington noted that the 'new lab has a serious shortage of appropriately trained technicians and investigators needed to safely operate this high-containment laboratory.' Though critical of the serious deficiencies they saw, the diplomats were broadly supportive of the Institute's work because, they argued: 'From a public health perspective, this makes the continued surveillance of SARS-like coronaviruses in bats and study of the animal-human interface critical to future emerging coronavirus outbreak prediction and prevention.'[19]

But these prophetic words were written in 2018. Two years later in April 2020, when the *Washington Post* article appeared, the world was a changed place. We were in the middle of a global pandemic and the CCP was frantically trying to spin a narrative that it had omnipotently mastered the virus and thereby saved the world from an even worse catastrophe. In that context, anything that cast doubt on this version of events had to be either eliminated or supressed. And so, within days of the *Washington Post* article being published, the rather bland and innocuous account of the US diplomats' visit that had been posted on the Wuhan Institute of Virology's website was erased. Xi's authoritarian China brooked no criticism; not even a reminder of criticism.

However, as previously noted, nothing of significance ever happens in a tightly controlled authoritarian state like China, without the approval of the Party leader. And, when the 'Paramount' leader expressly draws attention to an issue there is always something significant behind it. Within a few weeks of the Wuhan lockdown, Xi Jinping addressed the Communist Party's powerful Politburo Standing Committee, where he highlighted the need for reform in an area that he never mentioned before: biosecurity. 'Biosafety and biosecurity is vital to people's health,' Xi told the Politburo members, 'national security and long-term stability of the country, and must therefore be included into the national security system … Legislation on a biosecurity law must be accelerated to establish the legal and institutional frameworks needed to ensure biosafety and biosecurity of the country.'[20]

We don't know – and, perhaps, never will – precisely what had happened in the Wuhan labs to prompt this unusual reference by Xi Jinping to biosecurity and biosafety in February. But its timing so close to the Wuhan virus outbreak is unlikely to be coincidental. Within a couple of days of Xi's speech, the Party's English language paper *Global Times*, reported that the Ministry of Science and Technology had issued new guidelines 'strengthening the management of bio labs, especially on viruses, to ensure biosafety'. In a case of what sounds like an instance of "protesting too much", the article was at pains to stress that all of this had 'nothing to do with some saying that the coronavirus leaked from the Wuhan Institute of Virology', nevertheless, it went on to state that the 'release of the guideline deals with chronic loopholes at laboratories.'[21]

Conspiracy Theories

Because of visceral public fear and large gaps in our knowledge, conspiracy theories have always accompanied pandemics and outbreaks of plague. Covid-19 would be no exception. From the beginning there were serious doubts about the claim that the Wuhan seafood market was where SARS-CoV-2 had its origins. By May, even Chinese authorities had finally ruled out the market as the source of the virus. Gao Fu, the director of the Chinese CDC, told Chinese state media: 'At first, we assumed the seafood market might have the virus, but now the market is more like a victim. The novel coronavirus had existed long before.'[22] Even before the seafood market had been finally taken off the list as the location where the virus had originated, conspiracy theories regarding other sources of the virus abounded. But with the seafood market eliminated and no realistic or viable alternative being proffered by any credible authority, in the ensuing information vacuum conspiracy theorists had a field day.

Though we don't burn witches any more to try to stop a pestilence, today's most common ritually sacrificed victim is common sense. In the inevitable time-gap it takes to assemble a cohesive data-based picture of an outbreak, conspiracy theorists rush in where scientific angels fear to tread. As Abraham Lincoln pointed out 160 years ago, 'You can fool all of the people some of the time, and some of the people all of the time' – and it's this latter group that conspiracy theorists seem to target. Their proliferation on social media means that entirely unsubstantiated claims about the virus, including its origins, have acquired legs.

The pandemic also brought forth the usual assortment of quacks and charlatans promoting various elixirs as remedies for Covid. When health fears spike among the general public for whatever reason, 'alternative' remedies proliferate on social media. We saw earlier how in China at the height of the epidemic a Chinese herbal remedy had been promoted by the Wuhan Institute of Virology (see chapter 1). Purported cures for Covid-19 also included many of the usual suspects; teas, essential oils, tinctures of all kinds, herbal therapies, and many miracle mineral supplements. As the National Centre for Complementary and Integrative Health (NIH) pointed out; '**There is no scientific evidence that any of these alternative remedies can prevent or cure COVID-19**. In fact, some of them may not be safe to consume' (emphasis in original).[23]

It was the presence of not one but two biosecurity labs in the city that was the epicentre of the Covid-19 pandemic that provided the real grist to the conspiracy-theory mill. The internet has been awash with provocative and unsubstantiated suggestions as to the origins of Covid-19 virus. In the absence of any definitive knowledge as to where the virus actually originated, debunking these conspiracy theories is extremely difficult. This is especially so as some of the more *outré* propositions have become part of a wider geopolitical blame game between the United States and China.

The most popular extreme speculation doing the rounds in Western social media was that the virus was engineered in a Chinese laboratory as a bioweapon. Unfortunately, in view of the Communist authorities' dissembling behaviour and record of deception from the outset of the pandemic, trust in China is at an all-time low. Part of the effect of this has been to lend credibility to some of these wackier suggestions. With no publicly available evidence to support the bioweapon hypothesis, however, it can be safely ignored until definitive evidence for it emerges, if ever.

Allied to this are the claims that the virus was engineered in a lab, but not as a bioweapon. There is at least circumstantial evidence for this proposition. The Wuhan Institute of Virology, as we have already seen, did engage in gain-of-function experimentation which involved re-engineering the genetic structure of these highly pathogenic viruses. In an attempt to scotch the rumours that the particular viral genome that causes Covid-19 was a chimeric or engineer virus, numerous international virologists have weighed in. They have provided commentaries and analyses which have indicated that the SARS-CoV-2 virus was the product of natural evolution and had not been engineered in a laboratory.

In a letter published in *Nature Medicine* in March, a group of distinguished Western scientists stressed the importance of having a 'detailed understanding of how an animal virus jumped species boundaries to infect humans.' Following a detailed review of the virus's comparative genomic data, their conclusion was that, 'our analyses clearly show that SARS-CoV-2 is not a laboratory construct or a purposefully manipulated virus.'[24] There were several other statements and papers by other reputable virologists who made similar arguments, none of which seemed to dissuade those committed to the belief in an 'engineered virus'.

Then in an unusual statement, the Office of the Director of National Intelligence, which oversees the sprawling U.S. intelligence network said, 'The Intelligence Community also concurs with the wide scientific consensus that the COVID-19 virus was not manmade or genetically modified.' In its statement, however, it pointedly refused to rule out the possibility that the virus had escaped from the complex of laboratories in Wuhan. It promised to 'continue to rigorously examine … whether the outbreak began through contact with infected animals or if it was the result of an accident at a laboratory in Wuhan.'[25]

Even staunch believers in dialectal and historical materialism were anxious to jump on the conspiracy theory band-wagon. Chinese officials began claiming that the virus might have been introduced by members of the US Army who had visited Wuhan in October 2019 to participate in the World Military Games. The spokesman for the Ministry of Foreign Affairs, Zhao Lijian, suggested in a tweet that, 'It might be US Army who brought the epidemic to Wuhan. Be transparent! Make public your data! US owe us an explanation!'[26] Ironically, Zhao Lijian put forward this unsubstantiated conspiracy theory on Twitter, a platform that is banned in China. Though Twitter, in its recently vastly expanded editorial capacity has assiduously blocked or censored tweets it has deemed to contain 'unsubstantiated claims', so far there is no evidence it has applied this editorial policy to such unsubstantiated conspiracy claims by China.

In latter months, the CCP has promoted another false narrative that the virus had multiple origins in different locations around the world and had come into China in frozen food packages. There is no credible scientific evidence to support this 'multiple origins' theory yet it is being pushed very hard by the CCP which has managed to have it included in the terms of reference of the WHO-led international inquiry.

As bilateral relationships between the superpowers deteriorated dramatically, diplomacy entered a far more combative phase. In the competition between the US and China to control the narrative of the virus, China was resorting to one of its stock-in-trade disinformation tactics. Simply put, Zhao Lijian's tweet was an 'up-yours' response by China to repeated references by President Trump and other senior administration officials to the 'Wuhan virus' and the 'China virus'. Around the same time, an article in the Chinese state news agency, *Xinhua*, said; 'instead of focusing on fighting the epidemic in their own country, some in the United States are trying to shift the blame and politicize humanity's common challenge by stoking pernicious anti-Chinese sentiments.'[27] More significantly, this type of megaphone diplomacy by both sides signified for many that a new Cold War was underway.

But the most persistent, and potentially most credible theory is that somehow the virus had escaped from a biosecurity lab in Wuhan. I say potentially, because just as in the case of the Wuhan seafood market, there is no hard evidence that the virus did in fact escape from a lab. Without providing any, Secretary of State, Mike Pompeo said in a TV interview 'I can tell you that there is a significant amount of evidence that this came from that laboratory in Wuhan.'

In his inimitable, enigmatic, circumlocutionary fashion, President Trump made similar claims: 'We're going to see where it comes from. We have people looking at it very, very strongly. Scientific people, intelligence people, and others. We're going to put it all together. I think we will have a very good answer eventually.' When pressed at the White House briefing for an explanation as to what he meant, and specifically did he have evidence that the virus had escaped from a Chinese lab, he ended his dance-of-the-seven-veils explanation by saying: 'I can't tell you that. I'm not allowed to tell you that.'[28] So the proof was there, somewhere; but in the meantime, the public was going to have to accept innuendo.

Origin of the Species

Chinese scientists have identified the origin of the SARS virus in horseshoe bats located in the remote caves of southern China. Researchers led by Shi Zhengli of the Wuhan Institute of Virology found that this species of bat carried the virus that had a similar genetic make-up to that of SARS.[29] This breakthrough discovery was widely welcomed as it enhanced the potential to develop a successful treatment or vaccine.

Unfortunately, this has proved to be a forlorn hope as to date no vaccine for SARS has ever been developed. Because Covid-19 is genetically similar to SARS, scientists are convinced that it too had its origins in the same horseshoe bat population.

However, mystery still surrounds the mechanism through which the virus jumped from bats in South China to humans in Wuhan. Authoritative scientific opinion presumes that this happened by way of an intermediate species such as had happened with SARS: the intermediate host species in that instance turned out to be civet cats. For Covid-19, a number of species have been suggested as candidates for this intermediate animal host, but to date scientific investigations have failed to come up with any contender for this intermediate species.

This has left an obvious and important missing link in the chain of events that resulted in the virus infecting people in Wuhan. It was precisely this important issue that two researchers from the South China University of Technology, Botao Xiao and Lei Xiao, addressed in an important paper: 'The possible origins of 2019-nCoV coronavirus', which was published online in February 2020. For these Chinese academics, 'It was critical to study where the pathogen came from and how it passed on to humans.' They noted the important epidemiological information in *The Lancet* which had stated that of the 41 laboratory-confirmed infectious Wuhan patients, '27 of them had contact with Huanan Seafood Market.'

However, they also noted that the bats in which the virus originated 'were more than 900 kilometres away from the seafood market' and as the academics' own research indicated; '{A}ccording to municipal reports and the testimonies of 31 residents and 28 visitors, the bat was never a food source in the city, and no bat was traded in the market.' Additionally, they argued that no information on an intermediate host animal had yet emerged. The internal logic of their argument led the academics to investigate whether there were any other possible sources of the virus in the vicinity of the seafood market.

Having consulted Google Maps, the researchers noted that, unlike the P4 lab at the Wuhan Institute of Virology, the Wuhan Centre for Disease Control (CDC) biolaboratory was situated a mere 278 metres from the seafood market in city centre. They even provided a map to emphasise how close the two premises were to each other. The laboratory carried out experiments on animals for research purposes, part of which included pathogen collection and identification. The researchers at that laboratory collected their own bats, including horseshoe bats, on which they conducted their experiments. According to the academics' study, surgery was performed on these animals 'and the tissue samples were collected for DNA and RNA extraction and sequencing.'

One of the virologists at this CDC lab, Tian Junhua, acquired quite a reputation as a bat collector whose exploits became the subject of articles in newspapers and a television documentary during the preceding two years. During his nocturnal explorations, he had a number of mishaps which he described on his Internet blog. By his own admission, according to one newspaper report, 'Apart from knowing bats in books, Tian Junhua's knowledge of bats can be said to be almost zero.' On one occasion, 'he was attacked by bats and the blood of the bat shot on his skin. He knew the extreme danger of the infection so he quarantined himself for 14 days.' On another occasion he was urinated upon by bats and again had to quarantine himself for 14 days.[30] Though the paper doesn't say so explicitly, clearly the safety standards at this CDC laboratory in Wuhan seem to have been less than optimal.

At this point in their paper, the academics seem to be following the logic of Sherlock Holmes' advice that, 'when you have eliminated the impossible, whatever remains, however improbable, must be the truth.'[31] Without pointing the finger explicitly, but clearly having the CDC lab in mind, the academics came to the explosive conclusion that 'the killer coronavirus probably originated from a laboratory in Wuhan.'

Though the academics themselves state that none of what they had written amounted to proof that the virus escaped from a Wuhan lab. However, they argued that, at the very least, it raised the issue that, 'Safety level[s] may need to be reinforced in high-risk biohazardous laboratories.' Given the lax safety standards and all the other issues and the circumstantial evidence surrounding this biolaboratory that are detailed in the paper, the possibility that the virus escaped from this CDC lab has warranted urgent investigation. As far as can be ascertained, none has been carried out. Instead, the messengers were silenced. In the light of the controversial nature of their paper – and especially its conclusion – it comes as no surprise that this academic paper did not escape the attention of Chinese censors. It was removed very shortly after the researchers had posted it online – but, luckily, not before I managed to make a copy of its contents.[32]

There is one Western commentator who, since January 2020, has made similar claims to these Chinese researchers from the South China University. Jamie Metzl is a technology futurist and geopolitical expert who served on the Clinton Administration's National Security Council and is a current WHO advisor on genome editing. He has consistently claimed that the virus is most likely to have escaped from one of the labs in Wuhan. In making his claims, Dr Metzl readily admits that the lack of open access to the detailed evidence has been a severe limitation. Nonetheless, he has stated; 'I have no definitive way of proving this thesis but the evidence is, in my view, extremely convincing.' His level of confidence that the virus was a lab leak is very high: 'I would say there's an 85% chance the pandemic started with an accidental leak from the Wuhan Institute of Virology or Wuhan CDC and a 15% chance it began in some other way.'[33]

There are a number of aspects of Dr Metzl's claims that distinguish them from virtually all others made by non-Chinese commentators. The arguments supporting his hypothesis are carefully crafted; steadfastly maintained for over a year; and have been given sporadic airing in reliable Western (mainly US) media outlets. Most importantly, they have not received any credible rebuttal from an equally authoritative source. Nor is Dr Metzl some kind of closet Trumpian or compulsive conspiracy theorist: his Democratic credentials extend to having served as Deputy Staff Director of the U.S. Senate Foreign Relations Committee under President Biden when he was a Senator.

In the hyper-partisan atmosphere that has surrounded all aspects of the origins of SARS-CoV-2 – at both the geopolitical level between the US and China, and within the frenzied US presidential race context – Dr Metzl's arguments deserve to be taken seriously. On the basis of the investigative logic of both Occam's Razor (the simplest explanation is always the best), and that of Sherlock Holmes quoted above, Dr Metzl, and Dr Botao Xiao and Dr Lei Xiao of the South China University of Technology have, independently, arrived at similar plausible explanations for the vitally important question of the origins of the disease that has caused such global mayhem. In my view, it is the closest that we have yet come to finding a smoking gun. Unfortunately, the likelihood of either of the two major inquiries into the origins of the virus even investigating the laboratory escape hypothesis are very remote.

Finally, the WHO Enquiry Gets Underway

In the light of the unprecedented combination of death, disease, misery and economic devastation caused to the people of the world, an explanation of the origins of the virus is essential. This is not only for present purposes, but for future protections from such spillover events. Despite the WHO statement in January 2020, following the meeting between Dr Tedros and President Xi Jinping in Beijing, claiming that arrangements for a WHO-led investigation would be made 'as soon as possible'. One full year later, in January 2021 the WHO team were finally given the go-ahead to enter China. However, in the eyes of many, is a fundamentally compromised inquiry because both its terms of reference and its membership have effectively been dictated by the CCP. In other words, this has all the hallmarks of being a CCP-controlled investigation that will end up being a whitewash. It may even lead to a further muddying of the already murky waters of the origins of the virus.

Dr Peter Daszak, CEO of EcoHealth Alliance has worked for over 15 years with the Wuhan Institute of Virology on bat research, including gain-of-function experiments. He has reportedly said that 'The idea that this virus escaped from a lab is just pure baloney.' In an article in the *Guardian*, he has argued that theories of an escape from a lab in Wuhan are conspiracy theories which have resulted in 'political posturing against China, with calls for an inquiry'.[34] Peter Daszak is one of the leading members of this WHO inquiry team.

In March, *The Lancet* published a 'Statement in support of the scientists, public health professionals, and medical professionals of China combatting COVID-19'. Its central message was crystal clear: 'The rapid, open, and transparent sharing of data on this outbreak is now being threatened by rumours and misinformation around its origins. We stand together to strongly condemn conspiracy theories suggesting that COVID-19 does not have a natural origin.'[35] In July, *The Lancet* launched its own investigation, *The Lancet* COVID-19 Commission, and set up various task forces charged with delving into aspects of the pandemic. One of these was assigned to look into the origins of the virus. In September, the Commission released its first interim report, one of whose conclusions was; 'The origins of severe acute respiratory syndrome coronavirus 2 (SARS-CoV-2) are yet to be definitively determined, but evidence to date supports the view that SARS-CoV-2 is a naturally occurring virus rather than the result of laboratory creation and release.'[36] The Commission's task force charged with seeking the origins of the virus is chaired by the same Peter Daszak.

Both of these investigations are inherently flawed. The most egregious defect is with the WHO investigation whose complete superintendence by the CCP will render its findings virtually worthless. But the fact that Dr

Daszak has a prominent role in both the WHO and *The Lancet* investigations represents a fundamental conflict of interest. At its simplest, Dr Daszak has worked closely for over a decade and a half with the Wuhan Institute of Virology, one of the principal laboratories from which the virus may have leaked. While his personal integrity is not in question, the fact that he has vehemently and publicly denied even the possibility of such a leak should have rendered him ineligible as member of either investigation. His appointment to both does not augur well for the type of open-minded investigation that this global crisis demands, and the people of the world expect.

As the WHO investigation got under way in China, the CCP ratcheted up the volume considerably in the advancement of its own cack-handed attempts to promote the notion that the virus had not originated in China at all. This newly intensified propaganda campaign seems to have abandoned the previous unfounded claim that it was US army members attending the World Military Games in Wuhan in October 2019 that brought the virus with them and introduced infection to the city. In a dramatic switch, the CCP began asserting an equally spurious claim that the virus had emerged in multiple locations around the world and had entered China through imported frozen food packages.

Spokespersons from the Foreign Ministry, and the CCP-controlled media swung into action to promote a false narrative that had now received official sanction. The irrepressible Foreign Ministry spokesperson, Zhao Lijian (see above), who would leave Sean Spicer, Sarah Saunders and Kaleigh McEnany in the ha'penny place when it comes to telling porkies on behalf of their boss, led the propaganda charge once more: 'Although China was the first to report cases', he told the world's press, 'it doesn't necessarily mean that the virus originated in China … Origin tracing is an ongoing process that may involve multiple countries and regions.' The frozen food scenario and the multiple locations narrative with which it is linked, has as least two benefits from the Communist authorities perspective: first, it deflects attention away from labs and gives a new lease of life to the notion that the virus source was the Wuhan seafood market where frozen food was on sale. Second, if provides a perfect excuse for China to place extra customs restrictions and costly delays on the frozen food imports of whatever country it wishes, for whatever reason, to target.

On January 18, 2021, BBC's resident Correspondent, John Sudworth queried the Foreign Ministry spokeswoman, Hua Chunying, directly on the new narrative: 'Can you tell us why China is promoting this narrative in the absence of scientific evidence, and with the WHO inquiry into the origins barely just begun?' It was a simple and direct question, but Ms Hua responded to the question with less than equanimity: 'Your question reveals your prejudice against China. Why can't the Chinese media report on this? The British media have reported on these stories, haven't they? ... What are you implying with your question?'[37]

As is often the case with such exchanges, the Foreign Ministry spokeswoman's response said little while revealing a multitude. However, one thing Ms. Hua was adamant about was that the virus had not escaped from a lab in Wuhan. As evidence she referred to Peter Daszak, whom I just mentioned above: 'Peter Daszak, a prominent American expert on virology who has been cooperating with the WIV for 15 years, said in an interview last April that there is no virus in the Wuhan lab that could trigger the outbreak, so it's impossible that the virus came from the lab', said Ms. Hua, triumphantly.[38]

Meanwhile the CCP's international mouthpiece, the *Global Times*, reported at the end of November that a study conducted by scientists at the Chinese Academy of Sciences 'was about to be published in top medical journal The Lancet, [which] suggested that the Indian subcontinent might be the place where the earliest human-to-human novel coronavirus transmission occurred, three or four months prior to the outbreak in Wuhan.'[39] More than two months after the Chinese scientists' paper had been published in a number of non-peer reviewed (pre-print) publications, the controversial article has still not seen the light of day in *The Lancet*. Given that *The Lancet* and its editor, Richard Horton, got into considerable hot water in the past by publishing controversial papers that had to be withdrawn subsequently, it may be understandable that, on this occasion at least, the very contentious claims in this paper will be scrutinised with a fine-tooth comb before they receive the imprimatur of *The Lancet* – if they ever do.

Dr Daszak had dismissed out of hand the possibility of a lab leak even before he arrived in China as part of the WHO investigation. However, some other Chinese scientists have made a reasoned scientific case for at least the possibility that a lab leak of some kind happened, in a paper that has received insufficient attention in the West. The substantive aspect of their argument is worth quoting in full:

'... we were surprised to find that SARS-CoV-2 resembles SARS-CoV in the late phase of the 2003 epidemic after SARS-CoV had developed several advantageous adaptations for human transmission. Our observations suggest that by the time SARS-CoV-2 was first detected in late 2019, it was already pre-adapted to human transmission to an extent similar to late epidemic SARS-CoV. However, no precursors or branches of evolution stemming from a less human-adapted SARS-CoV-2-like virus have been detected … It would be curious if no precursor or branches of SARS-CoV-2 evolution are discovered in humans or animals …*Even the possibility that a non-genetically-engineered precursor could have adapted to humans while being studied in a laboratory should be considered, regardless of how likely or unlikely.*'[40] (emphasis added).

Against that background, the terms of reference under which China has agreed to allow the WHO to conduct an investigation do not inspire a great deal of confidence. Indeed, they would appear explicitly to rule out any investigation of the possibility that the virus that has crippled the world could have leaked out of a lab in Wuhan. Apart from some innocuous generalities that the WHO investigation 'will contribute to improve the understanding of the virus origins' and suchlike, the terms of reference set for the WHO investigators seem to be focused exclusively on the natural or 'zoonotic source of the virus'. Just as ominously, the terms of reference state that this 'global origin tracing work is therefore not bound to any location and may evolve geographically as evidence is being generated, and hypotheses evolve.' The terms of reference's next paragraph begins: 'Where an epidemic is first detected does not necessarily reflect where it started.' It then continues, 'the possibility that the virus may have silently circulated elsewhere cannot be ruled out.'[41] These statements can clearly be interpreted as pandering to the CCP claim that Covid-19 had multiple origins around the world before it was detected in Wuhan: a claim that has not been substantiated by any independent objective scientists.

To bolster its case for what in the West would be categorised as just another conspiracy theory, the CCP has drafted in the 'Bat Woman' herself, Shi Zhengli, to give a veneer of scientific credibility to these unsubstantiated claims. In a recent article in *Science Magazine*, she wrote 'Given the finding of Sars-Cov-2 on the surface of imported food packages, contact with contaminated uncooked food could be an important source of Sars-Cov-2 transmission'. For good measure she also wrote that there is evidence that 'SARS-CoV-2 existed for some time before the first cases were described in Wuhan.'[42]

Dr Daniel Lucey, a physician and infectious disease professor at the Georgetown Medical Centre in Washington, is extremely apprehensive about what the methodology being followed by the WHO. He suggests that the WHO investigation is merely going through the motions in which the stage is being set for a foregone conclusion: 'In my view, if you line up side-by-side the WHO's terms of reference with the Shi Zhengli Science article, then it is clear that the overarching strategic narrative is that the origin of the virus is outside of China.'[43]

Writing in *The Wall Street Journal*, two other internationally recognised experts, Dr Alina Chan, of MIT and Harvard and acclaimed science journalist Matt Ridley, have voiced similar misgivings about the WHO investigation. 'The world needs an inquiry that considers not just natural origins but the possibility that SARS-CoV-2, the virus that causes Covid-19, escaped from a laboratory.' As a scientist and a science writer, they 'believe that both natural and lab-based scenarios of Covid-19's origins must be rigorously investigated, not only to avert future pandemics but for the sake of science's reputation. The formal investigation launched by WHO is only taking steps to look into natural origins. That needs to change.'[44]

What is urgently needed is not merely a circumscribed investigation into the natural or zoonotic aspects of the outbreak, such as the one the WHO is conducting. What whole the world needs is a forensic investigation. Writing in the *Bulletin of the Atomic Scientists*, Filippa Lentzos, Senior Research Fellow of King's College London, a world expert on the international governance of biological threats, has made the case for a forensic investigation. Dr Lentzos also outlined what such an inquiry would entail: 'Investigating the range of possible spillover sites—from the wet market, to an accidental lab or fieldwork infection, or an unnoticed lab leak—requires a forensic investigation ... A forensic investigation would additionally involve auditing and sampling viral collections at relevant labs that had been studying coronaviruses, examining the types of experiments carried out and the viruses used, and reviewing the safety and security practices in place.'[45]

None of this bodes well for the WHO investigation. Given the strong possibility that this investigation will be managed and manipulated by the Chinese Communist Party, it seems likely that any hopes that we might have to learn the truth about the outbreak of the virus will not be realised – or, at least, not by this investigation.

Chapter 14: The WHO Lied

Funding the WHO

The WHO is mandated by the United Nations to act as a coordinating authority on international health issues. It is supported by two kinds of funding; assessed contributions which are then supplemented by additional voluntary contributions, primarily from its 194 member states. But it also receives very substantial financial assistance under this heading from private donors. According to Reuters, as a proportion of its 2018-19 biennial budget of US$5.6 billion, 15% came from the US, 11% was contributed by the EU, and 0.2% was paid in by China.[1]

The United States is the single biggest funder of the WHO, contributing more than $400 million per annum to the organisation. This breaks down roughly into an annual assessed contribution of between$100 and $120 million, topped up by variable additional voluntary contributions of between $100 and $400 million. For most of the period covered by the Obama administration, the US average annual contribution was $320 million while during the first three years of the Trump administration, that figure increased by over 30% to $422 million annually.[2] Apart from providing substantial finance, the US has long been an active member of the WHO, providing technical support and being actively involved in its governance structures.

In mid-April, President Trump announced the suspension of funding for the WHO pending a formal review of the global body's response to the coronavirus pandemic which he characterised as 'severely mismanaging and covering up the spread of the coronavirus'. The President went on to highlight the US funding of the WHO which he compared to that of China. 'American taxpayers provide between $400m and $500m per year to the WHO; in contrast China contributes roughly $40m a year, even less. As the organisation's leading sponsor, the United States has a duty to insist on full accountability.'[3] But the President's principal charges of severe mismanagement and cover-up centred on his claim that 'Through the middle of January, it parroted and publicly endorsed the idea that there was not human to human transmission happening, despite reports and clear evidence to the contrary.'[4] A storm of criticism quickly followed the President's announcement – all of it directed at him.

Most of the criticism centred on the fact that a reduction in funding on this scale would have a detrimental effect on the WHO's ability to maintain its level of operations and that it would impair the WHO's attempts to combat the coronavirus pandemic. Without equivalent cost saving measures to make up the funding shortfall, these criticisms had considerable validity. But most of his critics failed to engage with the President's substantive argument, that the WHO was blithely following the Beijing line that, there was no human-to-human transmission throughout January.

One of the few to do so was *Science* magazine. While it gave voice to the standard criticisms that ranged from 'this is a short-sighted decision which would be disastrous for the agency', to the more overtly political 'a transparent attempt to shift the blame for the U.S. administration's own failings', it also disputed the central tenet of the President's position.

The article states that 'His [Trump's] criticism conflicts with the fact that the WHO warned the US and other countries as early as January 10 that there was a risk of human-to-human transmission.' This is not correct. The WHO statement of January 10 states that 'preliminary investigation suggests that there is no significant human-to-human transmission'. This is virtually the same phraseology the WHO used in its first major statement of the outbreak on January 5 and again in its statement of January 12 and in a tweet of January 14. In fact, the first time the WHO confirmed human-to-human transmission was in a statement of January 23 which said; 'Human-to-human transmission is occurring … and the extent of human-to-human transmission is still not clear.'[5] This was after Dr Tedros' visit to meet Xi Jinping in Beijing, and the same day that the CCP locked down Wuhan.

It is also worth remembering that this WHO statement came three days after the renowned epidemiologist, Dr. Zhong Nanshan, had been on China's national television channel CCTV and gave the first official public confirmation that there was human-to-human transmission. Despite these dramatic developments, in its statement of the next day, January 24, the WHO reiterated its standard travel advice, 'WHO advises against the application of any travel or trade restrictions on China based on the information currently available on this event.'[6]

In many peoples' eyes, the WHO had effectively become a willing accomplice in the CCP's attempts to bend the world to its viewpoint.[7] This willingness to go along with Beijing's revisionist undertaking to rewrite the coronavirus narrative in China's favour has been repeatedly signalled by the public statements of Dr Tedros. His comments that China was 'setting a new standard for outbreak control', and lauding the leadership of the CCP for its 'openness to sharing information' with the WHO, looked decidedly at odds with the mounting evidence that China had in fact played fast and loose with information about the outbreak. In adopting the attitude that China-can-do-no wrong, the Director General of the WHO had fatally crossed the line separating advice from advocacy – a lapse that has reflected very badly on the credibility of the WHO.[8]

Even more problematically, while Dr Tedros was acting as advocate-in-chief on behalf of the CCP internationally, back in China doctors were being arrested for 'rumour-mongering' and 'seriously disrupting social order'. And hundreds of millions of Chinese social media posts were excoriating the communist authorities for their dismal performance in withholding information. On January 21, the headline on a Bloomberg report read: 'China Faces Social Media Backlash With New Virus Outbreak'.[9] The deluge of criticism was so enormous that the normally efficient communist censors were being overwhelmed.

From the beginning, the WHO has reported consistently that China had always been transparent with it about the outbreak as, for instance, a Dr Tedros tweet on January 23; 'I thank the Government of #China for its cooperation and transparency.'[10] In statement after statement by the WHO, and in press conferences and interviews, Dr Tedros has repeatedly suggested that China informed the WHO about the outbreak on December 31, 2019. This has been seized upon by China which then went the next logical step by claiming that it actually had informed the WHO on December 31.

It has also been repeated ad nauseam in publication after publication, including for example, the prestigious scientific magazine *Nature* which, as late as mid-April said in an article that 'The WHO was notified of a cluster of pneumonia cases by China on 31 December.'[11] Similarly, *The Washington Post* 'China notified the WHO on Dec. 31.[12] Apart from assertions by both the WHO and China that this happened, there is no independent corroboration of China ever having informed the WHO as it was legally obliged to do under the WHO International Health Regulations rules.[13] In fact, it now turns out that this claim is completely false.

To ascertain what was going on, we need to look briefly at what the WHO actually said. Its first statement about the outbreak was a tweet sent out on January 4, which read: '#China has reported to WHO a cluster of #pneumonia cases —with no deaths— in Wuhan, Hubei Province. Investigations are underway to identify the cause of this illness.' There is no ambiguity about the statement that 'China has reported to WHO a cluster of pneumonia cases.' The following day, January 5, a lengthy two-page statement began as follows: 'On 31 December 2019, the WHO China Country Office was informed of cases of pneumonia of unknown etiology (unknown cause) detected in Wuhan city, Hubei province of China.'

In the context of what was happening in China at the time, the casual reader of that sentence could not be faulted for inferring that it was the Chinese authorities that had informed the WHO. You will remember from your school days, I'm sure, that the use of the passive voice in a sentence means that, as in this example, the subject 'the WHO' is acted upon by the verb 'informed' while the object, whoever did the 'informing', is omitted. This sentence structure is unlikely to have been accidental. Whoever wrote it was being deliberately evasive about who or what the source was that had informed the WHO. But the unambiguous impression created, especially in the context of the previous day's tweet, was that the People's Republic of China had informed the WHO about the outbreak of the disease on December 31 – as it should have done under the WHO's 2005 International Health Regulations. This was the understanding that the rest of the world has taken for granted ever since.

From the start of the outbreak the WHO has maintained a timeline on its website which highlighted the major events of the Covid-19 pandemic crisis with which the organisation had been involved. As the pandemic progressed, it was modified from time to time with appropriate updates. In the timeline statement of April 27, the first entry under the date 31 Dec 2019 stated 'Wuhan Municipal Health Commission, China, reported a cluster of cases of pneumonia in Wuhan, Hubei province. A novel coronavirus was eventually identified.' That same timeline statement also contained an unusual and surprising qualification: 'This statement is no longer maintained. An updated version was published on June 29.'[14]

On its June 30 updated version of the timeline, the entry under the same date, 31 Dec 2019, is very different from what the WHO had been saying for the previous six months. The one short paragraph in the original timeline is replaced by a longer four paragraph version. In this, verbs like 'informed' or 'reported' have been dropped completely and replaced by the more informal 'picked up'. So, instead of saying, as its first tweet did in January that 'China has reported to WHO…' The opening line of the revised version in June states, 'WHO's Country Office in the People's Republic of China picked up a media statement by the Wuhan Municipal Health Commission from their website …' And then comes the critical revelation. The WHO 'also picked up a media report on Pro-MED (a programme of the International Society for Infectious Diseases) about the same cluster of cases of "pneumonia of unknown cause", in Wuhan.' The reference to ProMED in the completely revised WHO version events at the end of June is of considerable significance.

You are unlikely to have ever heard of ProMed, but it is a very interesting organisation.[15] It is a non-profit, internet-based organisation that reports on infectious disease outbreaks around the world. Unlike the WHO which is an international quango with a hierarchical reporting structure, ProMED is a distributed network of independent operators. It comprises a collection of professional disease experts who volunteer their services to an organisation that operates on a shoestring. The difference between ProMED and the WHO in terms of its operational procedures and above all its budget, is like chalk and cheese. ProMED's disparate sources of information are worldwide and include media reports, official reports, online summaries, reports from local observers. Once something of interest crops up relating to a possible disease outbreak, a report is written which is then reviewed and edited by expert moderators and, if approved, is disseminated to ProMED subscribers by email. It is simple, fast and very effective.

Founded as a charity just 25 years ago, ProMED's mission is to serve global health through the immediate dissemination of information about infectious disease outbreaks as they occur. It has a peerless track record in the very early detection and reporting of infectious disease outbreaks around the world; including well know ones such as SARS, MERS, Zika, and Ebola.[16] Its success has not gone unnoticed. In February, researchers at the French Ministry of Health[17] analysed ProMED's reporting performance between 2007 and 2018 and compared it with the WHO's reporting of infectious diseases. The analysis concluded that throughout that period, the WHO's reporting of a disease outbreak was on average 18.5 days behind that of ProMED.[18]

On the evening of December 30, one of a dedicated coterie of ProMED's editors, the epidemiologist Dr Marjorie Pollack, received an email from a trusted contact that was familiar with China and spoke Mandarin. Her informant talked about a sudden uptick in posts on Chinese social media regarding a notice issued that day by the Wuhan Municipal Health Committee regarding 'an urgent notice on the treatment of pneumonia of unknown cause.' Dr Pollack immediately alerted the ProMED network regarding the discussions on Chinese social media, indicating there was a possibility of a significant pneumonia outbreak happening and seeking help with confirmation. Within hours she had received the type of corroboration that the strict ProMED reporting rules required before a report of a disease outbreak could be filed on its network. It provided independent verification that the Chinese social media posts were true - something major was happening in China.

The source was a reputable Chinese financial magazine, *Sina Finance*, which had carried a comprehensive account of the disease outbreak in Wuhan just hours earlier. The article talked openly about SARS and described in some detail the likely SARS symptoms. It also stressed that SARS had not yet been confirmed by the health authorities and cautioned against any panicked reaction by people.[19] Satisfied with the verification of the troubling news, Dr. Pollack completed her ProMED report. At one minute to midnight on December 30, 2019 she pressed the send button on her computer. With its subject title 'Undiagnosed pneumonia – China', this email was the first warning to the world that the deadly SARS virus may have returned.[20] In her report that night, the vastly experienced Dr Pollack added a prescient note to her post: 'Having been involved in moderating the SARS-CoV (Severe acute respiratory syndrome - coronavirus) and the MERS-CoV (Middle Eastern Respiratory Syndrome - coronavirus), the type of social media activity[in China] that is now surrounding this event, is very reminiscent of the original "rumors" that accompanied the SARS-CoV outbreak.'[21]

It now transpires that what the WHO had been promoting for six months, that 'China has reported to the WHO…' is a falsehood. According to this extraordinary admission, the WHO only became aware of the potential seriousness of the outbreak in Wuhan by accident, 'picked up' from media reports as the organization's updated statement of June 30 states. Astonishingly, this might also be an indication that China may never have formally reported the outbreak to the WHO at all. But this unprecedented revelation also raises fundamental questions about what was going on between the WHO and China: in essence, it comes down to a choice of incompetence or collusion.

As the Georgetown Professor of Global Health Law, Lawrence Gostin sees it 'WHO just routinely repeated as if it were its own information, as if it were verifying it … By uncritically citing Chinese data, WHO officials lent credibility to information that was false.'[22] Prof. Gostin, who also provides technical advice to the WHO, put it even more bluntly in February; 'We were deceived … Myself and other public health experts, based on what the World Health Organization and China were saying, reassured the public that this was not serious, that we could bring this under control, he continued. 'We were,' he added, 'giving a false sense of assurance.'[23]

In a further interesting twist to the story, a senior executive director of the WHO, Dr Michael Ryan, confirmed publicly that the actual source of the WHO's information about the disease outbreak in Wuhan was indeed ProMED. He did this at a virtual press conference in Geneva on April 20 in response to a *Le Monde* journalist's query about an email from Taiwan. This press conference took place almost two months before the WHO's official timeline was modified.

During the conference, the straight-talking Irishman, Dr Ryan, confirmed that, 'On 31st December information on our epidemic intelligence from open-source platform partners, PRO-MED, was received indicating a signal of a cluster of pneumonia cases in China.' He also went on to explain Taiwan's involvement in these events. 'On the same day we had a request from health authorities in Taiwan and the message referred to, news sources indicated at least seven atypical pneumonia cases reported in Wuhan media …'[24] He went on to say that while outbreaks of atypical pneumonia are very common throughout the world, in the light of the ProMED information and the email from Taiwan, they requested 'our country office[in China] for follow-up with Chinese authorities and on 1st January we formally requested verification of the event under the IHR…'

Lest there was any risk that the assembled media had got the wrong end of the stick from Dr Ryan's remarks that Taiwan should be given any credit as the first country to alert the WHO to the outbreak in China, Dr Tedros intervened in order to, as he put it, summarise. He was at pains to knock the Taiwan email on the head: 'one thing that has to be clear is the first email was not from Taiwan … The first report came from Wuhan, from China itself so Taiwan was only asking for clarification …'[25] This was clearly the basis of the WHO's repeated public statements since early January that 'China reported to WHO'. It was crystal clear, even from the information given at this press conference, that this was not the case. The WHO's first inklings came from ProMED and the email from Taiwan. On foot of these, the WHO in Geneva contacted its office in China and as Dr Ryan confirmed, 'on 1st January we formally requested verification of the event under the IHR.' Despite Dr Tedros' attempt to muddy the waters, it was the WHO that first contacted China and not the other way around as the WHO and its Director General had been repeating for months.

Part 2

The Global Pandemic

Chapter 15: Asian Neighbours

The Asian Tigers

Since the 1960's the East Asian societies of Hong Kong, Singapore, South Korea, and Taiwan recorded spectacular levels of economic growth such that in recent years they have joined the ranks of the wealthiest nations on earth. Such was their success in regularly achieving double-digit growth figures, they were dubbed the 'Asian Tigers'. Explanations for their incomparable economic success were many and varied, with economic analyses invariably describing it as 'miraculous'. When practitioners of the 'dismal science' are reduced to invoking the spiritual as explanations for economic phenomena, we can be certain that we are looking at very exceptional performances indeed.[1]

Fuelled by exports and rapid industrialisation, the basis of their economic success was specialisation. Within a few decades they went from being dependent on agriculture and low-grade manufacturing to producing complex products such as memory chips, motor vehicles, computer servers, and sophisticated financial products. South Korea and Taiwan focused on electronic components and information technology and became essentiall hubs in the global manufacturing supply-chain. Hong Kong and Singapore took a different route by becoming two of the world's most important financial centres. Such has been the speed and scale of the growth of their GDP per capita, that measured on the basis of this important metric, all four have surpassed Japan.[2]

Their achievements in not just lifting their populations out of poverty but giving them a lifestyle comparable to any developed Western society was not lost on the behemoth of the region, China. China's overbearing presence in the region has also meant that three of them, Hong Kong, South Korea, and Taiwan have had to contend directly with the thorny issues of geopolitics. Rising tensions in the region are largely a consequence of the adjustments been forced upon the incumbent superpower, the US, as it contends with a rising and increasingly assertive challenger, China. Directly in Beijing's immediate line of fire was Hong Kong, which though part of China, is nominally a self-governing region. But the most obsessive focus of Beijing's political ire has been Taiwan which, for most of its existence since 1949, has had to operate in a diplomatic no-man's-land. Since the 1990s, as a consequence of China's successful foisting of its 'one China principle' on most of the world, Taiwan has been cast into the diplomatic outer darkness.

At the start of a highly infectious disease epidemic there's only one thing worse than being at its epicentre – being next door to the epicentre. The 21st century's first major novel infectious disease to become a global pandemic was SARS. It originated in southern China in November 2002, reaching Hong Kong in February 2003, and then spread rapidly to a total of 30 countries across five continents. Of the ten most seriously affected countries, seven were in Asia with, apart from China, Hong Kong and Taiwan being the worst affected. South Korea largely escaped SARS but was hit by the MERS outbreak in 2015. China's Asian neighbours had learned three important lessons from their experience with SARS and MERS. First, a highly infectious disease spreads rapidly through air travel. Secondly, early reporting of the outbreak to neighbouring countries and the WHO is vital to contain the international spread of a virus. Thirdly, efficient contact tracing combined with appropriate quarantine measures are essential to control an epidemic.[3]

In 2019, neighbouring countries looked on with increasing alarm as the number of infections in Wuhan continued to escalate. Their concerns were magnified enormously as China's most significant annual holiday, Lunar New Year, was just weeks away. By January 20, apart from a big jump of new cases in Wuhan, the virus had also spread to several other locations across China. Beijing had been infected as had the southern city of Shenzhen, part of the sprawling Pearl River Delta megalopolis that borders Hong Kong. But a step-change in the onward march of the virus had taken place the previous week on January 13 with the announcement by the WHO that the virus had spread internationally.

As we have seen earlier, the Chinese government suspended all public transportation in and out of Wuhan on January 23. The following day it suspended all group travel within the whole of China. But in these travel restrictions there was one glaring omission. It did not prohibit groups of Chinese citizens from travelling abroad for the Lunar New Year holidays until January 27. This turned out to be a disastrous three-day delay, permitting a mass exodus of Chinese holiday makers in the midst of an infectious disease crisis. Popular foreign holiday destinations, especially in Thailand, saw a surge in infections. Even worse, China imposed no restrictions at all on individuals travelling overseas –to anywhere. So, planes carrying infected Chinese travellers landed in Thailand, Japan, South Korea, Italy, Spain, France, UK, Australia, as well as North and

South America. As China itself was locking down city after city to prevent the contagion spreading, its failure to impose similar restrictions on international travel seeded the virus across the world.

With the consequences of the SARS epidemic indelibly marked on their collective consciousness; neighbouring countries began ramping up their surveillance efforts from the moment they got wind of the Wuhan outbreak in December. With the Lunar New Year approaching fast and tens of millions of Chinese tourists preparing to go abroad, China's neighbours began to batten down the hatches. Their experience of what happened two decades previously made them less inclined to take at face value Chinese health authority assurances that there was no evidence for person-to-person transmission and that no health workers were infected. Seungtaek Kim, a virologist at the Institute Pasteur South Korea in Seongnam, made a gloomy if prescient assessment of what was happening, 'This could be the beginning of a disaster.'[4]

The first recorded laboratory-confirmed instance of the virus outside of China was reported by Thailand on January 13. As the Chinese Lunar New Year holidays got into full swing, Chinese tourists poured into Thailand. Thai authorities were on full alert and began checking the temperatures of all arrivals from China. On January 8, a 61-year-old Chinese woman who had travelled from Wuhan arrived at Bangkok's Suvarnabhumi international airport with some family members and was found to be suffering from a fever. Subsequent tests confirmed that she had the pneumonia caused by the Covid-19 virus. Despite this being a travel-related instance of the spread of the virus, in its statement of January 13 announcing details of the Bangkok case, the WHO advised 'against the application of any travel or trade restrictions on China based on the information available.'

Professor David Hui Shu-cheong, a respiratory specialist from the Chinese University of Hong Kong, wanted to know whether the Chinese woman had visited the Wuhan seafood market. Because, he speculated, if she had not, it would be a big problem as it meant game meat in other markets in Wuhan could also be infected with the virus, which then spread to people. This was a logical inference for the Hong Kong Professor to have made because with China and the WHO still insisting that the virus was not being passed from person-to-person, how were people being infected? From animals? But if she had not been to the Wuhan seafood market then where did she acquire the virus? In response to one of its citizens testing positive for the virus in Thailand, the Wuhan Municipal Health

Committee issued a statement on January 14 which stated 'clear evidence of human-to-human transmission has not been found, and the possibility of limited human-to-human transmission cannot be ruled out, but the risk of continued human-to-human transmission is low.'[5]

On January 16, three days after the case in Thailand, Japan also reported that a person who had travelled to Wuhan had been diagnosed with the disease. As the geographical spread of the Wuhan virus continued, the chorus of demands for more information from China grew louder.[6] Yoshihiro Kawaoka, a virologist at the University of Tokyo argued that it was' crucial that China identifies the animal source of the virus so that proper measures can be taken to limit its spread.' Scientists outside of China were getting increasingly desperate, especially for epidemiological information. 'China needs to share more appropriate information and as soon as possible,' he said. 'The disease is no longer confined within the country. A virus doesn't know borders.'[7] A little over a week later, Chinese scientists provided the first detailed epidemiological analysis of the initial batch of 41 infected patients from Wuhan which was published in *The Lancet* on January 24(See chapter 7 for the details).

Hong Kong

Memories were still vivid regarding what happened in Hong Kong towards the end of February 2003 as SARS suddenly struck the island. The story of how the unfortunate Dr Liu came to be a super spreader of the disease had not been forgotten. Hong Kong authorities were acutely aware of the dangers to the colony once they heard what was going on in Wuhan. On January 22 Hong Kong reported its first two cases of the coronavirus. One was a mainland Chinese tourist from Wuhan and the other was a Hong Konger who had visited Wuhan and came back positive. On the same day, Macau also reported a case; that of a Wuhan businesswoman visiting the casino island.

However, on January 4, 18 days before its first coronavirus case had even been detected, Hong Kong launched its Preparedness and Response Plan for Novel Infectious Disease and activated its Serious Response Level protocol. This was all done under a disease prevention and control system that had been established following the 2003 SARS crisis and operated by a newly designated organisation, the Center for Health Protection (CHP).[8] The trigger for this was 'the urgent notice on the treatment of pneumonia of unknown cause' statement issued by the Wuhan Health Commission on

December 30. Unlike the WHO, which was hidebound by its bureaucratic and legalistic procedures, Hong Kong's CHP did not need, as it were, 'further and better particulars' – it could read the clear message between the lines of the Wuhan statement – a major SARS-like infectious disease is on the way, get ready.

Independently of any government action, Hong Kong's population itself had reacted spontaneously through increased use of face masks and the adoption of social distancing. With these and other measures, Hong Kong managed to keep its infection rate low for January and February, despite its land border with China and the intense level of human interactions across it. Even two months later, on March 20, which was considered the peak of the crisis up to that point, only 48 new cases were reported on that day bringing the total in Hong Kong to 256.

As the world grappled with the effects of the pandemic, China's puppet government in Hong Kong began a serious crackdown on dissidents. The proposed legislation to allow Hong Kongers to be extradited to mainland China that had initially provoked the street protests in June, was finally withdrawn. Emboldened by this victory, the mainly student protesters extended their demands to include an expansion of democracy, and an investigation into the behaviour of the police during the protests.

Following almost 6 months of constant street protests, the local elections in November were an opportunity for people to express themselves through the ballot box. Pro-democracy candidates won a landslide victory, taking 87% of the council seats. The result completely undermined the legitimacy of the Beijing-backed Hong Kong government and its pro-Chinese policies. The CCP and its local allies were convinced that the daily street protests had antagonised the public, but Beijing had completely misread the mood of Hong Kongers The CCP took the election result as a clear sign that Hong Kong was slipping from its grasp. As with all Communist dictatorships facing a democratic revolt, the CCP's reflexive response was crackdown.

Though the coronavirus outbreak had effectively put an end to the street protests, on April 15, a number of prominent pro-democracy dissidents were arrested. These were not students, the arrested were democratic heavyweights which included the 'Father of Democracy', the 81-year-old lawyer Martin Lee, the media tycoon Jimmy Lai, and former opposition legislators, Albert Ho, Lee Cheuk-yan and Leung Kwok-hung.

Never before had so many long-standing pro-democracy leaders been arrested in one swoop.

By moving decisively to silence the pro-democracy movement, the arrest of these democracy veterans was also a way for the CCP to call America's bluff. Chris Patten, Hong Kong's last colonial governor said; 'this is not the rule of law. This is what authoritarian governments do. The world should make clear how this further undermines any residual trust that we still have in the Chinese Communist dictatorship.'[9] But as often happens in such cases, the 'international community' sat on its hands. Emboldened, the CCP planned an even more fundamental assault on Hong Kong's institutions: one that would effectively put an end to the 'one country, two systems' agreement signed with the British that was less than half-way through its 50-year term.

Singapore

Like Hong Kong, following the 2003 SARS outbreak, Singapore had put in place an institutional infrastructure capable of dealing with any future pandemic. Singapore too was fast out of the blocks. 21 days before any case was detected, on January 2, the Health Ministry requested doctors to notify it regarding patients with pneumonia symptoms and a history of travel to Wuhan. As an immediate precautionary exercise, all passengers from Wuhan were subjected to temperature checks at airports.

From January 23, with the identification of Singapore's first infection case, a tourist from Wuhan, the city-state began a speedy escalation of public policy initiatives to contain the threat. Initially, all flights between Singapore and Wuhan were suspended. Then on February 1, all visitors to Singapore with a history of travel to China within the previous 14 days were denied entry or transit through Singapore.[10] All other travellers entering Singapore by air, land, or sea were subjected to temperature checks and any symptomatic passengers showing fever or breathing difficulties were given a swab test.

The test kits used in this process had been developed by a Singaporean company in just three weeks in January had an accuracy of 99%, and could produce results within three hours.[11] As a precautionary system designed for use at borders, the test kits only tested for the presence of the virus and not its severity. To complement its mitigation measures, from February 4, the Singaporean government allocated 4 free facemasks to every household each week. An extensive electronic contact tracing system was also put in place, which was accompanied by very strict quarantine policies, including up to 6 months in prison for quarantine violations. Because of its comprehensive array of measures including, extensive border controls, swab tests on arrival, rigorous quarantine, and intensive systematic contact tracing, Singapore was able to avoid locking down its society and economy. Nor did it have to close its schools.

Up to March, Singapore had a record low numbers of cases at 266, and zero deaths – it was being hailed as a global pandemic success story. During April, however, Singapore was hit by a second wave of infections. The figures went through the roof with the number of infections increasing by 13-fold and included both imported cases and community transmission. The cause of the huge spike in infections was an enormous number of clusters found among Singapore's very large migrant workforce.

Mainly from India, Bangladesh, Myanmar and China, at 1.4 million, these foreign workers represented almost one-third of Singapore's total labour force. With up to 320,000 of them living in cramped, crowded dormitories with 10 to 20 men to room, and most sharing unsanitary facilities, these were perfect conditions for the virus to spread unchecked. By the end of April, these migrant workers accounted for 85% of Singapore's almost 15,000 infections and were increasing at the rate of 1,000 per day. The island city-state of just under 6 million people had gone from having the lowest to the highest number of reported Covid-19 infections in Southeast Asia. The infection rate among the migrant workers had become Singapore's largest humanitarian health crisis ever.

But despite the escalating infection rate, one statistic continued to stand out. Though Singapore had become the most infected nation in Asia, apart from India and China, its death rate remained remarkably low. In June, it had only 26 deaths out of more than 42,000 infection cases, a mortality rate of just 0.62 deaths per 1,000 infections, compared to a global average of 70 deaths per 1,000 infections for the time. Even more strikingly, it was miniscule when compared to both the US and China's average of 56 deaths per 1,000 infections.[12] The reasons for the incredibly low death rate are two-fold. Though the migrant workforce accounted for the vast majority of infected cases, they are young and healthy and so their infections are generally mild and non-lethal. Older people, the most vulnerable group, had by and large heeded the government's warnings and stayed at home and thus avoided the virus, keeping mortality rates down.

South Korea

Like Hong Kong and Singapore, South Korea reacted swiftly to the early signs of an epidemic emerging in Wuhan. Without having to resort to extensive travel bans or lockdowns, South Korea managed to largely contain the virus despite having quite a high rate of infections. Its success is largely attributed to a sophisticated programme of mass-testing with an initial capacity to carry out 20,000 tests per day. Similar to Hong Kong and Singapore, its rapid response was also honed by an earlier pandemic, but unlike them, South Korea had been hit in 2015 by MERS (Middle East Respiratory Syndrome). Its state of readiness was such that by mid-April South Korea had tested over half a million people.

Once credible reports of a SARS-like viral pneumonia started to emerge from Wuhan, South Korea began implementing increased surveillance for travellers from the city. As a result of these prevention and control measures, the first suspected case of the disease was discovered on January 8. This Chinese visitor was confirmed infected by the virus on January 20. A week later, there were three more confirmed cases all of whom had travelled from Wuhan. But by early February, cases of local transmission were being recorded

Unlike any of the other Southeast Asian countries, South Korea had to deal with an unusually large cluster of outbreaks in one urban area. On February 18, a middle-aged woman, known as 'patient 31' tested positive for Covid-19. She became South Korea's first super spreader and infected hundreds of people in the southern city of Daegu. By mid-March, the government designated the city itself and the surrounding region a 'special disaster zone' – a categorisation normally used for natural disasters. The disease spread so fast throughout the city that by the end of March, over 70% of all confirmed Korean Covid-19 cases were in the area of Daegu.

The woman was a member of a religious cult called the Shincheonji Church of Jesus and during a religious ceremony she had come into contact with over 1000 people. She refused to be tested for the coronavirus on three occasions, claiming she had not recently travelled to China. However, a Ministry of Justice investigation discovered that the sect had a secret office in Wuhan and that 42 members from there had visited South Korea during the previous six months.

Due to the cult's initial failure to cooperate with authorities the South Korean CDC had difficulties tracing members who had travelled to the ceremony from other regions. When this finally happened, the cluster associated with the Shincheonji sect amounted to over 5000 – over half of South Korea's total number of infections. The fringe doomsday cult was certainly living up to its public image. As the number of infections associated with the Shincheonji Church of Jesus exploded, the sect went from being a theological curiosity to a national pariah. As a consequence of its behaviour, the sect is being sued by the city of Daegu for damages to the tune of $82 million.

As in the other South East Asian examples, a key component of South Korea's success in combating Covid-19 was a combination of free testing and intense compulsory tracing. Following the Shincheonji debacle in Daegu, the government set up a network of 40 drive through testing facilities, where people could be tested in their own cars at the rate of 10 per hour. Additionally, the authorities pursued an intrusive contact tracing regime as allowed for under its infectious disease laws which were amended in 2015 following the MERS outbreak. This legislation permitted the CDC to use mobile phone data, CCTV camera footage, and information from credit card companies to track down individuals who may have been in contact with an infected person. Strict electronic monitoring of all quarantine patients was also instituted. One controversial aspect of the South Korean system was the publication on the web and via text messages of information relating to confirmed cases in people's vicinity. Though no names were used, detailed personal information such as age, sex, and the neighbourhood where the infection took place were all released publicly.

Taiwan

As early as December 31, Taiwan began health surveillance of incoming airline passengers checking for signs of fever and pneumonia-like symptoms. It was a further 21 days before the first case was detected – a Wuhan-based Taiwanese businesswoman returning home. As an indication of its success in combating the disease, two months later Taiwan had just 59 confirmed cases and one death. This was despite the fact that, even more than Hong Kong, there was extensive travel for business and tourist reasons between the island and mainland China. Over 1 million Taiwanese live and work in China, many making the 130-kilometre journey across the Taiwan Straits regularly, and 2.7 million Chinese tourists also visited the island every year. Yet, by July Taiwan had a total of 451 cases, an incredible 19 per 1 million population, and only seven people had died of the disease. So how did Taiwan succeeded in avoiding the massive outbreak of infections and deaths that paralysed its inordinately greater neighbour?

Like the other countries discussed above, on first hearing of the problems emerging in Wuhan, Taiwan was alert to the enormous dangers involved and reacted quickly. It implemented early travel restrictions with Wuhan and began screening all passengers arriving from the city in December 2019. On January 23, when the lockdown was imposed on Wuhan, Taiwan suspended all flights to and from the city and Wuhan residents were prohibited from entering the country. In tandem with its focused travel restrictions, it also instituted aggressive testing and screening, and enforced strict quarantine rules. By January 26, Taiwan became the first country to exclude all Chinese citizens from entering the country.

As a democracy, police-state tactics were not an option, so it actively engaged with its people through a comprehensive communications campaign, including neighbourhood text messages. The importance of constant communications during a pandemic was emphasised by epidemiologist Chang Shan-chwen, convener of Taiwan's Central Epidemic Command Center (CECC), 'One of the most important factors in the success of our response has been transparency ...In [China's] autocratic system, every citizen will stay at home when told so. But this is something which cannot be easily achieved in free and democratic countries.'[13] An analysis carried out by US medical researchers on Taiwan's response to Covid-19 and published in the peer-reviewed *Journal of the American Medical Association* (JAMA), concluded 'Taiwan is an example of how a society can respond quickly to a crisis and protect the interests of its citizens.'[14]

Apart from the overriding priority to protect the health of its people, the Taiwanese government's approach to tackling the pandemic also preserved the health of its economy. It avoided the socially disruptive, economically devastating and costly lockdowns that most other countries were forced to resort to because of their initial tardy and inadequate response to the wildfire spread the disease. As the seasons passed and autumn gave way to winter, the vast majority of countries that had suffered grievously during the first wave had to endure it all again during a second wave accompanied by an inevitable second lockdown. Yet, even by November, Taiwan was still completely confounding these international trends

Conclusion

Despite being among the first to be hit by the Covid-19 virus, these four Asian societies were also among the most successful in combating it; recording relatively few cases, and significantly less deaths than elsewhere. But their individual success was underpinned by policy approaches that were broadly common to all: early intervention, including travel restrictions and bans, rigorous testing and contact tracing, and extensive and regular communication with their public. If we were to identify a single set of policy initiatives that really set these Asian societies apart from most other countries, it was their rigorous approach to testing and contact tracing. A modelling exercise carried out by *The Economist* found that countries that tested more rigorously detected more cases and reported lower death rates.[15] The following comparison is an instructive case in point. South Korea and the United States reported their first coronavirus case on the same day, January 20. Six weeks later on March 1, South Korea, with a population of 51 million had carried out over 100,000 tests, while the United States with a population of 327 million had tested just 472 people.

On a final note, before we leave Asia for the far from sun-lit uplands of coronavirus Europe and the rest of the world, Taiwan deserves a special mention. In some of the early predictive modelling done by John Hopkins University, it identified the countries and regions at the highest risk of importing the Covid-19 virus 'with the primary risk posed to southeast Asia.' Because of their geographical proximity and extensive flight connections with China, the study then compared the numbers that their model had predicted with what the actual outcomes were for Singapore, Hong Kong, South Korea and Taiwan. For the first three of these countries the reported number of cases was higher than the model had predicted; in the case of Singapore, almost twice as high. With an outcome better than the model had predicted, Taiwan was the exception.[16] Taiwan was not only doing well at beating the contagion; it was also confounding the modellers.

Even before China admitted that there was person-to-person transmission of the disease, Taiwan assessed the risk of importing the disease from its epicentre in Wuhan as the most serious threat that it faced. Taiwan first banned flights from Wuhan city and then extended the flight-ban to the whole of China by the end of January – an initiative the WHO had repeatedly advised against. But Taiwan is disbarred from WHO membership, and even its observer status at the WHO was withdrawn by the WHO in 2016 under pressure from the CCP. Yet this vibrant democracy of 26 million people has been an exemplar to the world by not just successfully keeping the worst excesses of Covid-19 at bay, but doing so without resorting to authoritarian measures or locking down its economy. The economic fruits of these achievements were abundantly clear by the end of the year when, for the first time in 30 years, Taiwan's GDP grew at a faster rate than that of China. On the basis of these stellar achievements, you would have thought that the WHO would be citing Taiwan as *the* example for the rest of the world to emulate – you would be wrong.

In February, the WHO published a report on a joint WHO-China mission, the purpose of which was to identify 'next steps in readiness and preparedness for geographic areas not yet affected.' The WHO experts' report states 'In the face of a previously unknown virus, China has rolled out perhaps the most ambitious, agile and aggressive disease containment effort in history.' The report went on to claim that China's strategy 'demonstrated that containment can be adapted and successfully operationalized in a wide range of settings.' The WHO was not only endorsing the CCP's authoritarian crackdown in Wuhan with its open disdain for individual rights and liberties, it was actually proposing that it could be adopted (operationalized) by other countries.

Citing the potential human rights breaches of following the CCP's pandemic strategy, Georgetown University's Prof. Lawrence Gostin and Director of the WHO Collaborating Center on National and Global Health Law suggested that, 'The most important thing in public health is not to drive the population underground and make them fearful ...You want them to believe that the government is there to help them and not to violate their rights. It's very, very difficult to control an epidemic once you've lost the trust of the population.' Unfortunately, Prof Gostin and many others like him forget that having control of the People's Liberation Army, Xi Jinping's can rule China based on a version of Caligula's dictum: *oderint dum metuant* – 'let them hate me so long as they fear me.' In these circumstances, it is a travesty of international justice and fair play that the behaviour of the CCP dictatorship continues to be privileged by the WHO's Dr Tedros over the far superior achievements of democratic Taiwan.

Chapter 16: Europe Gets Hit

Come Fly with Me

Before we analyse what was happening within Europe, we need to look briefly at the important, yet thorny, issue of travel restrictions and bans during an infectious disease epidemic. Virtually all the evidence, including the brief summaries given here, points to the fact that the single most important vector for seeding country after country around the world with the SAR-CoV-2 virus was air travel. It is incontrovertible that international air travel was instrumental in transforming a Chinese epidemic into a global pandemic. A number of recent scientific papers have come to similar, though in some cases, more nuanced conclusions.

By June, the coronavirus pandemic had spread to over 100 countries in all inhabited continents. The scale of the infection was largely due to the innate transmissibility of the virus combined with globalised air travel. But other characteristics of the virus have conspired not only to magnify its scale, but also the speed with which the pandemic has been able to propagate. Two features in particular have assisted this process; the respiratory nature of the disease, and the high frequency of pre-symptomatic and asymptomatic cases.

In April, *Science* published a study that looked at the impact of travel restrictions on the national and international spread of the pandemic. It concluded that the travel ban introduced in Wuhan on January 23 only delayed the progression of epidemic by 3 to 5 days within China. But international travel restrictions did help to slow spread elsewhere in the world, at least until mid-February. In the case of Wuhan, this is an unsurprising conclusion given that by the time the lockdown was imposed on January 23, as many as 5 million Wuhan residents had already departed the city and dispersed across China. Despite the severity of the lockdown, its modest 3 to 5-day curtailment effect was simply due to the fact that the stable door was being closed after many of the horses had bolted. On the other hand, the international ban on flights from China was more effective in that it reduced cases of disease importation by almost 80% up to mid-February.[1]

In July, another set of international researchers published an analysis of the first 288 cases discovered outside of China during the very early phase from January 3 to February 13, when China was still the primary epicentre of the pandemic. The study concluded that, 'Our findings indicate that travel bans and containment strategies adopted in China were effective in reducing the exportation growth rate.' In particular, 'We found a rapid exponential growth of importations from Hubei, up to the closure of Wuhan airport preventing further travel of cases.' Their detailed number crunching clearly indicated, 'that strict travel bans may be beneficial by reducing importations to manageable levels and by giving countries the time to prepare and strengthen their surveillance systems in the short term.' With regard to ongoing policy formulation, the report concluded that, 'Though effective in reducing international spread, the travel ban in Wuhan did not prevent the seeding of the pandemic in other countries, later becoming new epicenters of the pandemic.'[2]

Another paper that investigated how travel patterns affected the propagation of the pandemic concluded that the spread of Covid-19 in Europe was closely aligned with air travel patterns. Furthermore, it argued that the severe travel restrictions implemented across the continent had resulted in substantial decreases in the spread of the disease. Its authors were of the view that any deficiencies in the use of travel restrictions were not due to the restrictions themselves, but in the timing of their implemented – invariably, they were introduced too late.

Yet, despite all this evidence, the WHO has persisted with the same travel mantra that it enunciated right from the beginning of this outbreak in Wuhan: 'WHO advises against the application of any travel or trade restrictions on China based on the current information available on this event.'[3] On February 29, the organisation issued a comprehensive update on its recommendations for international traffic during the Covid-19 pandemic. It reiterated its position that the 'WHO continues to advise against the application of travel or trade restrictions to countries experiencing COVID-19 outbreaks.' It went on to argue that, 'evidence shows that restricting the movement of people and goods during public health emergencies is ineffective in most situations.'

Despite its insistence on an evidentiary basis for its 'no travel ban' policy, the WHO neither cites references nor quotes any scientific analysis in its many statements relating to travel. It is therefore difficult, if not impossible, to make an independent evaluation of the reasonableness or otherwise of the organisation's travel policy recommendations. One thing, however, is very clear: many of its members were not prepared to take its advice, and were in flagrant breach of the WHO's recommendations on international travel. In its end of February statement, from which the above quotations have been taken, the WHO itself pointed out that, 'as of

27 February, 38 countries have reported to WHO additional health measures that significantly interfere with international traffic in relation to travel to and from China or other countries.'[4]

Europe Leads the Way

Mongolia is a sparsely populated, landlocked, central Asian country that is almost 3 times the size of France. It is sandwiched between Russia to the north and China to its south with whom it shares a 2,700 km border. Following the announcement of the Covid-19 outbreak in central China on January 27, the Mongolian government closed the border with China and banned all flights originating from there. A range of other epidemic control measures were also implemented including, temperature checks for all other passengers entering the country, a ban on mass gatherings, internal travel restrictions, and extensive school closures.

The government's containment strategy was so effective (helped by its sparse population) that by June Mongolia recorded only 200 cases of infection, and no deaths. What was strange about these figures, however, was that Mongolia had no recorded cases of community transmission among its 3.6 million population – all the instances of the disease had been imported. The first case of Covid-19 in Mongolia was a French citizen who had travelled there via Moscow and had tested positive for the virus on March 2.[5] It was ironic that, despite its geographical proximity and extensive contiguous border with the original source of the epidemic, China, Mongolia's first case of the infection had come all the way from Europe. Europe as the primary source for the international spread of the disease was a pattern that became established quickly, and was soon in evidence across the globe.

The first recorded case in Latin America was on February 27 in Brazil when a 61-year-old resident of Sao Paolo, who had just returned from Italy, tested positive for the virus. The Ministry for Health also noted that 59 other cases had undergone laboratory testing, and were negative. But the statement also referred to a further 20 suspected cases of coronavirus that were being actively monitored by Brazilian health authorities, and of these cases, 12 had travelled to Italy and 2 to Germany.[6]

On March 5, the South African government announced its first coronavirus case. A 38-year-old man had tested positive for the virus on his return from a skiing trip to Italy, which he had made with his wife in the company of a group of 10 others.[7] A few days later, his wife also tested positive, while the rest of the group were being actively monitored. On March 10, the South African government announced they had a total of seven cases of coronavirus – all were part of the skiing trip to Italy.

But for many African countries, and for some countries in the Middle East, the biggest threat of disease importation during the early phase of the pandemic was from China. This was a direct consequence of the enormous success in Africa and parts of the Middle East of China's 'Belt and Road Initiative', an infrastructure investment programme which has resulted in an enormous increase in the volume of air traffic between China and parts of Africa. A comprehensive modelling exercise published in *The Lancet* detailed the extreme vulnerability of many African countries of importing the disease directly from China. The analysis was based on the extent of their air traffic volumes with infected Chinese provinces which showed Egypt, Algeria, South Africa, Ethiopia, and Nigeria to be at highest risk.[8]

In the meantime, Europe had become the new epicentre of the pandemic and, more worryingly, it had also become a porous purveyor of the virus around the world. An analysis by an online news publication *Intercept* reveals that, 'Travel from and within Europe preceded the first coronavirus cases in at least 93 countries across all five continents, accounting for more than half of the world's index cases.'[9] Travellers from just one European country, Italy, accounted for the first coronavirus case in at least 46 other countries. This compares with travellers from China accounting for the first case in 27 countries. The focal point of the propagation of the disease had shifted inexorably from East to West.

The European Union (EU) likes to see itself as an oasis of progressive values positioned between the Charybdis of American selfishness and the Scylla of Communist collectivism. The European Commission has ambitious plans to carve out a meaningful role for the block as a serious actor on the global stage. However, its ambitions in this regard far exceed its institutional capabilities. Having relied on the US-dominated NATO for military protection since the end of the Second World War, the members of the EU are disinclined to either organise, or fully pay for, their collective defence.

As a result, in the geopolitics of superpower contestation, the EU is listened to politely but, devoid of any serious firepower, it is ultimately sidelined. Whether this is desirable or not is entirely a matter of opinion, the point is that it is the logical outcome of the manner in which the institutional structures of the EU have been arranged. In terms of international affairs, what this means is that the EU does not seek power – it aspires to have influence.

Likewise, Europe's capacity to respond in a timely and meaningful way to the onset of the pandemic was institutionally limited. This is primarily due to the EU's subsidiarity rules in which certain spheres of action, such as health, are deemed to be the primary responsibility of the individual member states. Lacking appropriate structures, Europe's leaders were reduced to filling the vacuum by issuing heart-warming platitudes in response to the contagion.

Speaking in the European Parliament in March, Ursula von der Leyen, President of the European Commission said, 'We must look out for each other, we must pull each other through this. Because if there is one thing that is more contagious than this virus, it is love and compassion. And in the face of adversity, the people of Europe are showing how strong that can be.' The opening remarks by Charles Michel, President of the European Council, at the EU's *Global Response Pledging Event against Coronavirus* in May, were not untypical: 'Only a shared spirit of global solidarity and responsibility will defeat the COVID-19 crisis.'[10] Though difficult to disagree with, these sentiments were poor consolation to the elderly residents of Europe's care homes, which were being ravaged by the virus for months.

By mid-March, as the number of cases in Europe exceeded that of China, it gave an opportunity for Dr Tedros to shift the focus from China to Europe. Both at a press conference in Geneva, and later in a tweet, the WHO's Director-General noted that: 'Europe has now become the epicenter of the #COVID19 pandemic, with more reported cases and deaths than the rest of the world combined, apart from China. More cases are now being reported every day [in Europe] than were reported in CN at the height of its epidemic' So how did this happen? To get an answer, we need to look at the reaction of the organisations designated by the EU to deal with an infectious disease epidemic like the one that emerged from Wuhan. Their thoughts and actions were reflective of the prevailing mindset of senior health officials across the continent.

Within days of the confirmation that the Wuhan virus was being transmitted from person-to-person, the European Centre for Disease Prevention and Control (ECDC) said that the likelihood of the introduction of the disease to the EU was 'moderate'. While the EU-funded Platform for European Preparedness Against (Re-)emerging Epidemics

(PREPARE) believed there was 'a credible threat for a pandemic also in Europe.' Despite the threat, the organisation's coordinator, Herman Goossens was very upbeat, especially about the availability of diagnostic tests: 'the diagnostics test was developed very fast and we're already discussing the clinical protocol. I've never seen this kind of response in previous epidemics or pandemics.' He went on to explain when the diagnostic kits would be available: 'before the end of January and beginning of February, when cases are more likely to be reported.'[11] With regard to flights coming into Europe from infected areas of China, in January the ECDC had a relaxed attitude telling Euronews by email that 'a targeted approach focussing on passengers from direct incoming flights may be considered.'

It is a well-known phenomenon that generals have a tendency to fight the last war. This was in evidence right across Europe as senior health officials reassessed the 2002-3 SARS pandemic for guidance and insights into how to deal with the Covid-19 outbreak. Though SARS was indeed a global pandemic that affected 30 countries across several continents, the stark reality was that SARS was largely an Asian phenomenon in which Europe was a bit player. Looking to this example, from which Europe emerged virtually unscathed, as a basis for modelling outcomes in the current pandemic was only ever going to lead to a false sense of optimism in Europe's ability to contend with the crisis. At minimum, when time-critical decision-making was of the essence, it could lead to confusion.

The ECDC's first risk assessment report was issued on January 22, and contains some evidence for both complacency and confusion. Under the heading 'Preparedness' it states, 'In general, evidence does not support entry screening as an efficient measure for detecting incoming travellers with infectious diseases ... However, three of the four cases of nCoV-2019 detected outside of China were found using entry screening procedures at destination airports. Therefore, a targeted approach focussing on passengers from direct incoming flights from Wuhan may be considered in the respective countries to facilitate early identification.'[12]

The ECDC's position seems to have been that, on the one hand, there is no evidence that entry screening works to detect infectious diseases but, on the other hand, there is evidence that it works for Covid-19, so we're going to do it in some ill-defined 'targeted' way. We should remind ourselves that this report was issued on January 22, just two days after China finally publicly admitted that there was human-to-human transmission and that medical personnel were being infected. And, as we have already seen, for those states living cheek by jowl with the source of the contagion in Southeast Asia, airport screening of incoming passengers was not some optional extra, it was a core aspect of their initial response to the outbreak in Wuhan, because they had compelling practical evidence that it worked.

On February 24, based on information it had received from member countries, the EU Commission stated that 'there is a strong overall level of preparedness with countries having response measures in place to provide treatment for the cases in the EU and to mitigate any further transmission within and into the EU.'[13] Early on the morning of the day before, Sunday, February 23, a cargo plane took off from Vienna bound for China. It was loaded with 25 metric tons of PPE equipment that included masks and gloves, and was part of a 50-metric ton consignment of PPE supplies being donated by EU member states to China.

Just three days after the flight to China had departed, Italy made an urgent request to the European Commission for masks and other PPE supplies as its hospitals were being overwhelmed, and its frontline medical staff had insufficient protection. Italy's request to the Commission went unanswered – there was no PPE available. Janez Lenarčič, the European commissioner responsible for crisis management made an astute observation regarding the complete silence that had greeted Italy's urgent cry for help: 'not only is Italy not prepared … Nobody is prepared … The lack of response to the Italian request was not so much a lack of solidarity. It was a lack of equipment.'

The European Commission's health security committee, which comprises representatives of the various ministries of health of member states, had its first coronavirus conference call on January 17; more than half of the EU member states were absent, including Italy. On the advice of the ECDC, airport screening of passengers was deemed to be largely ineffective so it was agreed to target only the 12 weekly flights from Wuhan to Europe.[14] One month later on February 18, the guardians of Europe's collective health, the ECDC's Technical Advisory Committee held a two-day meeting at the organisation's headquarters in Sweden. The minutes of the meeting show that the committee considered the risk to Europe's population from Covid-19 to be 'low'. A sense of unperturbed calm seems to have prevailed at the meeting at which measures to control the virus were postponed until meetings scheduled for two and three weeks later.[15]

Within three days of that meeting, February 21, the disease had erupted across the continent with nine countries reporting a combined total of 45 confirmed cases. The vast majority of these had been either infected directly in China or were part of two major clusters, one in Germany and one in France, each of whose index cases had travelled from Singapore and China, respectively.[16] But this was just the tip of the iceberg because these were merely the recorded cases.

Meanwhile, the disease continued to sweep across Europe undetected, and virtually unhindered. The reason for this was simply that the testing criteria had been defined too narrowly. The technical committee of the ECDC had decided in February that only those people with coronavirus symptoms who had a history of travel to Wuhan were eligible for testing. While people exhibiting the principal coronavirus symptoms who did not have such a travel history were not tested – this was a virus detection net with a very large hole.

Just a day later, on February 22, there was a bombshell from Italy. Clusters of cases were being reported from a number of regions in northern Italy including, Piedmont and Veneto, to which Emilia-Romagna was added the following day. Covid-19 infections had been detected in multiple municipalities throughout these regions. But the news out of Italy also contained information which was to alter radically the whole trajectory of the pandemic in Europe. The Italian health authorities were not reporting instances of disease importation by people travelling from an already infected country, these were home-grown cases of community transmission. Even more portentously, the disease was being transmitted within hospitals where both healthcare workers and patients were being infected.[17]

On February 25, just three days after the details of the catastrophe that was unfolding in Italy had been released, the ECDC testing criteria were changed. But in little over a week later, on March 5, the outbreak in Italy had grown exponentially to 3,858 cases with 148 deaths – and the numbers were tripling every 48 hours. The virus had broken through the permeable ramparts of the European citadel, and it was going to prove very difficult to dislodge. On March 12, the first report of a panel of experts established to advise the EU President on the crisis had a very blunt message for Ms von der Leyen, 'It is no longer possible to stop the pandemic, only to delay it.'[18]

In a dramatic move on March 17, for the first time in its history, the EU closed its external borders in an attempt to contain the fast-spreading virus. At least for now the 'happy talk' of Ms. von der Leyen and M. Michel was abandoned as they jointly announced the unprecedented temporary sealing-off of the EU from the rest of the world. In a series of decisions that only a few weeks earlier would have been considered inconceivable in western democracies, European countries instituted lockdowns, imposed curfews and closed whole swathes of their economies in a desperate attempt to stem the flow of the epidemic.

The EU had been prompted to take the extraordinary step of closing its external borders in an attempt to dissuade an increasing number of individual member states from closing their internal borders with each other. As a visceral fear of the contagion took hold of people across the continent, they demanded that their governments impose strict border controls. Many states needed little prompting to do so, as border checkpoints re-emerged almost spontaneously across Europe. These actions were, of course, in direct contravention of one of the key pillars of European integration: the free movement of people. The coronavirus had tested the limits of European solidarity which for many states, for now at any rate, stopped at their own frontiers. In the existential crisis brought about by the epidemic, Westphalian norms were reasserting themselves, much to the consternation of the European federalist elites.

Contrary to their self-confident assurances of preparedness of a few weeks earlier, Governments across Europe were caught flat-footed as acute shortages of PPE and other medical equipment and supplies began to emerge. Having finally woken up to their dire predicament, they responded with ill-concealed panic.

Simultaneously, the world market for various types of PPE had gone into spasm as countries, including China, tried to corner the market for all available supplies. In response, the EU and various individual member states began to impose restrictions on the export of PPE equipment. In tandem with the critical medical supply shortage, the much vaunted 'European solidarity' was also in very short supply – an early casualty of the pandemic.

President Macron, the self-appointed cheerleader for a revitalised and more integrated Europe, had to execute an ignominious about-face. On March 3, he announced that the French state was requisitioning all stocks of masks as well as the production of protective masks which were to made available solely for use within France. This involved the confiscation of a Swedish company's entire stock of 6 million masks stored in a warehouse in Lyon, which had been purchased by other European countries such as Italy, Spain, the Netherlands and Portugal. The following day, the German Chancellor, Angela Merkel, followed suit and banned the export of medical protection gear including masks and gloves to mitigate Germany's looming shortages. All this led to accusations by some other member states that France and Germany were 'stealing' vital medical supplies from them. The two so-called 'pillar states' of Europe had resorted to a very un-European form of economic distancing.

As with the debt crisis of a decade previously, and the more recent immigration crisis, effective burden-sharing within the EU became a major bone of contention. When it came to the discussions about paying for the economic and financial crisis caused by the pandemic, the EU's north-south fissures quickly re-opened. Highly indebted southern countries such as Spain, but especially Italy, had suffered the most from the devastation wrought by the virus. Italy's economy, already severely weakened following decades of economic stagnation, was hit hardest of all by the pandemic. Its imposition of a most severe lockdown decimated what remained of its economy. As in the previous financial crisis, however, northern debtor nations proved just as disinclined to underwrite the enormous debts of what they saw as their profligate fellow southern member states. As the politicians procrastinated, the European economy was being brought to its knees. One by one, EU governments shut down their economies, and once again the lights went out all over Europe: like Sir Edward Grey a century earlier, many wondered when they would see them come on again.

Like much of the rest of the world, European countries struggled to cope as they were assaulted by several waves of viral attacks throughout the ensuing months right up to the autumn of 2020. As a result, in November of that year, when it was announced that a successful vaccine had been developed, the relief was palpable. However, when it came to acquiring vaccine supplies, for what seemed like ideological reasons, the EU Commission insisted that it would take sole responsibility for securing all the collective vaccine requirements of the entire EU bloc. However, due to a combination of weak European political leadership and its own extraordinarily lethargic bureaucracy, the Commission failed to move quickly enough to secure sufficient vaccine supplies. By January, as member-states began screaming for vaccine supplies that were simply unavailable, the EU leadership seemed to panic. It accused the vaccine manufacturer, AstraZeneca, of failing to meet its delivery obligations – the particular rights and wrongs of that claim are irrelevant to what happened next.

In a dramatic development, the EU announced that it was prohibiting the export of vaccines to Britain from Pfizer. This was a company that had nothing do with the EU's commercial dispute with AstraZeneca, and, in the process, the EU had targeted a country that was not even directly involved. These Pfizer vaccines had been legally purchased by the UK and so the EU was effectively commandeering vaccine supplies over which they had no apparent claim in law – this behaviour was all-too reminiscent of what had happened with PPE supplies at the very start of the pandemic in Europe.

Then came a truly exceptional and unexpected announcement. In order to ensure that no vaccine supplies could reach the UK via the 'back-door' of Northern Ireland, the EU said it intended to exclude Northern Ireland from the single market and effectively create a border between it and the Irish Republic. This was the very thing it had argued against for years, on the grounds that such a border would undermine the Northern Irish peace process and lead to the likely resumption of the IRA terror campaign. That was, admittedly, a rather dubious assumption, but it was one that EU had clung to persistently throughout the entire Brexit negotiations.

To cap it all, President Macron went on a bizarre solo run, making wild claims that the AstraZeneca vaccine - which the EU was simultaneously demanding should be delivered immediately, - 'doesn't work as expected' and was 'quasi-ineffective' for over 65s. The French President's claims had no scientific basis: indeed, President Trump had been thrown off Twitter for much less. It seemed that those on the Remain side of the Brexit debate in Britain who had argued that Brexit would lead inevitably to insular thinking, increased protectionism, and a massive growth in hubristic chauvinism, had turned out to have been right all along. However, it wasn't Britain that was displaying these negativities, it was the EU. Maybe lockdown isolation and too many zoom meetings had induced a collective nervous breakdown in the EU leadership. By any standards, this was an extraordinary episode in which the EU's reputation as a rules-based, globalist international trading entity had become seriously tarnished. It seems inevitable that the repercussions of this fiasco are likely to continue long after the particular circumstances that produced it have long passed.

Chapter 17: Carnage in Italy

Italy was the first European country to be seriously affected by the virus. The epicentre of the pandemic had shifted from China to Europe, and Italy became its epicentre in Europe. The first recorded cases of Covid-19 in Italy were on January 31 when two Chinese tourists from Wuhan were diagnosed with the disease. That same day, the Italian government suspended all flights to and from China. But almost immediately, the virus began rampaging through Italy's heavily populated northern province of Lombardy. Like most countries, Italy was ill-prepared for the arrival of the Covid-19 pandemic. In terms of hospitalisations and deaths, Covid-19 was a singular disaster for the country.

CREDIT: Instagram

Chin-Chin: Zingaretti and friends.

Having gone through yet another one of its perennial political crises in the late summer of 2019, Italy's political class had managed to cobble together a new government by September. The new left-wing coalition was composed primarily of the left-leaning populist Five-Star Movement, and the heirs to the former Communist Party, the Democratic Party.

On February 27, the leader of the governing Democratic Party, Nicola Zingaretti, posted a picture on Instagram of himself and a group of friends in Milan, clinking glasses with the message, 'Let's not lose our habits, we can't stop Milan and Italy. Our economy is stronger than fear: let's go out for an aperitivo, a coffee or to eat a pizza.'

Four days previously, Italy's pandemic tally had been; 17 dead, 650 infected, and 10 neighbouring towns just south of Milan in quarantine. Nine days after his display of braggadocio in Milan, Mr. Zingaretti posted another announcement on social media; this time confirming that he had tested positive for the virus. By then, there were 4,636 other confirmed cases, and almost 200 dead across northern Italy. Whether Mr Zingaretti's bravado was just whistling past the graveyard, or he genuinely failed to appreciate the scale of the carnage the pandemic would wreak on his country and people, we'll never know. But one thing's for sure, he wouldn't be the only European politician to haughtily distain the virus – and live to regret it.

As already indicated, Italy's first reported cases of coronavirus were on January 31 when a Chinese couple from Wuhan had tested positive for the virus. However, in mid-June, Italy's National Institute of Health (ISS) announced that samples taken as early as December 18 from the sewage systems of Milan and Turin contained genetic traces of the virus. If accurate, this meant that the virus was circulating in Italy almost six weeks before it was formally detected. This was just a little over two weeks after the first Covid-19 patient had been hospitalised in China on December 1, and just as importantly, two weeks before China supposedly reported the outbreak to the WHO on December 31. According to Reuters, samples of sewage taken from Bologna, Milan and Turin in January and February also showed positive traces of the virus, but samples taken earlier in October and November 2019 had been negative.

Further scientific evidence emerged that the virus had been passing between humans at the end of 2019, and was spreading rapidly throughout the world shortly after it first emerged in China. Corroboration that the virus was being transmitted extensively and rapidly from early on in the epidemic also came from a study conducted by researchers at University College London. The UCL study added to a growing body of evidence that, despite undergoing small genetic mutations, the virus shared a common ancestor. Additionally, the UCL researchers concluded that the ancestral virus had emerged at the end of 2019, which was the likely date when it made the jump from its animal host to humans in China.[1]

The clear message from these and other scientific papers was that once the coronavirus had jumped the species barrier in China, it spread very rapidly around the globe. And, as we shall see, too rapidly for western governments and their bureaucracies to mount effective defences to counter it. Their failed efforts at containment necessitated falling back on an array of mitigation measures, so called 'flattening the curve', which slowed the progress of the virus, but failed to deliver a decisive *coup de grace*.

The cordon sanitaire that had been placed around the 11 neighbouring towns south of Milan was strictly enforced with police checkpoints everywhere. 50,000 people within the sealed-off zone were told to stay in their houses, and anyone entering the zone was advised by police that they would not be permitted to leave. By the third week of March, Italy's death toll had surpassed that of China. The morgues of the region were being inundated with coffins. As the crematoria were unable to cope with the influx, coffins began to pile up in churches. A local newspaper in Bergamo, one of the worst hit towns, normally carried one page of death notices, now had death notices that took up a full 10 pages of the newspaper.

The health system of northern Italy was being overwhelmed. Intensive care units were full to over-capacity and so other wards were turned into makeshift ICU's. Patients were scattered everywhere, on beds, on trolleys and sitting on chairs: most were elderly and all were struggling to breathe. An intensive care specialist in one of the hospitals said, 'it's a massive strain for every health system, because we see every day 50 to 60 patients who come to our emergency department with pneumonia, and most of them are so severe they need very high volumes of oxygen.' Surveying the scene that surrounded him, he concluded grimly, 'Here they are calling it the apocalypse, and this is what it looks like.'[2] With no let-up in the volume of pneumonia patients arriving each day, and insufficient ventilators to cater for them, soon medical staff were being forced to decide who would live and who would die.

Italy's government had completely underestimated the gravity of the outbreak from the beginning. As the number of infections and deaths grew exponentially, the government struggled to control the situation. On March 9, Prime Minister Conte ordered a national lockdown, imposing severe travel restrictions on Italy's 60 million inhabitants, the effect of which he said would be, 'The whole of Italy will become a protected zone.' Echoing Churchill, he continued, 'it is our darkest hour, but we will make it'.

With the northern Italian health system unable to cope, what preoccupied many decision-makers were the potentially cataclysmic consequences that would ensue if the virus took hold in Italy's economically deprived southern regions. With a far less robust health system than that of Lombardy, Italy's southern Mezzogiorno region would be completely overwhelmed. It was a preoccupation articulated by Filippo Anelli, president of the National Federation of Doctors, 'If Lombardy is struggling, imagine what will happen in the south, where there are enormous disadvantages in terms of equipment and personnel.'[3]

Meanwhile, the spread of the virus continued to outpace the government's best efforts to contain it. Considerable vagueness in Rome's lockdown instructions gave enormous scope for politicians in the various regions to interpret them differently. As with all Italian government regulations, matters were not helped by the Italian public's widespread scepticism as to how strictly and uniformly the new measures would be applied and enforced. The end result was that a 'national' lockdown ended up with substantial regional variations in approach, and, inevitably, different outcomes. But nationally, the human cost of the pandemic continued to mount. Other European governments looked at what was happening in Italy with amazement, and an increasing sense of foreboding – was Italy's fate to be theirs as well?

Beware the Ides of March

The Ides of March was the watershed moment for many in Europe. As we have already seen, on March 17 the EU took the unprecedented decision to seal its borders with the rest of the world. It was done, according to Commission President, Ursula von der Leyen, in order 'to reduce the huge pressure on our healthcare system.' What the connection was between Europe's external borders and its healthcare system was never made clear. Given that the coronavirus disease was already rampant across Europe with infection rates rocketing in almost every member state, closing the EU's external borders looked like a case of too much, too late. It was a politically inspired action, driven as much by the EU leadership's need to be seen to do something of relevance in the midst of an existential European crisis for which it had very little legal competence under the rules. Though ostensibly temporary and limited to 30 days, the ban was largely intact several months later.

Meanwhile, those with the competence and the duty to safeguard their peoples from the worst depredations of a pandemic that was threatening to become a viral tsunami were in full Westphalian mode. In the days immediately preceding the European Commission President's announcement, state after state had followed the Italian example and imposed draconian lockdown restrictions of varying degrees of severity. France, Germany and Spain led the charge.

Many, perhaps inevitably, drew on martial metaphors. President Macon of France, having botched his initial response to the coronavirus pandemic (as did most countries), went on national television on March 16 to declare that France was 'at war' with the virus. 'We are at war ... the enemy is there, invisible, elusive, progressing. And that requires our general mobilization' he insisted. Rising to his task, and probably for the shock-effect, President Macron even insisted on banning that most quintessential of Gallic greeting traditions, kissing.[4]

In the midst of all this pandemic-induced fear, war-talk, political panic, and posturing, we have tangible evidence for the phenomenon of 'the dog that didn't bark.' Probably in deference to the dead and dying, and a fear of being accused of crassness, few politicians thought to mention, not to mind calculate, the economic and financial costs of all this. While death stalked the land, any mention by political leaders of the economic calculus involved would have led to their immediate garroting on social media, and the mainstream media would have had a field day. But, the issue of who pays the ferryman was one that would have to be faced up to, sooner rather than later. For Italy, the spiralling costs of the lockdown hung over the country like the sword of Damocles.

Since the 2008-9 banking and sovereign debt crisis, Italy had always been considered the most likely European candidate to require a future bail-out. Escalating public debt used to finance endless over-spending by politicians, when combined with virtually no economic growth for decades, had turned Italy into the economic sick-man of Europe. The result was a debt level of 132% of GDP, the second largest in the Eurozone after Greece, and youth unemployment of over 30%. While successive governments had made half-hearted attempts to reduce both, their efforts had failed to make a dent on either.

Other European politicians view modern Italian politicians' attitudes to matters economic as being reminiscent of their Imperial Roman predecessors, whose feckless overspending had the combined effect of debasing the currency and crashing the Roman economy which in turn hastened the demise of the Roman Empire. The recurring nightmare of the more frugal northern European states was that modern Italian politicians were also working off the same script, and so could visit similar ruination on the Euro and the whole European project.

Following the financial and sovereign-debt crises of 2009 where private bank debts ended up being transferred to the balance sheet of sovereign states, attempts to rectify the glaring gaps in the monetary architecture of the Eurozone became the focus of acrimonious and divisive debate. The indebted member states of the South demanded European solidarity, while the wealthier northern states refused any form of burden sharing without it being linked to significant structural economic reforms. Under the pressures of the pandemic, the political tensions of this unresolved stalemate over debt mutualisation between the rich and not-so-rich states of Europe re-emerged with renewed clarity. On top of the general issue of 'principle', there was the particular problem of funding an Italian government functionally dependent on the populist Five Star Movement which was both euro-sceptic and pro-China.

The recent rise of populist parties of the left and the right in Italy has been accompanied by a new rhetorical discourse. As disenchantment with the EU has grown among the Italian public, some populist politicians and the Five-Star Movement have championed a new narrative in which an alliance with China is promoted as a valuable counterweight to what they see as an increasingly malign EU. A favourable opinion of China was also gaining considerable traction with the Italian public. An opinion poll carried out in May suggested that China's popularity had risen 42 percentage points since the previous year, and now found favour with 52% of Italians. The corresponding figure for the USA dropped by 12 points and was favoured by just 17% of Italians. When asked 'who should Italy align with in the future?' 30% said the US and 36% said China. These are quite dramatic figures, particularly in the context of similarly drastic reductions in support for the EU among Italians in recent years.

Mask Diplomacy

In early February, the Chinese government took control of the production and distribution of all medical supplies, including PPE, and decreed that henceforth they were for domestic use only. Because of China's pre-eminent role as the global supplier of PPE equipment, this reduction in exports created immediate shortages of these critical medical supplies across the globe. However, as the pandemic in China began to taper off, the government announced that it would release some supplies to designated countries which would be selected 'according to political calculations.'[5]

One of the first to benefit from China's diplomatic efforts to extract PR benefits from the prevailing shortages of medical protection equipment was Italy. In the middle of March, as the pandemic was crucifying Italy, and the EU had effectively abandoned Italy to its fate by failing to respond to its urgent plea for medical supplies: the CCP seized the opportunity. In a phone call to President Conte, Chairman Xi Jingping promised that China would 'send more medical experts to Italy and do its best to provide medical supplies and other assistance [and] ... to contribute to international cooperation in combating the epidemic and to the construction of a Health Silk Road.[6]

CREDIT: Shutterstock

Chinese Medical Personnel and Supplies Arrive in Italy

Less than three weeks after the plane had taken off from Vienna with 25 metric tons of PPE bound for China, another plane took off from Shanghai and landed at Rome's Fiumicino airport. On board were Chinese medical personnel and 31 tons of cargo that included, intensive care unit equipment, PPE supplies, and antiviral drugs. Speaking at a press conference surrounded by the Chinese medics, Italy's Foreign Minister and leader of the governing Five Star Movement, Luigi Di Maio said, 'If you are in solidarity, you will receive solidarity. Today China will rise again, we will soon rise again.' A founding member of the EU and its third largest economy, Italy had become a battleground in the fast-developing information war that China was mounting with increased gusto.

Though a trained physician, Ursula von der Leyen's bedside-manner video message to Italians on March 11 left a lot to be desired. 'Dear Italians, at this difficult moment, I want to tell you that you are not alone … In Europe we are following what you are doing with concern but also with profound respect and admiration …Italy is part of Europe, and Europe is suffering with Italy.' Addressed to a member state in which unprecedented numbers of its elderly citizens were dying lonely coronavirus deaths without the consoling presence of either kith or kin, it simply didn't cut it. At the geopolitical level, the words of the President of European Commission showed she lacked authority, power, and charisma – in international power politics, Europe looked to be floundering. A couple of days later as the tons of medical supplies from China were rolling off the China Eastern Airbus A-350 at Fiumicino airport, Foreign Minister Di Maio made the pointed comment, 'This is what we call solidarity.'[7]

The Sino-Italian Affair

Italy's fixation with China had long pre-dated its more recent urgent need for PPE. Italy's leftist Europhile (the terms were virtually synonymous in Italy) and two-time Prime Minister, Romano Prodi, pursued the then fashionable globalist agenda of cosying up to the CCP. In 1997, he led an unprecedentedly large 100 company delegation on a 10-day trade mission to China. It was a preoccupation shared by many of his socialist Prime Ministerial colleagues including, Massimo D'Alema, Matteo Renzi, and Paolo Gentilioni. The exception was Italy's right-wing Prime Minister, Silvio Berlusconi, who favoured looking to the US rather than China (but this didn't stop him selling his beloved AC Milan to Chinese investors in 2017).

In the wake of the 2008-9 financial and sovereign-debt crisis, populist parties of both left and right became serious contenders for political power in many countries around the world. In Europe, they became major domestic actors in virtually all EU states, including; France, Germany, Italy, Spain, Austria, the UK, the Netherlands, Greece, Poland, Hungary, Slovakia, Sweden, Finland and Denmark. Usually, a country's dominant populist strain tended to be either right, such as the National Front in France, or left such as Syriza in Greece – Italy got two for the price of one. Following Italy's 2018 earthquake General Election in which the political landscape was transformed, the left and right populists, Five Star Movement and Lega, formed Italy's 66th government in 73 years. Italy's resurgent populist politicians and parties who had been deeply enamoured of Xi Jinping's China for years, brought Sino-Italian relationships to an entirely new level when in government.

China's Belt and Road Initiative (BRI) is the centrepiece of an ambitious global programme of economic diplomacy which exemplifies Xi Jinping's assertive foreign policy. The BRI is an elaborate programme of direct investment in, and funding of, large-scale infrastructure projects around the world, but with a particular focus on developing countries. Through it, China is acting as a lender-of-last-resort for countries whose current level of indebtedness has given them limited access to traditional debt markets. In return, China earns kudos and considerable influence in the intensifying information war and, worst case, in the event of default China can simply repossess the underlying infrastructure asset.

CREDIT: Foreign Ministry PRC

President Xi Jingping and President Giuseppe Conte Meet in Rome

Within a year, Europe's first Eurosceptic-led government had invited Xi Jinping on an official state visit to Italy. The climax of the state visit was the signing of a memorandum of understanding on collaboration and investments across strategic industrial sectors such as ports, shipping, telecommunications and pharmaceuticals as part of the Belt and Road Initiative. This $900 billion investment project was an illustration of what Edward Luttwak refers to as the shift from geopolitics to geo-economics, using the logic of conflict but the grammar of commerce.[8] The signing represented an enormous feather in the cap of Xi Jinping. Italy had become the first European country, and the first member of the G7 club of industrialised nations to endorse his signature geo-strategic initiative. This was a major diplomatic coup for the CCP and, correspondingly, a very humiliating public poke in the eye for the EU. The deal provoked anger in Washington and alarm in the EU at the prospect of China gaining privileged access to highly sensitive telecommunications infrastructure and, critical maritime and other transport hubs.

The EU's response to this provocative intrusion by China was a classic piece of confused analysis, borne of political callowness and instinctive appeasement: a combination that would have shocked the past European giants of political realism such as Thucydides, Machiavelli, Hobbes, and Max Weber. In March 2019, clearly stung by the Sino-Italian deal, the European Commission defined its relationship with China as follows: 'China is simultaneously a cooperation partner with whom the EU has closely aligned objectives, a negotiating partner, with whom the EU needs to find a balance of interests, an economic competitor in pursuit of technological leadership, and a systemic rival promoting alternative models of governance.'[9] The EU's all-things-to-all-men approach was a clear indication that it had fundamentally misread the fact that Xi Jinping's China was primarily a 'systemic rival' which was actively seeking to undermine the EU's fundamental objectives. And with Italy on board, it could now begin to do it from within.

The Mask Slips

The smiles, handshakes and bonhomie at the signing ceremony in Rome and the subsequent much publicised mask diplomacy were winning hearts and minds in Italy. In its growing love affair with China, little thought was given in Italy, or anywhere else, to the possibility that the avuncular Xi was really a wolf in panda's clothing. But evidence for a much darker side to the CCP's activities also came to light.

In mid-January, before China admitted that there was person-to-person transmission of the disease, the CCP issued an urgent instruction to its vast network of Chinese embassies and consulates and companies to purchase all available stocks of PPE worldwide.[10] The drive was so successful that within just five weeks beginning January 24, China was able to import up to 2.5 billion items of personal protection equipment, including over 2 billion masks. A Chinese customs' report dated March 3, records that 'From January 24 to February 29, the national customs inspected and released 2.46 billion pieces of epidemic prevention and control materials, worth 8.21 billion yuan. Among them, there are 2.4 billion pieces of protective equipment, mainly including 2.02 billion pieces of masks and 25.38 million pieces of protective clothing.'[11]

While China kept the rest of the world in ignorance of the severity of the 'pneumonia of unknown cause', the CCP had issued instructions to hoover up as much as possible of the global stocks of PPE equipment: they spent over one billion euros ($1.17 billion) on this hoarding exercise. It was a covert operation to stockpile masks and other medical protection supplies at a time when prices were at their lowest as there was no competing demand. There was no competing demand for these supplies around the world because those with the knowledge that would create such demand kept it secret. This was insider trading on a global scale. The highly questionable moral and ethical nature of the behaviour involved in this duplicitous scheme are obvious. Less obvious were its costs, which were not measured in monetary terms but in the dead bodies of frontline healthcare workers around the world who, as they battled to save the lives of their patients, died because they were deprived of this essential protective equipment early on in the pandemic.

Under the aegis of its diplomatic services, China had recruited the services of other actors, including overseas Chinese citizens and commercial Chinese owned companies for this hush-hush operation to corner as much as possible of the global supply of medical protection equipment. On February 3, *Xinhua*, China's state news agency published a stirring account of the 'patriotic' efforts of foreign-based Chinese to acquire these scarce supplies: 'They are racing day and night, racing against time, to send back batch after batch of scarce epidemic prevention materials for the motherland.'[12]

This operation was orchestrated by an organisation called the United Front (UF)[13] which reports directly to the Central Committee of the CCP, and has been described by Xi Jingping as one of the party's 'magic weapons.' The United Front focuses its activities on intelligence gathering and influencing members of the overseas Chinese communities, especially those in important positions in commercial, social or academic institutions who can support the interests of the CCP and, conversely, keep an eye on dissidents and critics. The United Front's mask operation was confirmed in a report of the CCP's mouthpiece, the *People's Daily*, at the end of March: 'At the beginning of the outbreak of the new corona pneumonia, there was a sharp shortage of medical protective materials such as masks, protective clothing and goggles in China. Many overseas Chinese did their best to donate and mail medical materials to the country regardless of cost.' [14]

In a retrospective effort to take the sting out of this CCP-directed enterprise, the *People's Daily* went on to make a song and dance about the United Front's reciprocal action later on to assist in overseas' shortages of PPE. The article claimed that the United Front 'quickly raised 1 million masks. At present, 700,000 pieces have been donated to overseas Chinese in severely affected countries such as Italy, Spain, the United Kingdom, and France, and the remaining 300,000 pieces will be shipped quickly in batches according to the needs of overseas Chinese.' Apart from the openly ethno-centric, if not downright racist aspect of this exercise, of the two billion masks the CCP had netted covertly in early January, this donation constituted a mere 0.05% - significantly short of the magnanimity threshold.

Chapter 18: Britain is Blindsided

The *Global Health Security Index* (GHSI)[1] assessed the risks of high-consequence and globally catastrophic biological events for 195 countries. Its first report was published on 24 October, 2019, just six weeks before the first confirmed case of the coronavirus pandemic was detected in Wuhan. One of its major conclusions was that 'National health security is fundamentally weak around the world. No country is fully prepared for epidemics or pandemics, and every country has important gaps to address.' However, in its overall rankings, the GHSI put the UK almost at the top of the class. The report gives the UK an extremely high score of 77.9 and places it second from the top of the 195 countries, after the US. In its assessment of 'Rapid Response' capabilities, the UK received an exceptionally high 91.9 compared to the global average of 38.4.[2] But this was a paper exercise, one year later in the real world, the pandemic had infected over 2 million people and killed over 67,000 in the UK.

As in most other countries, the response of the government and health authorities in the UK was initially lethargic, indicating a serious failure to appreciate the scale of the impending threat. This was undoubtedly due in part, at least, to China's initial cover-up and subsequent downplaying of the seriousness of the outbreak, aided and abetted by the WHO (see chapter 14). Based on the understated information emanating from the WHO, on January 22, Public Health England (PHE) changed the status of the threat of the virus to the UK public from 'very low' to 'low'.

The first two cases of coronavirus in the UK were on January 31. They were both Chinese nationals from the same family who had fallen ill at the Staycity Aparthotel in York. Both patients, one of whom was a student at York University, were treated at the Infectious Disease Centre based at Newcastle's Royal Victoria Infirmary. Throughout February, most of the other confirmed cases of the disease were infected while abroad.

Then on February 28, the first recognised case of local community transmission was diagnosed. That same day witnessed the first British citizen to die from the virus. He had been infected with the disease while aboard the cruise ship Diamond Princess ship which had been moored off the coast of Yokohama, Japan (See below chapter 19). He had been one of four infected passengers from a group of 30 Britons and two Irish who were repatriated by the British government and quarantined in a special NHS isolation facility. At that point, with a total of 691 passengers and crew infected by the virus, the Diamond Princess was the location of the largest Covid-19 outbreak outside of China. Most of these inbound travel-related infections in the UK were found to have occurred in the period mid-to-late March.[3]

On March 5, the first coronavirus death in the UK itself was that of a woman in her 70s who had underlying health conditions. Throughout March, the spread of the contagion picked up substantially. On Friday, March 13, the number of infections rose by 200 in one day, and the UK's major supermarkets appealed to the public not to panic-buy grocery items and to refrain from stockpiling food. One week later, the number of confirmed cases had risen to 3,269 and the numbers of deaths, which had increased by 40% in one day, now stood at 144. Like almost all other countries, the momentum of the pandemic caught the UK government and its health authorities completely off-guard.

By this stage, many scientists were predicting that the UK was on the same epidemic trajectory as Italy, just lagging events there by about two to three weeks. If accurate, it was an ominous portent of things to come, as Italy had just instituted an unprecedented lockdown of its 60 million inhabitants. Then, two weeks after Italy had imposed its national lockdown, the UK government did the same on March 23. The question was, had it acted in time or, had it been behind the coronavirus curve?

Just as in Asia, the issue of importing infections through air travel was a critical issue during the early stages of the spread of the disease in the UK. A study published in June, confirmed that about one third of the incidences of the disease in Britain were the result of inbound international travel, with two thirds of those coming from Spain, France and Italy; almost half of whom were returning UK residents. During a period that included the February half-term school holidays, when substantial numbers of British schoolchildren traditionally travelled to the continent in groups – skiing trips to northern Italy being one of the most popular destinations – there were no travel restrictions in place.

It was only on March 17 that the UK government *advised* against all non-essential overseas travel and almost a week later, on March 23, it advised British travellers overseas to return to the UK. But there were no government bans on air travel. However, by March, fear of the virus had dissuaded most people from flying in any case, and airline companies responded to the drop in demand by curtailing their services – but there were still some flights to most destinations. It was also a time when Covid-19 was globally rampant. Or as the June study understatedly puts it, 'there was a period in mid-March when inbound travel to the UK was still substantial and coincided with high numbers of active cases elsewhere.'[4] When it came on March 23, the lockdown was probably too late. In the absence of severe travel restrictions in the weeks prior to the lockdown, a highly infectious virus had been given access, and time to take root.

CREDIT: PA

Cheltenham Racegoers High Stakes Gamble in March

As a result, the UK was hit extremely hard. Within a few months it was recording the second-highest number of coronavirus deaths in the world. By July 10, the death toll in the UK stood at almost 51,000, with the majority of deaths being among people aged 65 years and over (45,528). This enormous tally was second only to the United States, which had registered 133,847 by the same date, but that was out of a population over five times the size of the UK. On a like-for-like comparison based on population size, the US had 404 deaths per million while the UK was almost twice that number at 750 deaths per million.[5]

Though Italy had imposed its national lockdown on March 9, in the UK the Cheltenham Festival took place over four days from March 10-13 and was attended by over 250,000 people – just 5.5% fewer than the previous year. Tens of thousands of people packed tightly together while loudly cheering on their favourite nag looked decidedly inappropriate on the same day (March 11) that the WHO had declared the coronavirus to be a global pandemic. The reason why Cheltenham and other large sporting events were allowed to go ahead was because SAGE (see below) had advised the government that 'There is currently no evidence that cancelling large events would be effective.'[6]

The reason the WHO gave for making, what many regarded as a very belated decision in any case, was 'because of the speed and scale of transmission'. In making the announcement, the WHO's Director General, Dr Tedros explained in a tweet that, 'The idea that countries should shift from containment to mitigation is wrong and dangerous.'[7] In the case of the UK, his fears were entirely misplaced: containment had hardly even begun.

The following day, March 12, in a scene that was to become a nightly staple for UK television audiences, Prime Minister Johnson admitted as much. Set against the backdrop of the wood-panelled walls of the state dining room at number 10 Downing Street, and flanked by two of his coronavirus new-best-friends, the Prime Minister addressed the nation: 'We have a clear plan that we are now working through. And we are now moving to the next phase in that plan … this is now not just to attempt to contain the disease as far as possible, but to delay its spread and thereby minimise the suffering.'[8]

With all hopes of containment firmly abandoned, the new mantra was 'flattening the curve'. The avowed purpose of the new mitigation phase was to delay the spread of the virus in order to prevent the health service being overwhelmed, as had been happening in Italy. It was a sombre recognition that this was the best that could be achieved under the circumstances. Another central plank of the containment strategy was also formally abandoned that day. Standing beside the Prime Minister, England's Chief Medical Officer, Prof. Chris Whitty announced that community testing was also to be jettisoned in favour of in-hospital testing of patients. This was also against WHO advice, and the experience of countries like South Korea and the other Asian Tigers.

The next day, March 13, the government's Chief Scientific Officer, the third member of the pandemic television trio, Sir Patrick Vallance, stirred up a right hornets' nest in an interview he gave to Radio 4. He said that the thinking behind the government's new approach was for up to 60% of the UK population to acquire a 'degree of herd immunity so that more people are immune to the disease.'[9] In contrast with what was happening internationally, the UK government seemed to be saying; 'Keep calm, carry on … and get infected.' That Friday the 13th proved to be lucky for some, but not so lucky for others. As the French owned, Irish trained *Al Boum Photo* was striding into equine history as the only horse ever to win the Cheltenham Gold Cup twice in a row, the Chief Scientific Officer was explaining to various media outlets what herd immunity actually meant:

that up to 40 million UK citizens would need to become infected with the disease – it caused uproar.

On March 16, Health Secretary Hancock sought to calm things down and clarify matters: 'We have a plan, based on the expertise of world-leading scientists. Herd immunity is not a part of it. That is a scientific concept, not a goal or a strategy.'[10] In spite of the Health Secretary's 'clarification', the controversy initiated an avalanche of criticism of the government's piecemeal approach to the pandemic. One critic, citing the success of South Korea, Hong Kong, Singapore and Taiwan in controlling the virus through extensive testing and strict social distancing measures said, 'That's what you need to be doing. You go all in, or not at all. And not at all ends up like Italy.'[11]

On March 23, the day after Public Health England had changed the status threat of the virus to the British public from 'very low' to 'low', the Health Secretary, Matt Hancock, told the House of Commons, 'The whole of the U.K. is always well prepared for these types of outbreaks.' Clearly, much of this official insouciance was an attempt by the government not to frighten the horses, as it were. But it was also a clear indication that the British government, having been very late out of the starting blocks, was trying to buy time to figure out how exactly it was going to handle this crisis. In the meantime, it had deliberately adopted the duck posture: floating serenely on the surface while paddling furiously underneath. The paddling got even more furious from March 16 onwards.

SAGE – Pandemic Wisdom on Tap

On March 16, in a non-descript government building on London's Victoria Street a meeting of a secretive government advisory committee took place. Among the 20 or so attendees were some of Britain's leading scientists, health experts, and government officials, as well as representatives from academia and industry. It had been given the acronym SAGE (Scientific Advisory Group for Emergencies) and when the government says that it is 'following the science', it is, more often than not, the advice of this committee to which it is referring.

Subsequently, when politicians and government officials sought to give their pronouncements on pandemic policy an air of oracular wisdom, or, more commonly, close down debate and fend off criticism, they invariably invoked the name of SAGE. Yet little was known about how this powerful committee made its decisions. Not only that, its membership was secret, its meetings were closed, its recommendations were private, and the minutes of its deliberations were rarely, if ever, subjected to public scrutiny – transparent it was not.[12] Under such conditions of opacity, it was impossible for anyone, scientist or layperson, to divine whether the science that was being followed was even optimal. But for good or ill, SAGE remained at the beating heart of the UK government's pandemic decision-making process.

According to Bloomberg, that Monday's meeting was presented with shocking new modelling data which indicated that the committee's pandemic policy was in need of a radical and speedy overhaul. The evidence showed that, contrary to previous opinion, virus transmission between children, parents, and teachers was far higher than had been supposed.

A severe lockdown along the same lines as almost every other European country was now unavoidable. In particular, it would mean that over 30,000 schools across Britain would have to close. Despite a rising crescendo of demands up to then, closing down schools was something that Prime Minister Johnson had staunchly resisted for weeks. Whatever the political fallout and loss of credibility that might be involved, the committee decided that a U-turn on school closures had to happen.[13]

But the real catalyst for the governments' volte face on the lockdown issue was the publication, also on March 16, of a report from a team of modellers from Imperial College London, led by Neil Ferguson. Its shocking prediction was that if unconstrained the virus could kill over half-a-million people. Without a rigorous lockdown, the NHS would be overwhelmed as new cases could double every five to six days. Furthermore, the report claimed that the UK was much further along the pandemic curve than had been assumed. The extent of the policy reversal that ensued was enormous. Just three days previously, according to the minutes of the SAGE meeting of March 13: 'SAGE was unanimous that measures seeking to completely suppress [the] spread of Covid-19 will cause a second peak. SAGE advises that it is a near certainty that countries such as China, where heavy suppression is underway, will experience a second peak once measures are relaxed.'[14]

The Imperial College modelling study was both credited and blamed for the government's rapid about-face on the lockdown. Some epidemiologists and specialists in computational biology were highly critical of the Imperial College model and its conclusions, and posed some uncomfortable questions about model-driven policy making. Questions were raised also about the underlying software code of the model, which had been written 13 years earlier to model an influenza pandemic. Whether fairly or not, the computer code was described as a tangled mess of undocumented steps, with no discernible overall structure. But much more importantly, as the model that was used as the basis for the implementation of a national lockdown on March 23, one of the most significant peacetime decisions in British history, it remained unavailable for scrutiny. Both Prof Ferguson and Imperial College refused to publish the underlying taxpayer-funded code for evaluation by other experts. On top of that, this important study had not been peer-reviewed at the time of the decision.[15]

Whatever about the accuracy, or otherwise, of Prof Ferguson's modelling methodology, he certainly seems to have had an aptitude for grabbing the headlines. He subsequently had to resign from SAGE because his married girlfriend had breached quarantine rules by visiting him on a number of occasions – he was seen to be in breach of his own lockdown. Later, on June 10, he told a Select Committee of the House of Commons that, 'The epidemic was doubling every three to four days before lockdown interventions were introduced. So, had we introduced lockdown measures a week earlier, we would have reduced the final death toll by at least a half.' It was a bold statement which immediately dominated the news agenda. But what was omitted from the subsequent news coverage was that under further questioning by MPs, Prof Ferguson admitted that he had no proper scientific basis for making his headline-grabbing statement. Indeed, he seems to have resiled from his bold claim that an earlier lockdown would have reduced the final death toll 'by at least half' when he explained further; 'I'm second guessing at this point, certainly had we introduced them earlier we would have seen many fewer deaths.' By any definition, 'many fewer' does not equate to 'at least a half'.

Lockdown Britain

Like many things to do with the pandemic, precisely identifying when something started or ended is difficult. These difficulties are compounded when some of the widely used terms, such as lockdown, lack any formal or agreed definition. In the case of the UK, for instance, there are competing claims as to when precisely the lockdown began. Health Secretary Hancock claimed it began on March 16, when four months later he told MPs that '16th of March is the day that I came to this House and said that all unnecessary social contact should cease. That is precisely when the lockdown started.' This claim of a March 16 start to lockdown is contradicted, however, – by none other than Mr Hancock himself. On June 2, he told the Commons that the mortality rate "is lower than at any time since lockdown began on 23 March.'

But Secretary Hancock's inconsistencies aside, there is a compelling argument for March 23 being the commencement date for lockdown in the UK. March 23 is the day when the Health Secretary's previous 'advice' became an 'instruction' from the Prime Minister. Smarting from a storm of criticism for his laissez-faire attitude to the lightening spread of the disease, a sombre Prime Minister announced the most draconian restrictions on the British public since World War II. Britain was about to align with the rest of Europe where, in a desperate effort to stem the contagion, lockdowns had become ubiquitous. Italy had been in full lockdown since March 9, Denmark since March 11, Spain's began on March 14, and France on March 17.

In a live television address to the nation that evening, Prime Minister Johnson announced 'From this evening I must give the British people a very simple instruction - you must stay at home.' He went on to define, in considerable detail, what was about to happen. People were only allowed to leave their homes to get essential food items and medicines, or to travel to work. And there was to be no socialising. All non-essential retail outlets were to close and all social events, including religious ceremonies, were to cease. In the event that the rules were not being followed, the Prime Minister warned, 'the police will have the powers to enforce them, including through fines and dispersing gatherings.'[16] It was the most stringent set of curtailments on British life in living memory. That day there were 6,650 confirmed cases of infection and 335 deaths in the UK – a 600% increase in a week.

On the same day, the Foreign Office advised up to 1 million Britons who were abroad on holiday or business, to make urgent plans to return home immediately. The Foreign Secretary, Dominic Raab, couldn't have been clearer; 'We are strongly urging UK travellers overseas to return home now where and while there are still commercial routes to do so … If you are on holiday abroad the time to come home is now while you still can.'[17]

Meanwhile, 7,563 former clinicians had answered the call to return to the NHS to assist in the crisis. With only 8,000 ventilators there was an urgent plea to British industry for a special 'wartime effort' to manufacture

30,000 additional machines to alleviate the shortage and cater for the expected peak demand in the NHS. And emergency legislation was introduced at Westminster which gave sweeping powers to the government to enforce the lockdown, many of which had not been used since the Second World War. The Coronavirus Act 2020 was passed by the House of Commons on March 23 without a vote.

Public Health England

We have developed a bifurcated attitude to the administrative state. On the one hand, we want to let public servants and the experts 'get on with it', but then when things go wrong, we blame the politicians. For public servants this can often lead to a case of heads we win, tails you lose. Public Health England (PHE) is the expert national public health agency of the Department of Health and Social Care, which deals with both health protection and health promotion. It commenced operations on April 1, 2013 and was modelled on the US CDC. During the pandemic it had a number of important functions, one of the most critical being its sole responsibility for testing and contact tracing.

From the beginning, PHE's capacity to test and trace was extremely limited. At best, it could cope with 50 new cases a week which amounted to just 8000 contacts being isolated. This was woefully inadequate for a fast-spreading infectious disease and so, unsurprisingly, on March 12 the government had to abandon its test-and-trace strategy. Giving evidence to a Commons health committee in May, the government's Chief Scientific Officer admitted, 'If we had managed to ramp testing capacity quickly, that would have been beneficial. For all sorts of reasons that didn't happen.' The chairman of another Commons committee, Greg Clark, summed up concisely what had happened: 'capacity drove strategy, instead of strategy driving capacity'. [18] Just as the UK was throwing in the towel on testing, speaking to the media in Geneva on March 16, the WHO's Dr Tedros said 'You cannot fight a fire blindfolded. And we cannot stop this pandemic if we don't know who is infected. We have a simple message for all countries: test, test, test.'[19]

On March 25, giving evidence before a House of Commons committee, a director of PHE, Sharon Peacock, was asked why the organisation had abandoned the South Korea model and relied solely on its own laboratories and those of the NHS and did not avail of private and university laboratories to relieve the bottleneck. The chair enquired, 'Can you explain why we rejected the South Korean model in favour of that approach?' To which Ms. Peacock replied, 'that's a good question.' When pressed by the chair on the scientific rationale for this critical decision and whether it was published so that it could be 'scientifically interrogated'. She said 'The straight answer is that it is not published at the moment', but she promised to make it available to the committee in the next few days – if never materialised.[20]

Public Health England also has regulatory responsibility for the almost 300,000 residents in some 9,000 care homes in England. On February 25, it issued advice on care homes which contained no restrictions on visits while claiming that it was 'very unlikely that people receiving care in a care home or the community will become infected.' This relaxed attitude to the virus extended to the use of face masks. 'During normal day-to-day activities facemasks do not provide protection from respiratory viruses, such as COVID-19 and do not need to be worn by staff in any of these settings.'[21] Throughout March there was no prohibition on visits, it was only on April 2 that visiting was restricted to exceptional circumstances only: 'family and friends should be advised not to visit care homes, except next of kin in exceptional situations such as end-of-life.'[22] It was also only in April that it emerged that the national statistics being collected had missed out completely on one of the most vulnerable sectors of the health system – care homes. On the simple principle that if you don't measure, you can't manage, this was disastrous. The high rates of infection and, most importantly, the high death rates that were occurring throughout the care home sector were being completely missed.

There are occasions when loss of life above and beyond the norm is acceptable. In an exceptional influenza season, or during an intense heat wave, people with various illnesses and the elderly are at high risk and, unfortunately, experience higher than normal levels of mortality on such occasions. Though tragic, these deaths are looked upon as largely the unavoidable consequences of naturally occurring circumstances. But what if a massive spike in the deaths of highly vulnerable elderly people were the result of policy failures, and bureaucratic bungling? That, in the minds of the public, would be an entirely different matter.

In its many forms, tragedy has been a constant companion of the coronavirus pandemic. But like accidents, many tragedies don't just happen, they are caused. Most of the tragic consequences that flowed from the pandemic were the result of failures of both action and inaction, omission and commission. In the UK, the failure to act sufficiently early had dramatic consequences, and ultimately narrowed the available policy options to the blunt instrument of lockdown. Even within that, although there was much public lip-service, in reality there was a complete failure to cater for the extreme vulnerabilities faced by the residents of the nation's care homes. Nowhere has the coronavirus tragedy played out which such devastating consequences than among the 400,000 people who resided in these healthcare facilities.

The extent of the death toll among care home residents in England and Wales is evident from the figures released by the Office of National Statistics (ONS) in early July. Between March 2 and June 12, 2019, 37,000 care home residents died, the figure for the same period for 2020 was over 66,000 – almost 30,000 higher. While 20,000 of these deaths specifically mentioned Covid -19 as the cause of death, previous ONS analysis indicated that many of the other 10,000 deaths could also be Covid-19 related.23 A more recent study found that in care homes with higher levels of infection among staff and where there was a higher use of agency personnel, the levels of infection among residents were correspondingly higher.24 Britain's tardiness in shutting things down, combined with its relatively less stringent lockdown rules, meant that the virus was able to spread faster and farther, which ultimately made it much harder to suppress in care homes, as elsewhere.

Despite these appallingly high figures, on a pan-European comparison of these grim statistics, with 21% of total Covid deaths being in care homes, the UK fared reasonably well in percentage terms. The equivalent numbers in many other European countries were shockingly higher: Sweden 45%, Spain 66%, Belgium 51%, France 50%, and Germany 37%. [25] In terms of the absolute figures, as the UK had the highest number of total Covid deaths, the absolute number of care home deaths was also the highest in Europe.

By the end of June, with a figure of almost 47,000 the UK had the worst record of total coronavirus deaths in Europe, surpassing even Italy's 35,000. Britain was also top of the European leader board for deaths in another age-related category – under 65s. Possibly a reflection of high levels of obesity and weight-related diseases, even younger people in Britain had much higher death rates than any other European country. With 5.1 deaths per 100,000, Britain had more than double that of the next worst case, Spain (2.1).

In this context, there is a further statistic that we need to consider before we leave the UK. It has a significance not just for Britain, but for each and every country that has been affected by the Covid-19 pandemic. In their singular focus on the deaths and illness caused by the virus, governments worldwide have only belatedly begun to consider one of the most negative unintended consequences of the pandemic: the deaths of people with other serious health conditions who were denied access to critical medical care because of the lockdown. Certain medical treatments for serious diseases such as cancer were suspended by the NHS. In addition, there was a reported drop of up to 50% in attendances at A&E departments by stroke and heart attack victims.

A study published by researchers at Sheffield and Loughborough Universities in conjunction with Economic Insight, estimates that some 21,000 additional U.K. deaths were attributable, not directly to Covid, but to the lockdown, and especially lack of access to critical medical care. The purpose of the lockdown was to "flatten the curve" of coronavirus cases to prevent the National Health Service from being overwhelmed, but far from being overwhelmed the NHS was underutilised by many of those suffering from other serious conditions.

The researchers from Sheffield and Loughborough Universities have calculated that as a direct consequence of the lack of access to critical healthcare and the drop in A&E attendances has resulted in a further 2,700 people dying each week. Having analysed the official data, the writers of the report came to the disturbing conclusion that 21,000 people had died because of lack of access to critical health care. Figures released by the NHS confirm that there was a fall-off in A&E attendances during April of 57% - the lowest figure ever recorded.

Ultimately what this means is that 'success' on the Covid front would have to be balanced by an assessment of the profound negative impact on the health outcomes of those patients suffering from other serious conditions. The campaign to 'flatten the curve' of coronavirus cases, in order to prevent the NHS from being overwhelmed succeeded, but at a yet to be calculated cost. The sad irony of all this is that, as it turned out, those with serious conditions such as cardiac, stroke, and cancer died not because there were insufficient beds or trained medical staff to treat them, but because many elderly people were too afraid to go to hospital and so died lonely deaths at home. This was an outcome that surely was not 'guided by the science'.

Chapter 19: Down Under

CREDIT: Shutterstock

From One Disaster to Another

By early March, the flames of the raging bushfires that had ravaged parts of Australia for months were being finally extinguished. The wildfires had shrouded swathes of New South Wales in a pall of acrid smoke that at times stretched from the Blue Mountains to Australia's most populous city, Sydney. The volunteer 'firies' who had battled heroically against these infernos were exhausted. Those not directly affected by the fires themselves were still reeling from the scale of the devastation in terms of homes, forests, loss of life and wildlife that the unprecedented bushfires had caused. But just as the embers of that disaster were dying out, another one that had been smouldering for about a month began to ignite.

As with most other countries, the first recorded coronavirus case in Australia was imported: a Chinese man who had returned from Wuhan to Melbourne on January 25. One month later, Feb 27, there were 22 confirmed cases of Covid-19 in Australia. Of these, 15 were connected to Wuhan, but in an unusual twist, the remainder were passengers who had been on board a virus-stricken cruise ship from which 200 Australian citizens had been evacuated about a week previously. The prelude to the story of Australia's fateful connection between cruise ships and the coronavirus began in February in Japan.

The Diamond Princess in Yokohama

The drama on board the Diamond Princess cruise ship began on the evening of February 3 at dinnertime, while the vessel was docked at Yokohama, Japan. That evening's diners listened in stunned silence as the captain announced that a previous passenger who had disembarked from the cruise ship in Hong Kong had been diagnosed with coronavirus. Following an initial round of testing, 20 of the remaining 2,666 passengers then on board also tested positive, and so the vessel was quarantined for 14 days by the Japanese authorities. An eerie silence fell over the once bustling luxury cruise ship as the passengers were confined to their cabins where they were served meals three times a day while they anxiously awaited news of their uncertain future.

Though isolated in their cabins, the virus continued its inexorable spread throughout the ship. A week later, on February 10, there were a total of 135 confirmed cases of coronavirus on board. That's a 575% increase in infections in just one week: it made the Diamond Princess the single biggest coronavirus cluster outside of China. Meanwhile, many of those on board were able to observe from their balconies the distressing sight of their newly infected fellow passengers being ferried away in ambulances. Witnessing these daily scenes and living with the uncertainty of what was going to happen to them, and the ever-present fear of getting the infection, had turned what for many had been a trip of a lifetime into a floating hell.

The final Covid tally of the Diamond Princess cruise was 700 passengers and crew infected and fourteen dead. As the international passengers were repatriated by their governments to various parts of the world, the Diamond Princess outbreak engendered a fire-storm of publicity around the world. As well as exposing major shortcomings in its pandemic response, the Diamond Princess contagion was a publicity disaster for Japan. At the time, Japan was completing its final preparations for the 2020 Olympics which were just months away at that stage. At the end of February, when for the remaining almost 3700 passengers and crew were allowed to disembark the Diamond Princess, their ordeal had finally come to an end – or so they thought.

Sydney's Viral Storm in a Port

Though the Diamond Princess was the first cruise ship to grab the international headlines for all the wrong reasons, by the end of April over 40 other cruise ships had reported confirmed coronavirus cases. Governments advised their citizens not to take cruises, and port after port around the world started to prohibit cruise ships from docking. Passengers and crews on board many vessels that were already on the high seas were effectively stranded there.

On March 15, the federal government of Australia banned all cruise ships arriving from foreign ports from docking in Australia. However, it made four exemptions for those cruise ships that were already at sea and *en route* to Australia. One of the exceptions was the sister ship of the Diamond Princess, the Ruby Princess which was bound for Circular Quay in Sydney Harbour. There were other nationalities on board, including US citizens, but the majority of the passengers were Australian. The ship had been forced to cut short its voyage because a number of passengers had reported feeling unwell with respiratory problems – though the reason the passengers were given for the curtailment was that there was an approaching storm.

CREDIT: Getty Images

Australia's Plague Ship Ruby Princess

Following its docking in Circular Quay the previous evening, on March 19 all 2,700 passengers aboard the Ruby Princess were allowed by NSW health authorities to disembark in Sydney. This was in spite of the fact that over 100 of them were showing signs of flu-like symptoms. Within weeks, many of them became Australia's single largest source of the coronavirus infection.

Four days earlier, on March 15, the Prime Minister, Scott Morrison, had announced that all travellers entering Australia had to self-isolate for 14 days. This order, of course, applied to the Ruby Princess passengers. Yet they were all allowed to disembark some, according to reports, coughing and sputtering as they left the ship.[1] They then dispersed on buses, trains, and planes to various parts of Australia and overseas. Most of these passengers were completely unaware that there had been an infectious disease outbreak on board their ship.

They had been kept in the dark by the captain and crew on board, and by the cruise-ship owners and health authorities onshore. Most passengers only discovered when they got home that they had been living with the deadly coronavirus for days: one passenger only found out as she was waiting to collect her bags at Heathrow airport. Under the shadow of the iconic vaulted arches of the Sydney Opera House, countless numbers of undetected infected passengers were allowed to stream off the Ruby Princess in Circular Quay: this viral storm was about to sweep into the centre of Australia's largest city and continue right across Australia. By May, over 700 passengers from this ill-fated voyage had tested positive for the virus and 21 had died – it transpired that a total of 26% of all passengers had been stricken by the virus. Even more disturbing, this catastrophe was allowed to happen just one week after the WHO had declared the coronavirus outbreak a global pandemic.

But this was not a completely unforeseen event; there were ample chronicles of a disaster foretold. Global news had been preoccupied with the saga of its sister ship, the Diamond Princess, which had been quarantined in Yokohama docks for most of the month of February because of a similar massive outbreak of coronavirus infections among its passengers. The Japanese authorities hadn't quite covered themselves in glory, but they had coped – at least they hadn't allowed infected passengers to wander all over the country and the world.

But there was another warning a little earlier, that was even closer to home. In fact, it was an exact replica of what happened on March 19: it involved the same Ruby Princess cruise ship; arriving at the same destination, Circular Quay; from the same New Zealand voyage – all that was different was the date: 11 days earlier on March 8.

According to email information obtained by 7NEWS, the Port Authority of NSW had been aware that the Ruby Princess had arrived that day with '158 people who were sick and 13 of whom had a temperature.' The email confirmed that because of those numbers, NSW Health deemed the Ruby Princess a 'medium risk' and so nine of those who were ill were tested by for Covid-19: they were found to be negative. As a result, the cruise ship was allowed to depart Sydney and set sail for another round trip to New Zealand with its new batch of passengers on board.[2] It was the return leg of this voyage that disgorged its infected passengers into Sydney city centre. Surprisingly, this second arrival of the vessel was designated 'low risk' by NSW health authorities – it was anything but. Very soon the number of cases that resulted from these Ruby Princess infected passengers accounted for over 10% of Australia's total Covid-19 infections. The Ruby Princess had become Australia's plague ship. On April 5, the NSW police Commissioner announced that a criminal investigation was being launched into the Ruby Princess coronavirus disaster.

As the fog of financial and economic war intensified in the wake of the global stock market crash on 'Black Friday' October 10, 2008, the then Prime Minister, Kevin Rudd received some simple advice from his Treasury Secretary: 'go early, go hard, go households.'[3] It was important advice that helped Australia to weather the worst of the ensuing economic turmoil and become one of the few G 20 countries to pull through the financial crisis relatively unscathed. It was a triad of advice that would have had equal salience for those political leaders who, 12 years later, were confronting the even more daunting task of a simultaneous health, economic and geopolitical crisis.

The current Prime Minister, Scott Morrison, recognised that the coronavirus pandemic was a 'once-in-a-hundred-year event'. In order to combat the virus effectively across federal and state jurisdictions, one of his early moves was to form a cabinet of national unity comprising of the prime minister and his state and territory counterparts, – the first since 1945.[4] The national cabinet was designed to bring the full force of Australia's nine governments together in a coordinated political effort to combat the coronavirus – it was a novel form of executive federalism.

It was a smart political move as well. Though the national opposition Labour Party was not directly part of it, the newly-formed national cabinet was essentially a bi-partisan institution in that it had five Labour members sitting beside four Liberals as part of the one team. For a country whose states guard their independence with an obsessive jealousy, this was a unique experiment in federal political cooperation inspired by a collective Australian desire to defeat the demon virus. In this regard, the national cabinet's most significant contribution has been to largely eliminate the divisive rancour that has bedevilled the US federal/state response to the pandemic. With little coordination (and much distrust) between the President and many of the State's governors, US efforts at both managing the crisis and communicating coherently to the American people were severely hampered.

A surge of new infections around the world soon showed that international efforts to contain the virus were failing. On February 27, Prime Minister Morrison announced details of the government's plan for a phased approach to tackling the coronavirus threat. He detailed a series of escalating lockdown measures that would come into effect as the transmission of the virus intensified. But for now, the Prime Minister reiterated, 'Australia has acted quickly, Australia has got ahead of this at this point in time.' With just 27 recorded cases of infection and no deaths at the time he addressed the nation, there was considerable justification in Prime Minister Morrison's optimistic claim – the question was, how long would it last?

The answer came a few weeks later. By the end of the third week of March, community transmission had completely supplanted importation as the principal source of the spreading contagion. The number of infections jumped by 500% in just one week. It went above 1,000 infections for the first time, and deaths had more than doubled from three to seven. On cue, the government began the lockdown measures it had previously announced. Beginning on March 22, all 'non-essential' services were closed down including; pubs, clubs, cafes and restaurants, but excluding takeaways. Gyms, indoor sporting venues, cinemas, casinos and nightclubs were closed the next day, but schools remained open – for now. Soon the travel advice against international travel became a travel ban.

The optimism that the government's plan was working was given a considerable boost by a University of Sydney modelling exercise that showed Covid-19 peaking in mid-April and reducing virtually to zero by July. But critically, the study assumed there would be extensive testing and 90% compliance by Australians with social distancing rules. In fact, the mid-April peak that the model had suggested was surpassed, as the peak actually happened a couple of weeks earlier, towards the end of March. From mid-March to mid-April the total number of infections went from 302 to 6,416, and deaths increased from 5 to 63. But from that point onwards the number of daily reported infections began to drop off significantly.

From mid-April to the end of June the total number of infections went from 6,416 to 7,767 – an average daily increase of only 30, while deaths from Covid-19 averaged just one a day. But even this low average death rate disguised an important trend. The litmus test for measuring success or failure in combating an infectious disease like Covid-19 is the mortality rate. There had been no deaths from Covid-19 for almost a month, and only two for the whole of June. The figures were conclusive, border closures, mandatory quarantines and an extensive lockdown had worked – at least the death curve had been flattened. Understandably, the Prime Minister was buoyant when signalling an easing of lockdown, 'You can't stay under the doona (duvet) forever'.

The virus was well and truly in retreat and so lockdown restrictions were gradually relaxed between April and May. Following an unprecedented period of over six weeks spent indoors, millions of Australians emerged into the autumn sun, blinking and restive. Almost instinctively, they headed in droves to the newly re-opened beaches to celebrate the easing of the harsh restrictions. Optimism abounded that the remaining curtailments on the Aussies' famous outdoor lifestyle were soon to be lifted entirely.

With the virus virtually eliminated in large parts of the country, Australia was being held up as an international exemplar on how to confront the pandemic. The exhortation to 'go early, go hard, go households' had been followed and, seemingly, it worked again. As autumn gave way to winter across the big sky country that is Australia, just one Covid cloud remained on an otherwise equable horizon. It hung menacingly over Victoria's state capital and Australia's second largest city, Melbourne.

For weeks Australia's most populous state, New South Wales and its capital Sydney, had reported no infections. Nationally the curve had almost disappeared, it had been flatlining since the end of April right up to the end of June. But in early July things began to go awry. There was a surge in new infection cases due south of NSW in the state of Victoria. Melbourne, a city of 5 million people, had suddenly become the epicentre of a new coronavirus resurgence.

Australia had instituted strict quarantine procedures since it closed its international borders in March. All citizens and residents returning to the country had to undergo a mandatory quarantine period of 14 days in specially designated quarantine hotels situated in their place of arrival. For those flying in from abroad that meant Sydney and Melbourne, the cities with the largest international air terminals. The numbers were not insignificant, over 20,000 passengers had gone through the quarantine hotel system in Melbourne alone. But there was an important difference between how Sydney and Melbourne operated their quarantine systems. In Sydney, the police were in charge, standing guard outside the hotels to ensure there was no illegal egress by the quarantined residents. In Melbourne, private contractors were employed to guard the hotels, many of whose employees did not have the requisite training.

It wasn't long until the press began to report that 'all-night parties' were taking place in some of the quarantine hotels, with guests freely visiting each other in their rooms. There were also reports of considerable nocturnal 'socialising' between the guards and the guests, some of whom were infected with the virus. City officials were forced to investigate what they referred to delicately as 'infection-control breaches'. With health officials linking most of the city's new virus clusters to either guards or guests, a retired judge was appointed to head a public inquiry into the operation of Melbourne's quarantine programme that was the source of the rapidly escalating catastrophe.

As the number of infections continued to expand, just one month after it had re-opened, Melbourne was locked down again for a further six weeks – this time it was a stage-four lockdown which included night curfews. Neighbouring states, NSW to the north and South Australia to the west, closed their borders, effectively hemming in Victoria's population. It was the first time that the borders had been sealed since the Spanish flu epidemic in 1918. Despite these measures, the spike in infections continue with 723 new cases and 13 deaths occurring on July 30 – it was Australia's deadliest day of the pandemic.

Victoria was in a serious battle to supress the revivified contagion which had Melbourne at its epicentre. At the height of the first wave of infections in March there were 450 people in hospital with Covid-19 across Australia. A new record was set during the first week of August when 600 people were being treated in hospital for the virus – 575 of these were in Victoria. A month-long spell of no deaths from Covid was broken by the death of a Victorian man on June 24, virtually all subsequent deaths in Australia have occurred in Victoria. As had been the case globally, the vast majority of those who died were over 70, with most fatalities happening in care homes.

As the experience of Victoria illustrates, the coronavirus is unforgiving and exacts swift retribution for any lapses in the struggle against it. The graph below of the history of infection cases in Victoria is a stark reminder that this highly infectious pathogen, with grave and vastly disproportionate consequences for the elderly, cannot be taken for granted. Though Australia overall had achieved a significant victory over this virus, its raging resurgence in Victoria was an important lesson for the world that the price of Covid 'peace' was eternal vigilance.

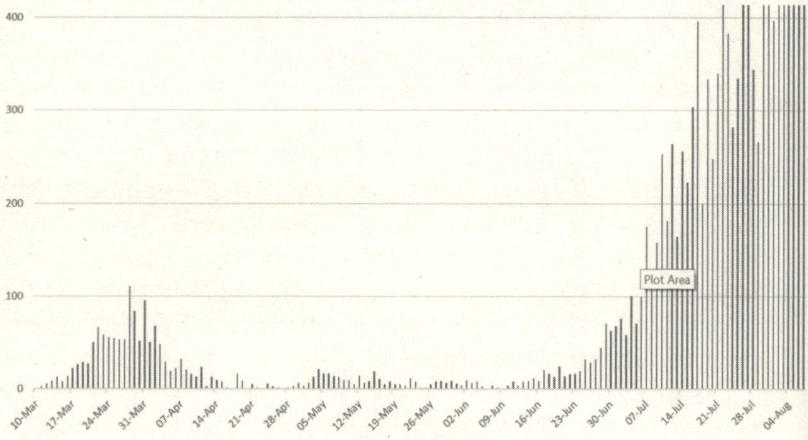

Victoria infections

Chapter 20: America First

PUBLIC DOMAIN

Vice-Premier Liu He and President Trump Sign Trade Deal in the White House, January 15, 2020

On January 13, a delegation of Chinese 'high representatives' arrived in Washington for the signing of the Phase 1 trade agreement with President Trump at the White House. The signing, on January 15, marked a truce in the 18-month trade war between the world's two superpowers in their struggle for economic supremacy. But while peace was breaking out on the geopolitical front, domestically the political contestation between the President and the Democrats was reaching a crescendo. On the same day that the historic trade agreement was being signed in the White House, around the same time at a different ceremony being held in the House of Representatives over on Capitol Hill, Speaker Nancy Pelosi was signing another set of historic documents: the articles of impeachment of the 45th President of the United States, Donald J. Trump.

The prospect of an impeachment trial of President Trump on charges of abuse of power and obstruction of Congress had been consuming Washington, the media, and the people of the United States for months. Following an anonymous complaint by a whistle-blower in August, Speaker Pelosi announced a formal House impeachment inquiry on

September 24. In the wake of the impeachments of Presidents Johnson (1868) and Clinton (1998), this would be just the third impeachment trial of a sitting President in US history. With a Republican majority in the Senate, where the trial would ultimately take place, there was little real prospect of the Democrat's impeachment gambit succeeding, but it offered an irresistible opportunity to inflict maximum reputational damage on President Trump. For the Trump administration, it was a massive distraction from the day-to-day business of government, and it remained so until February 5 when, as expected, the Senate voted to acquit the President on both counts.

Coincidentally, on January 15, two days after the Chinese trade delegation had arrived in Washington DC, a 35-year-old male resident of Washington State had also flown in from China where he had been visiting family. Though he was in good health when he landed at Seattle-Tacoma International Airport, within days he developed a dry cough and a fever and so sought medical assistance. When he informed the doctors that he had just returned from Wuhan, the CDC was alerted and following a positive test on January 20, he became America's first officially recognised case of Covid-19. In their subsequent briefings to the media, the CDC said that the risk to the American public remained low.[1]

One month later on February 24, there were 53 confirmed cases of the infection in the US. The first 14 cases confirmed in the United States included 12 travellers returning from China and two individuals who had close contact with some of those travellers. Towards the end of February, the vast majority of US infections were either associated with Wuhan or with those who had been repatriated from the Diamond Princess in Yokohama, Japan: this latter group constituted 39 of those 53 infections. Though it was far from clear at the time, this was the beginning of a public health disaster whose social, economic, and political consequences would continue to reverberate for a very long time.

But there was one group in the US during that fateful mid-January period that was intimately aware of the disastrous scale of the havoc that the virus could wreck. Among the Chinese trade delegation in the East Room of the White House in mid-January were some of the most senior members of the Chinese Communist Party. Vice-Premier Liu He, who led the delegation, is a former member of the Party's Central Committee and a current member of its Politburo. Many of those senior CCP officials standing in the room with the President and his senior advisors, with no masks and no social distancing, had just arrived from a country experiencing a raging outbreak of a highly infectious disease. Yet, there are no reports that the contagion elephant in the room was ever even mentioned, referred to and certainly not discussed by the Chinese with their American hosts. Meanwhile, the Trump administration and the whole US media was entirely consumed by Speaker Pelosi's impeachment charges against the President.

Xi Jinping later confirmed that when speaking to the Politburo 'on January 7 ... I put forward requirements for the prevention and control of the novel coronavirus pneumonia epidemic.'[2] Which is confirmation that the senior leadership of the CCP was fully aware of what was happening with the virus from very early January, at least. But from December right up to the third week in January, at Xi Jinping's insistence, the CCP kept its own people in the dark and only released partial information to the international community when circumstances gave it no choice. Xi's personal absence from the historic signing in the White House is, in retrospect, a clear indication that in mid-January, the General Secretary of the Communist Party had more pressing matters to deal with back home in China.

Though an infectious viral storm had been raging fiercely in China in the weeks immediately preceding their visit to Washington, members of the Chinese trade delegation showed no compunction about working in close proximity for days with the President and senior members of his administration in the White House. The health risks posed by this episode were obvious and considerable. Even more pertinently, there is no indication whatsoever that any of the Chinese representatives availed of the opportunity to alert members of the Trump Administration as to the serious dangers of the viral epidemic that was bringing large parts of their country to a standstill. Xi's insistence on 'omerta' regarding the epidemic in China was adhered to rigidly by his comrades in Washington.

But it remains a moot point whether a confidential word by Vice Premier Liu He to President Trump would have elicited anything other than a bombastic dismissal along the lines of, 'We'll be fine'. The reason for this is not simply due to the personality of the President. Throughout January and February, the attitude among the US political elite of all stripes, including the most senior infections disease adviser to the President, was uniformly one of general nonchalance with respect to the coronavirus and its possible consequences. In all of their publicly state views, the virus was important, but not urgent.

Fauci and Friends

CREDIT: Doug Mills/The New York Times

The diminutive Dr Fauci has President Trump's full attention at White House Briefing

If anyone could navigate their way around the political quagmire of the Washington 'swamp', it was Dr Anthony Fauci. He has been director of the National Institute of Allergy and Infectious Diseases (NIAID) for over three-and-a-half decades, a length of tenure that few administrative officials can match. During this period, he has advised six Presidents on various aspects of existing and emerging infectious diseases.

As Covid-19 made its unrelenting advance throughout the United States, Dr Fauci's avuncular bedside manner endeared him to the US public, and he quickly became a media darling. As a consequence, his pronouncements on every aspect of the pandemic became the nearest thing to scientific holy writ. Standing beside the, at times, brooding presence of the President at the increasingly regular White House media briefings, the diminutive Dr Fauci seemed to be growing in stature by the day.

By then, most of the US media no longer bothered to disguise their disdain for a President whose election they failed to foresee and could not now abide. For them, Dr Fauci was the perfect foil to President Trump who, in their eyes, was congenitally mendacious and could do no right. This was a made-for-media contest featuring the about to be octogenarian teller of scientific truth to a power-obsessed President whose election they deemed, in any case, to have had only a veneer of legitimacy. In the process, Dr Fauci morphed from being the President's most senior adviser on the infectious disease pandemic into one of the most sought-after media pundits in America. In terms of Dr Fauci's self-declared favourite 'book of philosophy', Mario Puzo's *The Godfather*, the media had made him an offer which he found impossible to refuse.[3] In a media world obsessed with 'breaking news', Dr Fauci was rarely off the airwaves or the front pages, and some of his pronouncements make interesting reading.

From an early stage in the pandemic-induced health crisis, Dr Fauci willingly shared his views with an ever-appreciative media. In an interview on January 21 with the cable news channel, Newsmax TV, speaking about the threat that the virus posed to the US, Dr Fauci said 'But this is not a major threat for the people in the United States and this is not something that the citizens of the United States right now should be worried about ... Bottom line, we don't have to worry.'[4]

It's a message he reiterated in a radio interview a few days later on Sunday, January 26. The dulcet tones of Dr Fauci's Brooklyn accent could be heard offering New York radio listeners some comforting reassurances; 'It's a very, very low risk to the United States ... It isn't something the American public needs to worry about or be frightened about. Because we have ways of preparing and screening of people coming in [from China]. And we have ways of responding - like we did with this one case in Seattle, Washington, who had traveled to China and brought back the infection.' That same day, January 26, a newspaper headline ran with the story 'Government health agency official: Coronavirus 'isn't something the American public need to worry about'.[5]

Three weeks later, on February 19 America's biggest circulation newspaper, *USA Today*, carried the headline 'Top disease official: Risk of coronavirus in USA is 'minuscule'; skip mask and wash hands'. According to the article itself, Dr Fauci's concern was with the more urgent threat posed by seasonal flu; 'Fauci doesn't want people to worry about coronavirus, the danger of which is "just minuscule." But he does want them to take precautions against the "influenza outbreak, which is having its second wave ... At the same time people are worrying about going to a Chinese restaurant. The threat is (we have) a pretty bad influenza season, particularly dangerous for our children.' None of these statements have been retracted so, their accuracy is assumed.

Two months later, in an interview with MSNBC on April 13 the host, Rev. Al Sharpton, asked Dr. Fauci when it occurred to him that the coronavirus had become a serious problem: to which Dr. Fauci replied, 'probably toward the middle to end of January'. In an illuminating follow-up question Rev. Sharpton enquired, 'and did you begin advising the administration ... that this could be a major problem at that time?' 'You bet,' came Dr Fauci's emphatic reply. This claim that Dr Fauci's serious concerns about the virus began 'toward the middle to end of January' is at odds with many of his public statements as outlined above. These show that as late as the third week of February he was telling the American public that they should be more concerned with the seasonal flu than the coronavirus.

So how do we explain this disparity? It's important because these were the opinions of the most senior infectious disease adviser to the President and his administration around which, presumably, pandemic policy responses and statements to the public were being crafted. One thing we can safely rule out is, as a professional of the highest integrity, that Dr Fauci was advising one thing to the President and saying something completely different to the American public at the same time. The most likely explanation is that Dr Fauci's late February statement to MSNBC was a retrospective 're-calibration' of the timing of his advice to the President – even Homer nods. In the absence of evidence to the contrary, it is a reasonable conclusion that right up to at least the third week in February Dr Fauci's advice to President Trump was similar to the message conveyed by the *USA Today* headline, 'Risk of coronavirus in USA is 'minuscule''.

It is important to note that the concerns of the 'data-driven' disease expert, Dr Fauci, about the flu rather than the coronavirus were solidly grounded in the facts – they were, so to speak, data-driven. The CDC's influenza figures for 2019-20 for the US were horrendous: 39-56 million infections; 18-26 million medical visits; 410-740,000 hospitalisations and between 24,000 and 62,000 deaths.[6] Even for a population of 330 million these are not trifling numbers, especially considering that they occurred within a relatively short four-month period. However, as shocking as these numbers were, they were nothing out of the ordinary as flu seasons go – the previous year 95,000 people had died, according to the CDC.

But in a very real sense, the flu is different. At one time or another we've all had it and recovered so, psychologically, it is not as frightening. The flu is also seasonal and therefore predictable. We know roughly when it will arrive every year and, no matter how bad it gets in terms of morbidity or mortality, we know it will go away. Psychologically, the coronavirus is entirely different. Not only did it possess the 'shock of the new', but our considerable ignorance regarding the disease fed directly into one of our primeval response mechanisms – fear of the unknown. Flu has a risk that we can quantify and we are therefore more comfortable with it, but Covid-19 is surrounded by uncertainties that engender visceral fears, some of which are likely to prove unfounded. Fundamentally, it is the difference between risk and uncertainty: risk can be measured and therefore managed, but uncertainty is, by definition, unmeasurable and unmanageable.

A week after the *USA Today* article was published in the third week of February, at a coronavirus White House press briefing on February 26 there was confirmation that what Dr Fauci had been saying in public was also what he was advising the President in private. 'I spoke with Dr. Fauci on this, and I was really amazed, and I think most people are amazed to hear it: The flu, in our country, kills from 25,000 people to 69,000 people a year', the President informed the press. Of course, in his inimitable style President Trump immediately went on to gild the lily. In his comments on the then recorded 15 cases of coronavirus, he made the fatuous prediction that 'the 15 within a couple of days is going to be down to close to zero, that's a pretty good job we've done.' His anticipatory boast did not elicit a spontaneous round of applause from the assembled White House media. But they loved it all the same: President Trump had fashioned yet another stick with which they could beat him with, later.

But President Trump and Dr Fauci weren't the only members of the US elite who were downplaying the threat from the virus during January and February. The House Speaker, Nancy Pelosi, was doing likewise in her San Francisco constituency where fear of the virus had caused people to stop eating in Chinese restaurants and from visiting the city's famous Chinatown district for fear of being exposed to the virus. By some estimates, business in San Francisco's thriving Chinatown had dropped by up to 50%. Ms Pelosi's set it as her mission to assist her constituents by helping to boost their businesses and get people back visiting Chinatown again.

NBC's report on Speaker Pelosi's Chinatown walkabout had her saying 'That's what we're trying to do today is to say everything is fine here, come because precautions have been taken. The city is on top of the situation.' The next day, February 25, ABC's broadcast of the Speaker's

Chinatown visit carried the same message: come to Chinatown it's safe to visit, adding "I trust Dr. Fauci at the National Institutes of Health, and he seems to have confidence in what we are doing.'

At the time, California had a total of 21 cases of Covid-19 either in hospital or in quarantine. As a result of these numbers, other local politicians did not share Speaker Pelosi's insouciance about the virus. On February 25, the same day as Ms Pelosi's message that everything was hunky-dory in Chinatown was aired on ABC, the Democrat Mayor of San Francisco declared a state of emergency in the city because of coronavirus fears. In a further surprising development, later autopsy reports showed that two deaths caused by the virus had occurred much earlier than had previously been thought. The two coronavirus victims had died on February 6 and 17, respectively, in Santa Clara County, California - they were the first recorded deaths from Covid-19 in America.[7]

In an excellent *New York Times*, article published on March 17, Rem Rieder rehearses the principal statements President Trump had made about the coronavirus up to that point. It began; 'This is a pandemic," President Donald Trump said at a March 17 press conference. "I felt it was a pandemic long before it was called a pandemic.'

'Jan. 22: "We have it totally under control. It's one person coming in from China. We have it under control. It's going to be just fine." — Trump in a CNBC interview.

Jan. 30: "We think we have it very well under control. We have very little problem in this country at this moment — five — and those people are all recuperating successfully. But we're working very closely with China and other countries, and we think it's going to have a very good ending for us ... that I can assure you." — Trump in a speech in Michigan.

Feb. 10: "Now, the virus that we're talking about having to do — you know, a lot of people think that goes away in April with the heat — as the heat comes in. Typically, that will go away in April. We're in great shape though. We have 12 cases — 11 cases, and many of them are in good shape now." — Trump at the White House.

Feb. 14: "There's a theory that, in April, when it gets warm — historically, that has been able to kill the virus. So we don't know yet; we're not sure yet. But that's around the corner." — Trump in speaking to National Border Patrol Council members.

Feb. 23: "We have it very much under control in this country." — Trump in speaking to reporters.

Feb. 24: "The Coronavirus is very much under control in the USA. We are in contact with everyone and all relevant countries. CDC & World Health have been working hard and very smart. Stock Market starting to look very good to me!" — Trump in a tweet.

Feb. 26: "So we're at the low level. As they get better, we take them off the list, so that we're going to be pretty soon at only five people. And we could be at just one or two people over the next short period of time. So we've had very good luck." — Trump at a White House briefing.

Feb. 26: "And again, when you have 15 people, and the 15 within a couple of days is going to be down to close to zero, that's a pretty good job we've done." — Trump at a press conference.'

On the predictive aspects of some of these pronouncements, clearly the President was getting carried away by a sense of his own omniscience. More generally, for the period January to late February, the tenor of the above statements is not fundamentally at odds with similar statements I quoted earlier which were made around the same time by Speaker Pelosi and Dr Fauci - making allowances for the President's incomparable capacity to mangle English syntax. As the man with the ultimate political responsibility, however, I'm not trying to minimise President Trump's liability for the ensuing pandemic failures. What I am arguing is that, at this early stage, despite the overwhelming evidence before them, the US political elite and many in the senior administrative ranks did not appreciated the scale of the existential threat they were facing - and neither did the American public. As the headline in *The Washing Post* article quoted above states: 'If Trump lied, so did Dr Fauci' - and for good measure one could add; and so did Speaker Pelosi.

Chapter 21: Homeland Insecurity

For more than a century and a half, all of America's wars were fought 'over there'. For Americans, both people and politicians, the sanctity of an inviolable homeland was an article of faith that had become deeply ingrained in their psychic. In a sense, it had become the flip side of the "Manifest Destiny" coin. That may explain why attacks such as Perl Harbour and 9/11 were not just surprises, they were visceral shocks that traumatised American's sense of collective security in a way that was disproportionate to the loss of lives or material damage involved. For most Americans, both episodes qualify, in President Roosevelt's words, as dates 'that will live in infamy.' It also helps to explain the overwhelming US responses that both of these attacks elicited: which had more than a hint of Old Testament retribution about them. But these were rare events; exceptions that proved the rule. Once they were over and done with, the American public was more than happy to slip back into the comfort zone of thinking of the USA as a safe and impenetrable fortress.

When Americans think of security, they tend to have a particular definition in mind. The concept of 'Fortress America' is predicated upon the guarantees it offers against invasions or attacks from external enemies. The security issue is deeply ingrained in American culture. Every citizen is still obliged to swear an oath to defend the country 'against all enemies, foreign and domestic'. Their patriotism is not limited to having a flag in the front porch. Having a family member volunteer to join the US armed services remains a matter of intense pride, and similar, in some respects, to an Irish Catholic family in previous generations having a son of the priesthood: an occasion to be celebrated by photographs on proud display throughout the house. There is little political resistance to enormous amounts of tax-payers money being spent on defence budgets. And wars and rumours of wars are a regular and integral part of the political and media discourse. Yet in all this, security from natural disasters, especially epidemics and pandemics, hardly gets a look in.

The Spanish Flu, for instance, was one of the deadliest natural disasters in human history. It was a global pandemic that killed up to 100 million people at a time when the world's population stood at 2 billion. It was the 20th century's greatest disaster. In the United States alone, about 670,000 people died from the disease which lowered Americans' life expectancy by more than a decade. In fact, more US soldiers died from influenza than were killed in battle in 1918. Yet, this biblical-scale pandemic exists today largely as a footnote to the history of the First World War. Despite being traumatised by this overwhelming public health catastrophe, one hundred years later, American memories of it have all but faded. So how do we account for this collective amnesia?

It may be explained, at least in part, by the concept of the 'availability heuristic' developed by the psychologist Daniel Kahneman who argues against the assumption of human rationality.[1] This 'heuristics and biases' argument is based on the notion that if we can recall something it is important, while something we have difficulty recalling we assume to be unimportant.[2] Wars which are, sadly, a relatively common occurrence we can recall easily, but since pandemics are relatively uncommon, we can have some difficulty remembering them. This may be a significant part of the reason why Americans (and the rest of us) have not traditionally considered the visceral threat to their security that the silent invasions of viruses entail. The 2020 coronavirus pandemic is likely to change all that, and not just for Americans. To put it in terms that their collective memory would appreciate; for only a second time since the Civil War, the homeland had again become a war zone.

The Administrative State

The word 'global' has become a buzzword during the last few decades, but rarely has its true meaning been confirmed so rigorously as with Covid-19. The virus which began in Wuhan at the end of 2019 had, by mid-2020, become a truly global event: every single country in the world had been infected by it. Its continental sweep has been breath-taking. By early March, the number of coronavirus-related deaths in Europe surpassed that of Asia. Six weeks later (mid-April) there was a surge of virus fatalities in the United States which soon afflicted every state in the union. The toll in human lives continued to escalate such that by mid-August the number of Covid deaths was over 160,000. The situation continued to deteriorate with December turning out to have the highest number of deaths in one month since the start of the pandemic – by then the death toll had risen to over 300,000.

Yet on paper the United States was exceedingly well prepared for any war against an invisible enemy like Covid-19. Partly funded by the Gates Foundation, the *Global Health Security Index* (GHSI)[3] is a detailed assessment of the preparedness of 195 countries to tackle an infectious disease pandemic (see chapter 18). Published in October 2019, just prior to the virus outbreak in Wuhan, the GHSI ranked the US as number one in the world, scoring 100 (average 16.9) in the category 'Emergency preparedness and response planning'.[4] It is important to remember, this study was an independent evaluation by international experts of the capabilities of the administrative apparatus of the United States to fight a pandemic, not of its political capabilities. On this basis, as we've seen, the US passed with flying colours. According to the GHSI, the US health Leviathan was itself in rude good health.

As indicated earlier, when the virus was establishing itself in the US during January and February, the political and health elites seem to have been overtaken by a strange impassivity, even nonchalance, with respect to the deleterious consequences of the virus for the nation's health. During this early phase, President Trump, Speaker Pelosi, and even Dr Fauci were actively downplaying the threat of the virus. But, in the subsequent three-cornered fight between the Democrats, the media, and the White House, the political responsibility for the pandemic debacle was quickly placed squarely and solely on the shoulders of the President.

This was an outcome not in the least bit helped by the President's own gratuitous exaggerations, championing of off-beat cures, and a recurring tendency to mangle his syntax during explanations of complex issues. These performances were a gift to his many enemies, both across the political aisle and in the media, which they gratefully accepted and repaid with interest. The polls were soon reflecting the fact that the public was also of the view that unlike his handling of the economy, the President's pandemic performance was being rated as dismal. By August, President Trump was trailing his Democratic presidential opponent, former Vice President Joe Biden, by as much as 10 points in some national polls. And this was an opponent some of whose own foot-in-mouth media performances were unsettling for many.

But whether you place all, part, or none of the blame for the catastrophically inept US response to the Covid-19 pandemic on President Trump is ultimately a political question to which there was a comprehensive electoral response on November 3. Though he is highly unlikely to be thanked for it, there is one bequest that President Trump had gifted the incoming Democratic administration, and from which it is likely to benefit enormously – vaccines. But that said, the new Biden administration will face similar difficulties with respect to the abysmal failings of the administrative state in its handling of the country's unprecedented health crisis. Because these failings may well become manifest again when it comes to delivering a mass vaccination programme, it is worth looking at how they arose.

The Chinese soldier-philosopher, Sun Tzu had many salient observations on strategic warfare. Arguably, one of his most pertinent and insightful was that 'the supreme art of war is to subdue the enemy without fighting'. In the case of combating a highly infectious virus, this initially involves surveillance and detection in order to prevent community spread – in practical terms, it means extensive testing and contact tracing. As if to confirm Field Marshal von Moltke's aphorism that no battle plan survives contact with the enemy, whatever plans the US health bureaucracy had devised to deal with a pandemic, it more or less disintegrated on first contact with Covid-19.

Size Does Not Matter

Contrary to some popular beliefs about other aspects of life, in the case of the virus, size does not matter, but scale does. Broadly speaking, Covid-19 attacks people in two phases. During the first phase, the virus manages to slip past the body's natural defences and silently secure a foothold. There is then a critical four to six-day period when there are no outward signs that someone has become infected. Following that, the immune system seems to rally and attempts to expel the invading pathogens. The resultant civil war causes all sorts of headaches, sniffles, sneezes, and an overwhelming feeling of tiredness, but for the vast majority of people it is not fatal. Ultimately, their immune systems are able to cope.

For those with compromised immune systems, however, especially the elderly, a weakened defence system means that victory invariably goes to the virus during this important first-phase battle. It then enters a second and potentially very serious phase. It is at this point that Covid-19 performs its unique and devastating trick: it replicates so fast and on such a scale that it can completely overwhelm the immune system. This is largely what gives the virus its uncommon lethality. As we shall see, the mechanism through which one of the smallest organisms on the planet invades and compromises an individual's immune defences is not vastly different from how the virus attacks and devastates countries.

Disease dynamics are all about numbers. Though there are differences from country to country in how the number of infection cases and deaths are recorded, they still offer the best metric available for making international comparisons. The US figures for both infections and deaths from Covid-19 are exceptional; for all the wrong reasons. About 4.25% of the world's population lives in the US yet, by mid-August, the country accounted for almost 25% of the global figures for both infections and deaths from the virus. How do we account for this enormous disparity and the vastly disproportionate consequences, especially the high mortality, that the virus has inflicted on people living in the United States?

Some of the standard reasons presented in the media for these gargantuan failures to protect the American people are the following; President Trump got rid of epidemic expertise[5]; a chronically underfunded health service was unable to respond; endemic racism made African-Americans especially vulnerable; low-paid employees had little choice but to remain working to survive financially. Some of these have an undoubted salience and some, frankly, have more than a whiff of partisan politics about them. But the biggest problem with these well-rehearsed arguments for the failures of the US response is that they fail to address the Covid-19 elephant in the care home.

In the NIAID, with its budget of almost $6 billion, the US has the largest biomedical research organisation in the world. It is run by Dr Fauci who, according to its website 'oversees an extensive research portfolio of basic and applied research to prevent, diagnose, and treat established infectious diseases.'[6] With a budget of almost $12 billion, the even better endowed Atlanta-based Centre for Disease Control and Prevention (CDC) has a global reputation as a public health agency that is second to none. Its pronouncements and guidance on matters of public health are listened to and emulated across the world, as a matter of course. With this level of expert health and disease firepower, it is no wonder that the writers of the October 2019 GHSI report on national preparedness for epidemics and pandemics placed the United States number 1 out of 195 countries. Yet, just months after this glowing report on America's preparedness for a pandemic, when Covid-19 struck in January 2020, the US administrative health system failed utterly to live up to its top billing.

Anatomy of a Disaster

The performance of the US federal government compares very unfavourably with those countries that had to face the devastation of the pandemic much earlier, especially in Asia. There were glaring systemic failures within the federal administrative state structures that included, but are not limited to: inadequate preparation and planning; poor leadership and coordination; an inexplicable sluggishness; and regulatory failures at critical junctures. Like other Western countries, one of the most consequential failures was testing.

At its first press briefing on the virus held by the CDC on January 17, Nancy Messonnier insisted, 'This is a serious situation ... we know it's crucial to be proactive and prepared.' Ms Messonnier went on to confirm that, 'We're working on a specific diagnostic test to detect this virus and we'll be distributing this test to state health departments.' As the diagnostic test was an important tool in the fight against the virus, when questioned by journalists as to its likely availability, she confirmed; 'We expect to have that imminently.[7]

One of the most commonly used adjectives throughout these press briefings by the CDC was the word 'proactive'. It is a standard feature of bureaucratese, calculated to give the impression that immediate purposeful action is underway when, in reality, little of real consequence may actually be happening. But 'proactive' has a soothingly reassuring sound to it and, for inertia-prone bureaucracies, it helps buy time. Thus, in its press release of January 24, the organisation announced the important news that the 'CDC has been proactively preparing for the introduction of 2019-nCoV in the U.S. for weeks ... [and] has developed a diagnostic test to detect this virus in clinical specimens.'[8]

Ed Jong of *The Atlantic* did not mince his words in his description of what actually happened: 'The CDC developed and distributed its own diagnostic tests in late January. These proved useless because of a faulty chemical component. Tests were in such short supply, and the criteria for getting them were so laughably stringent, that by the end of February, tens of thousands of Americans had likely been infected but only hundreds had been tested ... It's hard to overstate how thoroughly the testing debacle incapacitated the U.S. People with debilitating symptoms couldn't find out what was wrong with them. Health officials couldn't cut off chains of transmission by identifying people who were sick and asking them to isolate themselves.'[9]

This testing fiasco was a calamitous failure at the critical early stage of the pandemic. Such was its enfeebling effect that the US never really regained the initiative in its protracted pandemic struggle – the viral horse had bolted and it was anyone's guess where it would end up. But the missteps of the federal health system in this regard went even deeper. As

Jong also points out, 'Diagnostic tests are easy to make, so the U.S. failing to create one seemed inconceivable. Worse, it had no Plan B. Private labs were strangled by FDA bureaucracy.'[10] So, while one arm of the administrative state failed to deliver on its publicly stated promises, another arm actively inhibited an alternative from being deployed to help solve the crisis.

The Care Home Catastrophe

From the experience of those other countries which were forced to contend with the virus earlier, it was apparent that the elderly constituted by far the most vulnerable group in society. There was conclusive evidence from as early as January in China that the occupants of care homes and elderly nursing institutions were especially susceptible to the Covid-19. Yet, in the US no effective action was taken to avert a care home catastrophe. By June, the gruesome statistics confirmed the scale of the calamity that had occurred and was still occurring in US care homes.

Residents of nursing homes account for approximately 1% of the US population. Yet by June, out of the total of around 120,000 of the Covid deaths that had happened up to then, 50,000 of them were in facilities for the elderly – a harrowing 43% of all virus fatalities. Inevitably, in a Presidential election year, a grim political blame game ensued from which it is extremely difficult to separate partisan claims from contributary causes; and almost impossible, for now, to establish responsibility or assign culpability. But the contours of the most salient contributory factors can be identified.

The decision by some state Governors to move elderly recovering Covid patients out of hospitals and into nursing homes, though taken for the best of reasons – to free up hospital beds for more acute cases – but it was a significant contributory factor. However, this alone cannot account for the overall high rates of fatalities in care homes across the nation. This is because it was only carried out in a minority of states, and by governors who happened, in the main, to be Democrats – hence it got lots of partisan political airtime.

In addition to complaints of inadequate supplies of PPE for care home staff, another serious issue emerged relating to unacceptable time lags in the receipt of test results carried out on staff and residents. A survey conducted by the American Health Care Association at the end of June found that its members were still experiencing troubling delays in getting test results returned. In the context of the criticality of test results for both staff and residents in care homes, these delays were significant: 63% of care homes experienced lag times of between two and four days, and almost a quarter had to wait five days or more to receive their test results. In a work environment that, by definition, involved regular daily close personal contacts between staff and residents, an inability to identify who were the positive carriers of the virus for days at a time was a glaring hole in the system – one that was tailor-made for the coronavirus to exploit.

The Coronavirus Aid, Relief, and Economic Security (CARES) Act was passed by a massive bipartisan majority in Congress and became law at the end of March. Its primary objective was to keep workers paid and employed during the period of the coronavirus emergency. At $2.4 trillion it was the largest rescue package in US history – almost 3 times the size of the 2009 financial crisis stimulus package.

The Act contained a number of health-related provisions, including paid sick leave and insurance coverage for coronavirus testing. It also made substantial funds available to hospitals and other healthcare facilities to help offset the financial burdens of the pandemic. Long-term care workers are predominantly female and constitute some of the lowest paid workers in America. Because of the personal nature of their work in a congregate indoor environment with a highly transmissible disease, they were particularly exposed to Covid-19 infections.

Astonishingly, through a complicated system of exemptions and exclusions care homes workers were largely excluded from the provisions of the Act. Under these rules, health care providers, 'including employees of nursing and retirement facilities, may be excluded from paid sick leave.' [11] The law also provided for substantial federal funding for hospitals and other care facilities to purchase PPE, but it did not allocate any of these funds to long-term care facilities. In addition, the care and nursing home sector is one that is most reliant on migrant, often illegal, labour. Though these employees had paid their taxes using an individual taxpayer identification number (ITIN), they were excluded from getting the stimulus payment because it only applied to those with a Social Security number.

This is particularly strange given that so many of the political and other key players – Trump, Biden, Fauci, McConnell and Pelosi – are themselves of advanced years. So, what lies at the root of this failure to offer financial protection to this exposed, low-paid group of workers looking after the highly vulnerable elderly? A simple but unpalatable explanation may be that a wealthy, or at least, financially very secure elite, was afflicted by an endemic form of social purblindness.

Since March, long-term care facilities had implemented a range of strict protocols, not only to prevent the virus from entering facilities, but also to prevent it spreading once it got inside. Some of these policies included universal testing for residents and staff, tight visitor restrictions, and the isolation of positive-testing residents. Yet, in spite of these measures, care homes continued to see a rise in cases.'[12] The asymptomatic spread of the virus from staff to residents was the most likely explanation for the continuing high prevalence of the disease in care homes. Because of this, most experts believed that routine, repeat testing of staff was the key to controlling Covid-19 in these facilities.

David Grabowski is Prof. of Health Care Policy at Harvard Medical School and a specialist in long-term care for the elderly. Speaking to a House Oversight Committee in June he said, 'rather than prioritizing the safety of the 1.3 million individuals who live in nursing homes and the staff that care for them, we failed to invest in testing, PPE and the workforce.' His reasoning for the ongoing health crisis in elderly care homes was simple, straightforward and difficult to fault: 'The secret weapon behind COVID is that is spreads in the absence of any symptoms ...If COVID is in a community where staff live, it is soon to be in the facility where they work', he explained to the lawmakers. He also put the politicians present on notice that, 'Until we get rapid and accurate testing for all staff and residents, we won't be able to contain COVID'.[13]

In any subsequent investigation of this particular issue, people need to remind themselves that the death certificates of all those who died in care homes did not specify whether the deceased were Republican, Democrat or Independent – they were simply vulnerable elderly US citizens. Nationally, almost 700 care home staff have also died from Covid. Working for close to the minimum wage, risking their health and their lives, care home workers are the forgotten heroes of this tragedy. When all the political bluster and self-serving bureaucratic spin has dissipated, it is hard to escape the sad conclusion that both the staff and residents of US care homes have ended up being mere collateral damage in the coronavirus wars.

Part 3

Cost and Consequences

Chapter 22: The Care Home Calamity

Chinese Whispers

For decades the Chinese Communist Party has manipulated all kinds of statistics for political purposes. From the beginning, the figures coming out of China for both coronavirus infections and deaths lacked basic credibility. For that reason, official figures such as those for early March 2020, which claimed just 80,000 cases of infection and 2,912 deaths for a population of 1.4 billion were widely disbelieved. As the virus ravaged country after country around the world, the scepticism of international governments and other observers deepened as they witnessed the devastating pandemic tallies that were being racked up in their own countries. For months, US intelligence agencies had been briefing President Trump that China had vastly understated the spread of the coronavirus and the damage the pandemic had caused.[1]

In response to widespread international incredulity about these low numbers, the Communist Party did an amazing about turn by revising upwards the number of deaths that had occurred at the epicentre of the outbreak, Wuhan city. The volte face was delivered by an anonymous official in mid-April, and a report of which was carried by China's national news agency, *Xinhua*. The statement announcing the revised figures declared that, 'under the strong leadership of the Party Central Committee and the State Council ... it insists on seeking truth from facts and actively making corrections.' Among the principal reasons the statement gave for making the correction to the Wuhan death figures was 'the credibility of the government'.[2]

Following a long-winded explanation, the official figure for the number of Wuhan dead was increased from 2,579 to 3,869. Mathematically precise to one decimal point, the revised number of Wuhan dead was exactly 50% higher than the previous one (try it: multiply 2,579 by 1.5). This statistical sleight of hand was little more than a belated effort to save the CCP's blushes in the light of continuing international disbelief about China's Covid numbers. It was the kind of statistical sleight-of-hand perfectly described by the Grand Poobah in Gilbert and Sullivan's comic opera, *The Mikado*, as one that merely provided, 'corroborative detail, intended to give artistic verisimilitude to an otherwise bald and unconvincing narrative.'[3]

But the statistical saga of Chinese Covid-19 infections didn't end there. In April, a seroepidemiological survey carried out by the Chinese CDC to check for the presence of Covid-19 antibodies in the Wuhan population came up with some astonishing results. This retrospective analysis checked how many people had actually succumbed to the virus at the height of the epidemic in the city. It concluded that 4.43% of the city's inhabitants had been infected – that is almost half a million people.[4] This was ten times the official figure of 50,354 infected Wuhan residents that the Wuhan Municipal Health Commission was still claiming on its website in the very same week that the CDC report was published.[5] Though the CDC analysis had been carried out in April, the report was not published until eight months later, in December.

Following ten months of a rampaging virus, the massive recorded infections of other countries made the low Chinese official numbers lack any credibility. Was the release of this CDC report another belated attempt by the CCP to provide some further corroborative detail to take the bald look off an official statistical narrative that had become utterly discredited?

Uncounted – They Don't Count

Chinese statistics apart, there have been inherent difficulties with virtually all coronavirus numbers from the outset of the pandemic. This has given rise to a phenomenon known as infodemic: a term defined as an excessive amount of information about a problem that is typically unreliable, spreads rapidly, and makes a solution more difficult to achieve. Classically, for instance, official Covid-19 data-sets have, for instance, greatly understated or entirely omitted asymptomatic and mild cases of the infection. These and other coronavirus data discrepancies have, in many cases, compromised statistical modelling and skewed the results.

If the important analytical process that leads from data, to information, to knowledge, starts with data that underreports the true pandemic picture then policy responses will be, to put it mildly, less than optimal. In such circumstances, mantras such as 'evidence-based' and 'data-driven' end up being mere catchphrases. As we have seen, time and again during the pandemic, once a policy prescription has been adopted, the administrative state bureaucracy finds it almost impossible to change course, even when the underlying evidence for that policy turns out to be flawed.

Nevertheless, in the fog of pandemic war we have to accept that faulty, inaccurate, even erroneous data are an inevitable, if unfortunate, part of the mix. But what is indefensible, is not having any data at all. Astonishingly, this is the situation that many governments found themselves in when it came to dealing with the single most vulnerable group to be exposed to the onslaught of Covid-19 – the elderly residents of various types of institutional care homes.[6]

These elderly people are almost invisible in modern societies in any case, but during the pandemic they were struck down in disproportionate numbers by the silent Covid killer. This grim reality was shrouded in statistical silence at a critically early state of the pandemic. In many countries, the attention of the relevant authorities was only drawn to the unfolding care home calamity by media reports. These were often led by local newspapers carrying distressing reports of individual facilities being completely overwhelmed by the rapidity and scale of the death toll.

By mid-year some of the hardest-hit European countries such as Italy, Spain and France which accounted for up to one-third of global Covid infections were not testing the elderly residents of care homes as a matter of routine. Bergamo in Italy was the epicentre of that country's Covid-19 contagion. But, during one week in early March, 400 people died from the disease, yet only 91 had tested positive for the virus. Even countries as far apart as Slovenia and New Zealand, which were relatively successful in containing the spread of the virus more generally, failed their care homes. Despite having low levels of Covid fatalities, the vast bulk of those who died were in care homes, 81% and 72% respectively.

A retrospective hospital study showed that the virus had been active in France from as early as December 2019. But the event that was instrumental in spreading the disease throughout the country was a meeting in mid-February of 2,500 members of an evangelical megachurch in eastern France: about half of those who attended the meeting became infected. As elsewhere, the disease spread rapidly, and by March 12, President Macron had imposed a lockdown. Yet, it was not until several weeks later when French care home statistics were first published that the sombre reality of what had been happening in these institutions was revealed. Like virtually all other countries, deaths from Covid-19 in France's care homes were staggeringly large.

Less than two months into the French lockdown, 9,471 residents of these facilities had been swept away by the disease. These deaths represented the single largest cohort of Covid deaths and accounted for almost two-fifths of all Covid deaths in France at that stage. The same grim picture was repeated across most other European countries where over one third of all official deaths were recorded in care home facilities. Belgium was the worst case: over half of all its deaths happened in care homes.[7]

In the UK, there was an almost complete focus on the NHS from the outset – which meant that the rapidly escalating crisis in care homes was virtually ignored. This was despite the fact that the rudimentary figures that were becoming available from countries which were a little further along the coronavirus path such as Italy, Spain and France, were indicating that up to half of all deaths from the coronavirus were happening in residential homes for the elderly. The dire situation in UK care homes was made immeasurably worse by the decision to free-up hospital beds by transferring elderly patients into care homes without being tested in advance. As a result, this influx of both symptomatic and asymptomatic elderly people was a significant factor in spreading the disease throughout the care home network.

By the end of April, the WHO had also woken up to the 'the deeply concerning picture that has been emerging of COVID-19 in long-term care facilities in the European Region and globally in recent weeks.'[8] The WHO's assessment of the situation in care homes was based on estimates, and despite the ongoing lack of detailed statistics, its disturbing conclusion was that 'up to half of those who have died from COVID-19 were resident in long-term care facilities.' The WHO report concluded: 'This is an unimaginable human tragedy.'[9]

From what had happened already in China, and then in Italy, it was widely known that elderly people with existing health issues were especially exposed to the virus. But even without formal statistics which, by definition, only become available after the fact, there were alarming and clear warning signs from an early stage in Europe and elsewhere. On March 23, when military personnel were sent into care homes in Madrid to disinfect them, they found that many had been virtually abandoned with dozens of elderly residents dead in their beds: their cries went unheeded, and they died alone. The scandal only became known through media reports, as Spain had not even included deaths in care home facilities in its official statistics.[10] For these people, little seemed to have changed in almost seven centuries when, during the mid-14th century

Black Death, Boccaccio recorded that 'many there were who departed this life without witness.'[11]

The official count for the number of deaths in UK care homes up to May stood at 8,314. However, researchers from the London School of Economics found that this was a very significant underestimation of the real level of care home mortalities from Covid-19. This was evident in the failure to explain the 'excess mortalities' in these institutions in 2020, when compared with the same period in previous years. A further problem was that the official figure did not include the deaths of care home residents from Covid-19 who died in hospitals. When all these factors were taken into account, the care home death count from the virus was in excess of 22,000, more than double that of the official figure.

This high mortality rate among care home residents arose from a number of factors. Inadequate staff training, shortages of PPE, absence of isolation facilities, close quarter living conditions, and completely inadequate testing of both staff and residents. All of which was compounded immeasurably by care homes being required to take in Covid-19 patients who were regularly being discharged from hospitals. By mid-June the virus had killed 5.3% of the total number of care home residents in the UK. In Spain, the equivalent number was even higher at 6.1%.

In complete contrast, the percentage of care home residents who died of the virus in Germany was just 0.4%: an outcome that was 13 times better than that of the UK.[12] One of the most significant explanations for this staggering difference is that, unlike the UK, elderly patients being discharged from hospitals in Germany were not admitted to care homes unless they tested negative for Covid-19. If they tested positive, they were required to quarantine in designated centres or repurposed hotels for 14 days. Care homes across Europe not only ran out of various types of equipment and materials that would have protected both staff and residents from the virus. In a macabre indication of Europe's structural failure towards its elderly citizens, the *Associated Press* reported that some facilities had even begun to run out of body bags.

A Global Trend

The sad truth is that the inordinately high rates of the deaths from Covid-19 that had occurred among residents of long-term care institutions was a worldwide phenomenon. In the United States, the virus had also proved particularly deadly for long-term care residents in assisted living facilities. The first major outbreak of Covid-19 in the US was in a Washington State care home that had been engulfed by the coronavirus during the second half of February. The deadly outbreak caused 129 infections among residents, staff and visitors of whom up to 40 died from the disease. The international pattern quickly established itself in the US as American care homes also bore the brunt of the pandemic fatalities.

As with many other countries, the available US figures for this category are incomplete since only 33 states report deaths in nursing home settings. Almost unnoticed, because of the dearth of figures, these care facilities for the elderly became coronavirus incubators. Soon the virus was able to infect a large proportion of more than a million residents of US care homes. In the absence of comprehensive official data, it has been estimated that at least one in five of the 15,000 US residential care facilities had become infected by the virus at an early stage. By August, the available statistics revealed that while residents of these care homes accounted for just 8% of total national coronavirus cases, they constituted 45% of all Covid-19 deaths.

As these care facilities were struggling to cope, on March 25, Governor Cuomo of New York issued an executive order forbidding nursing homes from refusing admission to elderly patients who were being discharged from hospitals, 'solely based on a confirmed or suspected diagnosis of COVID-19.' The purpose of the order was to free up hospital beds for an expected surge in Covid-19 cases. In the event this surge never materialised but the impact of Governor Cuomo's decision was soon felt in the care homes of New York State. The New York Health Department refused to release the numbers involved, but the *Associated Press* carried out its own survey and concluded that up to 4,500 Covid-19 patients were discharged from hospitals directly into nursing and care homes as a result Governor Cuomo's order.[13]

Given the lack of equipment, appropriately trained staff, and little or no isolation capacity in many of these facilities, Cuomo's order was a recipe for disaster. To make matters worse, the Governor's order barred the care homes from testing the patients to check whether or not they were contagious. New York was the only state in the Union to prohibit such testing. In the weeks that followed, the disease spread rapidly through New York State's care and nursing homes where out of a population of 100,000 residents more than 6,000 people died. In the meantime, Governor Cuomo received an Emmy award for his media appearances during the pandemic.

For the remainder of the year the taint of the deaths of so many of New York's care home residents remained with Governor Cuomo. The belief that his policies had contributed directly to the deaths of many of these elderly New Yorkers persisted. Then in January 2021, there was a bombshell. His own Attorney General, a Democrat, Letitia James, released a 76-page report accusing Governor Cuomo of deliberately under-counting the numbers of deaths in state nursing homes by as much as 50%, in order to minimise his own culpability. The real figure for the numbers of New York care home deaths was up to 15,000. A media darling in November, Gov Cuomo now faced calls for his resignation and the prospect of a Department of Justice investigation and a possible criminal prosecution.

The good news, if it can be called that, is that deaths in these facilities peaked during the early stages of the pandemic in April and May, with June and July seeing a decrease in both infections and deaths. This relative improvement is likely to have resulted from more vigilance among the staff, visitor restrictions and more comprehensive and effective testing regimes for both staff and residents. The improvements resulting from these measures were also reflected across the United States where the number of coronavirus infections in care homes had accounted for 1 in 5 of all cases. By August, that figure which by August had dropped to 1 in 10. But then, ominously, during that same month, there was a surge of cases and mortalities in care homes and nursing homes as some states became coronavirus hotspots again. The care home situation simply reflected a revival of widespread community transmission with almost a 60% increase in care home cases mirroring the same trend in the wider community across the country.

In some Canadian provinces, the military were called in to assist with manning levels in care homes because some had simply become overwhelmed. The available official statistics suggest that up to 80% of all the coronavirus-related deaths in Canada were linked to long-term care homes and residences for the elderly.[14] By July, out of a total of 8,700 Covid deaths 7,050 were among the residents and staff of Canada's care homes. Prime Minister Trudeau accepted that Canada had failed its elderly: 'We shouldn't have soldiers taking care of seniors', he said, 'In the weeks and months to come, we will all have to ask tough questions about how it came to this.'

In a major study of the available international evidence published by the London School of Economics, the researchers' first key finding was,

'Official data on the numbers of deaths among care home residents linked to COVID-19 is not available in many countries but an increasing number of countries are publishing data.' The analysis went on to conclude that 'on average the share of all COVID-19 deaths that were care home residents is 47% (based on 26 countries).'[15]

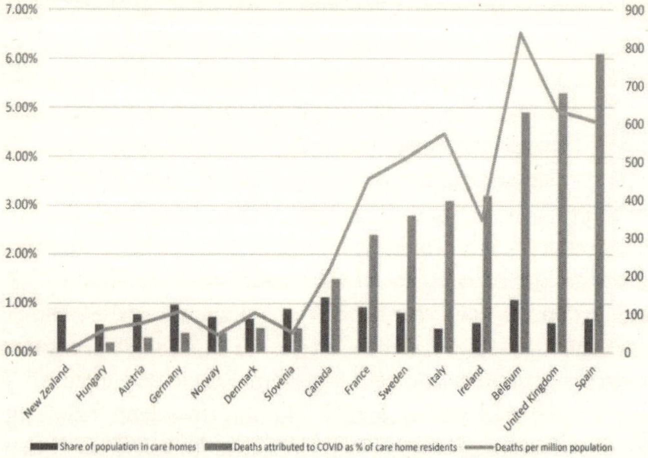

SOURCE: ltccovid.org

The first bar along this graph shows the percentage of the total population living in care homes. The second bar shows the percentage of care home residents who died from Covid-19. While the grey line tracks the share of the total population who have died from the disease (per million). The graph makes some important trends very clear. First, there is no correlation between the number of people in a country who are resident in care homes and the number of people who died in those facilities. However, there is a very close relationship between the total number of deaths in a country (the continuous line) and the numbers of care home residents who died. Put simply, those countries which did badly managing in their overall attempts to control the virus in the community, also did badly in preventing deaths in care homes.[16]

Care workers are one of the lowest paid employees in most societies. Because of low wages they regularly work part-time shifts in several facilities and because they not entitled to sick pay, many continued to work even when feeling unwell. In these circumstances, they became agents of the disease, spreading it from the community into the care homes in the first instance, and then between care homes. These were some of the conditions that created such a perfect viral storm. Undoubtedly, the care home crisis was exacerbated when staff became infected and had to quarantine themselves – leaving residents with insufficient carers to look after them. Shocking images soon appeared of elderly residents having to be evacuated on stretchers by emergency workers because the virus had decimated both staff and residents, rendering their care home a deadly and inoperable petri dish.

In contrast to the depressingly dismal picture in the rest of the world, as in their overall handling of the pandemic, Hong Kong, Singapore, South Korea and Taiwan were also stand-out successes in safeguarding the residents of their care homes. By mid-year, Hong Kong was able to report no deaths in its care homes. Even more astonishing, there had been no infectious outbreak in any part of its network of care homes up to then. It was a similar story in Taiwan, which also prevented any Covid-19 outbreak in any of its 1091 care homes. These are incredible achievements when set against what was happening at the same time in care homes across Europe. During one 24-hour period, on May 18, 2020 in Belgium, 19% of all new Covid admissions to hospitals were from care homes. In Ireland 24% of all confirmed cases of infection were from care homes, in France the figure was 52%. By May almost 36% of care homes in England had experienced infectious outbreaks, in Scotland it was 59% and Sweden 14%.[17]

This raises an obvious question: to what can we attribute the singular achievement of these Asian countries in protecting the lives and well-being of their elderly care home residents? It turns out there was nothing extraordinary about what they did to achieve their extraordinarily positive outcomes. They did the simple things well and consistently, but above all they were prepared. Taiwan has a deep awareness of and commitment to disease prevention and control in its care home network. It has well-established routines and procedures in place which are practised and tested diligently. There are clear regulations, self-audits, and accreditation standards that are strictly enforced. Staff training is routine and hand-washing is mandatory before and after each patient encounter. There are ample supplies of alcohol-based hand liquids, medical masks, gloves and gowns on site.[18] In short, all of the things that most of the rest of the world struggled with and largely failed to put in place on time. It was a gargantuan failure at many levels that has resulted in horrific unintended consequences. In the recent history of 'social' Europe and the rest of the developed world, rarely have so many innocents died on such a scale for want of so little. The unpalatable and deeply disturbing truth is that the care home calamity was both so tragic, and yet so preventable.

Chapter 23: Trump and Therapeutics

Since the last century, vaccines have been our most effective means of successfully combatting dangerous viruses. It is no surprise, therefore, that virtually all of the world's hopes were pinned on the development of an effective vaccine. Dr Fauci stated that hope clearly in a White House coronavirus press briefing in April when he told the media, 'Ultimately, the showstopper will obviously be a vaccine.' However, until that happy day arrived a number of therapeutic strategies were being actively investigated. One of the most common involved the repurposing of existing drugs for use in ameliorating the effects of the Covid-19.

The antiviral drug Remdesivir is a broad-spectrum antiviral drug that was originally developed to fight Ebola. It underwent several clinical trials to test its effectiveness against SARS-CoV-2. Remdesivir received an emergency use authorisation from the FDA in May, following a trial that showed hospitalised Covid patients recovered up to 30% faster when using the drug. In issuing its emergency use authorisation, however, the FDA stressed that they were doing so because, 'there are no adequate, approved, and available alternative treatments'.[1]

Based on three randomised controlled trials, one of which was carried out by Dr Fauci's NIAID in October, the FDA approved Remdesivir as the standard care treatment for Covid-19 in hospital patients.[2] By then, Remdesivir had either been approved or received an emergency use authorisation in up to 50 countries. However, just one month after the FDA's approval, the WHO issued a conditional recommendation against the use of Remdesivir for treatment of the virus. Based on evidence from four randomised trials, the WHO concluded that the drug had 'little or no effect on 28-day mortality or the in-hospital course of COVID-19 among hospitalized patients.'[3]

A further concern for some of those medical experts that, as a repurposed medicine, Remdesivir had an estimated manufacturing cost of about $1 per vial but a sales price to governments of $390, with health insurance companies paying $520 per vial. The experts worried that at such high prices it could divert resources away from other treatments.[4] Additionally, the break-through announcement of a vaccine in early November meant that faith in Remdesivir as some sort of Covid wonder drug was beginning to evaporate. However, Remdesivir may have given rise to one particular condition – buyer's remorse. Just a week prior to the

WHO announcement, the European Commission signed a €1 billion deal for the supply of Remdesivir. The manufacturing company, Gilead, had advance knowledge of the details the WHO's report, but the Commission was still in blissful ignorance when it signed the contract on October 8.

In June, researchers at Oxford University found that an off-patent steroid, dexamethasone, could cut the death rate of the most seriously ill patients on ventilators by one-third and by one-fifth in patients receiving oxygen. The steroid works at this critical stage of the disease by reducing inflammation, especially in the lungs.[5] The difference between Remdesivir and dexamethasone in terms of clinical outcomes and costs are very significant. Remdesivir reduced the length of stay in hospitals by three to four days and cost as much as $3,000 per course. Dexamethasone, however, was a fraction of that cost and reduced the number of extremely ill people dying from Covid-19 by up to one-third.

There was one other drug that had been used extensively as an anti-malarial treatment for about 50 years, as well as for a variety of rheumatological conditions. It was also very cheap. However, the use of hydroxychloroquine in the treatment of Covid-19 infections had been surrounded by intense controversy. On Friday May 22, a paper was published in *The Lancet* which found that hydroxychloroquine was associated with a higher risk of heart problems and death among those infected with Covid-19. The study, using an enormous database of 96,000 patients from an impressive 1,200 hospitals around the world, found not only that hydroxychloroquine didn't work, but it was actually dangerous.

One of the findings of the study was that hydroxychloroquine increased the risk of in-hospital death by 30% to 40%, and increased incidents of arrhythmia by a factor of 2 to 5. These were shocking figures which had an immediate impact across the medical-scientific community with massive consequences. Within 24 hours, the WHO suspended its hydroxychloroquine trial with immediate effect. And around the world all other hydroxychloroquine trials quickly ground to a halt.

But within days of *The Lancet* study being published, scientists began to identify serious and potentially fatal flaws in its methodology and its findings. In particular, there were database errors which exaggerated the number of deaths. More than 120 scientific and medical researchers sent an open letter to the editor of *The Lancet*, Richard Horton which raised up to 10 major concerns regarding the statistical methodology of the paper and the integrity of the data used. On foot of this, the paper was discredited. This was not the first time under Horton's editorship that *The*

Lancet was forced to withdraw a paper – this time, it came just one week after its publication.[6] Once the discredited *Lancet* paper was withdrawn, all trials were quickly resumed.[7]

Apart from the fraudulent paper published by *The Lancet*, there have been at least a couple of hundred research papers published worldwide on the use of hydroxychloroquine as a treatment for Covid-19. Most of these have been driven not by the demands of science, but by the enormous amounts of media coverage and social media commentary devoted to quasi-scientific and anecdotal reports that hydroxychloroquine works. Given the lack of a vaccine, and the morbid fear that the disease aroused among the general public, this clutching at the hydroxychloroquine straw was largely understandable.

The same Oxford researchers who had found the off-patent steroid, dexamethasone, to be of major benefit to seriously ill Covid patients also came to a very different conclusion with respect to hydroxychloroquine: 'there is no beneficial effect of hydroxychloroquine in patients hospitalised with COVID-19.'[8] As a consequence, the trial was ended. Most other studies to date have also shown that there is no evidence that hydroxychloroquine is of benefit to patients admitted to hospital who already have COVID-19.[9] Neither is there evidence that it offers protection as a prophylactic or preventative for those likely to be exposed to the disease, such as healthcare workers.[10]

The odds on hydroxychloroquine being assessed like any other potential treatment for Covid-19 shortened very considerably in March, when President Trump became one of its most ardent advocates. A Presidential tweet that month, which typically did not lack for hyperbole, said, 'HYDROXYCHLOROQUINE & AZITHROMYCIN, taken together, have a real chance to be one of the biggest game changers in the history of medicine.'[11] At a press conference in April, President Trump was openly encouraging people to take the drug; 'What do you have to lose? Take it'. In May, as if to lead by example, the President announced that he himself was taking hydroxychloroquine as a preventative measure against Covid-19. This was in contravention of the FDA advice that taking hydroxychloroquine in this manner was dangerous.

Once hydroxychloroquine had received the Presidential seal of approval, a previously innocuous anti-malarial treatment which was medically controversial for use against Covid-19 became politically toxic. In the intensely divisive partisan politics of the 2020 US presidential election, the Presidents' devotees and detractors had found yet another contentious issue to fight over. In that dichromatic political atmosphere, all other 50 shades of opinion were summarily excluded: hydroxychloroquine had become a simple black and white issue and an expression of fealty to one's chosen political tribe.

All the President's Meds

On October 2, there was a bombshell announcement. As usual, eschewing all official communications channels, at around 1 a.m., President Trump announced on Twitter that: 'Tonight, @FLOTUS and I tested positive for COVID-19. We will begin our quarantine and recovery process immediately. We will get through this TOGETHER!'[12] With just a month to go to poling day, this was a sensational development.

The media went into meltdown. Reminiscent of how sport's commentators from 200 metres away can confidently diagnose an 'anterior cruciate ligament' injury in a prone player while medics require MRI scans, medical experts with no more information than the general public were falling over themselves to pronounce on the President's condition. Many spoke darkly about a relapse and that it could all yet end in tears, with some suggesting that the fact that the President felt great was probably a drug-induced feeling of euphoria. Meanwhile, his medical team continued to give a consistently upbeat message that President Trump was doing well and had been up and about. As if to prove the media doomsayers wrong, despite his doctors' cautioning that he was not completely out of the woods, after just three nights, President Trump left the Walter Reed military hospital on the evening of Monday, October 5.

Though none of the media reports had the temerity to suggest he deserved it, expressions of sympathy for the President were in very short supply. Their attitude was probably best summed up by an article in the *Los Angeles Times*, 'News Analysis: A history of falsehoods comes back to haunt the COVID-stricken president'. The opening paragraph set the tone: 'Donald Trump's presidency began with a falsehood, and now, thousands of misstatements later, that history of prevarication is undermining the administration at a time when trust is needed most.'[13]

On October 2, following his dramatic disclosure that he and his wife, Melania, had contracted the Covid disease, President Trump received his first dose of the experimental drug Regeneron. Shortly afterwards he was taken by helicopter to the Walter Reed Military Hospital a few miles away where he began a five-day course of Remdesivir. As part of the President's treatment plan, he was also given the generic steroid dexamethasone. All of this was routine treatment for any American citizen that contracted Covid-19, except for two things: its speed and the inclusion of the experimental drug Regeneron.

Of the three principal medications the President's medical team prescribed for him, the least surprising, in some respects, was dexamethasone, a steroid drug that has been around for a very long time. It is an anti-inflammatory drug traditionally used for a range of ailments, including arthritis, kidney, blood and thyroid disorders and severe allergies. As we have seen, Oxford University researchers carried out a large-scale trial on the efficacy of dexamethasone in patients who had contracted the coronavirus disease. As reported by the *New England Journal of Medicine* in July, the results of the trials were compelling.[14] So compelling in fact, that three other trials were ended prematurely and their placebo participants given dexamethasone because it was felt medically unethical to deprive them of such a beneficial treatment.[15]

From an early stage in the pandemic, Remdesivir, an experimental anti-viral drug was seen by many as a treatment with the potential to transform the battle with the SARS-CoV2 virus. Unlike other therapeutics which were originally designed to deal with non-viral diseases, Remdesivir was originally developed as a treatment for Ebola, and so is purposely designed to tackle viruses. It works by inhibiting the replication mechanism of the virus. Though it was ultimately ineffective against Ebola, recent trials conducted by the US National Institute of Allergy and Infectious Diseases had shown positive results against SARS-CoV2. Though there was no statistically significant difference in the number of deaths between patients who were given the drug and the placebo group, Remdesivir was found to reduce the number of days that patients spend in hospital from 15 to 11 days.

The third significant medication on the President's list of drugs that his medical team released to the media was Regeneron. It was still in clinical trials at the time, but was given to the President on a 'compassionate use' basis. The trials comprised patients at various stages of the disease, including those who had been diagnosed with the infection, and were symptomatic but not hospitalised – just like the President. Regeneron mimics the immune systems' natural processes and creates the antibodies the body normally manufactures to fight off specific diseases. Though referred to as a 'cure' by the President, Regeneron was, at that stage, a therapeutic drug that was still undergoing clinical trials.

One the interesting and ironic features associated with the Regeneron drug is that, similar to the AstraZeneca and Moderna vaccines, it was developed with the aid of stem cells. In Regeneron's case, the HEK 293T cells that were used had been originally derived from the kidney tissue of a fetus that had been aborted in the Netherlands in the 1970s. In 2019, the Trump administration suspended federal funding for most new scientific research that used stem cells derived from abortions. Within days of his release from hospital, President Trump delivered an exuberant video statement from the White House lawn in which he largely attributed his 'miracle cure' to Regeneron. The whole experience, he claimed had been 'a blessing from God' because it gave him a whole new insight into the Covid-19 disease and the power of treatments like Regeneron to combat it. If so, then maybe this blessing was also an implicit 'compassionate use authorisation' from on High for the restoration of federal government funding for scientific research based on stem cells of all types.

Chapter 24: The Race for a Vaccine

The emergence of infectious pathogens like the SARS-CoV-2 virus that causes the Covid-19 disease are random occurrences. Not only is their emergence unpredictable, but their structure and make up may be something with which science is completely unfamiliar. Devising effective therapies to counter viral disease outbreaks that are both arbitrary and indiscriminate is extraordinarily challenging. Up to the end of 2019, 76 million people have been infected with the HIV virus and about 33 million have died from it. Currently, around 38.0 million are living with HIV and up to 770,000 continue to die from it annually. Yet, despite billions being spent on research and clinical trials during the last three decades, there is still no vaccine for the HIV/AIDS. There have, however, been many false dawns.

Vaccine development is not linear. Chance, even accidents can play a role. Canadian scientists trying to understand the Ebola disease put its genes into an otherwise harmless virus and injected mice with it. Instead of the animals getting the disease, as the scientists had expected, the mice became immune to Ebola. That serendipitous event led eventually to the development of a vaccine for this highly contagious disease. Because of the seriousness of the threat that Ebola posed to humanity, that vaccine went through the critical-phase trials from I to III in a record 10 months.[1] The vaccine was approved for use throughout the world and proved effective in combatting an Ebola outbreak in 2018. Prior to the advent of the vaccine, according to the WHO, the Ebola virus had killed 11,310 people in West Africa over a three-year period. At its first peak during April 2020, Covid-19 was killing almost as many people in a single day.[2] By January 2021, it was killing even more.

A Jab in the Dark

Normally, vaccines take a long time to develop. Some have taken decades, and some, as we've just noted, have never come to fruition at all. It is also salutary to remind ourselves that after 100 years of research, we still do not have a completely effective treatment for influenza. On the positive side, recent years have seen substantial technological innovations which are likely to streamline the vaccine development process and shorten vaccine delivery timescales – that, at least, has been the hope.

During the past two decades alone, more than $14.5 billion has been spent in pursuit of an AIDS vaccine. This has resulted in almost 150 different vaccines being brought to various stages of development. One hundred of these were abandoned at an early stage, while 46 survived to the preclinical or clinical evaluation phase. Ultimately, all of these failed to deliver a vaccine for AIDS, but the enormous scientific effort expended over the decades has not been in vain.

This meant that, when the coronavirus pandemic arrived, virologists and immunologists around the world were far better prepared to tackle the scientific challenges it presented. By July 2020, there were 160 vaccines under development. By any standards this marked an impressively rapid response to a pathogen that was completely unknown to the scientific community just six months earlier. What was even more impressive, was that 21 of these vaccines were being evaluated in clinical settings. In their battle with AIDS, researchers had gained an enormous amount of scientific knowledge about the human immune system. It had allowed many to re-purpose their vaccine technologies, research and scientific expertise in their quest for a Covid-19 vaccine.

In the past, developing a vaccine was a laborious and potentially dangerous task. Scientists worked on actual versions of a virus and so these explorations had to be carried out in purpose-built containment laboratories surrounded by exhaustive safety procedures that were designed to avoid infections to researchers or a virus escape into the community. More recently, the development of new technologies such as gene sequencing, however, has reduced the need for much of this hazardous work. And, less need to work with actual samples of the pathogen, has resulted in vaccine research becoming much more manageable, safer, and, above all, faster.

One of the most common strategies is to use an existing molecular platform into which the genetic sequence of the coronavirus can be slotted. This has eliminated significant bottlenecks at the scientific investigation stage. Most critically, it has permitted the scientists to produce small-scale quantities of a new vaccine in a matter of weeks, a process that heretofore would have taken over a year. The real significance of all of this, of course, is that a new vaccine can commence the all-important clinical trial phase much sooner.

The gold standard for clinical trials is a double-blind randomised placebo-controlled trial. This is where some participants are given the treatment being tested while others are administered a placebo, and neither researchers nor participants being aware of who is in which category – hence the term double-blind. In the case of infectious disease outbreaks, fast-tracking or emergency use of a new therapy may be permitted. Such decisions are ultimately based on a balance of the risks of patients suffering serious side effects set against the known high mortality rates of the disease. That assessment would, for instance be very different for a disease like Ebola that has a 70% fatality rate, when compared to an infectious disease with less than 2% mortality rate.

Even with those assessments successfully completed, there are substantial hurdles still to be overcome. The challenges involved in mass-producing a vaccine are enormous. Accessing production capacity on the scale required to deliver global immunisation is a potentially severe constraint. There are also the formidable logistics required to deliver a vaccine, possibly repeatedly, to consumers. Under all these circumstances, the search for an effective Covid-19 vaccine was an enormous scientific and commercial gamble. And as if that wasn't enough, there was the very considerable additional pressures of a US election in which President Trump was pressing to have companies supersede an already ambitious timeline to come up with a vaccine prior to November 2020.

The Geopolitical Proxy War

The competition was not confined to commercial companies. In a global pandemic, the search for a vaccine inevitably involved geopolitics, as competition between various blocks and 'value systems' re-surfaced with renewed vigour. The United States, Europe, China, and many individual countries, each pursued their quest for a vaccine with a degree of aggressiveness that had become somewhat unfashionable in recent decades. What had been presented at the beginning as a noble scientific endeavour to help extricate all humanity from the deadly embrace of a silent global killer quickly developed into a geopolitical proxy war.

China has used the pandemic as an ideal opportunity to showcase its new assertiveness under Xi Jinping. Few of its actions exemplify this more than its concerted efforts to develop a Covid vaccine. Well over 1,000 Chinese scientists have been working on this project since January. For a regime in which the boundaries between private and state activities are fluid to the point of irrelevancy, this provides an indication of the political, ideological, and personal importance to President Xi that China's search for a vaccine should be militarised. Though there were a number of candidate vaccines being progressed simultaneously in China, the front runner was one being developed with the support of the People's Liberation Army Academy of Military Medical Sciences.

The CCP's theoretical journal, *Qiushi*, stressed the importance of all of this scientific endeavour as a means of demonstrating the innate superiority of what the Party likes to call 'socialism with Chinese characteristics'. Victory in the scientific quest to develop a vaccine was just another means for the CCP to 'fully leverage the institutional advantages and governing efficiency of Chinese socialism.'

The cultural expression of this muscular assertiveness combined with enormous national pride in Chinese scientific achievements, led to the production of an 2017 action movie that broke all box-office records in China. The heroine of *Wolf Warrior II* was a Chinese military scientist who developed a successful vaccine for a deadly virus that was sweeping across Africa. As a result, the movie character, Dr Chen became an overnight hit across China. The film was a not-very-subtle reference to a real military scientist, conveniently also named Dr Chen, who two years earlier had gone to Sierra Leone to help develop a vaccine for Ebola.

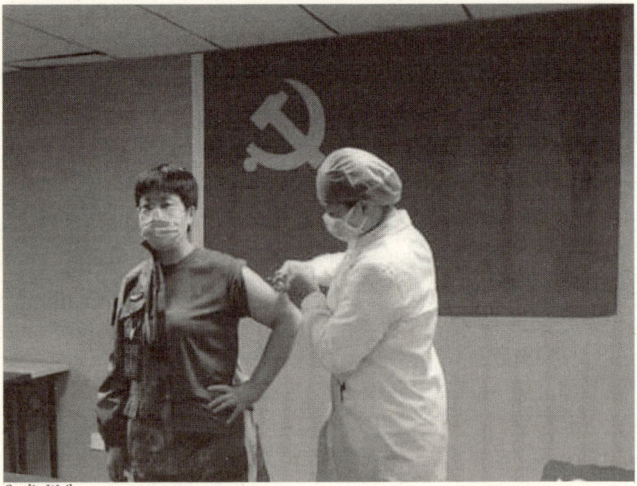

Credit: Weibo

Wolf Warrior Chen Prepares for Battle in Wuhan

As one of China's top virologists and a bioweapons expert, the PLA's Major General Chen Wei stepped back into the limelight once more to lead the battle against the outbreak of the coronavirus in Wuhan. Dr Chen and a team of PLA scientists were quickly dispatched to Hubei province in mid-January where they established their base at the Wuhan Institute of Virology. In this photo Dr Chen, dressed in battle fatigues, can be seen receiving a booster injection in advance of her journey to Wuhan to tackle the infectious disease outbreak. The picture of the scene, adorned with the hammer and sickle red flag of the CCP, was released by the People's Liberation Army on its Weibo account as an obvious part of an official propaganda exercise. But propaganda is a two-way street. This same photo of Major General Chen Wei being injected with a vaccine was also widely circulated on social media as evidence that she and other PLA members had subjected themselves to a vaccine that had not been tested, not even on animals.[3] The claim has been fact-checked by the Associated Press and found to be false.

From the epicentre of the contagion, the PLA scientific team immediately began work on developing a vaccine. In March, the Communist Party's English language publication, *Global Times* announced that 'A research team led by a Chinese military major general … has achieved a major breakthrough in developing a vaccine to the novel coronavirus (COVID-19)'[4]. The vaccine was developed by a joint venture comprised of the Chinese military and the Hong Kong quoted company CanSino Biologic. According to *China Daily*, the team conducting these human vaccine trials was led by Major General Chen Wei.[5] This first Chinese-made coronavirus vaccine began human trials immediately in March in Wuhan.

In an exercise that received little fanfare, China began an extensive programme in July. This involved distributing two experimental coronavirus vaccines to hundreds of thousands of people. This was done in spite of the fact that the vaccines had not yet completed phase III trials to confirm their safety and efficacy. According to Chinese state media, the move had received the blessing of the WHO in late June. In response to questioning, the WHO explained that any country has the right to issue, on its own account, an emergency use authorisation for an experimental vaccine: it was hardly the ringing endorsement that the Chinese authorities had sought.

The primary basis for an emergency use authorisation is that there was no alternative effective treatment available for, in this case, a highly infectious disease that is life-threatening. However, China has been claiming for months that it had completely suppressed the Covid-19 virus with negligible cases occurring during that period. If those claims were true, then the CCP was stretching the definition of emergency use authorisation far beyond any previous interpretation. Indeed, the apparent shortage of positive cases in China forced a number of these vaccine developers to carry out the phase clinical III trials overseas. Making a virtue of necessity, China now claims that this emergency use strategy that was claimed originally to be 'designed for China' was really one designed 'to provide the vaccine to the world'.[6]

Meanwhile, as the four principal Chinese candidate vaccines continued their phase III trials, Reuters reported that China was in active discussions with the WHO to have these vaccines included in the WHO's list of emergency use vaccines. Inclusion in the WHO's emergency use list would allow these unlicensed vaccines to be made available internationally for public health emergencies. Reuters also reported that hundreds of thousands of people in China had been given these vaccines even though 'clinical trials had not been fully completed, raising safety concerns among experts.'[7]

The CCP's English language newspaper, *Global Times*, reacted to such sceptical comments by claiming that all of those tens of thousands of vaccine recipients 'have shown no abnormal reactions ... [which] once again proves that China's COVID-19 vaccines were safe ... a strong response to some Western countries' slander on the quality and safety of Chinese vaccines.' In its opening paragraph the *Global Times* countered by pointing out something that had been widely reported in western media: the trials 'of a coronavirus vaccine developed by AstraZeneca and Oxford University [were] paused after a volunteer fell ill during trials.' The *Global Times* emphasised, however, that the CanSino Biologics vaccine which uses the same recombinant adenovirus vector platform as the AstraZeneca/Oxford one, was entirely safe.[8]

In May, the EU launched the impressive-sounding Coronavirus Global Response, the objective of which was 'to gather significant funding to ensure the collaborative development and universal deployment of diagnostics, treatments and vaccines against coronavirus.' The headline on the Commission's press announcement contained the even more impressive claim that, '€7.4 billion [had been] raised for universal access to vaccines'[9]

The opening paragraph, however, told a different story: it seemed that the €7.4 million had not actually been raised, it had only been 'registered' as 'pledges from donors worldwide'. The total figure involved a 'pledge of €1.4 billion by the Commission.' And this figure, it went on to explain, consisted of €1 billion in grants and €400 million in loan guarantees all of which was being done 'through reprioritisation of Horizon 2020 (€1 billion), RescEU (€80 million), the Emergency Support Instrument (€150 million) and external instruments (€170 million).'

Supported by US government funds, the French pharmaceutical giant Sanofi joined with UK rival GlaxoSmithKline in an unusual move to form one of the leading partnerships in the search for a vaccine. Sanofi, however, got into hot water in May when its CEO, Paul Hudson, told Bloomberg: 'The U.S. government has the right to the largest pre-order because it's invested in taking the risk, that if we've helped you manufacture the doses at risk, we expect to get the doses first … I've been campaigning in Europe to say the U.S. will get vaccines first. That's how it will be because they've invested to try and protect their population, to restart their economy'[10]

On hearing this, Gallic political indignation knew no bounds. French Secretary of State for Economy and Finance, Agnes Pannier-Runacher said, 'it was unacceptable for this country or that to have privileged access on a pecuniary pretext.' Sanofi's CEO was soon summoned to the Elysée Palace to explain himself. Later, Sanofi confirmed that it's CEO had been lobbying the EU to adopt a US-like approach to financing vaccine development, and that it was still in discussions with the Commission 'to speed things up.'[11] On September 18, it was announced that both Sanofi and GSK had signed a purchase agreement with the EU to supply up to 300 million doses of a Covid-19 vaccine, once the vaccine had been approved. However, in December, Sanofi/GSK announced that their vaccine had not met expectations and would not be available until the end of 2021. Not only was this a blow to French national pride, it also left a massive hole in the EU's vaccine supply, amounting to a shortfall of 20%.

Operation Warp Speed

By May, the US economy had almost shuddered to a halt with unemployment sky-rocketing. The contagion had killed over 100,000 and 1.5 million people had been infected. In the same month, on May 15, President Trump unveiled 'Operation Warp Speed'. It was the Administration's Manhattan Project-style effort to radically cut the development time of a coronavirus vaccine. The basic objective was to manufacture and make available hundreds of millions of safe and effective vaccines to US citizens by January 2021. *Science* magazine made clear what the President was trying to achieve: 'Warp Speed intends to deliver the first 100 million doses of a vaccine in November and another 200 million over the following 2 months.'[12] It was a public-private partnership with a major logistics role for the US military. Warp Speed was led by Moncef Slaoui, a venture capitalist and 30-year pharma industry veteran from GlaxoSmithKline.

A vaccine had never been developed before in such a short time. But President Trump refused to be bound by conventional wisdom on vaccine-development timeframes. Instead, he insisted on break-neck speed. The *New York Times* reported that 'Mr. Trump's order came after he grew frustrated by warnings from Dr. Anthony S. Fauci, the director of the National Institute of Allergy and Infectious Diseases [NIH], and other experts on the coronavirus task force, that development of a vaccine would take a year to 18 months, and that even that schedule might be ambitious.'[13] The whole project was funded by US taxpayers to the tune of $18 billion.[14] But, in any case, funding was unlikely to have been a problem for what had become a signature policy of the President's 'America First' political agenda.

For its many critics, Warp Speed was not only unrealistic, it was reckless, and possibly dangerous – principally because they feared corners would be cut. A vocal critic who counselled that 'we should not cut corners' was Dr Nicole Lurie. Her job in the President Obama's administration was, until 2016, Assistant Secretary of Health with specific responsibility to 'lead the nation in preventing, responding to and recovering from the adverse health effects of public health emergencies and disasters.' The critical comment by Peter Hotez of the Baylor College of Medicine and a member of the US health administration's NIH initiative, Accelerating COVID-19 Therapeutic Interventions and Vaccines (ACTIV), was not untypical. According to Hotez: 'Some of the language coming out of the White House is very damaging … I don't see a path by which you can collect enough efficacy and safety data by the end of the year.' Despite this and similar criticisms, President Trump, along with what the media inevitably dubbed his 'vaccine czar', Moncef Slaoui, a registered Democrat, pushed ahead relentlessly.

By early October, there were 151 potential vaccines in preclinical trials with 48 in human trials and ten of these in Phase III trials.[15] From all of these, 14 of the most likely candidates were selected. By June, these initial 14 participants had been whittled down further to just five; Moderna, Pfizer, AstraZeneca, Johnson & Johnson, and Merck. It soon became evident that the three front runners were Pfizer, Moderna and

AstraZeneca. All three companies were in receipt of massive funding from the US taxpayers either through direct development grants or pre-development purchase agreements; Moderna has received $2.5 billion, Pfizer/BioNTech $2 billion, and AstraZeneca/Oxford $1.3 billion. In return for this advance funding, the US had been granted guaranteed access to hundreds of millions of these vaccine doses.

While the sights of health experts and the hopes of billions of people around the world were set firmly on the delivery of a Covid-19 vaccine by mid-2021, there was one person had a much more ambitious delivery deadline: November 3. To expect the vaccine development cycle to align itself perfectly with that of the Presidential election cycle was undoubtedly asking too much. No matter how hard he willed it to happen, science would not bend to the President's will. In September, nine of the leading pharmaceutical companies involved in the race for a vaccine issued an unprecedented joint public declaration, stating that they would uphold the highest scientific and ethical standards in their quest for a coronavirus vaccine.

Despite a concerted campaign of what amounted to cyber bullying of his own administration's health experts on Twitter, President Trump's unrealistic hopes for a vaccine to be available prior to polling day, were dashed. Instead, surrounded on all sides by recalcitrant private pharmaceutical companies; politicians from both sides of the aisle that needed to be placated: and by an administrative state that refused to do his bidding, President Trump must at times have looked wistfully at General Secretary Xi's command and control capacity to summon up Wolf Warriors and order them to cut corners for the greater glory of People, Party and President.

Then on November 9, the world breathed a collective sigh of relief as, against the odds and his own projected timeframe, Dr Fauci's 'showstopper' event was realised. Pfizer/BioNTech announced that its vaccine was 90% effective against Covid-19. In an imperfect world, blighted for a year by a persistent pestilence, this seemed as close to perfection as it gets: it also augured well for those other vaccines that were coming up fast behind the victor. While few contemporaries seem willing to give him any credit, history will show that it was that most imperfect of American Presidents, Donald J. Trump, whose shockingly bold vaccine gamble was instrumental in delivering a vaccine for Covid-19 in a timeframe that was historically unprecedented. Though the virus would continue to exact a very heavy price for many months into 2021, its days as a plague on humanity were probably numbered.

Chapter 25: A Century of War and Plague

Economics is a profession that is deeply enamoured of laws. It would seem that there are laws for almost everything in economics: the Law of Diminishing Returns; the Law of Diminishing Marginal Utility; the Law of Comparative Advantage; not to mention the canonical Law of Supply and Demand. The general public is unfamiliar with the precise workings of this host of laws; they are known only to the Elect of what has been termed the Dismal Science. Economic history, however, is not afflicted by this psychosis of absolute certitude. It knows only one law – the Law of Unintended Consequences.

From time immemorial, humanity has been blighted by the Bible's Horsemen of the Apocalypse. During the last 100 years two of these Horsemen have made a particular impact: War and Plague. The human misery and economic distress that have flown from humanity's encounters with both of these forces have been incalculable. But in our numerate and calculating age we are far better placed to assess the consequences and costs of these recurring catastrophes. However, this is not an exact science and, inevitably, because our responses to such disasters involve the law of unintended consequences – which means that precision continues to elude us.

War

As a young man, one of the 20th century's best-known economists, J.M. Keynes attended the 1919 Versailles Peace Conference as part of the British Treasury delegation. He saw that the victorious Allied Powers were determined to impose a 'Carthaginian Peace' whose economic provisions were designed to crush Germany. Keynes resigned in frustration and despair, and returned to England in May, before the Versailles Treaty had been finalised. Within two months of his arrival back in England, he had written one of the most prescient and consequential history books of modern times. *The Economic Consequences of the Peace* was an immediate best seller on both sides of the Atlantic, selling over 100,000 copies and was translated into 12 languages.[1] One of its principal conclusions was that the Treaty of Versailles would have serious economic and political unintended consequences for Germany, Europe and the world at large.

The Covid-19 pandemic has already caused massive economic dislocation and has the potential to precipitate even greater economic misery as its repeated waves persist. The resultant economic shocks that have impacted upon the world's economy means that future political repercussions are inevitable. So, while we await the publication by some aspiring (or current) celebrity economist of a tome titled, *The Economic Consequences of the Pandemic*, how do we begin to assess the medium and long-term macroeconomic consequences of the current crisis? Looking at past pandemics[2] and wars may offer some instructive guidance, and, unfortunately, the 20th century provides more than a sufficiency of both.

It is clear that the human costs of war are horrendous, but its economic ramifications are also massive. Though war creates employment, increases GDP, and spurs technological innovation, these short-term gains are soon wiped out by the tremendous economic dislocation and destruction of capital caused by the war itself. To pay for all this massive expenditure, taxes are invariably increased. This association between war and tax is a long one. Income tax, for example, was first introduced by William Pitt the Younger in 1799 as a temporary measure to pay for the wars against revolutionary France. By the end of the Napoleonic wars, income tax had become so unpopular it was abandoned – but only temporarily.

Modern warfare is a very expensive business, and taxes alone are insufficient in themselves to cover the colossal costs involved. The US had to finance World War II through a combination of borrowing and increased taxes. By the end of that war, US debt had grown to 120% of GDP and taxes had gone up threefold to over 20% of GDP. But the vast bulk of modern wartime military expenditure is financed by government borrowing, and so the biggest medium and long-term economic burden that war bequeaths is an enormous debt burden. For major wars, this deficit financing has created inordinate levels of public debt which have often taken generations to repay. It's only recently, for example, that the United Kingdom has paid off the last of its War bond debt obligations for the First World War – which ended more than a century ago.

Plague

While war and a pandemic both result in enormous levels of public debt, they also differ in one very important respect. A war tends to boost both production and employment, but a pandemic does the opposite: it stifles production and curtails employment. When a sharp drop in consumption is added to the mixture, the economy can suffer the equivalent of an anaphylactic shock. The sort of trauma that follows must be counteracted quickly if the economy is to avoid permanent structural damage. This is why governments nowadays reach out immediately and smash the glass marked 'Emergency Stimulus'. That releases floods of money into the economy which is intended to prevent a painful, long drawn-out recession. The severity and extent of a recession caused by a pandemic is ultimately determined by four things: the mortality rate, the age cohort that is mainly affected, the containment measures implemented to stem the spread of the virus, and the actual duration of the outbreak.

The world has been hit by three contagious respiratory illness pandemics during the 20th century and one in the first few years of the 21st century. These have varied in their intensity, lethality, geographical spread, and economic consequences. In order of occurrence, they were: the Spanish flu in 1918, the Asian flu in 1957 and the Hong Kong flu in 1968, and then SARS in 2002. The most severe by far was the Spanish flu for which the estimates of the numbers who died vary from 17 million to 50 million people. Some even argue that the number who died could be as high as 100 million. Based on these studies and a WHO document on influenza pandemics, I think the total death toll was probably somewhere between 20 and 50 million.

Although it happened over a century ago, on a like-for-like comparison with the current pandemic, the Spanish flu provides an interesting template for assessing the macroeconomic fallout we are likely to experience today. In contrast with the current pandemic and its two immediate predecessors, one of the peculiarities of Spanish flu was that it disproportionally killed young adults who had no underlying or pre-existing health conditions. This, coming on top of the enormous numbers of young males who died in the immediately preceding WW1, meant that a large section of the active labour force was eliminated.

Modern researchers have estimated that the Spanish flu pandemic may have been the fourth worst macroeconomic shock that the world has experienced since 1870. It comes after World War 1, the Great Depression of the early 1930s, and the Second World War. Though they happened around the same time, and partially overlapped, the disaggregated analysis for World War I and the flu pandemic indicates that the pandemic reduced per capita GDP by 6%, while World War I causing an even greater reduction of 8.1%.[3] In terms of their respective effects on the stock market, the pandemic knocked 26 percentage points off stock prices while the Great War had a lesser impact, reducing stocks by 19 percentage points.

The current death toll which has surpassed two million, puts Covid-19 on a par with those pandemics caused by its viral cousins during the latter half of the 20th century. But even this high mortality rate, when it is assessed in relative terms to the total population, the death toll from Covid-19 will be substantially smaller than in the worst pandemic of the recent past, the Spanish flu which killed about 2% of the then global population. If Covid-19 had a similar mortality rate of 2%, based on the world's current population of 7.8 billion, it would cause the deaths of over 150 million people – a horrific figure that no one is suggesting.[4] But there were two other pandemics that happened during the second half of the 20th century which have some pertinence for today.

The Asian flu (H2N2) of 1957-8, for instance, was a global pandemic which originated in Guizhou, China and killed at least a million people worldwide. It was the first pandemic to occur within the era of modern virology and so, for the first time a rapidly spreading global virus was subjected to scientific laboratory investigations. As a result, the public was confronted by a microbial pathogen which was deemed to have a singular lethality: a virus that did not need bacterial assistance to kill people. Although it had a low mortality rate of 0.07%, among the most vulnerable groups were those with underlying heart conditions and pregnant women.

Then in 1968 along came the Hong Kong flu (H3N2). Though its first recorded case was in Hong Kong, there are strong suspicions that it too originated in mainland China.[5] It also killed about 1 million people most of whom were 65 years or older. Like its predecessor from which it is directly descended, that virus continues to circulate worldwide as a seasonal influenza virus which jointly have become the leading cause of seasonal influenza illness and death over the last 50 years.

Both viruses experience small but frequent genetic mutations as a result of which the body's immune system fails to recognise the new flu variant and reinfection occurs. For this reason, flu vaccines must be reviewed and updated annually in a constant effort to stay ahead of the influenza curve. The strains derived from the Hong Kong version have had the greatest effect on the public health of subsequent generations. In recent years, it has led to more than twice the number of hospitalisations than those influenzas derived from the earlier Asian flu version. Part of the reason for the greater impact of Hong Kong influenza derivatives has been their tendency to mutate more rapidly, as well as their disproportionate effect on the elderly.

The Third Millennium

The first few years of the Third Millennium were eventful ones. The 9/11 attack on the Twin Towers in 2001 triggered a lengthy and extremely costly War on Terror. It has lasted for almost two decades, during which US-led combat troops have carried out military operations in some 24 countries.6 These operations have been conducted outside the borders of the US – in Afghanistan, Iraq, Syria and Pakistan. However, the USA has still paid a hight price for its 'war on terror'. It is estimated to have cost American taxpayers $6.4 trillion, and also resulted in the deaths of almost 1,000,000 people, mainly civilians.[7] In a major publishing coup in December 2019, the *Washington Post* secured access to over 2,000 official documents. These showed conclusively that government officials had lied egregiously to the US public throughout this whole period.[8]

One year after the Taliban had been driven from power in Afghanistan, the first serious threat to global health security emerged at the end of 2002 in China. The inauspicious origins of this first known case of what was called 'atypical pneumonia' in Guangdong in November 2002 offered no hint that it would become a landmark event in modern Asian history. The catalyst for its global spread, however, was three months later when it crossed from mainland China into Hong Kong. It had been carried by a doctor who stayed in the Metropole Hotel, Kowloon (See Chapter 6).

Though SARS had relatively low mortality and morbidity, it had very significant economic consequences for the region. Hong Kong, a thriving regional economic hub, was worst hit, and its services sectors such as hospitality, retail, and tourism were devastated. The 'demand shock' caused by SARS knocked an estimated 0.5% of Hong Kong's GDP. Across the region the primary cause of the economic downturn was the high level of uncertainty and fear that SARS engendered in the general public as people across Asia absented themselves from schools, universities, offices, factories, and retail outlets, and airports fell eerily silent.

Most studies on the economic impact of SARS have focused on its effects on particularly badly affected sectors such as tourism and retail. It is true that fear of infection caused a very substantial drop in consumer spending in travel and retail. But the economic damage caused by a global disease such as SARS goes far beyond particular sectors of disease-affected countries. More broadly, a pandemic's economic impact has been evaluated through the prism of its demographic consequences, especially with respect to the labour force. These effects need not necessarily be entirely negative. A pandemic, for instance, that largely kills the elderly but leaves the economically active part of the population largely unaffected can lead to an initial increase in per capita GDP.

This means that any in-depth analysis of major historical pandemics needs to have a very broad purview – one that is beyond our purposes here. But, suffice it to say that with fewer than 900 deaths worldwide, the relatively low mortality of SARS had a concomitantly low economic impact on the global economy.[9] Thus the economic consequences of the pandemic are not due to the impact the disease itself on those directly affected but rather on the behaviour of the rest of the population. In this regard, a significant factor in the ultimate costs of the current pandemic will be its persistence. We have already experienced a second wave and third wave confirmation in December that Covid-19 had mutated to become more infectious. In these circumstances, the adverse effects on people's psychological behaviour becomes extended over time and consumer confidence gets further eroded. With consumer spending constituting at least 60% of GDP in most developed economies, a significant decline on that front will have a determinative effect on economic performance.

Compared to the 2008-9 financial crisis and the macroeconomic response to it, the Covid-19 pandemic has even greater potential to become a causative agent of significant and long-term social, economic, and political change. So how will the outcomes of the current pandemic differ from its predecessors? Without even considering the figures, it is clear that the economic fallout from this pandemic will be massive. They will also be global, for two reasons: first, the virus itself has struck every country in the world and secondly, the globalised nature of modern trade has ensured that the economic shock waves will be propagated seamlessly across political frontiers.

Chapter 26: Who Pays the Ferryman?

Bad and all as things were during the financial crisis of 2008-9 – and they were very bad – most of the world's major economies have experienced a shock of far greater magnitude due to Covid-19. Unemployment during the financial crisis peaked at 10% in the US. In April 2020, US unemployment had reached almost 15%. Just a few months earlier, it had stood at its lowest rate for 50 years at 3.5%. During the entire recession of 2008-9 there were 8.6 million jobs lost in the US. In April 2020 alone, 20 million jobs were eliminated. A staggering total of 33 million people filed for unemployment assistance as the pandemic caused massive business closures and layoffs on a catastrophic scale across the US.

A Tale of Two Streets: Wall Street and Main Street

It Was the Best of Times, It Was the Worst of Times

While the US economy was grinding to a halt, the stock market was reaching new heights of exuberance. During the height of the financial crisis the S&P 500 fell about 40% from its peak. In the pandemic of 2020, it fell by just 14%. This sense of a parallel universe between the stock market and the real economy was perfectly encapsulated in a screenshot taken in early April 2020 from the MSNBC *Mad Money* programme hosted by Jim Cramer. The screen in the background screams 'The Dow's Best Week since 1938', while the rolling news ticker at the bottom of the picture announces the staggering loss of 16 million US jobs in a period of just 3 weeks.

Throughout the pandemic while the economy remained extremely fragile and dependent on government stimulus support, the stock market has rapidly recovered from its initial plunge. By any standards, this was an extraordinary feat during what the *Wall Street Journal* described as 'one of the most catastrophic economic collapses in U.S. history.'[1] Reflecting the optimism for a speedy recovery following the announcement of a vaccine in November, stock market valuations increased further. So, how do we explain what for most people is a puzzling contradiction: a declining economy combined with rising stock markets.

Historically low interest rates are certainly a big factor, as central banks have kept them at close to zero. With little chance that they will rise anytime soon, cheap money has driven up the prices of longer to medium-term assets, and this was especially technology stocks like Facebook, Amazon, Alphabet (Google) etc. Large corporates were being supported by the unprecedented US Federal Reserve policy of buying corporate bonds. All of this has meant that despite an unprecedented economic crisis, corporate bankruptcies have remained very low. This raises the obvious question: where is the crisis?

They may loom large due of their absolute size, but the corporates that are traded publicly on stock exchanges only represent part of the economy. The real economy is mainly composed of small and medium sized businesses who employ the largest number of people in retail, services and small-scale manufacturing. It is these businesses and their employees that have borne the brunt of the economic pain caused by the pandemic lockdowns. The scale of this tragedy will only become fully evident as government stimulus funds begin to dry up and businesses that have been built up over generations get wiped out along with the incomes of their employees. Those who were fortunate enough to have owned assets at the start of the pandemic, probably had a 'good' pandemic financially, while small business owners and their workers are likely to pay a heavy financial price. This is the sad reality behind many of the macroeconomic figures, which themselves paint a very scary picture.

By mid-2020, the extent of the economic carnage inflicted on the developed world by the coronavirus was becoming clear. A series of dismal records were being smashed across the globe. In the first six months of 2020, the UK's GDP slumped by an unprecedent 22%, Spain's fell by 22%, and France's by 19%. Germany was the least badly affected, falling by just

12%. Across the Euro area as a whole, GDP fell by a whopping 15%. From these figures, it was hard to avoid the conclusion that the recovery in Europe would be slow and uneven. The US economy also slumped to a post-war record, losing 15% of GDP during the first half of 2020. Meanwhile, China, the world's second largest economy and the original source of the contagion, also managed to notch up its own economic record by taking a viral hit to its GDP of almost 10% during the months of the lockdown. This followed a record period of nearly four decades of exceptionally high economic growth.

A Crisis Like No Other

Though, as we have seen, not all sectors of the economy were impacted to the same extent, an extended recession will likely result in permanent changes to the way in which goods are produced and consumed. This is because the negative impact experienced by those sectors that have been affected directly affected will eventually ripple through to the rest of the economy. On the supply side, serious disruptions to the globalised supply chain that come from, for example, China, will almost certainly lead to some permanent realignments in this critical area. Such an extended period of uncertainty will also lead to the deferment of investment decisions by both corporate businesses and individual households. A downward negative spiral could easily develop in which uncertainty about the trajectory of the pandemic will be compounded by the fear and anxiety caused by people seeing, for instance, house prices and other assets decline. The net result could be a further drop in investment and spending and a concomitant increase in savings by households and businesses as basic survival instincts kick in.

What all this could mean for individuals was spelled out starkly by the World Bank: 'The pandemic is expected to plunge most countries into recession in 2020, with per capita income contracting in the largest fraction of countries globally since 1870.'[2] If the Bank is correct, that will be the biggest hit to incomes for 150 years. And the Bank even qualified its disquieting prognosis with an important caveat: 'Should COVID-19 outbreaks persist, should restrictions on movement be extended or reintroduced, or should disruptions to economic activity be prolonged, the recession could be deeper.' In such an eventuality, the Bank concluded that the hit to global economic growth could be as high as 8%.[3]

The sharp contraction in consumer demand and a concomitant rise in unemployment has forced governments to intervene directly by pumping unprecedented levels of financial support into both households and businesses. In developed economies, central banks have undertaken far-reaching monetary and fiscal measures to improve liquidity and maintain investor confidence. Indeed, the fiscal and monetary supports that central banks and governments have provided were far greater than those enacted during the 2008-9 financial crisis. In 2012, at the height of the Eurozone crisis, the then European Central Bank Chairman, Mario Draghi, used the famous phrase 'Whatever it Takes'. That phrase seems to have been dusted down and slightly reformulated for the pandemic crisis as, 'Whatever it Costs'.

The costs of both mitigating the disease and alleviating the economic damage it has caused have been very substantial. Most advanced economies, including the US, China, and the Eurozone already had significantly high debt to GDP ratios, but most still threw fiscal caution to the wind and borrowed even further to fight the pandemic. To solve the financial crisis of 2008-9 and bailout the banks, the US Congress passed stimulus packages to the tune of $1.5 trillion. With $3.3 trillion already allocated and spent, and a Biden fiscal rescue package of $1.9 trillion in the pipeline, the final tally for pandemic stimulus spending will be $5.2 trillion. This level of debt-funded fiscal relief amounts to an astonishing 25% of GDP – orders of magnitude greater than that of the financial crisis – and by far the highest amount spent by any other country during the pandemic. This enormous quantity of US fiscal stimulus has already created a debt to GDP ratio of over 100% - a debt level not seen since end of the Second World War.[4] The extreme danger in all of this is that, as Milton Friedman so pithily pointed out, there is nothing so permanent as a temporary government program.

With debt levels in many countries already at historic highs, this additional debt-financing could create a further unwelcome dimension to the pandemic as systemic financial stress leads to cascading defaults: layering a banking crisis on top of everything else. In the event of such a scenario unfolding, an economic rebound and a return to more normalised financial conditions will be greatly delayed. The 2008-9 financial crisis was the most severe shock to hit the global economy in more than 70 years, and because of subsequent investment shortfalls, the recovery was slow.[5] With the pandemic recession said to be at least twice as severe as the financial crisis, it is very likely to cast a much longer shadow.

A Cautionary Economic Tale

In the immediate aftermath of the 2008-9 financial crisis, Western governments pursued Keynesian stimulus programmes that involved borrowing huge amounts to finance additional government spending and the funding of tax cuts in an effort to revive their economies. Many worried that this burgeoning mountain of public debt was merely storing up major problems for the future. Though the phrase had been around for decades, 'kicking the can down the road' became the metaphor *du jour* for the predicament. Yet governments were stayed from taking more immediate action because of concerns that a premature withdrawal of the stimulus spending risked tipping the economy back into recession. Politicians, whose primary instinct is usually their own survival, were in a quandary: damned if they did, and damned if they didn't. Then, from the groves of academe came an economic benediction that offered the prospect of, if not quite political salvation, at least a respectable cover for action.

In 2010 two economists, Carmen Reinhart of the University of Maryland and Kenneth Rogoff of Harvard wrote a highly influential and a much-cited research paper titled, 'Growth in a Time of Debt'.[6] One of its principal conclusions was that, if a country's public debt exceeded 90% of GDP, then its economic growth would decline dramatically. This was interpreted by many as a critical tipping point for government indebtedness. Any further borrowing beyond this level would lead to a precipitous drop in economic growth. For fiscally frugal politicians, the paper was a godsend that offered deliverance from the horns of the dilemma on which the crisis had impaled them. For conservative governments, who were never comfortable in any case with what they considered a dangerous dalliance with socialist statism, it provided a way back to the path of economic righteousness. The transition from stimulus to austerity could be seamlessly executed, following which the sunlit uplands of sustained economic growth beckoned.

The Reinhart and Rogoff paper provided much of the theoretical cover for the stringent programmes that were subsequently implemented by most Western governments. In a *Financial Times* Op-ed article, the duo recognised that their cure had risks, but insisted it was the correct thing to do: 'Given the likelihood of continued weak consumption growth in the US and Europe, rapid withdrawal of stimulus could easily tilt the economy back into recession. Yet, the sooner politicians reconcile themselves to accepting adjustment, the lower the risks of truly paralysing debt problems down the road.'[7]

This was a confident assertion by two celebrated economists, but soon afterwards, some lesser lights at the University of Massachusetts discovered that the Reinhart-Rogoff analysis had some serious statistical flaws. These included some straightforward miscalculations as well as some unconventional data-averaging methods that undermined their headline conclusion that debt levels of over 90% of GDP were a threat to sustainable economic growth.[8] Accused by left-leaning economists such as Paul Krugman, of promoting austerity politics, the academics defended themselves: 'Nowhere did we assert that 90 percent was a magic threshold that transforms outcomes, as conservative politicians have suggested.'[9] This defence cut little ice with Prof. Krugman: 'What the Reinhart-Rogoff affair shows is the extent to which austerity has been sold on false pretenses.'[10] Though the controversy took some of the sheen off Reinhart and Rogoff's principal macroeconomic conclusion, it had by that stage, in Prof. Krugman's words, 'achieved almost sacred status among self-proclaimed guardians of fiscal responsibility.'[11]

But the rights and wrongs of the economic arguments were of far less significance than the political reverberations that ultimately flowed from it. The strict and over-zealous application of budget-reduction austerity by governments for whom the 90% of GDP rule had become an *ex-cathedra* prescription had some significant political consequences, which few had considered.

Rigid adherence to budgetary discipline and public debt reduction became the hill on which many politicians and governments had chosen to die – and in the ensuing political backlash, many of them did just that. In both Europe and the US, as well as other countries of size and significance around the world, the political centre was pushed to the political margins as populism of both left and right varieties made enormous political advances. Undoubtedly, like Tolstoy's unhappy families, each of these polities was 'unhappy in its own way', but most analysts now accept that the over-egging of the austerity agenda was a significant factor in the rise of so-called populism.

Flattening the Debt Curve

But 12 years later, as the pandemic lockdowns became more severe, many governments stepped up their emergency financial lifelines to protect people, preserve jobs, and minimise business bankruptcies. These discretionary fiscal measures were designed primarily to cushion the drop in household incomes caused by the derailing of most of the major economies. With the global economy largely closed for business, government incomes also took a big hit as a black hole suddenly appeared in their revenues. The effect of this fiscal pincer movement was to drive government debt to levels not seen outside of wartime.

At a time of ultra-low interest rates, the temptation to consider debt as being cost-free is considerable. However, the historical evidence shows that loading up with excessive debt has considerable risks which can force governments to implement disruptive fiscal adjustments at the least opportune moment. However, Reinhart and Rogoff's (2009) warnings on the perils of excessive public debt that we discussed above were put aside for the duration of the crisis. Part of the argument for this was that the fiscal costs of borrowing were not an issue so long as the interest rate stayed below the rate of economic growth. This benign scenario would obviate the need to increase future taxes in order to pay for past borrowing.

With interest rates at an all-time low, debt appears to be cheap: but it is not free. It is also important to remember that historically, elevated levels of public debt have been one of the most important harbingers of impending financial crises. In addition, as a recent IMF paper reiterated, the risks associated with high levels of debt have not gone away: ' beyond certain debt levels the likelihood of fiscal crises increases significantly irrespective of whether the interest-growth differential is highly positive or negative.'[12]

But such concerns seem quaintly old-fashioned in the context of the pandemic. The reality is that governments across the developed world have embarked on unprecedented levels of borrowing. It would also seem that a decade is a long time in economics. Carmen Reinhart, who co-authored the paper referred to earlier on the dangers of excessive debt and the threat it posed to economic growth, had a new job. As the newly minted Chief Economist at the World Bank, appointed in the middle of the pandemic, Ms. Reinhart, the long-time debt critic was singing a very different tune: 'While the disease is raging, what else are you going to do?

First you worry about fighting the war, then you figure out how to pay for it.'[13]

These extraordinarily large interventions by government were effective in the short term and prevented the economic crisis from spiralling out of control. But the size of the economic mitigation measures was unheard of outside of wartime. Governments spent huge sums on extended unemployment benefits, wage subsidies, and targeted cash transfers to both households and struggling businesses. This vast increase in expenditure has taken place while, simultaneously, the income of the state has been drastically reduced. On the revenue side there have been temporary deferrals of personal and corporate income tax and social security payments for periods of up to 12 months. Before the pandemic, what for many countries had been a fiscal gap soon turned into a yawning chasm that has continued to deepen. In many cases, governments have found themselves accumulating debt burdens as high as 150% of GDP, and in some cases even more.

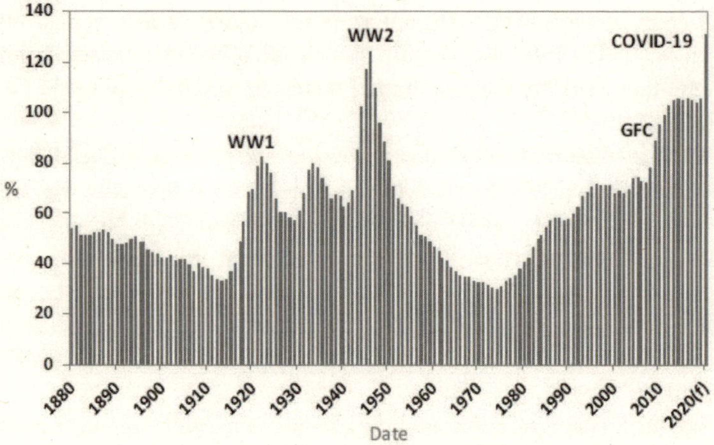

Public Debt as a % of GDP 1880-2020 Source IMF

As the above graph shows, we are in an exceptional era of debt-financed government spending which, for now at any rate, remains unconstrained by the threat of high interest rates. By the end of 2020, the IMF has estimated that the public debt of developed countries will amount to $66 trillion. As a once-in-a-century crisis, it seems clear that the current global pandemic warrants a committed policy response of deficit-financing in order to weather the economic storm. But ramping up government debt to the unprecedented levels not seen for over seven decades does not mean that this is a consequence-free option.

So, what will the post-pandemic economic landscape look like when the disease finally begins to ebb away? With austerity no longer a politically tenable option and interest rates at a historical low, the red ink has begun to flow in earnest as governments rack up significant amounts of sovereign debt to pay the enormous costs of the pandemic-induced economic crisis.

To remain within the currently defined boundaries of prudential economic management, governments in the developed world will need to tread a careful path between stimulus and restraint. The fact that for now, and for the foreseeable future, interest rates remain low and the threat of inflation is extremely low, means that governments can borrow to prop up their failing economies. This has the additional attraction of avoiding the necessity of debt reduction through austerity with its associated toxic political fallout.

For now, though, the Holy Grail of prudent management of the public finances, a balanced budget, will certainly end up getting kicked down the road like the proverbial can. But preparing for the eventual day of reckoning, whenever and however it arrives, will most likely be the defining challenge of our post-pandemic future. In the past, countries like Britain dealt with their war debts by letting inflation take care of them, but that option is no longer available. Today, the most effective way that governments have to reduce their debt mountains is through sustained economic growth at levels that are higher than prevailing interest rates. However, on past performance, this is a challenge that many will discover to be beyond their capacity to handle with ease.[14]

The promise of economic salvation from the arrival of effective vaccines in November has to be weighed, however, against the prospect of financial perdition that these unparalleled levels of public debt will entail. The ascent from the deep recession of 2020 back to pre-pandemic levels of economic growth will be long, uneven and difficult. There is also the considerable danger of significant permanent economic scarring.

One of the consequences of all this will almost certainly be an increase in inequality. To get an idea of the pandemic's adverse economic effects, it is worth reminding ourselves that the financial crisis of 2008-9 caused the global economy to shrink by 0.1%. In October, the IMF was predicting that by the end of 2020, the pandemic will have caused global economic output to drop by 4.4% – an outcome that's a whopping 44 times worse than that of the financial crisis.

JM Keynes booklet, *How to Pay for the War* was published in 1940. In it Keynes analysed the consequences of the manner in which the British government used a combination of inflation and higher taxes to pay off the enormous war debts from World War I. Keynes was at pains to stress that 'allowing prices to rise (inflation) … merely means that consumers' incomes pass into the hands of the capitalist class.'[15] In outlining his radical proposal, Keynes said, 'I have endeavoured to snatch from the exigency of war positive social improvements.' The booklet was a recognition by Keynes that the way in which the British government paid off its war debts had important implications for income and the distribution of wealth in society. The booklet was essentially an economic policy proposal which Keynes saw as an opportunity to introduce much-needed redistributive reforms that would maintain the vitality of the capitalist system.

The massive quantitative easing embarked upon to solve the economic fallout from the 2008-9 financial crisis, resulted in a spike in inequality because the "new money" boosted asset values such as stocks and bonds while wages continued to remain static. In tandem with this, the relentless pursuit of austerity policies provoked an unanticipated political backlash. How governments around the world proceed to deal with the unprecedently large pandemic debt mountain will also pose formidable challenges. The most demanding of these will be; how to avoid the cure being worse than the disease. In other words, will the disruption and chaos of the pandemic be replaced by a sustained period of debilitating political contagion?

During the initial stage of the pandemic as people watched Wuhan and city after city across central China being forced into draconian lockdowns, few had any conception that such a thing could even be contemplated in a modern democracy. They were quickly disabused of this conceit, as China-style lockdowns were imposed, first in Italy, and then across the whole of Europe. By November, it was happening all over again as Lombardy became Europe's coronavirus hotspot once more: indeed, its infection rates even worse than before. As Italy drowned in another wave of the virus, an estimated 16.5 million people in the densely populated Lombardy region, which includes Milan, experienced yet another episode of lockdown. By December, the virus had mutated and the UK faced the unenviable prospect of a Christmas lockdown, and even 'the hope of some sort of parole over the Christmas period was extinguished. By January mutant variants of the virus were causing consternation across the globe. Even China, which had managed to keep minor outbreaks under control through mass testing for all of 2020, was struck by levels of infection that had not been seen since the previous January.

Businesses that had been severely hit during the first wave came under renewed financial pressure by the year's end. Despite many jobs being protected through government furlough schemes, unemployment began to increase as more and more businesses buckled under the intense strain. As more firms fell into bankruptcy, their bad loans, in turn, placed enormous stress on the banking system. In economic terms, the second and third waves presaged a double-dip recession, with service companies such as restaurants, bars, hotels, and airlines again bearing the brunt of the crisis. The OECD estimated that between 70 and 80% of these businesses were adversely affected by being completely shut down in most countries. The likely outcome of all this was explained in November by ECB president, Cristine Lagarde: 'firms that have survived up to now by increasing borrowing and drawing on their savings could decide that remaining open no longer makes business sense.'[16]

To a much greater extent than the financial crisis, the pandemic recession has been a regressive economic crisis. It has disproportionally affected low-income households and smaller business enterprises which have less assets to fight off the threat of insolvency. Fitch, the ratings agency, has estimated that in the light of the collapse of GDP, without government furlough schemes, much of Europe would have experienced a surge in unemployment of up to 14%. Government subsidies to maintain workers incomes helped businesses to survive and averted mass unemployment by effectively freezing the labour market in place. But once the furlough schemes started to be dismantled, the true impact on the labour market quickly emerged as paid inactivity got transformed into unemployment. As Warren Buffet said in the context of a previous economic crisis, 'it's only at that sage, when the tide goes out that you find out who's been swimming naked.'

Chapter 27: The Costs of Lockdown

It was a full seven weeks after the first Covid-19 patient had been admitted to a hospital in Wuhan before the CCP finally allowed one of China's most renowned epidemiologists to go on the main state-controlled tv channel to announce that the disease did have human-to-human transmission. Zhong Nanshan's statement only confirmed what most Chinese may have already suspected for many weeks, but the official confirmation was still shocking. Having lost weeks of invaluable time during the early phase of the highly infectious outbreak by covering up and dissembling, the Party leadership knew it was too late for mitigation, the only response left was a draconian form of suppression – lockdown.

Within three days Wuhan, a city of over 11 million people, was hermetically sealed. The following day, more than 60 million people across Hubei province and surrounding areas were subjected to the same drastic policy of lockdown: a policy that was vigorously, and at times, violently enforced. Quarantining such a large number of people had never been tried before; in the words of one WHO official, it was 'unprecedented in public health history.' But what that official omitted to mention was a lockdown on this scale and with this intensity was tailor-made for an authoritarian police-state equipped with the world's most extensive techno-surveillance capabilities. Meanwhile, as the peoples of the world looked on with a mixture of fascination and apprehension at what was happening in China, they had little inkling that before long they too would be experiencing lockdown, albeit in a much less authoritarian form.

Out of Options

The release of the Imperial College report in mid-March led the UK government to abandon any further talk of herd immunity as it embarked on a new strategy of 'suppression'. This involved radical measures such as school closures and quarantining infected people. These measures were not expected to change the overall number of infections or deaths; instead, these would just be spread out over a longer period. This so-called 'flattening of the curve' was designed to prevent the hospital system from being overwhelmed by a sudden inundation of Covid patients. As the lead epidemiologist in the study, Dr Neil Ferguson put it 'Based on our estimates and other teams', there's really no option but follow in China's footsteps and suppress.'

To a large extent, the panic induced by the Imperial College projections was understandable – if those projections had turned out to be true, the effects would have been horrendous. But as time went by real data became available – even though they were still imperfect data. The actual figures reflected reality in all its glorious misery, but bad as they were, the reality was nowhere near what had been projected. The reality was grim, but not so apocalyptic and alarmingly grim as the Imperial College projections had led governments to believe. This begs the question: when the dire projections upon which the lockdown policy had been predicated did not happen, why was it persisted with? Even more pertinent: as further waves began to sweep across many countries, why did governments resorted yet again to lockdown – as if they and their advisers become one-trick lockdown ponies. They were failing to learn from experience; not even the kind of experience described by the US journalist Franklin P. Jones; 'Experience is that marvelous thing that enables you to recognize a mistake when you make it again.'

To have a reasonable chance of success, containment necessitated three essential elements: the early detection of cases through extensive testing, the immediate tracing of an infected individual's contacts, and then quarantining them for up to 14 days. The handful of countries that were successful in controlling the disease through containment distinguished themselves in two principal ways: they were aware and they were prepared. Since they were aware of the existential threat posed to them by any SARS-like disease, once they got the whiff of an outbreak in Wuhan, these Asian states reacted immediately (see chapter 15). But, critically, they had already equipped themselves with the institutional infrastructure to combat a serious infectious disease outbreak from their previous experience with SARS, almost two decades earlier.

Because of SARS, China too had put in place an elaborate early infectious disease warning system and had tested it regularly in 'fire-drills'. But when a real outbreak happened in Wuhan, the system remained largely underutilised due to the CCP's visceral antipathy to any news that might tarnish the Party's omnipotent image. A month and a half after the first infected patients were admitted to hospital in Wuhan was simply far too late for any form of containment to be effective, and so the CCP was forced to embark on the largest lockdown in history.

For all those other countries which, for a variety of reasons, had also missed the containment window, a rigorous, though less repressive version of China's lockdown became the accepted norm. Indeed, any dissenting view was almost regarded as heretical. The suppression of the disease that ensued involved massive social and economic disruption, but was presented and discussed in less menacing terms such as mitigation or flattening the curve. The vast majority of countries around the world bungled their initial response to the disease and so were out of options almost before they began. Bewildered by the speed with which Covid-19 had blanketed their countries and infected their populations, but anxious to be seen to act decisively against this silent interloper, they embraced lockdown with a sense of mission, but with little or no consideration of the costs or consequences.

Any fundamental assessment of these costs, however, would bring us to a rarely discussed, morally fraught, and ethically troubling question of how much does a human life cost? This is not the place for a detailed investigation of such a vexed question. I raise it merely to highlight the fact that, when embarking on such a drastic all-encompassing policy as lockdown, we should at least countenance the reality that flattening the curve entails other costs that deserve an airing.

One can also, of course, make the very reasonable argument that when the house is on fire is not the time to start worrying about the cost of the water bill. But I'm not referring here to financial or monetary costs in that narrow sense – although public policies always come down to economic costs at the end of the day. What's at issue here is that consequential policy decisions should not be taken exclusively on the basis of just one criterion – however critical that criterion may be. A more thorough evaluation of the policy options should entail using a variety of factors. This should be done on the basis of a cost-benefit analysis which, without wishing to be pedantic, involves weighing up the costs on the one hand, as against the benefits on the other. In the case of the US and UK governments (many others followed the same logic), it was the questionable Imperial College epidemiological analysis that proved to be the clincher in pushing them to adopt the lockdown policy.

The speed with which the contagion spread in Italy was stupendous. On February 20, there were only three confirmed cases in the country. A mere 18 days later, Italy's Prime Minister, Giuseppe Conte announced a draconian national lockdown: 'all of Italy is a protected zone', he declared to a bewildered populace. Governments across the Western world looked on in amazement, not fully grasping the fact that what they were witnessing was a preview of their own near-term futures.

In Wuhan at the peak of the outbreak when the hospitals were being completely overwhelmed, the case fatality rate was 5.8%. At a press conference early in March at its Geneva headquarters, the WHO's Dr Tedros had some alarming information, 'Globally, about 3.4% of reported Covid-19 cases have died.' For a highly contagious disease, that was a frightening statistic. At that same press conference, the head of the organisation's health emergency programme, Dr. Mike Ryan, gave the WHO's clearest endorsement of the efficacy of lockdown in fighting Covid-19: 'Here we have a disease for which we have no vaccine, no treatment, we don't fully understand transmission, we don't fully understand case mortality, but … where countries have fought back, where they've put in place strong measures, we've remarkably seen that the virus is suppressed.'[1] Future events would cruelly undermine that degree of confidence in such "strong measures".

In the consternation and panic surrounding the initial phase of this infectious disease outbreak with its suspected high morbidity and mortality rates, it was entirely acceptable for governments to adopt extreme interventions on the basis of the precautionary principle alone. In the absence of virtually no empirical data, these decisions, *faute de mieux*, were based almost exclusively on modelling projections. But the evidential cupboard did not remain completely bare for long. Empirical data soon began to emerge which shed some much-needed light onto this dark epidemiological picture.

Fatality rates are calculated by dividing the number of deaths from Covid-19 by the number of cases of the disease. But the number of cases is highly dependent on how many people are being tested. And since most testing was concentrated on those with symptoms, and usually those with more severe symptoms, the significant number of people with Covid-19 who were asymptomatic were not tested at all. Overall, the logic of the statistics ran as follows: the less testing, the less reported cases, the higher the mortality rate. Thus, because of different testing regimes, in using case fatality rates to compare the experience of different countries we quickly come up against the statistical difficulties of comparing apples and oranges.

But in this pandemic the number of asymptomatic cases was shrouded in uncertainties. Later studies began to indicate that up to half of all those infected were asymptomatic and these people could go on silently and unknowingly spreading the disease for up to 14 days after becoming infected. The early figures missed these people completely, as testing was only carried out initially on those who were hospitalised, and later on those showing symptoms: in other words, the silent spreaders were being missed completely.[2]

Even at this early stage, there was no doubt as to who the at-risk groups were: the elderly with pre-exiting health problems topped the list, then came others with underlying health conditions, such as those with cardiac, hypertension, diabetes, and lung diseases, and those who were otherwise immune-compromised. But it was also very well understood at this time that at least 80% of the population were in no real danger from the disease and would experience only mild symptoms if they became infected. This was confirmed by a WHO report as early as March 2020. However, it was what would happen to the remaining 20% that was the most disquieting. The early indications suggested that the next 15% of infections would be severe. But most troublesome of all, the remaining 5% would require hospitalisation in an intensive-care unit.[3] The implications of this for national health services in every country were stark.

In the light of all of this, lockdown made considerable sense; if only for the perfectly justifiable reason that no realistic alternative at the time. Lockdown had almost an onomatopoeically reassuring ring to it. It sounded so extreme that it seemed it had to work. But that aside, given the imperfect knowledge about the virus and the disease it was causing, erring on the side of caution was the correct thing to do. We had missed the critical opportunity for effective containment right at the start of the outbreak and we would not be given a second chance. If there were any debate on the issue, it was one framed in terms of just one short-term objective: the safeguarding of scarce hospital resources in order to be able to deal with the anticipated massive influx of severely ill Covid patients.

At its most basic, lockdown is a mediaeval plague solution being applied to 21st century societies. Much else has changed in the intervening seven centuries but, perhaps, human nature is not one of them. In economic terms, as we have seen, the costs have been gargantuan and will take generations to pay off. But the lockdown did achieve its primary objective of preventing hospital systems from being overrun. It succeeded so well in fact that many of the 'pop-up' hospitals that were built with impressive speed went largely unused. But then, towards the end of almost six months of lockdown, as the more extreme restrictions were lifted, the virus re-emerged. Reflexively, most governments reached for the lockdown sledgehammer again.

Having relied on fear and panic to persuade their populations to comply with the lockdown rules the first time, it was nigh on impossible for governments to reverse engines and change their lockdown impulses – even when the available data suggested that they should. This policy persistence was certainly not data-driven, and its basis in the science was far from self-evident. More likely, fear of losing credibility with the electorate was a major consideration in this reluctance to consider other policies. However, in failing to change tack they also risked undermining the public's confidence in the very lockdown measures they sought to bolster – for policymakers and governments it had become something of a Hobson's choice. As a second wave manifested itself in more and more countries, an increasingly restive population began to baulk at the prospect of a second lockdown.

Cure v Disease

As with all policy prescriptions, lockdown involves trade-offs. The debate was largely seen as a trade-off between lives and livelihoods, and a question of how to preserve the health of the population while maintaining the health of the economy. Ultimately, this is a false dichotomy since the two are inextricably linked because of the social nature of this disease. A more comprehensive approach to policy evaluation needed to consider the health costs but also the social and the economic costs: all three as separate but linked categories of cost. As the rate of reproduction of the virus changed dynamically and the infection and mortality rates were affected either in reality or as a result of more accurate data becoming available, it was imperative that the policy response be more flexible.

For instance, we knew who the vulnerable people were from the start of this pandemic. If governments and policy makers were unaware or confused, they need only have asked any passing medical student who would have explained to them the high-risk categories. The ones most susceptible to most contagious upper respiratory viral infection are elderly people with underlying medical conditions and other immuno-compromised people. Covid-19 was a highly infectious disease that was mild for many, serious for a minority, and fatal for the few. Yet a perverse irony of the lockdown policy was that while it locked down everyone else, it failed to safely lockdown the largest cohort of the most vulnerable – those in nursing and care homes.

This failure on the part of those charged with implementing the policy is one of the most breath-taking aspects of the pandemic. It reveals a complete absence of critical thinking on the part of health administrations. They seemed unable to grasp a core concept of public health policy implementation: that any policy evaluation must include the 'costs' of the policy itself. There is no such thing as a completely neutral 'flattening the curve'. The motivation for lockdown, as epitomised by such slogans as 'protect our NHS' in the UK, was a supreme priority of reducing suffering and death. But a draconian policy that directed all resources to flattening one disease curve meant inevitably that the trajectory of other disease curves would rise – sometimes with shocking consequences.

The worry for an increasing number of sceptics was that the lockdown cure would turn out to be worse than the Covid disease. Had policy makers given sufficient consideration to the impact of what they were doing, as well as the impact of what they were trying to prevent – did they only calculate one side of the lockdown equation? People began to question how much of this dystopian lockdown world was based on science fact or science fiction. In particular, what was the basis for privileging suffering and death from Covid-19 over consequential suffering and death from other diseases?

In all of this there is the not inconsiderable issue of delayed or forgone healthcare. In order to make room for the much-anticipated flood of Covid patients, hospitals and health care systems decided to cease non-essential procedures and all elective ones. To the lay person this conjures up the idea that this type of hospital procedure involves operations that have been insisted upon by the worried well, or even by those who want some kinds of cosmetic surgery. They are not. In Britain, the public was exhorted to 'save the NHS' in the UK by avoiding going to hospital, even in emergencies. And all of the evidence suggests that the public followed that advice and stayed away in very significant numbers.

Many of the foregone procedures were cancer screenings, cancer treatments involving radiography or chemotherapy, hip replacements or knee replacements, cataracts etc. Astonishingly, even emergency room attendance dropped off markedly. Some of this decrease was undoubtedly due to other factors: there were, for example, less vehicle accidents due to less traffic, but that does not explain the massive decline in heart attacks or strokes turning up in hospitals. The presumption is that many of those affected died at home, and in the case of many elderly people, they died alone. There are reports that 40% of those who experienced strokes, which requires a one-to-six-hour window to optimise recovery, did not call an ambulance within that timeframe. This might be explained, not justified, by the fact that many of these people were of a generation for whom personal sacrifice for the good of the society was second nature – it may have cost many of them their lives, completely unnecessarily.

For many of those who questioned the appropriateness of radical lockdowns, the fear was that the number of actual deaths as a result of being denied access to routine clinical healthcare may ultimately be greater than the projected fatalities from Covid-19. The forestalling of medical diagnoses of life-threatening diseases such as cancer screenings, tumour biopsies, colonoscopies etc., in addition to deferred treatments such as chemotherapy were seldom factored in as part of the costs of lockdown. According to Reuters, 'Millions of patients postponed tests considered crucial for detecting early signs of disease, monitoring its progression and improving patient outcomes'. The drop-off in the numbers going for some preventative care screenings were very high: in the case of cervical cancer, it was 68%; for cholesterol 67%; for diabetes testing 65%.[4] The scale of the unintended consequences as measured in increased mortality or suffering is difficult to calculate, but it is unlikely to be trivial and may well eclipse the total for Covid-19.

Aside from exacerbating serious underlying health conditions in the wider population, with the inevitable suffering and death that flowed from them, there were wider societal considerations that were being largely ignored. Increases in substance and alcohol abuse were inevitably accompanied by growing instances of domestic abuse as whole populations were locked up at close quarters for lengths of time rarely before experienced. With schools closed, the children couped up at home added to the list of potential abuse victims in some households. Not alone were the most vulnerable kids losing out on education, for many, school was also where they received the regular nutritious meals that were often unavailable at home. In extremis, where child abuse is suspected, it is schools and teachers who have traditionally been in the front line of identifying and reporting suspected cases; lockdown removed this important social safety net as well. It is impossible, for now, to assess these 'costs' but they will emerge in time when the experts have completed their research, and there is little doubt that the published reports will make for some harrowing reading.

More broadly, the lockdown had considerable differential effects on various social groups within society. To minimise social interaction during the lockdown governments insisted that, as far as possible, people should work from home. Employers were urged to facilitate their employees in this regard, and the vast majority of businesses did so. These were employees who mostly worked all day sitting at a desk with a computer – they were, by and large, the professional or semi-professional middle-classes.

But not all jobs or employees could easily accommodate themselves to these radically-altered work circumstances. Apart altogether from the direct economic impact on their social lives and incomes, the pandemic differentially impacted on lower-paid employees to a far greater extent than other socio-economic groups.

If you worked in a supermarket, a factory, in construction, maintenance, or drove a van, a bus or a taxi, were a hairdresser, or a member of the police, emergency, health care, or postal services, or worked in a meat factory, or the myriad of other jobs that required your physical presence, working from home was simply not an option. On the other hand, managers, office staff and those in administration, finance and banking as well as large sections of the public service could largely work from home. Those on the frontline of delivering services to the public had to continue to turn up for work, and, in the process, were also exposing themselves to the predations of the virus.

None of the above is to suggest that the alternative to lockdown is a let-the-virus-rip policy in the hope of reaching the promised land of herd immunity. Not even Sweden, which famously eschewed lockdown, went anywhere near that. In the heady first few days of the outbreak when infection numbers were tiny, most governments affected a nonchalant attitude while reassuring their publics that they were well prepared. The truth is that they were not. They were completely unprepared in one fateful, and, ultimately fatal, respect – mass testing. Where it really mattered, the rhetoric did not match the reality.

It was this failure more than anything else that impelled governments across the world to rely on various forms of draconian lockdown. This was not a policy of choice; it was imposed on them by their own lack of preparedness right from the beginning. Even more damning, six months into the pandemic many governments were still bungling their efforts to deliver mass testing. There is a simple principle that if you don't measure then you can't manage, when second and third waves hit in the closing months of 2020, many societies had to be placed in lockdown, yet again.

Chapter 28: Testing Times

Breathing Space

The coronavirus survives in airborne particles and gets access to us through our respiratory tracts. As we must keep breathing to survive, this is a highly effective way for the virus to gain easy entry. There is nothing unusual in this; lots of viruses use the same trick. Influenza viruses have been invading human respiratory tracts for centuries causing us to cough, splutter, and sneeze when they do. But as a piece of parasitical biological engineering, the SARS-CoV-2 virus has some other interesting features: two in particular.

The SARS-CoV-2 virus differs from influenza viruses is that, in many instances, it does not announce itself. There are no tell-tale coughs, splutters, or sneezes to alert us that something is wrong. Anything up to 40% of Covid infections happen silently and unobtrusively. We are unaware that we have become infected – we are, in medical jargon, asymptomatic. But here's the real rub; we can be merrily spreading the virus during this asymptomatic phase completely unknown to ourselves. The second significant feature of the virus is that it particularly targets the elderly. Masses of evidence point clearly to the fact that those over 70 years of age are especially vulnerable – a vulnerability that increases with each passing year. If, as is often the case, these elderly people also have other serious underlying health conditions, then the danger of death increases exponentially. These two features, its surreptitious spread combined with its lethality for the elderly, make this virus both very dangerous and extremely difficult to control.

Testing 101

There are lots of different tests for the virus and, as we shall see, innovative scientific research is bringing more to market almost on a weekly basis. Since the start of the pandemic testing has been an absolutely vital aspect of controlling the spread of the virus – as I've already said: if you don't measure you can't manage. When it is combined with tracing, testing enables us to identify infected individuals, to isolate them and to pinpoint their close contacts. The concept of test and trace may seem simple, but, in practice, few countries have done it successfully.

Broadly speaking, the hundreds of individual tests that are available can be divided into three categories: diagnostic tests, antibody tests, and antigen tests. The most commonly used diagnostic test glories in the technical name of "reverse transcription-polymerase chain reaction RT-PCR", (henceforth, PCR). The PCR test is a molecular diagnostic test that looks for the genetic RNA material of the virus which, if found, confirms that the person is infected. In scientific argot, PCR is a nucleic acid diagnostic test, and an important diagnostic tool. This is especially true in hospital settings, as it allows medical staff to make informed clinical decisions about infected patients. Though PCR is thought of as the 'gold standard' of testing, like all medical tests it is not infallible. Studies have indicated that up to 30% of PCR results can be inaccurate, with false negatives being more common than false positives: a critical factor that can undermine efforts to contain the virus. A false negative result is more consequential because, if an individual is asymptomatic, they could continue to infect others, unwittingly.[1]

The second type is a serological antibody test. The coronavirus is easily recognised by its now famous corona spikes that make them look somewhat similar to an old-style floating naval mine. And just like the naval mine spikes that cause an explosion on contact with a ship, the corona spike allows the virus to colonise a human cell and cause a viral explosion. In response, antibodies are produced that attach themselves to the invading pathogens which can then be eliminated from the body. But the immune system's response is not immediate. It can take days and sometimes even weeks for the antibodies to develop. Significantly, from a testing point of view, these antibodies can remain in a person's blood for several weeks, long after they've made a full recovery. It is the presence of these tell-tale antibodies that is the key that picks the lock for the antibody test.

And lastly, there's the antigen test. This does not seek molecular or genetic markers; it looks for specific proteins that protrude from the surface of the virus such as the signature coronavirus spike. Antigen tests are cheap and can provide results much faster that a PCR test, but they are also less accurate. However, the fact that they can provide test results more rapidly and are relatively cheap makes them particularly suited to being used for mass testing programmes and in point-of-care locations. Because of this, the antigen test will be the focus of particular attention in the next chapter.

To summarise briefly on testing techniques: as a logical outcome of the basic molecular and genetic features of the virus, we can think of the three tests in terms of different time horizons. The PCR and the antigen tests are diagnostic tests and have an 'immediate' focus in that they can reveal whether or not someone is currently infected: with the trade-off between them being speed versus accuracy. On the other hand, the antibody test is 'retrospective' in nature and can confirm if a person has had the disease.

Preparing to Fail

Large scale testing using PCR is not easy. The practicalities of a PCR test involve a two-step operation which takes place in two separate locations: a sampling station and a laboratory testing facility. At the sampling station, some mucus is collected by inserting a type of cotton bud down the throat or up the nose of an individual. This mucus swab is then placed in a vial containing chemicals and sent to a laboratory for analysis. Because of the surge in PCR testing around the world there is now a materials supply problem resulting in worldwide competition for reagents, the chemicals used to detect the RNA signature of the virus. And a further bottle-neck has arisen with the supply of swabs.

Handling the swabs in the laboratories is pretty routine, but analysing the results requires trained expertise. The PCR test is also expensive, and because of the dual location it can be logistically challenging. It is, in other words, a labour-intensive process, involving several stages at which errors may occur giving rise to false negatives and positives. The test itself can produce results in 3 to 4 hours but the logistics involved in using specialist laboratories means that in practice, there is a minimum of 24 hours before results are available.

Because PCR testing demands very significant laboratory infrastructure, trained technical personal, costly machines, complex logistics and supply chain management, large-scale testing is effectively ruled out for most countries. For those burdened with centralised laboratory structures effective mass testing presents real difficulties. The public sector is not generally known for its project management skills or its ability to build complex systems at scale and at speed. Relying on the administrative state alone to solve a critical aspect of the pandemic response was asking for trouble: and those who did so were not to be disappointed.

At its most basic, controlling the Covid-19 pandemic is primarily an information problem – it's really about what have been termed "the known unknows". We know there are many people infected with the disease, we just don't know who they are. The only meaningful way to fill that critical information gap is through testing. And the more we test the smaller the information gap becomes and, crucially, the more the pandemic picture begins to resolve into something that can at least be managed. For the few countries that did this promptly and successfully – such as Taiwan or New Zealand – a version of normal life continued and draconian lockdowns were avoided. For the many who didn't and who missed the boat at the start, a comprehensive testing regime, even if belatedly instituted, still offered the real prospect of making up for lost time. Unfortunately, many of those countries did not manage to avail of this second chance because they continued to fail the testing challenge.

Public Health England's instinctive centralised command-and-control instincts kicked in at the start. Outside help from some of the world's best university scientists, diagnostic laboratories and pharma companies was repeatedly rebuffed. PHE started with just a single lab in January and were slow to expand testing to its lab network, and even slower to involve NHS labs. In contrast, mass testing and tracing was at the heart of Germany's pandemic strategy from the beginning. By slowing the outbreak, Germany's testing strategy bought precious time to allow healthcare capacity to adapt to the to the particular demands of a pandemic, without becoming overwhelmed.

Professor Anthony Costello of University College London, a former WHO director, explained that 'Testing is the basis of public health detective work to shut down an epidemic.'[2] A position reiterated by the WHO's Dr Tedros who insisted that the only way to break the chain of transmission of the virus was to test and isolate. 'You cannot fight a fire blindfolded. And we cannot stop this pandemic if we don't know who is infected. We have a simple message for all countries: test, test, test.'[3]

But, of course, it is not just testing per se that matters: the timing of the testing is also critical. A high rate of testing conducted early on in the outbreak can prove effective at controlling it: the logistics are less daunting at that stage as there are far fewer infections to deal with at that stage. For the same reason, the testing programme itself is also more manageable. The evidence of the Asian Tiger states who instigated precisely these types of early and extensive testing initiatives offers incontrovertible evidence that it can work. The evidence from the US, UK, much of Europe and the rest of the developed world provides disheartening proof that failure to act swiftly with testing can have calamitous consequences.

As the virus raged through central China, on February 11, the UK's Department of Health and Social Care sought to reassure the public that its command-and-control system had everything in hand: 'we have world-class systems in place to prevent supply problems', a Health Minister declared. And the statement finished with a flourish, 'The NHS and wider health system is extremely well prepared for coronavirus and follows tried and tested procedures of the highest standards to protect staff, patients and the public.'[4] At this early stage in the crisis, the administrative state's health apparatus was graced with full-spectrum optimism, which, unfortunately, turned out to be entirely misplaced and delusional.

Right from the start, the 'world-class' testing programme promised by British politicians was shown to be spectacularly deficient. The meeting of SAGE, the UK government's scientific advisory body held on February 18 was informed that Public Health England's testing system was woefully inadequate – incredibly, it was only able to test and trace five Covid-19 cases per week. Even more disquieting, modelling suggested that, at best, the system could only be 'improved' to handle a total of 50 infection cases per week.[5] It was decided to abandon testing altogether. Britain was now flying blind in the midst the biggest public health infectious disease crisis in a century.

This means that right at the beginning of the outbreak in the UK, this acute shortage of testing had immediate and insidious repercussions. Throughout the country, medical and hospital administrators were having to make the unenviable decisions to use their limited testing capacity only on their patients, and leaving their staff untested. Large numbers of doctors and nurses were then having to self-isolate at home, unsure whether or not they had become infected by the virus. Weeks later, when those staff who had been self-isolating were tested, only one in seven were found to be positive. This lack of testing had greatly exacerbated the critical shortage of frontline medical staff.[6] At that time, there were only up to 70,000 tests being carried out in Britain each week compared to the 500,000 being done in Germany.

By the time industry and government got around to ramping up production of diagnostic testing kits, they hit another wall: there was a shortage of the critical chemical reagents that were essential to ensuring the reliability of tests. Soon various materials that were also vital to maintain the integrity of the entire testing process were in short supply. These included the first step in the process, the specialist swabs needed to reach the back of the throat to collect the mucus – and without a sample, there could be no test. In the laboratory, technicians use complex chemicals to extract the RNA genetic material from the sample. But because of the vastly increased worldwide demand for these, they too were in short supply. Clearly, those in charge had failed to comprehend, or had forgotten, the basic lesson taught in every management course they had ever attended: fail to prepare, prepare to fail.

Failing the Test

In the United States, a similarly flawed testing saga was unfolding. Over the seven decades of its existence, the US Centre for Disease Control and Prevention (CDC) had established an enviable reputation as one of the world's most respected health agencies. With an annual budget of over $12 billion and a staff compliment of 15,000, it is, by any standards, a formidable health behemoth. Yet, for an organisation that was established with the specific remit of dealing with and preventing the spread of deadly pathogens, it ran into serious and fundamental difficulties more or less from the beginning of the coronavirus pandemic. During the worst global public health crisis in over a century, the CDC's reputation has been tarnished, and its institutional credibility undermined largely as a result of some significant own goals.

According to the *New York Times*, initial attempts to get comprehensive testing under way were severely hampered by a combination of 'technical flaws, regulatory hurdles, business- as-usual bureaucracies'.[7] As its name suggests, and its mission statement confirms, the CDC has as its primary purpose; 'to protect America from health, safety and security threats, both foreign and in the U.S'. To do so, it claims to be 'On the cutting edge of health security – confronting global disease threats through advanced computing and lab analysis of huge amounts of data to quickly find solutions.'[8]

In a little more than a month after the virus had crossed to the United States from China in January 2020, the CDC had developed a test which received fast-track approval from the FDA in earl February. As one commentator described it, this was 'a remarkable display of government competence and bureaucratic flexibility, [whereby] two federal agencies were able to create a test for a never-before-seen virus and approve it for nationwide distribution in less than a month.'[9] It was also at that point, however, that the centralised controlling instincts of the state bureaucracy came to the fore, and laid the foundations of what proved to be a fiasco on a gargantuan scale.

Right from the beginning of the outbreak in the United States, dozens of federal officials met daily in the White House 'situation room' to grapple with the crisis. The meetings were constantly reassured by the CDC members present that it had a diagnostic kit ready to be rolled out as a first step in tackling the pandemic. But as February passed into March, the promised testing kit failed to materialise. While the FDA had given fast-track approval to the CDC test, it put impassable bureaucratic roadblocks in front of all those other players who were also developing tests with the result that no other test received FDA approval until February 29.

In the meantime, major problems had emerged with the CDC tests when they were put into real-world operation. These took a further three weeks to resolve. Having bet the farm on the CDC test, the US was left with virtually no form of mass testing during this critical early stage of the pandemic, when the virus was spreading exponentially. By mid-March, almost six weeks into the pandemic, because of the bureaucratic bungling with the CDC diagnostic testing programme, the US had no idea how big the infectious disease outbreak was.

At this critical early stage, a month was lost in which no mass testing could be carried out. The wealthiest, most technologically advanced, and scientifically well-endowed nation on earth had simply no idea of the scale of the developing catastrophe. Just like the United Kingdom, the US had squandered its opportunity to implement mass testing and so was destined to remain behind the viral curve as it spread surreptitiously across the country.

The practicalities of a PCR test involve a two-step operation which takes place in separate locations: a sampling station and a laboratory testing facility. At the sampling station, some mucus is collected by sticking a type of cotton bud down the throat or up the nose of an individual. This mucus swab is then placed in a vial containing chemicals and sent to a laboratory for analysis. Because the surge in PCR testing around the world there was a materials supply problem resulting in worldwide competition for reagents, the chemicals used to detect the RNA signature of the virus. And a further bottle-neck had arisen with the supply of swabs. The US was discovering what the UK had found out a little earlier – global supply chains for these products had become dysfunctional.

While it took other European countries months to establish the type of coronavirus testing regime required to combat the pandemic – and some were still struggling even after 6 months – by contrast, mass testing and tracing was at the heart of Germany's pandemic strategy from the start and managed to maintained a high level of testing right throughout. By slowing the outbreak, Germany's testing strategy bought precious time to allow healthcare capacity to adapt to the to the particular demands of a pandemic, without becoming overwhelmed.

Testing is not centralised in Germany; it is run by each of the 16 federal states. By June, the country had 138 operating labs doing over 165,000 tests a day. Even with a resurgence of infections in October, its testing regime maintained a spare capacity of 400,000 tests per week, with a maximum capability to do 1 million PCR tests per week, if required.

So, what did Germany do differently? It started testing very early. It had a decentralised testing infrastructure with multiple small and medium-sized labs dispersed around the country. It had an 'open' testing policy whereby anyone could get tested whether they had symptoms or not, and so they were able to identify many of the asymptomatic carriers. Tests were paid for by the state, and anyone that was required to self-quarantine were paid full wages for up to six weeks. Underlying all of this, of course, is the fact that Germany has a thriving medical diagnostics industry and one of the best health care infrastructures in the world – incomparable advantages when having to tackle an infectious disease pandemic. Though infections did increase during the second wave in the late autumn, Germany still managed to avoid crippling its health system with a sudden surge in Covid hospitalisations, and it also maintained its record of low Covid mortalities.

Chapter 29: A Pregnancy Test for Covid

The worst pandemic in a century has precipitated both a health crisis and an economic crisis. Governments have, by and large, taken the view that both crises cannot be solved simultaneously. They have opted to solve the health crisis and put the economy on life-support. But a singular focus on the health side of this equation also carries inordinate risks; ones that in the throes of pandemic panic have been put to one side.

There was a window of opportunity at the beginning of the outbreak to contain the virus, but the chance was blown by governments all over the world. What the strategy of national lockdowns has revealed is that the alternative option of containment failed at an early stage. These lockdowns may eventually have proved productive by decreasing infections and mortality. But one crisis has only been superseded by another: how to exit lockdown without causing a viral resurgence. Unfortunately, once the restrictions began to be lifted this is exactly what happened and the demon virus returned with a vengeance. Since the second wave threatening to be worse than the first, there seemed little option but to implement further lockdowns.

Fear and Loathing

The first lockdowns had substantially reduced infection rates, but, as it transpired, that was only a temporary abatement. It became increasingly difficult to justify continuing the lockdown strategy when it was causing economies to have a near-death experience. It was also becoming apparent that people's faith in that strategy was being undermined significantly by the obvious failure of governments to offer credible ways to exit from it. What was sorely required was another strategy –one that could control and mitigate the spread of the virus while simultaneously permitting the economy and daily life to gradually return to some semblance of normality. To achieve this, lockdown, as the most extreme form of social distancing, needed to be complemented by a more nuanced approach.

From the beginning, the virus instilled an enormous amount of fear in people. It didn't matter that some of this may have been irrational or, for that matter, a consequence of governments' inept attempts to get people to comply with the lockdown rules. It maybe something that we don't like to admit it, but our visceral fear impulses are easily provoked.

Prolonged social isolation and a general atmosphere of persistent low-level anxiety about catching the virus was, experts believed, also contributing to significant psychological stress. Evidence was emerging that this stress and anxiety was even retard our antiviral defence mechanisms: in other words, pandemic induced stress could actually have increased our likelihood of becoming infected.[1] On top of all this, coping with the growing economic insecurities meant further debilitating consequences. These were various forms of mass psychosis that need to be addressed in a generalised way. In the short and medium-term, one of the most effective means to deal with these pervasive, doubts, insecurities and fears could have been through mass testing.

If the public had confidence that testing was being carried out on a sufficiently large scale to quickly identify and then isolate those who had become infected, their anxieties and fears might well have begun to subside. People could then go about their business confident in the knowledge that they ran a substantially reduced risk of becoming infected. It would have meant that the normal patterns of social and economic interactions could be sustained without having to endure pervasive debilitating disruptions. At the end of the day, it could also give people hope that a close approximation to normal daily life might be in prospect - sooner rather than later.

The financial costs of such an extensive testing programme would, in reality, probably have been irrelevant. No matter what the cost, it would have amounted to little more than a rounding error when compared to the colossal costs of locking down the economy for months on end. In the context of the billions of funding that had already been spent on testing programmes that turned out to be comprehensive failures, the sums involved in mass testing, would have seemed paltry by comparison. In its third stimulus package, for example, the US Congress has allocated a total of $25 billion to testing, and by November the UK's disastrous test and trace regime had devoured a whopping £22 billion.

Exiting Lockdown

The PCR test may be the gold standard in terms of accuracy, but it is also costly, logistically cumbersome and many countries do not have adequate laboratory capacity to support it. As the infectious disease curves headed skywards for a second time and third time, relying on PCR alone was not going to flatten them. This is because most tests are administered to those who have symptoms. It was the presence of these very symptoms that gave rise to the suspicion that they had Covid-19 in the first place, hence the test. But by that stage of their infection, most of these people had stopped transmitting the virus to others, and the damage, so to speak, had already been done. From a public health perspective, as a method of trying to contain a raging infectious disease epidemic, these tests are virtually useless. This is especially the case where tracing systems are either ineffectual or are not being complied with – and, in reality, the two usually go together.

Imposing lockdowns again and again and expecting different results also makes little sense. We need to try something different. It is important to reiterate that the transmission of SARS-CoV-2 occurs days after initial exposure and before there are any obvious symptoms. To have a realistic prospect of controlling the epidemic it is therefore essential to have frequent testing and the rapid availability of the test results. The alternative is an endless game of catch-up.

Because of limitations with PCR testing, researchers busied themselves on developing alternative testing techniques. Some of the most promising so far are based on a lateral flow assay (LFA) technology which is designed to identify the presence of a specific biological marker. Probably the best-known example of this technique is the pregnancy test. The LFA test works in a similar way by identifying the antigen protein of the virus directly and giving a positive or negative result in a matter of 15 minutes or less. These LFA antigen tests are inexpensive and offer an easily scalable solution for population-wide diagnostic testing. However, the LFA test is not a substitute for the PCR test, it works as both a complement and adjunct to it. As Dr Birx (she of the multiple scarfs) explained at a White House briefing in April, 'There will never be the ability on a nucleic acid test [PCR] to do 300 million tests a day or to test everybody before they go to work or to school, but there might be with the antigen test.'[2] And here's how.

To break the back of the pandemic and exit lockdown, a once-off universal testing programme was clearly needed. That would have allowed governments to get a reasonably accurate assessment of the true scale of the infections – it would have given them a comprehensive snapshot in time. Pandemic policy-making would then have been released from its total dependence on epidemiological modelling which, for the most part, has not had a good epidemic. Unlike existing testing systems which are highly centralised, that approach would have been decentralised and easy to use. It would have required no laboratory facilities or special instrumentation and would have provided results that were virtually instantaneous and be very cost-effective. With many companies already mass-producing so-called point-of-care Covid diagnostic tests, the technology is now available to institute such a mass testing programme in a relatively short timeframe.

There is also a phone app available on which a person's negative result can be stored as a QR code and read by barcode readers similar to the ones used by many airlines for boarding passes. Barcode readers placed at the entrance of retail premises would allow people to enter shops, restaurants, bars, cinemas, sports grounds and board airplanes confident that everyone else present was also virus free: people could even go on holidays again. If applied extensively, such a testing regime could herald the end of lockdown and the resumption of normal life with a substantially reduced risk of large-scale infections re-occurring. In instances where local outbreaks reoccur, then everyone in that area could be re-tested immediately and the asymptomatic spreaders, identified swiftly and isolated.

There are those who will argue that these rapid point-of-care tests are somewhat less accurate than the PCR ones, and this is true: but it may also be irrelevant. Some estimates put the number of those who are asymptomatic carriers of the virus as high as 40%. Mass testing on a sufficiently large scale will capture more and more of those infected by the virus who don't yet know it; and most importantly, are still at an early stage before they begin infecting others. If the epidemiological imperative is to control the epidemic by preventing transmission, then it seems that significantly more effort needs to be placed on universal testing. Whether through bureaucratic lethargy or the well-meaning but flawed advice of experts, at all costs we must avoid a situation where the perfect becomes the enemy of the good.

China Shows the Way, But Few Follow

If there were any residual doubt as to the potential of mass testing in the battle to defeat the virus, there was interesting news from China in October. Through the application of draconian suppression measures, including an unprecedent and massive lockdown of 60 million people in Hubei province in January, the CCP succeeded in controlling the outbreak in the first couple of months. Inevitably though, from time to time, there were some localised disease eruptions that needed to be contained.

One such flare-up occurred in mid-October in the port city of Qingdao in East China's Shandong Province. According to the CCP's international organ *Global Times*, the outbreak started at the Qingdao Chest Hospital, where it is thought that cross-infection occurred through the use of CT scan machines which had not been properly disinfected. The outbreak resulted in 12 people in total being infected; six had symptoms and six were asymptomatic. What is interesting about this episode is that Quingdao in north-east China is a city that – prior to reports of this outbreak – was almost unknown to the outside world. Even more astonishing, the local Communist Party authorities announced immediately that all of the city's inhabitants were to be tested – all 9 million of them. And, as if the scale of the undertaking wasn't enough, they also stated that this Herculean testing task would be completed within just five days.[3] Even allowing for some propaganda exaggeration of a million or so here or there, and a few extra days, this was still an incredible achievement.

In July there was a major outbreak in Xinjiang, the autonomous Uighur province in the west of China that borders Kyrgyzstan, Pakistan and Afghanistan. To supress the disease in the province's capital Urumqi, a war-time state of lockdown was imposed and brutally enforced with people being forcibly quarantined and handcuffed inside their buildings.[4] The extremity of this action was, of course, compatible with the inhumane treatment that the Uighurs have received for some years from the government in Beijing. Then in late October, a cluster of 137 asymptomatic cases was discovered in another city in Xinjinag, Kashgar. On this occasion, the Communist authorities opted for mass testing and, they tested all 4.75 million of the city's residents in just four days.

The Communist Party's original draconian lockdown of Wuhan and Hubei province was looked upon by some in the West as the best, if not the only, way to master the virus. These included, Dr Tedros of the WHO, the editor of *The Lancet*, Richard Horton, Neil Ferguson of Imperial College. But, perhaps, the most obsequious support of the severe actions of the Chinese government came from Martin Jacques, the former editor of *Marxism Today* and now a senior fellow at the University of Cambridge. Some of those supporters even went on CCP controlled media to voice their admiration for the governments' actions. There was little surprise when their interviews were instantly cited by CCP propaganda as 'evidence' that what the Party had done was not only 'correct', but endorsed by all reasonable Westerners.

It may have proved effective, but the appropriateness of police-state tactics in the enforcement of the Wuhan lockdown is fundamentally questionable. Such drastic actions remain inimical to the ethos and mores of free and democratic societies. But having contained the contagion through such severe methods, it should be acknowledged that China then followed the most effective means of maintaining its mastery of the virus – mass testing. To achieve such largescale compliance with millions of people in large cities lining up to be tested, is a very considerable achievement – even for a repressive and authoritarian state. It is well-known that China is a highly developed techno-surveillance state with millions of cameras constantly trained on the public and linked to supercomputers with massive databases. Face and voice recognition technology is used extensively to identify people and control their behaviour. But even that is insufficient in itself to explain the almost universal turnout at mass-testing sites.

While the raw power of a police state can be used to enforce effective lockdowns, but a more subtle method was required to ensure total compliance with a mass testing programme. In this regard, the CCP was unable to rely on the type of ideological mobilisation that characterised the Maoist era. Instead, it needed to devise a new means to control and shape people's behaviour. Since Xi came to power in 2014, the CCP has been building just such a system: they call it the Social Credit System.

This System is essentially a form of technology-enabled authoritarianism. Its basic objective is to engineer 'better' individual behaviour by rewarding trustworthiness and punishing disobedience. It operates on the principle of disproportionate punishment, so that if infractions happen in one place, restrictions and punishments can be imposed everywhere. Any behaviour considered negative can lead to a person being disbarred from say, purchasing a train or a plane ticket, buying a property, renting an apartment or applying for a loan.

Though some in the West take a benign view of this national social control system, Samantha Hoffman, a fellow at the Australian Strategic Policy Institute begged to differ: 'China's social credit system is a state-driven program designed to do one thing, to uphold and expand the Chinese Communist Party's power.'[5] Failing to show up for a mass Covid testing event during a pandemic is certainly the kind of behaviour that is likely to have a very negative impact on one's social credit status. The

Xinjiang residents who protested their severe treatment under lockdown in July by shouting from their windows were told, it was an 'illegal act' and 'warned that everything from social credit ratings to their children's school admissions could be affected.'[6]

From the outset, Xi Jinping sought to portray the CCP's response to the pandemic as emblematic of the fundamental superiority of his self-proclaimed 'socialism with Chinese characteristics'. For Xi and the Communist Party, the pandemic was a globalised opportunity to showcase the superiority, agility and effectiveness of authoritarian state capitalism when compared with the lethargic, inefficient and chaotic democratic capitalism in effectively combating the single most disruptive health threat faced by humanity in a century. Apart from a desire to show the rest of the world the innate superiority of communism's ability to defeat the virus, the CCP was also supremely motivated by the domestic fear that any failure on its part to overcome the disease risked losing its 'mandate from heaven' to operate as a one-party state in the most populous country on earth.

Though the focus of the pandemic aspects of the geopolitical struggle between China and the United States had been on the development of vaccines, the task of developing innovative diagnostic testing solutions was also seen by China as an important field in which is should compete with the West. The *Global Times* loudly proclaimed China's superiority in its daily testing capacity: 'China's daily Covid-19 nucleic acid testing capacity hit 4.84 million at the end of July ... According to US media outlets, the country's Covid-19 testing labs are in crisis again over the lack of supplies ... The highest daily test capacity in the past three months in the US was only 920,000.'[7]

The CCP has been relentless in its efforts to establish China's success in combating the disease when compared to the West's floundering attempts. According to Xi Jinping, this has 'fully demonstrated the clear superiority of Communist party leadership and our socialist system.'[8] The CCP has also sought to capitalise on its perceived pandemic achievements in combatting the virus by engaging in extensive 'disease diplomacy' designed to win hearts and minds beyond its borders. Initiatives have included, supplying masks and PPE at the start of the pandemic, and the provision of vaccines and diagnostic testing equipment at a later stage. Recent opinion polls, however, indicate that these efforts have completely failed to stem the rising tide of anti-CCP sentiment in the West.

An opinion poll carried out in July and August by Pew Research found that among the populations of the top 14 developed Western countries, unfavourable opinions of China had grown massively during the pandemic. Of those polled, 78% had 'not too much or no confidence in Xi to do the right thing regarding world affairs.'[9] When asked about the specifics of China's handling of the pandemic, a YouGov-Cambridge poll of 26,000 people in 25 countries indicated that the vast majority of them believed that China was responsible for the outbreak and had not been open or transparent about it from the beginning. The majority of those polled believed that the pandemic could have been prevented if China had responded more quickly. The percentage of respondents who offered praise for China in this poll ranged as follows; Sweden (1%), Great Britain (1%) Germany (2%), Australia (2%) and Japan (3%).[10]

As these polls confirm, one of the most astonishing outcomes of the first 100 days of the pandemic has been that the initial attempts at cover-up by the CCP have led to a fundamental re-evaluation of China by people across the Western world. But the polls also show that what exercised many people in particular was the fact that while China locked down Wuhan and Hubei province, and grounded all internal flights to and from the highly infected region, it allowed international flights to continue to operate as normal. The knowledge that it was people on board these flights who were directly responsible for infecting over 90 other countries has caused profound reputational damage to the leadership of the CCP and China.

For over two decades China's double-digit economic growth has lifted hundreds of millions out of poverty and, as a result, had garnered immense respect, even admiration, among western countries and their peoples. But in a matter of just a few weeks, that enormous wellspring of goodwill towards China was frittered away by Xi Jinping and the CCP allowing their authoritarian reflexes to seek to obfuscate what had really happened in Wuhan in late 2019. When a local outbreak of a highly infectious disease with the potential to cause a pandemic required absolute candour and transparency with the international community, none was forthcoming or in evidence. It was a calamitous blunder, which, as we will see next, has had, and will continue to have, enormous geopolitical implications around the world.

Chapter 30: China Rising

Since the end of the Second World War, the international world order has been dominated by the United States. For most of that time the Soviet Union was the only effective challenger to US global hegemony. Indeed, based on the principle that my enemy's enemy is my friend, it was this intense rivalry that spurred a new strategic rapprochement between the United States and Communist China, beginning in 1972 with President Nixon's historic visit to China.

The opening up to China marked an irrevocable change in the dynamics of the Cold War in favour of the US. Meanwhile, in China, Deng Xiaoping began the radical economic reforms that created a socialist market economy and opened it up to global trade. By the time the Soviet Union collapsed in 1991, China was being integrated into the international rules-based system. It was being done with America's enthusiastic encouragement and considerable assistance. Believing that this was the best way to control the Dragon, the United States chose to ignore Napoleon's 200-year-old advice: 'Let China sleep, for when she wakes, she will shake the world.'

In May 2000, during the twilight days of his second term as President, Bill Clinton believed he had achieved one of the legislative highlights of his political career. In the teeth of strong opposition from organised labour unions, but with the support of Wall St, President Clinton convinced the House of Representatives to support China's bid to join the World Trade Organisation (WTO). 'Today the House of Representatives has taken an historic step toward continued prosperity in America, reform in China and peace in the world ... it will open new doors of trade for America and new hope for change in China ... In 10 years from now we will look back on this day and be glad we did this.'[1]

Normalising trade with China also had the backing of one of America's leading trade economists, Paul Krugman[2]: 'You don't have to be a disciple of Friedrich Hayek to believe that free markets and a free society have some affinity.' In Krugman's view failure to normalise trade with China and allow it to join the WTO would be akin to saying to China 'Sorry; markets and democracy work for us, but we aren't letting any more countries into our club.' In any case he concluded, 'it's an issue whose symbolic importance is much larger than its direct economic implications.'[3] Krugman's comments have come to seem extremely naïve in the years since then. A subsequent research paper published 15 years later by the National Bureau of Economic Research with the arresting title, 'The China Shock', calculated that direct competition from China had cost almost 1 US million manufacturing jobs. When other indirect job losses were factored in, the total number of jobs lost was 2.4 million.[4] Cheaper T-shirts from China was poor compensation for the hundreds of thousands who became permanently unemployed across America's Rust Belt – this had gone far beyond symbolism. And telling the growing number of communities of unemployed manufacturing, steel, and coal workers that they needed to become software coders in order to survive seemed like the sort of advice that Marie Antoinette might have given.

In 21st century United States, the people that Hilary Clinton wrote off as a 'basket of deplorables' had a vote. What they needed was a figurehead and once they found him, they also found their voice. In 2016 that electoral voice was heard across the United States, causing profound shock to the establishment elites from sea to shining sea. Before long, in an attempt to fathom what had gone wrong, formerly neglected fly-over country was being scrutinised forensically, with a near-anthropological focus being devoted to white working-class males like never before. But it wasn't just their jobs that had gone, whole industries whose roots were intricately entwined within the overall economy and society had been deracinated. It took the pandemic to expose one of the major unintended consequences of this de-industrialisation.

Monopoly Medicine

Under the banner of globalisation China had thrived economically, becoming the manufacturing hub for a globalised world. In the process, it sucked in tens of millions of manufacturing and other jobs from across the western world. Lives were being upended and once thriving communities turned into industrial wastelands with distressing speed. This was simply considered the unfortunate but unavoidable price of progress.

One of the most astounding outcomes of these developments has been that China is now the largest global supplier of so-called 'active pharmaceutical ingredients' (APIs). These are the chemical building blocks for a whole range of medications from over-the-counter medicines to prescription drugs. This is not just a question of vitamin C or aspirin, but antibiotics, steroids, and cancer drugs. More than half of the 4,000 active ingredients that are required to manufacture most of the pharmaceutical products that are sold throughout the western world are uniquely sourced in China. Astonishingly, the active ingredient for the antibiotic ciprofloxin which, among other things, is used to treat anthrax, is also in China's hands. The WHO classifies ciprofloxacin as a critically important antimicrobial for human medicine, and is on the organisation's List of Essential Medicines.[5]

This is a complete reversal of the situation that prevailed prior to the mid-1990s when the U.S., Europe, and Japan manufactured 90% of the global supply of key ingredients for the world's medications. It is an astonishing reversal that has been driven by what the globalised market is very good at, keeping prices low. How did China achieve this preeminent position as the world's principal supplier of pharmaceutical products, and why should it be a concern?

The answer to the first part of the question is fairly straight forward – they cheated. Having masses of cheap labour was obviously an advantage, at least initially. But pharmaceutical production is not particularly labour intensive and so this did not confer any unique advantage. In fact, pharmaceutical production (not cutting-edge scientific research) is heavily automated, so the cost of capital is of more significance than the cost of labour. In China, banking is largely a state-owned and controlled industry, and therefore access to credit is effectively in the hands of the CCP. With their access to cheap state-subsidised capital, China's pharmaceutical companies had an immediate competitive advantage over those of the west.

Another very significant overhead that western manufactures have to deal with are the compliance costs of a robust regulatory regime that is systematically – and literally – policed. Industries in China have not been held to the same exacting compliance standards, and so are regularly tempted to cut corners: sometimes with disastrous consequences for end users in the West. Quality assurance for Nike shoes or iPhones is obviously important, but for products like medicines that we ingest or inject, quality assurance needs to be of an entirely different order of magnitude.

Heparin is an anticoagulant drug that prevents the formation of blood clots in blood vessels. It is used extensively in clinical settings, especially for dialysis patients. In the US, the drug was manufactured by Baxter Healthcare in New Jersey but the active ingredient that gave it its therapeutic value was imported. From the mid-90s, along with most other active pharmaceutical ingredients, the one for heparin was no longer made in the USA, as production had been transferred to China. In 2008, there was a medical disaster that affected as many as 11 counties in the developed world: contaminated heparin was responsible for many hundreds of adverse reactions in hospital patients and caused up to 150 deaths. An FDA investigation concluded that the contaminated ingredient used had been imported from China. The FDA also believed that the contamination was a direct result of an effort by the Chinese manufacturer to cut costs. In circumstances where regulatory supervision was virtually non-existent, the economic incentive proved irresistible: the contaminated ingredient cost $9 a pound, compared with $900 for heparin.[6]

The Wolf in Panda's Clothing

While China was being welcomed enthusiastically into the rules-based international system, it had simultaneously devised a novel form of asymmetric struggle designed to undermine the principal architect and paymaster of that very system. It was not war by other means, it *was* war. This was not the old-fashioned sort of war that is fought with bombs and bullets. However, this was the new 21st century asymmetric version that encompassed information warfare, cyber warfare, economic warfare, and, only as a last resort, kinetic warfare. The details of this new grand-strategic approach were first described in a book published in China by two PLA Colonels called *Unrestricted Warfare*, with the subtitle, *Two Air Force Senior Colonels on Scenarios for War and the Operational Art in an Era of Globalization*.[7] It took a long time for the US, and the West generally, to wake up to the fact that cyber espionage and the wholesale stealing of technological secrets, combined with currency manipulation, had been a not-so subtle but very cost-effective way for China to enhance its GDP.

Even when it became clear what the CCP was doing, the elites in the West, and especially in the US, turned a blind eye. Providing the capital for China's runaway economy had become an enormously profitable business for Wall St and the City of London. No matter what the costs were to other sectors of the economy, the powerful capital markets leaders lobbied hard to keep the good times rolling. Such was their success that Chinese companies, some of them with questionable links to the PLA, were allowed to float on US stock exchanges without having to meet the same legal, compliance or accountancy standards that American companies were obliged to follow. Incredibly, not only had the West utterly failed to move China towards its version of democratic capitalism,

Communist China had succeeded in bending the West to its way of doing business.

From the commencement of his reign in 2012, opinion on the new Chinese leader among western scholars was divided into two camps. Optimists argued that Xi would follow the open reforming route of Deng, while pessimists detected an authoritarian streak in Xi, which they believed would lead him down the path of Mao. It turned out that the pessimists had got it right.

Xi steadily began to assert his personal dominance, while maintaining the public illusion that the collective leadership tradition of the previous three decades was still intact. Any lingering doubts about Xi's intention to re-instigate Maoist style one-man-rule soon faded as he successfully abolished the constitutional ban on Presidential term limits. In Party statements, Xi was increasingly being referred to as the 'core leader' – communist-speak for an unrivalled leader. The stage was also being set for Xi to be made Chairman of the Central Committee, a title that, until his death in 1976, was only ever applied to Mao. But Xi' gradual adoption of the mantle of Mao went beyond mere nomenclature.

One of Xi Jinping's recurring themes is his concept of the Chinese Dream. His repeated formulations of the Chinese Dream are a direct counterpoint to the American Dream: the one individualist, the other collectivist. In Xi's socialist conception the ordained hierarchical order was very clear, the individual was subservient to the state because: 'only when the country does well, and the nation does well, can every person do well.'[8] His various authoritarian explications of the Chinese Dream are suffused with words such as 'freedom', 'democracy', 'equality' and 'rule of law' which are deployed as deliberate rhetorical mis-direction moves to deflect the unwary from his core agenda. This was to entrench the CCP's rule over China, and his personal rule over the CCP.

By 2018, under the guise of his anti-corruption campaign, Xi had eliminated all of his potential political rivals among the senior cadres of the Party. That year, he was sufficiently confident in his control of the CCP that, in a move straight out of the authoritarian playbook, he had the constitutional ban on term limits for the post of president removed. It consolidated his personal grip on power and opened up the possibility of rule by Xi for life. With this constitutional amendment safely in place, Xi controlled the important levers of institutional power in China; General Secretary, Chairman of the Military Commission, and President. In these roles he ruled over the Part, the PLA, and the political system.

October saw the re-emergence of a political phrase that had been shunned by Chinese leaders since the death of Mao. The communiqué issued at the end of that month's plenary session of the Communist Party Central Committee declared Xi to be 'the core navigator and helmsman'. It was an unambiguous statement that the collective leadership tradition of *primus inter pares* (first among equals), that been the norm for more than three decades since the death of Mao, had given way to a new era of one-man rule – the cult of personality had returned. Xi was decisively proclaiming his lineal ancestry to the Great Helmsman, Chairman Mao, the most ruthless tyrant of the 20th century.

Dictatorial Rule

From early in the 21st century it had become increasingly evident that the contest between democracy and dictatorship had not been finally resolved, as many in the west had naïvely assumed when the Soviet bloc collapsed. It seemed that history had not ended after all: instead, it continued to move forward. From the start of his accession to power, Xi Jinping regularly threw down the gauntlet to the West with his repeated assertions about the superiority of 'socialism with Chinese characteristics' compared with western liberal democracy. Clearly delineated ideological values were being placed remorselessly at the epicentre of an active information warfare campaign between China and the US.

In November 2020, America was deciding its four-year political future in a Presidential election that had the highest voter turnout in its 200-year history. At the same time, China's future was being determined secretly by an unelected cabal of the CCP's most senior members. The group, sequestered in the People's Liberation Army-run Jingxi Hotel in West Beijing was led by General Secretary Xi Jinping. The Jingxi Hotel is situated about 300 metres from the People's Liberation Army's Bayi Building, home to the Central Military Commission (also chaired by Xi Jinping) that runs China's military: in effect, this is the Chinese Pentagon.

The Jingxi Hotel has been a silent witness to some of the most momentous events in recent Chinese history and holds many of the Communist Party's secrets. It was the scene of Mao Zedong's infamous show trials during the Cultural Revolution (1966-76). In 1978, it was where Deng Xiaoping launched his pivotal economic reforms in which the Party formally abandoned the 'class struggle' in favour of rapid market-based economic development. In a very real sense, the Jingxi Hotel was where China was set on a course to become a global superpower. In time, that decision was to have transformative implications for the international geopolitical order.

In the Communist Party's rulebook of governance, minute attention is paid to political choreography. Nothing is left to chance, and there are few coincidences. Diagonally across from the Jingxi Hotel is the Military Museum of the Chinese People's Revolution. An exhibition celebrating the 70th anniversary of China's involvement in the Korean War was taking place while the Jingxi Hotel meeting was in session. A sign above the entrance to the exhibition had the slogan, 'Resist America and Aid Korea', while inside a huge banner proclaimed a Mao Zedong statement of the time: 'Chinese people were united as one. Don't you dare think of invading us. If you make us angry, we could get out of control.' Just a few days earlier in his own speech marking the same 70th anniversary, Xi Jinping quoted Mao's words verbatim.[9]

The October 2020 meeting of the grandiose sounding Fifth Plenum of the Communist Party's 19th Central Committee was held amidst tight security; behind high walls topped by barbed wire and the building was surrounded by troops in camouflage fatigues. The four-day Jingxi Hotel meeting had to decide the elements of the next 5-Year plan, but also to determine China's long-term goals through to 2035. These annual convocations of the Communist Party's top brass often concern themselves with the authoritarian housekeeping priorities of Party and government. However, as we have seen, on occasion they can also provide the outside world with an invaluable window into important changes of direction in an otherwise opaque political process. This Jingxi Hotel conclave turned out to be one such occasion.

In the four decades since the initial reforms of Deng Xiaoping in 1978, the Chinese economy has grown at an average annual rate of 10%. China's economic 'miracle' was founded on a combination of cheap labour, resource-intensive manufacturing, and exports. But as a model for delivering continuous growth into the future, it had inherent limitations. Soon, unambiguous signals began to emerge that the model's structural limitations had been reached, as both labour productivity and returns on investment began to decline. For the CCP there was an urgent need to make the transition away from low-end manufacturing to a new model based on higher-value-added manufacturing and services: one in which consumption replaced investment as the engine of growth.

The official communiqué issued at the end of October's Jingxi Hotel meeting paid lip service to 'unswervingly promote reform'. However, it's main new policy emphasis was focused on a concept referred to as 'dual circulation'. In the abstruse lexicon of the CCP, 'dual circulation' refers to an economic strategy in which China would henceforth rely primarily on "domestic circulation" but supported by external resources such as raw materials and capital acquired through "international circulation". Its primary objective was to increase self-sufficiency and reduce dependence on foreign demand.

This new strategic departure was an attempt to build a domestic economy that was demand-led in preparation for an expected "decoupling" from the U.S. economy, in the context of an increasingly fractious trade war. It represented a new inward focus on its domestic economy and was a modern re-formulation of the former Maoist era strategy of autarky. The adoption of a complete domestic demand strategy acquired a new urgency and was moved rapidly to the top of the political agenda because of events surrounding the pandemic.

During the pandemic, the CCP's increasingly assertive and threatening behaviour towards those countries it deemed to have offended Chinese sensibilities, had unnerved many. An acute awareness had developed in the West that reliance on an increasingly belligerent strategic competitor for critical supply chain deliveries carried unacceptable risks. The dawning realisation of the West's almost total dependence on China for the vast bulk of its essential pharmaceutical ingredients and medical products had been a slow and rude awakening, raising profound concerns about security of supply in times of geopolitical tension. Though it made no reference to China's own behaviour in contributing to this state of affairs, the communiqué astutely acknowledges these new geostrategic realities: "the world today is undergoing major changes unseen in a century .... The balance of international forces is profoundly adjusted.'[10]

Evidence of the extent of these 'profoundly adjusted' international forces has been the formation of a new informal alliance between the Indo-Pacific region's four leading democracies; the US, India, Japan and Australia, known as the Quad. This is a new strategic partnership based on 'shared values and interests, including, the rule of law, freedom of navigation, respect for territorial integrity and sovereignty, peaceful dispute resolution, free markets, and free trade.'[11] Such responses from the West have, in turn, concentrated minds within the CCP regarding China's own vulnerabilities, especially in high-end core technology, energy supply, and food production. These are areas where China already feels particularly exposed in the event of a blockade by the West.[12] And with relations coming under sustained strain, the portends were not good.

The CCP communiqué also recognised China's high-tech shortcomings and so insisted that 'innovation should be the core of our country's modernization drive, and that scientific and technological self-sufficiency is the strategic pillar of national development'.[13] Indeed, innovation had been the foundational hallmark of China's staggeringly successful economic development to date, so there was nothing new in that. China had excelled in how it used and applied technology, but virtually all of the core technologies that it has deployed have originated in the West. Chinese patents, for example, tend only to represent incremental improvements on more innovative work carried out by others. They are process driven improvements that make the original designs perform faster, better or more cheaply.[14]

What China has singularly failed to master is technological invention. Invention, as opposed to innovation, is the type of high-quality basic research that yields breakthrough scientific discoveries. Such innovations radically disrupt existing industries and lay the foundations for entirely new ones. In this crucial respect, China seriously lags behind the United States. And it is likely to continue to do so because, as the second part of the above sentence from the communiqué indicates, Xi is adamant that 'technological self-sufficiency' is its objective. This is little more than a version of Mao's disastrous self-reliance strategy being applied in the 21st century, with technology replacing agriculture as the target industry.

One of the most perceptive analysis of China's failure to come to terms with technological invention is provided by the renowned Chinese artist, Ai Weiwei. 'If a person has never had the right to choose their information, freely associate with any kind of ideology, and develop an individual character with some passion and imagination – how can they become creative? It is against human nature. If you are against every essential value of individualism and independent thinking, and the willingness to take risks and their consequences, and have a sense of responsibility – what kind of creativity do you expect? … It would be impossible to design an iPhone in China because it's not a product; it's an understanding of human nature.'[15]

Xi's aspirations for China to become a technological superpower, self-sufficient in high-end technology, received a significant set-back in 2000, as a series of Western countries refused to sell core technologies to companies such as Huawei and ZTE because of their close links with the CCP and the Chinese military. These included the world's largest semiconductor manufacturer, Taiwan Semiconductor Manufacturing Co (TSMC), which had to suspend supplying chips to Huawei because of US sanctions. At a stroke, this put an end to Huawei's vaunted ambitions to dominate the global 5G mobile networks market. Likewise, a number of such Chinese companies have been excluded from deploying their technology within western telecommunications infrastructures as intelligence agencies consider that they pose a serious security risk.

As the tensions continued to escalate between China and the West, high-blown Chinese rhetoric about achieving ascendancy in quantum computing, artificial intelligence and sophisticated semiconductor chip manufacturing seemed to be further removed from reality. Ho-Fung, Professor of Political Science at Johns Hopkins University and author of *The China Boom: Why China Will Not Rule the World*, summarises Xi's current strategy; 'It is the mentality of the great leap forward under Mao, and it's going to end in another disaster.'[16] The Professor continued, 'Xi overplayed his hand with wolf warrior diplomacy. He alerted the whole world to China's aggressive ambitions and now it is going to be much harder to secure foreign technology transfers. Without that, it is going to be very difficult for China.'[17]

This book began in China because that is where the virus originated. It also ends with China because one of the most significant outcomes of the pandemic has been that Communist China is unlikely to be afforded the same level of indulgence and aversion of Western eyes from its more unsavoury authoritarian predilections that it has been given for over three decades. During the pandemic, the CCP's carefully fabricated mask slipped, revealing the less benign and less palatable despotic face of China and its paramount leader, Xi Jinping.

Though it will be wildly unpopular in many quarters, I feel duty bound to, as it were, give the devil his due. It was the iconoclastic President Trump who very early on identified China as an existential threat to Western interests. Sorely lacking the suave articulacy of President Obama, whose policy aspirations were rarely backed up by actions, President Trump bombastically and chaotically called out China's nefarious activities on cyber spying, trade manipulation, and its lengthy record of failure to abide by agreements. He may have done so in a typically bombastic and even incoherent manner, but he still posed a profound challenge to the prevailing orthodoxy on China and its glib assumption that at some stage in the future (always unspecified), China would become democratic.

In just four years, the world has seen America execute a bewildering swivel from the largely empty rhetoric of Obama to the transgressive behaviour of Trump. While the one was comforting but ineffectual, the other was prescient but profoundly discomfiting: paradoxically, it is the latter that is likely to have the greater long-term purchase. Though President Trump is gone, Trumpism is likely to continue in one form or another for some time. One of its abiding legacies will be that a will not resume its prior position in the eyes of the West. Throughout his presidential campaign, President Biden made that abundantly clear. If, however, he fails to live up to his election promises and reverts to the old ways by kowtowing to China again, then that will truly signal the beginning of the end of what has been the global hegemony of America. Either way, one of the most significant consequences of the pandemic is that a new geopolitical reality is taking shape courtesy, ultimately, of a deadly virus.

Afterword: Lessons from a year of living pandemically

The truism that it takes two to tango is key to understanding the disease dynamics of a pandemic. The particular properties of a virus must be understood in tandem with the social behavioural patterns of human beings. The virus and human beings may belong to very different species, but they share the same primary objective: to survive, and, in that process, to increase and multiply. In order for the virus to do this successfully, it must invade our cells and subvert them to its purposes. But, in doing so, it is not in the virus's objective interests to be too lethal and kill too many people or it will run out of hosts and so endanger its own existence. It needs to strike a fine balance between lethality and transmissibility.

There are, of course, many vital differences between humans and viruses. We are sentient beings capable of independent thoughts and feelings, while viruses are not. Thanks to rapid advances in the science of molecular biology, we already know a great deal about how this particular virus operates. However, the human side of this relationship is harder to predict and control. We are, after all, driven by needs and desires that are mediated through a range of competing emotions. And the complexity of those emotions can only increase when humans are put under conditions of great stress. If nothing else, the current pandemic has reminded us forcefully that our knowledge and understanding of human nature remains problematic.

Just as we entered the holiday season of Christmas 2020 – and the prospect of some blessed relief from the lockdowns – unfortunately, the tidings were anything but of great joy. There came news that nobody wanted to hear: new strains of the virus had emerged that were both more transmissible and created a higher viral load in those infected by them. Even worse, modelling showed that because the new mutations were up to 70% more infectious, even lockdowns would not be effective in containing them. There was an additional concern: anecdotal evidence from frontline doctors indicated that young people and children with no underlying health issues were presenting with critical illnesses when infected by the new variants. Epidemiologists were adamant, the only effective solution to solve the problem this time would be a rapid mass inoculation programme. In the meantime, fear and panic had again sparked another round of extensive international travel restrictions. Britain, where one of the new variants had first taken root, was effectively treated as a pariah state, and had its transport links with the rest of the world severed for up to 72 hours.

Yet, as this new phase of pandemic anxiety began to unfold, another source of profound uncertainty had finally been resolved. After what seemed like an interminable delay – as one journalist put it, it was like being eight-and-a-half months pregnant for four years – a Brexit deal was finally achieved. With the final 20 hours of the negotiations seemingly spent counting herring in Brussels. Punch drunk from the pandemic; people across Europe greeted the news with a Gallic shoulder shrug as the European chief negotiator, Michel Barnier rolled out his oft-repeated metaphor one last time: 'The clock is no longer ticking.' But even as he spoke, for those with acute political hearing, a new ticking sound could be heard coming from the Commission's Berleymont building in Brussels. What had seemed unthinkable just a few short years beforehand had actually taken place: the EU had been compelled – however reluctantly – to accede to the democratically expressed wishes of one of its largest members, and the sky had not fallen in. Within the remaining EU, the ticking sound of democracy would likely grow louder with time.

When Donald Trump finally left the Presidency of the most powerful country on earth, he left behind one particular legacy that President Biden may modify, but is unlikely to change fundamentally. There will be no return to the pre-Trumpian era of indulging China and turning a blind eye to its multiple, covert and nefarious behaviours. President Biden's nominee for the powerful Secretary of State cabinet position, Antony Blinken, when speaking in late January at his confirmation hearing before the Senate Foreign Relations Committee even went so far as to praise President Trump's stance on China: 'Let me just say that I also believe that President Trump was right in taking a tougher approach to China, I disagree very much with the way that he went about it in a number of areas, but the basic principle was the right one, and I think that's actually helpful to our foreign policy.'

As Vice-President in charge of the so-called pivot to Asia under President Obama, President Biden had up to 25 hours of one-on-one private meetings with his 'old friend', Xi Jinping. But that was then and this is now, and in the closing years of his Presidency, Trump had taken a radically different approach. This was, after all, a pandemic world where China, the CCP and its leader were no longer looked upon so benignly, and where the West's belief in China's inevitable progress towards liberal democracy has been exposed as the product of wishful and politically naïve thinking. This irrevocable shift from President Obama's strategy that has occurred within the Democratic Party was in evidence during the presidential campaign when Joe Biden dismissed the Chinese leader – his erstwhile 'old friend' – as a 'thug'. It has become clear that the views of both the West's political elites and the wider public have changed utterly on China. What was previously a balance of cooperation and competition had become one of competition and confrontation.

As I have argued previously (Chapter 13), the WHO-led investigation into the origins of the pandemic in China has been compromised before it even began. A CCP-controlled investigation into its own behaviour is very unlikely to add much of significance to the sum of human knowledge on either the pandemic or the origins of the Covid-19 virus. But this does not mean that we need abandon all hope of getting to the bottom of this critically important question. In fact, for the newly elected President Biden this investigative hiatus offers a glorious opportunity to both make his own mark while, at the same time, reasserting America's leadership role in the post-pandemic world of international relations. As one of his first major acts on the national and international stage, President Biden should instigate a Presidential Commission of Inquiry into the Pandemic – similar to the 9/11 and other Commissions of Inquiry. Not only would it be a fitting way to remember the millions of people in the US and around the world who have suffered and died in this pandemic, it would also offer a road map on how we might deal with what most experts believe to be the inevitability of the next pandemic.

While the public was being led down the pandemic yellow brick road by politicians who claimed that they were 'science-based' and 'data-driven, there was really only one break-through moment. In the depths of winter with an unprecedented lockdown-Christmas fast approaching and festive cheer in short supply, there came news that lifted spirits across the world. The announcement that a vaccine had been developed that was 95% effective against Covid-19 was momentous – finally, it seemed there was light at the end of the pandemic tunnel. The cavalry – in the form of science, technology, and innovation – had arrived to deliver us from the deadly grip of a prolonged period of contagion.

However, we hardly had the time to savour the respite from our pandemic tribulations that human ingenuity had given us, when mother nature struck back. New virus mutations, that were significantly more transmissible, began to emerge in a growing number of countries. These faster-spreading variants not only raised anxieties about the effectiveness of the newly developed vaccines to combat them, they also boosted what seemed like the inexorable rise of both infections and deaths. By the end of January 2021, a gruesome global Covid-19 threshold was crossed when over 100 million infections and over 2 million dead were recorded. It was evident that we had entered a new, and potentially more dangerous, phase of the pandemic. In this new period of viral evolution, success or failure would come down, ultimately, to a race between variants and vaccines.

If SARS CoV-2 evolves in the same way as the four other human coronaviruses, it is likely to become less lethal with time. On this basis, the future trouble that Covid-19 might cause us would be on a par with that of the common cold – a nuisance whose principal indignity may be no worse than a runny nose. However, there is also a less benign scenario.

The mutations to date that have allowed the virus to spread more easily have already caused us great additional hardship. However, this development has also been a timely reminder that there is no room for complacency in our struggle with the virus. This is primarily because one of the things that this type of mRNA virus does best is mutation. It evolves in response to changes in its environment – so-called selection pressures. In this context, vaccines, somewhat counter-intuitively, may be a bit of a double-edged sword.

Vaccines have been welcomed, quite correctly, as a hugely positive development, but from the perspective of the virus their advent also represents a colossal transformation in the environment with which it has to contend. In order to be able to survive better in this radically altered set of circumstances, the virus will have to adapt further or die out. If it adapts, there is a far from negligible risk that it will mutate into a variant that is better equipped to evade our vaccine-enhanced immune systems.

The nightmare scenario would be one in which SARS CoV-2 becomes, not only more contagious, but more lethal as well.* If this happens, despite all the pain and suffering of the past year, we will face the real prospect of ending up in a worse position than we were over 12 months ago. Though it is undoubtedly an appalling vista, in order to avoid such a calamitous occurrence, it is clear that the world's governments must do what they so patently failed to do at the start of the pandemic: put in place comprehensive and universal testing regimes with the capacity to trap,

* As I write this, the British Government has announced that a new variant that is 30% more transmissible has been discovered – others will surely follow.

identify, and isolate any such mutant variant before it spirals out of control. But above all, they must act now because, in this context, delay is the deadliest form of denial.

And far from there being "an end in sight", as politicians keep telling us, the coronavirus wars may end up becoming a seasonal permawar, just like influenza. The hard evidence for this lies in the plans of the pharmaceutical industry which is increasing investment in research facilities, and, most significantly, massively expanding vaccine manufacturing capacity worldwide. Big Pharma, a sector not known for making sentimental investment decisions, is betting heavily on the virus being around for a while – it would be foolhardy for the rest of us not to take the hint.

Vaccine development is a high-risk business whose history has been characterised as much by failure as success. As an indication of the risks involved, one of the leading vaccine contenders, Merck, announced on Monday, January 25, 2021, that it was pulling out of the race to develop a vaccine because early clinical-trial data showed that its two experimental vaccines had generated disappointing immune responses against the virus in early-stage studies. So, to develop an effective vaccine in just ten months was wholly unprecedented. Few believed it was even possible. In a very real sense, the vaccine announcement represented a triumph of hope over experience. In this achievement, Big Pharma deserves some credit, but only some. The real work was done by a small, German biotechnology company – led by Turkish immigrants – that lives or dies by its ability to conduct scientific innovation, BioNTech. It was yet another example of what has been the modus operandi of Big Pharma for decades: rather than doing the innovative research themselves, they acquire new technology by snapping up smaller companies who have already done the leading-edge innovations. Vaccitech, played a similar role in the AstraZeneca/Oxford consortium by developing the specialist viral vector for its vaccine. Big Pharma brings the money and the marketing heft, small pharma delivers the goods – horses for courses.

In broader terms, the advent of a vaccine in record time meant that science had triumphed in humanity's latest battle with the age-old scourges of pestilence and plague. In turn, it raises the question, could science, technology and innovation also hold the key to removing that other, more recent, sword of Damocles that hangs over our collective global existence, climate change?

One of the most staggering revelations of the pandemic has been the colossal failures of almost all the world's governments and their administrative state apparatuses to deliver relatively uncomplicated solutions such as testing and tracing. Despite vast sums of money being expended – and sometimes squandered – on such projects, they have failed repeatedly to meet their modest targets. In the light of this, it seems extremely foolhardy to expect the same entities to deliver the even more critical, complicated and challenging targets that are needed to alleviate climate change.

By the same token, our experience of pandemic lockdowns has provided incontrovertible evidence that we are not well adapted or psychologically motivated to accept the kind of material privations that are being urged upon us by various retired politicians and young middle-class activists who regularly disrupt our city's streets. Despite such exhortations, we have made little serious effort to modify our behaviours – or at least on a sufficient scale to make a meaningful impact. Emissions target after target have been repeatedly missed. But the pandemic has also shown that there is a viable solution to climate change - one that works. The positive pandemic message, if we care to heed it, is that science, technology and, above all innovation are well capable of delivering timely and viable solutions to meet the climate change challenge. What the myriad of innovative technology companies around the world require is the fulcrum and lever of the correct incentives, and like Archimedes, they will move the world.

Appendix 1

The possible origins of 2019-nCoV coronavirus
Preprint · February 2020
DOI: 10.13140/RG.2.2.21799.29601

The possible origins of 2019-nCoV coronavirus

Botao Xiao[1,2*] and Lei Xiao[3]
1 Joint International Research Laboratory of Synthetic Biology and Medicine, School of Biology and Biological Engineering, South China University of Technology, Guangzhou 510006, China
2 School of Physics, Huazhong University of Science and Technology, Wuhan 430074, China
3 Tian You Hospital, Wuhan University of Science and Technology, Wuhan 430064, China
* Corresponding author: xiaob@scut.edu.cn
Tel / Fax: 86-20-3938-0631

The 2019-nCoV coronavirus has caused an epidemic of 28,060 laboratory-confirmed infections in human including 564 deaths in China by February 6, 2020. Two descriptions of the virus published on Nature this week indicated that the genome sequences from patients were 96% or 89% identical to the Bat CoV ZC45 coronavirus originally found in Rhinolophus affinis 1,2. It was critical to study where the pathogen came from and how it passed onto human.

An article published on The Lancet reported that 41 people in Wuhan were found to have the acute respiratory syndrome and 27 of them had contact with Huanan Seafood Market 3. The 2019-nCoV was found in 33 out of 585 samples collected in the market after the outbreak. The market was suspicious to be the origin of the epidemic, and was shut down according to the rule of quarantine the source during an epidemic.

The bats carrying CoV ZC45 were originally found in Yunnan or Zhejiang province, both of which were more than 900 kilometers away from the seafood market. Bats were normally found to live in caves and trees. But the seafood market is in a densely-populated district of Wuhan, a metropolitan of ~15 million people. The probability was very low for the bats to fly to the market. According to municipal reports and the testimonies of 31 residents and 28 visitors, the bat was never a food source in the city, and no bat was traded in the market. There was possible natural recombination or intermediate host of the coronavirus, yet little proof has been reported.

Was there any other possible pathway? We screened the area around the seafood market and identified two laboratories conducting research on bat coronavirus. Within ~280 meters from the market, there was the Wuhan Center for Disease Control & Prevention (WHCDC) (Figure 1, from Baidu and Google maps). WHCDC hosted animals in laboratories for research purpose, one of which was specialized in pathogens collection and identification 4-6. In one of their studies, 155 bats including Rhinolophus affinis were captured in Hubei province, and other 450 bats were captured in Zhejiang province 4. The expert in collection was noted in the Author Contributions (JHT). Moreover, he was broadcasted for collecting viruses on nation-wide newspapers and websites in 2017 and 2019 7,8. He described that he was once by attacked by bats and the blood of a bat shot on his skin. He knew the extreme danger of the infection so he quarantined himself for 14 days 7. In another accident, he quarantined himself again because bats peed on him. He was once thrilled for capturing a bat carrying a live tick 8.

Surgery was performed on the caged animals and the tissue samples were collected for DNA and RNA extraction and sequencing 4, 5. The tissue samples and contaminated trashes were source of pathogens. They were only ~280 meters from the seafood market. The WHCDC was also adjacent to the Union Hospital (Figure 1, bottom) where the first group of doctors were infected during this epidemic. It is plausible that the virus leaked around and some of them contaminated the initial patients in this epidemic, though solid proofs are needed in future study.

The second laboratory was ~12 kilometers from the seafood market and belonged to Wuhan Institute of Virology, Chinese Academy of Sciences 1, 9, 10. This laboratory reported that the Chinese horseshoe bats were natural reservoirs for the severe acute respiratory syndrome coronavirus (SARS-CoV) which caused the 2002-3 pandemic 9.

The principle (sic) investigator participated in a project which generated a chimeric virus using the SARS-CoV reverse genetics system, and reported the potential for human emergence 10. A direct speculation was that SARS-CoV or its derivative might leak from the laboratory.

In summary, somebody was entangled with the evolution of 2019-nCoV coronavirus. In addition to origins of natural recombination and intermediate host, the killer coronavirus probably originated from a laboratory in Wuhan. Safety level may need to be reinforced in high risk biohazardous laboratories. Regulations may be taken to relocate these laboratories far away from city center and other densely populated places.

Contributors

BX designed the comment and performed literature search. All authors performed data acquisition and analysis, collected documents, draw the figure, and wrote the papers.

Acknowledgements
This work is supported by the National Natural Science Foundation of China (11772133, 11372116).

Declaration of interests
All authors declare no competing interests.

References
1. Zhou P, Yang X-L, Wang X-G, et al. A pneumonia outbreak associated with a new coronavirus of probable bat origin. Nature 2020. https://doi.org/10.1038/s41586-020-2012-7.
2. Wu F, Zhao S, Yu B, et al. A new coronavirus associated with human respiratory disease in China. Nature 2020. https://doi.org/10.1038/s41586-020-2008-3.
3. Huang C, Wang Y, Li X, et al. Clinical features of patients infected with 2019 novel coronavirus in Wuhan, China. The Lancet 2019. https://doi.org/10.1016/S0140-6736(20)30183-5.
4. Guo WP, Lin XD, Wang W, et al. Phylogeny and origins of hantaviruses harbored by bats, insectivores, and rodents. PLoS pathogens 2013; 9(2): e1003159.
5. Lu M, Tian JH, Yu B, Guo WP, Holmes EC, Zhang YZ. Extensive diversity of rickettsiales bacteria in ticks from Wuhan, China. Ticks and tick-borne diseases 2017; 8(4): 574-80.
6. Shi M, Lin XD, Chen X, et al. The evolutionary history of vertebrate RNA viruses. Nature 2018; 556(7700): 197-202.
7. Tao P. Expert in Wuhan collected ten thousands animals: capture bats in mountain at night. Changjiang Times 2017.
8. Li QX, Zhanyao. Playing with elephant dung, fishing for sea bottom mud: the work that will change China's future. thepaper 2019.
9. Ge XY, Li JL, Yang XL, et al. Isolation and characterization of a bat SARS-like coronavirus that uses the ACE2 receptor. Nature 2013; 503(7477): 535-8.
10. Menachery VD, Yount BL, Jr., Debbink K, et al. A SARS-like cluster of circulating bat coronaviruses shows potential for human emergence. Nature medicine 2015; 21(12): 1508-13.

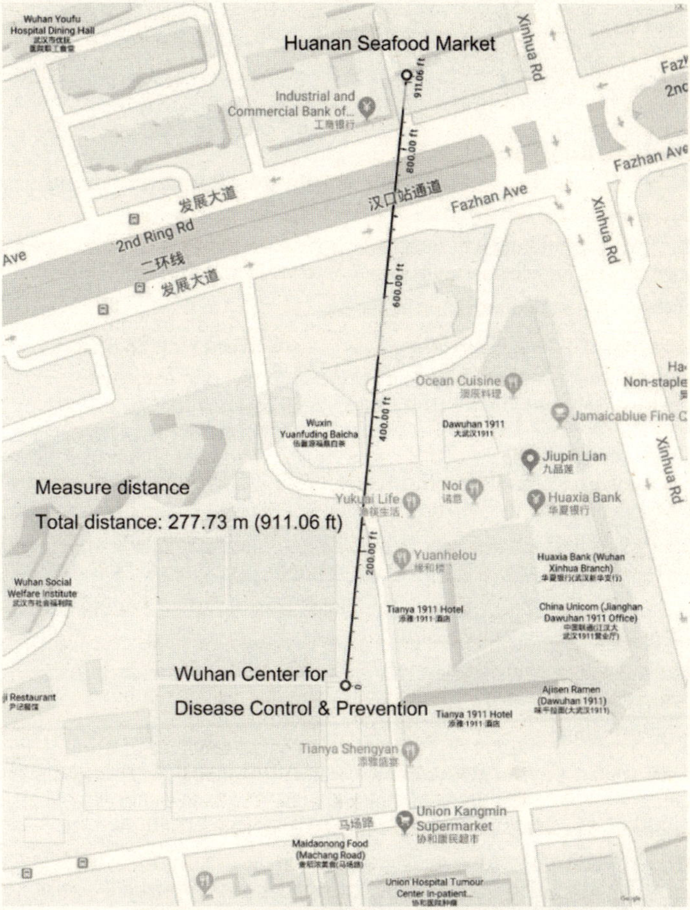

The Huanan Seafood Market is close to the WHCDC (from Baidu and Google)

Notes

Chapter 1: The Bat Woman of Wuhan

[1] https://www.telegraph.co.uk/global-health/science-and-disease/coronavirus-bats-evolved-become-perfect-disease-host/ Accessed 20.4.2020.

[2] https://www.scientificamerican.com/article/how-chinas-bat-woman-hunted-down-viruses-from-sars-to-the-new-coronavirus1/ Accessed 23.4.2020

[3] https://www.nature.com/articles/nature12711

[4] https://edition.cnn.com/2020/02/01/asia/chinese-traditional-medicine-claims-coronavirus-intl-scli-hnk/index.html Accessed 18.5.2020

[5] https://www.globaltimes.cn/content/1180037.shtml Accessed 18.5.2020

Chapter 2: Pandora's Box

[1] http://english.whiov.cas.cn/News/Events/201502/t20150203_135923.html Accessed 29.4.2020

[2] https://www.forbes.com/sites/kenrapoza/2020/04/14/the-washington-post-goes-rogue-china-lab-in-focus-of-coronavirus-outbreak/#65816df11ee1 Accessed 28.4.2020.

[3] https://www.legifrance.gouv.fr/affichTexte.do?cidTexte=JORFTEXT000000422695&categorieLien=id Accessed 17.5.2020.

[4] https://www.franceculture.fr/sciences/le-laboratoire-p4-de-wuhan-une-histoire-francaise Accessed 20.5.2020.

[5] http://www.xinhuanet.com/english/2018-08/08/c_137374368.htm Accessed 17.5.2020

[6] https://www.francetvinfo.fr/sante/maladie/coronavirus/covid-19-enquete-sur-le-p4-de-wuhan-ce-laboratoire-en-partie-finance-par-la-france-ou-a-ete-identifie-le-virus_3920783.html#xtor=CS2-765-%5Bautres%5D- Accessed 18.5.2020.

[7] https://www.washingtonpost.com/opinions/2020/04/14/state-department-cables-warned-safety-issues-wuhan-lab-studying-bat-coronaviruses/ Accessed 17.5.2020

[8] this part of the website has now been removed.

[9] https://www.gao.gov/assets/680/676705.pdf Accessed 11.5.2020

[10] https://eu.usatoday.com/story/news/2015/05/28/biolabs-pathogens-location-incidents/26587505/ Accessed 11.5.2020

[11] ' In 2018, about eight months after the opening of the P4 lab at Wuhan, another P4 facility became operational at Harbin which specialised in animal diseases.

[12] *Science* 21 Jun 2013: Vol. 340, Issue 6139, pp. 1459-1463 DOI: 10.1126/science.1229455

[13] https://www.nih.gov/about-nih/who-we-are/nih-director/statements/statement-funding-pause-certain-types-gain-function-research Accessed 11.5.2020

[14] 'Biosafety in the balance' https://www.nature.com/news/biosafety-in-the-balance-1.15447 Accessed 11.5.2020

[15] https://www.scientificamerican.com/article/how-chinas-bat-woman-hunted-down-viruses-from-sars-to-the-new-coronavirus1/

Chapter 3: Global Collaboration

[1] The GNL cost $167m to build and opened in 2008.

[2] https://www.scmp.com/news/china/science/article/3081036/coronavirus-wuhan-virology-labs-long-history-scientific Accessed 15.5.2020.

[3] https://www.houstonchronicle.com/news/houston-texas/houston/article/UTMB-scientist-acknowledges-safety-risks-at-15221826.php Accessed 15.5.2020.

[4] *Science* 19 Oct 2018: Vol. 362, Issue 6412, pp. 267. DOI: 10.1126/science. aav7120

[5] https://www.ncbi.nlm.nih.gov/genbank/ Accessed 15.5.2020

[6] Sharri Markson and Ashleigh Gleeson, 'The Covid Files: How the Red Army oversaw coronavirus research', *Daily Telegraph*, May 11, 2020. https://www.dailytelegraph.com.au/coronavirus/the-covid-files-australianfunded-coronavirus-paper-used-in-chinese-military-facility/news-story/7241a6b112816f3951495e0fa52ed2aa What also became clear at this time were the manoeuvrings of the Chinese government to position itself to gain the maximum commercial benefits from any new vaccine.

[7] https://www.nejm.org/doi/pdf/10.1056/NEJMoa2001191?articleTools=true Accessed 15.5.2020

[8] http://www.whiov.cas.cn/kyjz_105338/202002/t20200204_5497136.html Accessed 18.5.2020

[9] https://www.ncbi.nlm.nih.gov/pmc/articles/PMC7054408/ Accessed 18.5.2020

[10] https://www.ncbi.nlm.nih.gov/pmc/articles/PMC7054408/ Accessed 18.5.2020

Chapter 4: In the Beginning was … the Virus

[1] Their existence was discovered by a Russian botanist, Dmitri Ivanovsky. The newly discovered organism was given the name 'virus' by the Dutch microbiologist Martinus Willem Beijerinck, one of the founders of the science of virology.

[2] Forterre, P. 2010. 'Origin of Viruses' P24-7. In van Regenmortel, M. et al Desk Encyclopedia of General Virology, Academic Press.

[3] Villarreal and Witzany, 2010.

[4] Moelling, 2017. *Viruses: More Friends Than Foes* has a very readable account of all of these issues.

[5] Quammen 2013, 38-44. Quammen D. 2013, *Spillover: Animal Infections and the Next Human Pandemic*, Vintage Books, London

Chapter 5: Contagion Rules

[1] Cockburn A. The Evolution and Eradication of Infectious Diseases. Baltimore: Johns Hopkins, 1963.

[2] Burnet F, White DO. Natural History of Infectious Disease, 4th edn Cambridge: Cambridge University Press, 1972.

[3] The World Health Assembly is the governing authority of the WHO which decides the organisation's policies at its annual meeting in Geneva, Switzerland.

[4] https://www.ncbi.nlm.nih.gov/pmc/articles/PMC7165909/pdf/IMR-225-9.pdf Accessed 20.5.2020. This is an excellent historical summary upon which I have drawn extensively.

[5] Omran AL. The epidemiologic transition theory. A preliminary update. J Trop Pediatr 1983; 29:305–316.

[6] In fairness to the Surgeon General, Dr. William H. Stewart, though it has been repeated innumerable times throughout the literature, no definitive source for this statement has been found, and Dr Stewart does not recall having said it.

[7] Steven Pinker, 2018, *Enlightenment Now*, pp. 142, 306-7.

[8] Nichol, S.T., et al, 1993. 'Punctuated equilibrium and positive Darwinian evolution in vesicular stomatitis virus.' Proceedings of the National Academy of Sciences, 90(22), pp.10424-10428.

[9] Gould, S.J. and Eldredge, N., 1977. Punctuated equilibria: the tempo and mode of evolution reconsidered. *Paleobiology*, pp.115-151.

[10] This quotation has not been found in Lenin's *Collected Works.*

[11] Holland, J., Spindler, K., Horodyski, F., Grabau, E., Nichol, S. & Vande Pol, S. (1982) Science 215, 1577-1585

[12] Journal of Virology, 2013 Jun; 87(12): 7039–7045. doi: 10.1128/JVI.03273-12

[13] https://www.cdc.gov/flu/about/burden/index.html Accessed 8.5.2020

[14] https://www.who.int/csr/sars/country/table2004_04_21/en/ Accessed 22.5.2020

Chapter 6: Dress Rehearsal

[1] Ellen Nakashima, 'SARS Signals Missed in Hong Kong', *The Washington Post*, May 20, 2020. https://www.washingtonpost.com/archive/politics/2003/05/20/sars-signals-missed-in-hong-kong/50ff4807-4862-4229-8bbd-ec5932b5c896/

[2] Knobler S, et al., eds..2004. *Learning from SARS: Preparing for the Next Disease Outbreak: Workshop Summary.* Washington (DC): National Academies Press (US);

[3] Ibid. p258

[4] Henry Kissinger, 2014. World Order: Reflections on the Character of Nations and the Course of History.

[5] Gro-Harlem Brundtland, Past Director-General, WHO, Address at the 56th World Health Assembly, Geneva, Switzerland (May 18,2003).

[6] Brundtland 2005, 435. Gro Harlem Brundtland, 2005. Madam Prime Minister: A Life in Power and Politics, Farrar, Straus and Giroux.

Chapter 7: Censoring the Outbreak

[1] https://www.nytimes.com/2016/02/23/world/asia/china-media-policy-xi-jinping.html Accessed 23.5.2020

[2] The first two recorded cases in Italy were an elderly married Chinese couple who were visiting from Wuhan, China. Chiara Severgnini, 'Coronavirus, primi due casi in Italia «Sono due cinesi in vacanza a Roma» Sono arrivati a Milano il 23 gennaio', Corriere Della Sera, January 30, 2020. https://www.corriere.it/cronache/20_gennaio_30/coronavirus-italia-corona-9d6dc436-4343-11ea-bdc8-faf1f56f19b7.shtml

[3] Josephine Ma, 'Exclusive Coronavirus: China's first confirmed Covid-19 case traced back to November 17', South China Morning Post, March 13, 2020. https://www.scmp.com/news/china/society/article/3074991/coronavirus-chinas-first-confirmed-covid-19-case-traced-back Accessed 23.5.2020

[4] Huang, Chaolin, et al, 2020. 'Clinical features of patients infected with 2019 novel coronavirus in Wuhan, China.' *The Lancet* 395.10223: 497-506. https://www.thelancet.com/journals/lancet/article/PIIS0140-6736(20)30183-5/fulltext

[5] https://www.bbc.com/zhongwen/trad/chinese-news-51540821

[6] http://www.xinhuanet.com/english/2020-01/29/c_138741031.htm

[7] http://www.xinhuanet.com/2020-01/11/c_1125448269.htm

[8] Huang, Chaolin, et al, 2020. 'Clinical features of patients infected with 2019 novel coronavirus in Wuhan, China.' *The Lancet* 395.10223: 497-506. https://www.thelancet.com/journals/lancet/article/PIIS0140-6736(20)30183-5/fulltext

[9] https://mp.weixin.qq.com/s/IzzCnz4Yr2jEIYZePiu_ow

[10] Qun Li et al, 2020. 'Early Transmission Dynamics in Wuhan, China, of Novel Coronavirus–Infected Pneumonia', New England Journal of Medicine, January 29, 2020. https://www.nejm.org/doi/pdf/10.1056/NEJMoa2001316

[11] Sui-Lee Wee and Vivian Wang, 'China Grapples With Mystery Pneumonia-Like Illness', The New York Times, January 6, 2020. https://www.nytimes.com/2020/01/06/world/asia/china-SARS-pneumonialike.html?searchResultPosition=4

[12] Xu Wen, 'Wuhan disease control confirmed …' Beijing New Express, December 31, 2019. http://www.bjnews.com.cn/news/2019/12/31/668430.html

[13] Jim Geraghty, 'The Comprehensive Timeline of China's COVID-19 Lies' National Review, March 23, 2020. This provides an excellent synopsis of the early significant events in Wuhan. https://www.nationalreview.com/the-morning-jolt/chinas-devastating-lies/

[14] Qun Li et al, 2020. 'Early Transmission Dynamics in Wuhan, China, of Novel Coronavirus–Infected Pneumonia', New England Journal of Medicine, January 29, 2020. https://www.nejm.org/doi/pdf/10.1056/NEJMoa2001316

[15] Sui-Lee Wee and Donald G. McNeil Jr. 'China Identifies New Virus Causing Pneumonialike Illness', The New York Times, January 8, 2020.

https://www.nytimes.com/2020/01/08/health/china-pneumonia-outbreak-virus.html?searchResultPosition=7

Chapter 8: The Silence of the Labs

[1] http://virological.org/t/phylodynamic-analysis-176-genomes-6-mar-2020/356 Accessed 31.5.2020

[2] https://www.who.int/dg/speeches/detail/who-director-general-s-statement-on-the-advice-of-the-ihr-emergency-committee-on-novel-coronavirus Accessed 27.5.2020

[3] http://www.whiov.ac.cn/xwdt_105286/zhxw/202001/t20200129_5494574.html Accessed 13.6.2020

[1] https://www.theguardian.com/world/2020/apr/10/birth-of-a-pandemic-inside-the-first-weeks-of-the-coronavirus-outbreak-in-wuhan Accessed 11.6.2020.

[2] https://www.scmp.com/news/china/politics/article/3049606/coronavirus-doctors-death-becomes-catalyst-freedom-speech Accessed 26.5.2020

[3] https://www.scmp.com/comment/opinion/article/3048734/how-coronavirus-crisis-has-brewed-revolt-professionals-chinaAccessed 11.6.2020

[4] https://www.nytimes.com/2020/02/07/business/china-coronavirus-doctor-death.html Accessed 10.6.2020.

[5] https://www.economist.com/china/2020/02/13/li-wenliangs-death-exposes-the-costs-of-chinas-authoritarianism Accessed on 11.6.2020

[6] https://www.washingtonpost.com/world/asia_pacific/doctors-death-from-coronavirus-sparks-a-digital-uprising-rattling-chinas-leaders/2020/02/07/a4cb3492-4998-11ea-8a1f-de1597be6cbc_story.html Accessed 11.6.2020

Chapter 10: The Penny Drops

[1] Mao's Yangtze swim was a stunt. The over-weight, chain-smoking 73-year-old was in no shape to swim over nine miles down the fast-flowing river in the ludicrously short time claimed by Chinese media.

[2] Edward Gu and Lantian Li 2020, JOURNAL OF CHINESE GOVERNANCE, 2020, VOL. 5, NO. 2, 160–177. https://doi.org/10.1080/23812346.2020.1740468 Accessed 10.6.2020.

[3] Gu and Li 2000, 160.

[4] Gu and Li 2000, 171.

[5] http://www.gov.cn/premier/2020-01/21/content_5471097.htm Accessed on 14.6.2020.

Chapter 11: Wuhan Goes Viral

[1] These meetings are referred to as the 'Two Meetings (Sessions)', a common Mandarin expression for meetings of two of organizations which have close relations.

[2] https://www.ft.com/content/fa83463a-4737-11ea-aeb3-955839e06441 Accessed 14.6.2020.

[3] https://www.ft.com/content/fa83463a-4737-11ea-aeb3-955839e06441 Accessed 14.6.2020.

[4] https://www.medrxiv.org/content/10.1101/2020.03.03.20029843v3.full.pdf Accessed 20.6.2020.

[5] https://takungpao.com/news/232108/2020/0105/400593.html NB. This is a CCP-controlled newspaper and the article has been removed and the link does not work.

[6] https://www.nytimes.com/2020/01/22/health/virus-corona.html Accessed 18.6.2020.

[7] https://www.weibo.com/2656274875/IqCSrAXel?type=comment#_rnd1592906427411 Accessed 18.6.2020.

[8] https://www.who.int/thailand/news/detail/13-01-2020-thailand-responding-to-the-novel-coronavirus Accessed 19.6.2020.

[9] https://www.who.int/csr/don/16-january-2020-novel-coronavirus-japan-ex-china/en/ Accessed 19.6.2020.

[10] https://www.scmp.com/week-asia/health-environment/article/3045317/wuhan-pneumonia-asia-battens-down-chinese-new-year

[11] http://www.xinhuanet.com/english/2020-01/10/c_138694239.htm Accessed 14.6.2020.

[12] https://asia.nikkei.com/Editor-s-Picks/China-up-close/China-s-inaction-for-3-days-in-January-at-root-of-pandemic Accessed 12.6.2020.

[13] https://apnews.com/68a9e1b91de4ffc166acd6012d82c2f9 Accessed 11.6.2020.

[14] https://www.thepaper.cn/newsDetail_forward_5653949 (in Chinese) Accessed 18.6.2020.

Chapter 12: Dr WHO

[1] Marianne Schneider-Petsinger, 'Geoeconomics Explained' Chatham House, December 9, 2016 https://www.chathamhouse.org/2016/12/geoeconomics-explained

[2] According to an update issued by the China National Health Commission.

[3] This is the updated legal framework within which the WHO functions. I was ratified by WHO's 196 full members in 2005.

[4] International Health Regulations and Emergency Committees http://www10.who.int/features/qa/emergency-committees/en/

[5] Guardian, April 18,2020: https://www.theguardian.com/world/2020/apr/18/caught-in-a-superpower-struggle-the-inside-story-of-the-whos-response-to-coronavirus

[6] https://www.reuters.com/article/us-china-health-who/who-chief-says-widespread-travel-bans-not-needed-to-beat-china-virus-idUSKBN1ZX1H3 Accessed 21.6.2020.

[7] https://www.who.int/news-room/detail/28-01-2020-who-china-leaders-discuss-next-steps-in-battle-against-coronavirus-outbreak

[8] https://www.who.int/news-room/detail/07-07-2020-who-experts-to-travel-to-china

[9] https://www.reuters.com/article/health-coronavirus-who-mission-exclusive/exclusive-who-led-team-expected-in-china-in-january-to-probe-covid-19-origins-experts-idUSKBN28Q2IJ

[10] This is not correct. The Wuhan Virology Institute had decoded the genome of the virus by January 2 but it was not released to the WHO until 9 days later on January 11. This was only done because another lab had also decoded the virus and made it publicly available on the internet on January 10 through the auspices of Prof. Holmes of Sydney University. For defying the information clampdown, within days this lab was summarily closed by the Communist authorities 'for rectification'.

[11] https://www.ft.com/content/57c6a1d6-49a7-11ea-aeb3-955839e06441 Accessed 20.6.2020.

[12] https://www.ft.com/content/cc2be982-417d-11ea-bdb5-169ba7be433d Accessed 20.6.2020.

[13] https://www.newstatesman.com/politics/health/2020/02/coronavirus-and-geopolitics-disease Accessed 20.6.2020.

[14] https://www.ncbi.nlm.nih.gov/pmc/articles/PMC7106206/ Accessed 21.6.2020.

[15] https://www.who.int/news/item/30-01-2020-statement-on-the-second-meeting-of-the-international-health-regulations-(2005)-emergency-committee-regarding-the-outbreak-of-novel-coronavirus-(2019-ncov)

[16] https://www.fmprc.gov.cn/mfa_eng/xwfw_665399/s2510_665401/2511_665403/t1739548.shtml Accessed 23.6.2020.

[17] Donald G. McNeil Jr., 'To Take On the Coronavirus, Go Medieval on It', The New York Times, February 28, 2020.

[18] https://apnews.com/3c061794970661042b18d5aeaaed9fae Accessed 14.6.2020.

[19] https://apnews.com/3c061794970661042b18d5aeaaed9fae Accessed 14.6.2020.

[20] https://www.bmj.com/content/326/7398/1055.4 Accessed 16.6.2020.

[21] https://www.ft.com/content/8ede7e92-4749-11ea-aeb3-955839e06441 Accessed 15.6.2020.

[22] https://www.ft.com/content/8ede7e92-4749-11ea-aeb3-955839e06441 Accessed 15.6.2020.

Chapter 13: A Smoking Gun?

[1] Ji, W., Wang, W., Zhao, X., Zai, J. & Li, X. J. Med. Virol. https://doi.org/10.1002/jmv.25682 (2020). Accessed 25.6.2020.

[2] Lam, T.T., Jia, N., Zhang, Y. et al. Identifying SARS-CoV-2-related coronaviruses in Malayan pangolins. Nature (2020). https://doi.org/10.1038/s41586-020-2169-0 Accessed 25.6.2020.

[3] https://www.who.int/docs/default-source/coronaviruse/who-china-joint-mission-on-covid-19-final-report.pdf Accessed 12.5.2020.

[4] https://www.who.int/health-topics/coronavirus/who-recommendations-to-reduce-risk-of-transmission-of-emerging-pathogens-from-animals-to-humans-in-live-animal-markets accessed 10.5.2020

[5] https://www.who.int/ihr/biosafety/background/en/

[6] https://thebulletin.org/2019/02/supplementary-material-for-human-error-in-high-biocontainment-labs-a-likely-pandemic-threat/ Accessed 25.6.2020.

[7] https://wwwgao.gov/assets/680/679392.pdf Accessed 25.6.2020.

[8] Selgelid, M. J., 'Gain-of-function research: ethical analysis'. Sci Eng Ethics (2016) 22:923–964 DOI 10.1007/s11948-016-9810-1

[9] http://www.phe.gov/s3/dualuse/Documents/gain-of-function.pdf Accessed 25.6.2020.

[10] https://www.nytimes.com/2012/06/22/health/h5n1-bird-flu-research-that-stoked-fears-is-published.html Accessed 25.6.2020.

[11] Anthony S. Fauci and Francis S. Collins. 'Benefits and Risks of Influenza Research: Lessons Learned'. Science 336 (6088), 1522-1523. DOI: 10.1126/science.1224305. Accessed 26.6.2020.

[12] http://www.phe.gov/s3/dualuse/Documents/gain-of-function.pdf Accessed 25.6.2020.

[13] https://grants.nih.gov/grants/guide/notice-files/NOT-OD-17-071.html Accessed 25.6.2020.

[14] Menachery, V., Yount, B., Debbink, K. et al. A SARS-like cluster of circulating bat coronaviruses shows potential for human emergence. Nat Med 21, 1508–1513 (2015). doi.org/10.1038/nm.3985

[15] https://www.nature.com/news/engineered-bat-virus-stirs-debate-over-risky-research-1.18787 Accessed 26.6.2020.

[16] https://www.independent.co.uk/news/world/americas/dr-fauci-congress-coronavirus-testimony-grant-research-wuhan-lab-a9585886.html Accessed 26.6.2020.

[17] W. Liang, et al. "Severe Acute Respiratory Syndrome-Retrospect and Lessons of 2004 Outbreak in China," Biomedical and Environmental Sciences, 19, (2006): 445-451.

[18] https://www.who.int/csr/don/2004_05_18a/en/ 26.6.2020.

[19] Josh Rogin, 'State Department cables warned of safety issues at Wuhan lab studying bat coronaviruses', The Washington Post, April 14, 2020. https://www.washingtonpost.com/opinions/2020/04/14/state-department-cables-warned-safety-issues-wuhan-lab-studying-bat-coronaviruses/

[20] https://www.fmprc.gov.cn/mfa_eng/zxxx_662805/t1745270.shtml

[21] https://www.globaltimes.cn/content/1179747.shtml

[22] https://www.globaltimes.cn/content/1189506.shtml

[23] https://www.nccih.nih.gov/health/in-the-news-coronavirus-and-alternative-treatments Accessed 26.6.2020.

[24] https://www.nature.com/articles/s41591-020-0820-9 Accessed 29.6.2020.

[25] https://www.dni.gov/index.php/newsroom/press-releases/item/2112-intelligence-community-statement-on-origins-of-covid-19 Accessed 28.6.2020.

[26] https://twitter.com/zlj517/status/1238111898828066823?lang=en

[27] http://www.xinhuanet.com/english/2020-03/09/c_138859548.htm Accessed 29.6.2020.

[28] https://www.theguardian.com/us-news/2020/apr/30/donald-trump-coronavirus-chinese-lab-claim Accessed 29.6.2020.

[29] https://www.ncbi.nlm.nih.gov/pmc/articles/PMC5708621/

[30] http://www.changjiangtimes.com/2017/05/567037.html Accessed 20.6.2020. See also https://archive.is/ruSFu#selection-491.0-491.96

[31] Arthur Conan Doyle, Sherlock Holmes

[32] See Appendix1

[33] https://jamiemetzl.com/origins-of-sars-cov-2/

[34] https://www.theguardian.com/commentisfree/2020/jun/09/conspiracies-covid-19-lab-false-pandemic The Guardian, June 9, 2020

[35] https://www.thelancet.com/journals/lancet/article/PIIS0140-6736(20)31494-X/fulltext

[36] https://www.thelancet.com/article/S0140-6736(20)31927-9/fulltext

[37]

https://www.fmprc.gov.cn/mfa_eng/xwfw_665399/s2510_665401/2511_665403/t1847010.shtml

[38] Ibid.

[39] https://www.globaltimes.cn/content/1208404.shtml

[40] Shing Hei Zhan, et al. 'SARS-CoV-2 is well adapted for humans. What does this mean for re-emergence?' BioRxiv, May 2, 2020: https://doi.org/10.1101/2020.05.01.073262

[41] https://www.who.int/publications/m/item/who-convened-global-study-of-the-origins-of-sars-cov-2

[42] https://science.sciencemag.org/content/371/6525/120

[43] https://www.bbc.com/news/world-asia-china-55765875

[44] Alina Chan and Matt Ridley, 'The World Needs a Real Investigation Into the Origins of Covid-19', *The Wall Street Journal*, January 15, 2021.

[45] Filippa Lentzos, 'Will the WHO call for an international investigation into the coronavirus's origins?', *Bulletin of Atomic Scientists*, May 18, 2020.

Chapter 14: The WHO Lied

[1] https://www.newshub.co.nz/home/world/2020/06/europe-joins-us-in-moves-to-overhaul-the-world-health-organization.html Accessed 26.6.2020.

[2] https://www.kff.org/global-health-policy/fact-sheet/the-u-s-government-and-the-world-health-organization/ Accessed 27.6.22020.

[3] https://www.ft.com/content/693f49e8-b8a9-4ed3-9d4a-cdfb591fefce Accessed 27.6.2020.

[4] https://www.the-scientist.com/news-opinion/trump-suspends-who-funds-alleges-a-poor-covid-19-response-67426 Accessed 26.6.2020

[5] https://www.who.int/news-room/detail/23-01-2020-statement-on-the-meeting-of-the-international-health-regulations-(2005)-emergency-committee-regarding-the-outbreak-of-novel-coronavirus-(2019-ncov) Accessed 27.6.2020.

[6] https://www.who.int/news-room/articles-detail/updated-who-advice-for-international-traffic-in-relation-to-the-outbreak-of-the-novel-coronavirus-2019-ncov-24-jan/ Accessed 27.6.2020.

[7] https://foreignpolicy.com/2020/04/02/china-coronavirus-who-health-soft-power/ Accessed 29.6.2020.

[8] https://www.cfr.org/blog/who-and-china-dereliction-duty Accessed 29.6.2020 VG account of compromise of WHO

[9] https://www.bloomberg.com/amp/news/articles/2020-01-21/china-faces-social-media-backlash-with-new-virus-outbreak Accessed 29.6.2020.

[10] https://twitter.com/DrTedros/status/1220421162251051008 Accessed 29.6.2020.

[11] https://www.nature.com/articles/d41586-020-01121-1 Accessed 27.6.2020.

[12] https://www.washingtonpost.com/world/trumps-critique-of-who-may-be-a-diversion-but-it-resonates-beyond-the-white-house/2020/04/15/c3320360-7b30-11ea-a311-adb1344719a9_story.html Accessed 28.6.2020.

[13] The World Health Organization, INTERNATIONAL HEALTH REGUALTIONS (2005): https://www.who.int/ihr/publications/9789241580496/en/ Accessed 29.6.2020.

[14] https://www.who.int/news-room/detail/27-04-2020-who-timeline---covid-19 Accessed 30.6.2020. The publication date of the statement is 29 June 2020 but it states at the top of the page 'Last updated 30 June 2020.

[15] Debora Mackenzie 2020. Covid-19: *The Pandemic That Never Should Have Happened and How to Stop the Next One*, The Bridge Street Press. pp 1-3 contains very useful background on ProMED and its important role in alerting the world to the outbreak in Wuhan.

[16] Maryn Mckenna, 'How ProMED Crowdsourced the Arrival of Covid-19 and SARS', WIRED, March 23, 2020.

[17] https://wwwnc.cdc.gov/eid/article/26/2/19-1043_article#r3

[18] https://wwwnc.cdc.gov/eid/article/26/2/19-1043_article ; See also Chris Baraniuk,' A Free Email Service Broke the News of the Coronavirus in 2019', OneZero, March 26.2020. https://onezero.medium.com/a-free-email-service-broke-the-news-of-the-coronavirus-in-2019-ff2b595af606

[19] https://tech.sina.com.cn/roll/2019-12-31/doc-iihnzhfz9428799.shtml

[20] Pro-MED. PRO/AH/EDR. Undiagnosed pneumonia - China (HU): Request For Information. Archive Number: 20191230.6864153. 30 Dec 2019. 23:59. Available from: https://promedmail.org/promed-post/?id=6864153

[21] https://promedmail.org/promed-post/?id=6864153

[22] https://www.washingtonpost.com/world/trumps-critique-of-who-may-be-a-diversion-but-it-resonates-beyond-the-white-house/2020/04/15/c3320360-7b30-11ea-a311-adb1344719a9_story.html Accessed 28.6.2020.

[23] https://www.washingtonpost.com/world/asia_pacific/chinese-officials-note-serious-problems-in-coronavirus-response-the-world-health-organization-keeps-praising-them/2020/02/08/b663dd7c-4834-11ea-91ab-ce439aa5c7c1_story.html Accessed 28.6.2020.

[24] https://www.who.int/docs/default-source/coronaviruse/transcripts/who-audio-emergencies-coronavirus-press-conference-20apr2020.pdf

[25] Ibid.

Chapter 15: Asian Neighbours

[1] https://www.imf.org/external/pubs/ft/issues1/ Accessed 12.7.2020.

[2] https://www.economist.com/special-report/2019/12/05/after-half-a-century-of-success-the-asian-tigers-must-reinvent-themselves Accessed 11.7.2020.

[3] https://europepmc.org/article/med/15018125 Accessed 12.7.2020.

[4] https://www.nature.com/articles/d41586-020-00129-x Accessed 1.7.2020.

[5] https://recombinomics.co/topic/4356-2019-ncov-61f-patient-visited-other-markets-in-wuhan/ The full statement is available here; the original has been deleted from the Wuhan Municipal Health Committee web site.

[6] The new coronavirus disease was only given the name Covid-19 by the WHO on February 11, 2020

[7] https://www.nature.com/articles/d41586-020-00129-x Accessed 1.7.2020.

[8] https://www.coronavirus.gov.hk/eng/sars-report.html Accessed 12.7.2020.

[9] https://www.nytimes.com/2020/04/18/world/asia/hong-kong-arrests.html Accessed 11.7.2020.

[10] https://www.gov.sg/article/how-is-singapore-limiting-the-spread-of-covid-19 Accessed 12.7.2020.

[11] Yuen Sin, 'Coronavirus: Travellers with symptoms face quick test on arrival in Singapore', The Straits Times, March 6, 2020. https://www.straitstimes.com/singapore/quick-test-for-travellers-with-symptoms-on-arrival-in-spore Accessed 12.7.2020.

[12] Salma Khalik, 'Why Singapore has relatively low Covid-19 death rate', The Straits Times, June 25. 2020. https://www.straitstimes.com/singapore/why-spore-has-relatively-low-covid-19-death-rate Accessed 12.7.2020.

[13] https://www.ft.com/content/e015e096-6532-11ea-a6cd-df28cc3c6a68 12.7.2020.

[14] JAMA. 2020 ;323(14) :1341_1342. doi:10.1001/jama.2020.3151

[15] https://www.economist.com/graphic-detail/2020/03/07/tourism-flows-and-death-rates-suggest-covid-19-is-being-under-reported Accessed 11.7.2020.

[16] https://systems.jhu.edu/research/public-health/ncov-model-2/ Accessed 12.7.2020.

Chapter 16: Europe Gets Hit

[1] Science 24 Apr 2020: Vol. 368, Issue 6489, pp. 395-400 DOI: 10.1126/science.aba9757.

[2] Pinotti F, et al (2020) Tracing and analysis of 288 early SARSCoV-2 infections outside China: A modeling study.PLoS Med 17(7): e1003193. https://doi.org/10.1371/journal.pmed.1003193.

[3] https://www.who.int/csr/don/05-january-2020-pneumonia-of-unkown-cause-china/en/ Accessed 13.7.2020.

[4] https://www.who.int/news-room/articles-detail/updated-who-recommendations-for-international-traffic-in-relation-to-covid-19-outbreak Accessed 13.7.2020.

[5] https://www.reuters.com/article/us-health-coronavirus-mongolia/mongolia-confirms-first-coronavirus-case-a-french-national-idUSKBN20X03F Accessed 12.7.2020.

[6] https://www.saude.gov.br/noticias/agencia-saude/46435-brasil-confirma-primeiro-caso-de-novo-coronavirus Accessed 13.7.2020.

[7] https://www.gov.za/speeches/health-reports-first-case-covid-19-coronavirus-5-mar-2020-0000 Accessed 13.7.2020.

[8] Lancet. 2020 14-20 March; 395(10227): 871–877. Published online 2020 Feb 20. doi: 10.1016/S0140-6736(20)30411-6

[9] https://theintercept.com/2020/04/02/coronavirus-europe-travel/ Accessed 13.7.2020.

[10] https://www.consilium.europa.eu/en/press/press-releases/2020/05/04/speech-by-president-charles-michel-at-the-coronavirus-global-response-international-pledging-event/ Accessed 13.7.2020.

[11] https://www.euronews.com/2020/01/21/coronavirus-is-the-eu-prepared-for-an-outbreak Accessed 13.7.2020.

[12] https://www.ecdc.europa.eu/sites/default/files/documents/Risk-assessment-pneumonia-Wuhan-China-22-Jan-2020.pdf Accessed 12.7.2020.

[13] https://ec.europa.eu/commission/presscorner/detail/en/qanda_20_307 Accessed 15.7.2020.

[14] https://www.thebureauinvestigates.com/stories/2020-07-15/crisis-at-the-commission-inside-europes-response-to-the-coronavirus-outbreak Accessed 15.7.2020.

[15] https://english.elpais.com/society/2020-05-19/how-europe-underestimated-the-danger-of-the-coronavirus-pandemic.html Accessed 15.7.2020.

[16] https://www.ncbi.nlm.nih.gov/pmc/articles/PMC7068164/ Accessed 16.7.2020.

[17] https://www.ecdc.europa.eu/en/publications-data/outbreak-novel-coronavirus-disease-2019-covid-19-situation-italy Accessed 15.7.2020.

[18] https://ec.europa.eu/health/sites/health/files/preparedness_response/docs/ev_20200312_sr_en.pdf Accessed 16.7.2020.

Chapter 17: Carnage in Italy

[1] https://doi.org/10.1016/j.meegid.2020.104351 Accessed 17.7.2020.

[2] https://www.independent.co.uk/news/world/europe/coronavirus-italy-footage-video-hospital-bergamo-covid-19-a9414136.html Accessed

[3] https://theconversation.com/italys-darkest-hour-how-coronavirus-became-a-very-political-problem-133178 Accessed 18.7.2020.

[4] https://www.elysee.fr/emmanuel-macron/2020/03/16/adresse-aux-francais-covid19 Accessed 17.7.2020.

[5] https://crsreports.congress.gov/product/pdf/R/R46304 Accessed 19.7.2020.

[6] http://www.china.org.cn/world/2020-03/17/content_75823148.htm Accessed 18.7.2020.

[7] https://www.irishtimes.com/news/world/europe/italians-look-at-aid-from-china-and-a-series-of-slights-from-the-eu-1.4206136 Accessed 18.7.2020.

[8] https://www-jstor-org.elib.tcd.ie/stable/pdf/42894676.pdf Accessed 18.7.2020.

[9] https://ec.europa.eu/commission/presscorner/detail/en/IP_19_1605 Accessed 18.7.2020.

[10] Kate McClymont and Royce Millar, 'Billions of face masks sent to China during Australian bushfire crisis', The Sydney Morning Herald, April 2, 2020. https://www.smh.com.au/national/billions-of-face-masks-sent-to-china-during-australian-bushfire-crisis-20200402-p54gjh.html

[11] http://www.gov.cn/xinwen/2020-03/07/content_5488383.htm Accessed 18.7.2020.

[12] http://m.xinhuanet.com/fj/2020-02/03/c_1125524940.htm Accessed 18.7.2020.

[13] Its full name is the United Front Work Department

[14] http://bj.people.com.cn/n2/2020/0330/c233088-33914410.html Accessed 18.7.2020.

Chapter 18: Britain is Blindsided

[1] Is supported by the Open Philanthropy Project, the Bill & Melinda Gates Foundation, and the Robertson Foundation.

[2] https://www.ghsindex.org/wp-content/uploads/2019/08/United-Kingdom.pdf Accessed 22.7.2020.

[3] https://virological.org/t/preliminary-analysis-of-sars-cov-2-importation-establishment-of-uk-transmission-lineages/507 Accessed 20.7.2020.

[4] https://virological.org/t/preliminary-analysis-of-sars-cov-2-importation-establishment-of-uk-transmission-lineages/507 Accessed 20.7.2020.

[5] Because variations in the cause of death the number of confirmed deaths may not be an accurate reflection of the true number of deaths from COVID-19.

[6] https://www.economist.com/britain/2020/06/19/the-british-state-shows-how-not-to-respond-to-a-pandemic Accessed 20.7.2020.

[7] https://twitter.com/drtedros/status/1238110211291975681?lang=en Accessed 20.7.2020.

[8] https://www.gov.uk/government/speeches/pm-statement-on-coronavirus-12-march-2020 Accessed 20.7.2020.

[9] https://twitter.com/bbcr4today/status/1238390547783528448?lang=en Accessed 20.7.2020.

[10] https://www.telegraph.co.uk/politics/2020/03/14/must-do-everything-power-protect-lives/ Accessed 20.7.2020.

[11] https://www.theatlantic.com/health/archive/2020/03/coronavirus-pandemic-herd-immunity-uk-boris-johnson/608065/ Accessed 21.7.2020.

[12] Following mounting pressure, the minutes of SAGE were eventually made public at the end of May.

[13] https://www.bloomberg.com/news/features/2020-04-24/coronavirus-uk-how-boris-johnson-s-government-let-virus-get-away Accessed 21.7.20.

[14] https://www.newstatesman.com/science-tech/coronavirus/2020/06/where-science-went-wrong Accessed 22.7.2020.

[15] It was published and peer reviewed in Nature June 8, 2020. Flaxman, S., Mishra, S., Gandy, A. et al. Estimating the effects of non-pharmaceutical interventions on COVID-19 in Europe. Nature (2020). https://doi.org/10.1038/s41586-020-2405-7

[16] https://www.gov.uk/government/speeches/pm-address-to-the-nation-on-coronavirus-23-march-2020 Accessed 22.7.2020.

[17] https://www.gov.uk/government/news/foreign-secretary-advises-all-british-travellers-to-return-to-the-uk-now Accessed 22.7.2020

[18] https://www.ft.com/content/04d14587-44f0-4c97-a1ce-aacaa2c21706 23.7.2020.

[19] https://www.who.int/dg/speeches/detail/who-director-general-s-opening-remarks-at-the-media-briefing-on-covid-19---16-march-2020 Accessed, 23.7.2020.

[20] https://committees.parliament.uk/oralevidence/237/pdf/ Accessed 22.7.2020.

[21] https://www.gov.uk/government/publications/guidance-for-social-or-community-care-and-residential-settings-on-covid-19/guidance-for-social-or-community-care-and-residential-settings-on-covid-19 Accessed 22.7.2020.

[22] https://www.reuters.com/article/us-health-coronavirus-britain-carehomes/timeline-uk-government-advice-on-restricting-visits-to-care-homes-idUSKBN22R2F0 Accessed 22.7.2020.

[23] https://www.ons.gov.uk/peoplepopulationandcommunity/birthsdeathsandmarriages/deaths/articles/deathsinvolvingcovid19inthecaresectorenglandandwales/deathsoccurringupto12june2020andregisteredupto20june2020provisional Accessed 22.7.2020.

[24] https://www.ons.gov.uk/peoplepopulationandcommunity/healthandsocialcare/conditionsanddiseases/articles/impactofcoronavirusincarehomesinenglandvivaldi/26mayto19june2020 Accessed 22.7.2020.

[25] https://www.ecdc.europa.eu/en/publications-data/surveillance-COVID-19-long-term-care-facilities-EU-EEA Accessed 22.7.2020.

Chapter 19: Down Under

[1] https://www.bbc.com/news/world-australia-51999845 Accessed 24.7.2020.

[2] https://7news.com.au/lifestyle/health-wellbeing/coronavirus-australia-explosive-developments-in-ruby-princess-cruise-ship-saga-c-957325 See also, https://www.theaustralian.com.au/subscribe/news/1/?sourceCode=TAWEB_WRE170_a&dest=https%3A%2F%2Fwww.theaustralian.com.au%2Fnation%2Fcoronavirus-ruby-princess-cruise-ship-allowed-to-dock-in-sydney-despite-158-sick-on-board%2Fnews-story%2Ffbb1241af18873410c78dec3a3479e7c&memtype=anonymous&mode=premium Accessed 24.7.2020.

[3] https://www.smh.com.au/national/before-ken-henry-is-crucified-remember-the-good-he-did-20190208-p50whn.html Accessed 26.7.2020.

[4] It was not a government of national unity as it did not include the opposition Labour Party.

[1] https://www.theguardian.com/society/2020/jan/21/coronavirus-us-cdc-case-china-health Accessed 27.7.2020.

[2] http://www.qstheory.cn/dukan/qs/2020-02/15/c_1125572832.htm Accessed 28.7.2020.

[3] https://www.newyorker.com/magazine/2020/04/20/how-anthony-fauci-became-americas-doctor Accessed 28.7.2020.

[4] Marc A. Thiessen, 'If Trump lied, so did Fauci', The Washington Post, September 10, 2020. https://www.washingtonpost.com/opinions/2020/09/10/if-trump-lied-so-did-fauci/

[5] Edward Moreno, 'Government health agency official: Coronavirus 'isn't something the American public need to worry about', The Hill, 26 January, 2020. https://thehill.com/homenews/sunday-talk-shows/479939-government-health-agency-official-corona-virus-isnt-something-the

[6] https://www.cdc.gov/flu/about/burden/preliminary-in-season-estimates.htm Accessed 28.7.2020.

[7] https://www.sccgov.org/sites/covid19/Pages/press-release-04-21-20-early.aspx Accessed 28.7.2020.

Chapter 21: Homeland Insecurity

[1] Daniel Kahneman received the Nobel Prize in Economics for his work on the human errors that result from our heuristics and biases. See his best-selling book *Thinking, Fast and Slow* (2012) Macmillan. ISBN 978-1-4299-6935-2.

[2] Gilovich, T. D.; Griffin, D.; Kahneman, D. (2002). "Heuristics and Biases: The Psychology of Intuitive Judgment". New York, NY: Cambridge University Press

[3] Is supported by the Open Philanthropy Project, the Bill & Melinda Gates Foundation, and the Robertson Foundation.

[4] https://www.ghsindex.org/wp-content/uploads/2020/04/2019-Global-Health-Security-Index.pdf 22.7.2020

[5] This was raised by Vice President Biden in a *USA Today* op ed piece in January 27 'He (Trump)dismissed the top White House official in charge of global health security and dismantled the entire team.

[6] https://www.niaid.nih.gov/about/director Accessed 2.8.2020.

[7] https://www.cdc.gov/media/releases/2020/t0117-coronavirus-screening.html Accessed 5.8.2020.

[8] https://www.cdc.gov/media/releases/2020/p0124-second-travel-coronavirus.html Accessed 5.8.2020.

[9] Ed Yong, 'How the Pandemic Defeated America', *The Atlantic*, September 2020. https://www.theatlantic.com/magazine/archive/2020/09/coronavirus-american-failure/614191/

[10] Ibid.

[11] Sarah True, et al. 'COVID-19 and Workers at Risk: Examining the Long-Term Care Workforce', Kaiser Health News, Apr 23, 2020.https://www.kff.org/coronavirus-covid-19/issue-brief/covid-19-and-workers-at-risk-examining-the-long-term-care-workforce/

[12] Priya Chidambaram, 'Rising Cases in Long-term Care Facilities Are Cause for Concern' KFF, July 21, 2020. https://www.kff.org/coronavirus-covid-19/issue-brief/rising-cases-in-long-term-care-facilities-are-cause-for-concern/

[13] https://oversight.house.gov/news/press-releases/select-committee-briefing-confirms-urgent-need-for-federal-action-to-protect; See also, Maggie Flynn, 'House Briefing: COVID-19 in Nursing Homes 'Blasted the Doors Open of a System that Was Already Failing' Skilled Nursing News, June 11, 2020. https://skillednursingnews.com/2020/06/house-briefing-covid-19-in-nursing-homes-blasted-the-doors-open-of-a-system-that-was-already-failing/

Chapter 22: The Care Home Calamity

[1] Julian Barnes 'C.I.A. Hunts for Authentic Virus Totals in China, Dismissing Government Tallies' The New York Times, April 2, 2020. https://www.nytimes.com/2020/04/02/us/politics/cia-coronavirus-china.html

[2] http://big5.xinhuanet.com/gate/big5/www.xinhuanet.com/politics/2020-04/17/c_1125869575.htm

[3] Gilbert and Sullivan, *The Mikado*. https://www.gsarchive.net/mikado/webopera/mk208d.html

[4] https://mp.weixin.qq.com/s/LXTfDmsQLf3qZnu_S_MxcA

[5] http://wjw.wuhan.gov.cn/gsgg/202012/t20201229_1572409.shtml

[6] I use the term 'care home' to mean all non-acute residential and nursing facilities that cater for people with long-term care needs. There is no internationally agreed definition so the statistics vary somewhat from country to country.

[7] https://www.economist.com/europe/2020/05/09/many-covid-deaths-in-care-homes-are-unrecorded

[8] https://www.euro.who.int/en/about-us/regional-director/statements-and-speeches/2020/statement-invest-in-the-overlooked-and-unsung-build-sustainable-people-centred-long-term-care-in-the-wake-of-covid-19

[9] Ibid.

[10] Michael Birnbaum and William Booth, 'Nursing homes linked to up to half of coronavirus deaths in Europe, WHO says' *The Washington Post*, April 23, 2020. https://www.washingtonpost.com/world/europe/nursing-homes-coronavirus-deaths-europe/2020/04/23/d635619c-8561-11ea-81a3-9690c9881111_story.html

[11] *The Decameron of Giovanni Boccaccio*, The First Day, The First Story, trans. John Payne, Walter J. Black, New York NY.

[12] In reality the figure is lower because the 'care home' designation in Germany includes other communal settings such as homeless and refugee shelters and prisons.

[13] Condon, B., Peltz, and Mustian J.' AP count: Over 4,500 virus patients sent to NY nursing homes' May 22, 2020. https://apnews.com/article/5ebc0ad45b73a899efa81f098330204c

[14] https://www.bbc.com/news/world-us-canada-52814435

[15] Comas-Herrera, A et al 2020. 'Mortality associated with COVID-19 outbreaks in care homes: early international evidence' PP 2,27. https://ltccovid.org/wp-content/uploads/2020/06/Mortality-associated-with-COVID-among-people-who-use-long-term-care-26-June.pdf

[16] ibid.

[17] Maximilian Salcher-Konrad et al, 2020. 'COVID-19 related mortality and spread of disease in long-term care: first findings from a living systematic review of emerging evidence', https://www.medrxiv.org/content/10.1101/2020.06.09.20125237v1.full.pdf

[18] Peishan Yang and Lung Kuan Huang, 2020.' Successful prevention of COVID-19 outbreak at elderly care institutions in Taiwan', *Journal Formosan Medical Association*, 119(8): 1249–1250. https://www.ncbi.nlm.nih.gov/pmc/articles/PMC7241364/

Chapter 23: Trump and Therapeutics

[1] https://www.fda.gov/news-events/press-announcements/fda-issues-emergency-use-authorization-convalescent-plasma-potential-promising-covid-19-treatment

[2] https://www.fda.gov/news-events/press-announcements/fda-approves-first-treatment-covid-19

[3] https://apps.who.int/iris/handle/10665/336729

[4] https://www.bloomberg.com/news/articles/2020-07-30/remdesivir-gets-lukewarm-endorsement-from-experts-in-covid-fight

[5] https://www.ox.ac.uk/news/2020-06-16-low-cost-dexamethasone-reduces-death-one-third-hospitalised-patients-severe

[6] Melissa Davey, 'Covid-19 study on hydroxychloroquine use questioned by 120 researchers and medical professionals', *The Guardian*, 29.5.2020. https://www.theguardian.com/world/2020/may/29/covid-19-surgisphere-

hydroxychloroquine-study-lancet-coronavirus-who-questioned-by-researchers-medical-professionals

[7] https://www.thelancet.com/journals/lancet/article/PIIS0140-6736(20)31180-6/fulltext

[8] https://www.ox.ac.uk/news/2020-06-05-no-clinical-benefit-use-hydroxychloroquine-hospitalised-patients-covid-19

[9] https://www.recoverytrial.net/news/statement-from-the-chief-investigators-of-the-randomised-evaluation-of-covid-19-therapy-recovery-trial-on-hydroxychloroquine-5-june-2020-no-clinical-benefit-from-use-of-hydroxychloroquine-in-hospitalised-patients-with-covid-19

[10] https://academic.oup.com/cid/advance-article/doi/10.1093/cid/ciaa1571/5929230

[11] https://twitter.com/realDonaldTrump/status/1241367239900778501

[12] https://twitter.com/realDonaldTrump/status/1311892190680014849?ref_src=twsrc%5Etfw%7Ctwcamp%5Etweetembed%7Ctwterm%5E1311892190680014849%7Ctwgr%5Eshare_3&ref_url=https%3A%2F%2Fwww.npr.org%2Fsections%2Flatest-updates-trump-covid-19-results%2F2020%2F10%2F03%2F919898777%2Ftimeline-what-we-know-of-president-trumps-covid-19-diagnosis

[13] https://www.latimes.com/politics/story/2020-10-04/trump-coronavirus-diagnosis-trust

[14] https://www.nejm.org/doi/full/10.1056/NEJMoa2021436

[15] https://jamanetwork.com/journals/jama/fullarticle/2770275

Chapter 24: The Race for a Vaccine

[1] https://www.economist.com/briefing/2020/04/16/can-the-world-find-a-good-covid-19-vaccine-quickly-enough

[2] April 16 2020 saw 10,491 die of Covid-19. According to the WHO, in West Africa Ebola killed 11,310 over the years 2013-16.

[3] David E. Sanger, David D. Kirkpatrick, Sui-Lee Wee and Katrin Bennhold,' Search for Coronavirus Vaccine Becomes a Global Competition', The New York Times, March 19, 2020.

[4] https://www.globaltimes.cn/content/1181507.shtml

[5] Chi Jia, 'Human vaccine trial gets underway', China Daily 23.3.2020. http://covid-19.chinadaily.com.cn/a/202003/23/WS5e77f24aa31012821728112d.html

[6] Christian Shepherd, 'China rolls out experimental Covid vaccine as it eyes global market', Financial Times, 4.10.2020.

[7] https://www.reuters.com/article/us-health-coronavirus-who-china-idUSKBN26R19B

[8] https://www.globaltimes.cn/content/1200620.shtml

[9] https://ec.europa.eu/commission/presscorner/detail/en/ip_20_797

[10] James Paton, Riley Griffin, and Cynthia Koons, 'U.S. Likely to Get Sanofi Vaccine First If It Succeeds', Bloomberg. May 13,2020. https://www.bloomberg.com/news/articles/2020-05-13/u-s-to-get-sanofi-covid-vaccine-first-if-it-succeeds-ceo-says

[11] https://www.euronews.com/2020/05/14/coronavirus-vaccine-french-pharma-giant-sanofi-irks-paris-with-us-first-for-cure-comment

[12] Jon Cohen, 'Unveiling 'Warp Speed,' the White House's America-first push for a coronavirus vaccine', Science, May 12,2020. https://www.sciencemag.org/news/2020/05/unveiling-warp-speed-white-house-s-america-first-push-coronavirus-vaccine

[13] David E. Sanger, 'Trump Seeks Push to Speed Vaccine, Despite Safety Concerns', The New York Times, April 29,2020

[14] https://www.bloomberg.com/news/articles/2020-09-23/how-much-is-the-trump-administration-spending-on-a-vaccine

[15] https://www.who.int/docs/default-source/coronaviruse/risk-comms-updates/update37-vaccine-development.pdf?sfvrsn=2581e994_6

Chapter 25: A Century of War and Plague

[1] https://www.marshall.econ.cam.ac.uk/archives/economic-consequences-of-the-peace

[2] This brief analysis is focused on influenza pandemics and so omits the global AIDS/HIV pandemic which has killed 36 million since 1981, and the 1910-1 cholera pandemic which caused just under 1 million deaths.

[3] Robert Barro, Jose Ursua, Joanna Weng, 'Coronavirus meets the Great Influenza Pandemic' 20 March 2020. https://voxeu.org/article/coronavirus-meets-great-influenza-pandemic

[4] Other modern influenza outbreaks with global reach had much lower mortality rates as a share of the global population such as the East Asia (1957-58) at 0.07%, and Hong Kong (1968-69) at 0.03%.

[5] Chang, W. K. (1969). 'National Influenza Experience in Hong Kong, 1968'. *Bulletin of the World Health Organization.* WHO. 41 (3): 349–351https://apps.who.int/iris/bitstream/handle/10665/262470/PMC2427693.pdf?sequence=1&isAllowed=y

[6] 3 Barbara Salazar Torreon and Sofia Plagakis, *Instances of Use of United States Armed Forces Abroad, 1798*–2018, Washington, DC: Congressional Research Service, 2018.

[7] '20 Years of War' Watson Institute, Brown University, 2019. https://watson.brown.edu/costsofwar/files/cow/imce/papers/2019/US%20Budgetary%20Costs%20of%20Wars%20November%202019.pdf?utm_source=Daily%20on%20Defense%20(2019%20TEMPLATE)_11/15/2019&utm_medium=email&utm_campaign=WEX_Daily%20on%20Defense&rid=84648

[8] Craig Whitlock 'At War With the Truth', *The Afghanistan Papers: A secret history of the war. The Washington Post,* Dec 9, 2019. https://www.washingtonpost.com/graphics/2019/investigations/afghanistan-papers/afghanistan-war-confidential-documents/

[9] During these years AIDS was killing 3 million people annually around the world.

Chapter 26: Who Pays the Ferryman?

[1] Gunjan Banerji, 'Why Did Stock Markets Rebound From Covid in Record Time? Here Are Five Reasons', The Wall Street Journal, September 15, 2020.

[2] The World Bank. 'The Global Economic Outlook During the COVID-19 Pandemic: A Changed World', June 8, 2020. https://www.worldbank.org/en/news/feature/2020/06/08/the-global-economic-outlook-during-the-covid-19-pandemic-a-changed-world

[3] Ibid.

[4] Kate Davidson, 'U.S. Debt Is Set to Exceed Size of the Economy Next Year, a First Since World War II', *The Wall Street Journal*, September 2, 2020.

[5] Wenjie Chen, Mico Mrkaic, and Malhar Nabar 2019, 'The Global Economic Recovery 10 Years After the 2008 Financial Crisis' https://www.imf.org/en/Publications/WP/Issues/2019/04/26/The-Global-Economic-Recovery-10-Years-After-the-2008-Financial-Crisis-46711

[6] Carmen M. Reinhart and Kenneth S. Rogoff, 'Growth in a Time of Debt', *American Economic Review: Papers & Proceedings 100* (May 2010): 573–578. https://scholar.harvard.edu/files/rogoff/files/growth_in_time_debt_aer.pdf.

[7] Carmen Reinhart and Kenneth Rogoff, 'Why we should expect low growth amid debt', *Financial Times*, January 28 2010. https://scholar.harvard.edu/files/rogoff/files/why_we_should_expect.pdf

[8] Subsequent papers, without the errors, by Reinhart and Rogoff, as well as one by the IMF reached similar conclusions but with debt having less of an impact on GDP growth than the original paper suggested.

[9] Carmen M. Reinhart and Kenneth S. Rogoff, 'Debt, Growth and the Austerity Debate', *New York Times*, July 23, 2013. https://www.nytimes.com/2013/04/26/opinion/debt-growth-and-the-austerity-debate.html

[10] Paul Krugman, 'The Excel Depression', *New York Times*, April 18, 2013. https://www.nytimes.com/2013/04/26/opinion/debt-growth-and-the-austerity-debate.html

[11] Ibid.

[12] Marialuz Moreno Badia, Paulo Medas, Pranav Gupta, Yuan Xiang, 'Debt Is Not Free', IMF Working Paper January 2020.

[13] Jonathan Wheatley, 'Borrow to fight economic impact of pandemic, says World Bank's chief economist', *Financial Times*, October8, 2020. https://www.ft.com/content/0582e495-765a-46a1-98f9-ac48e80a139c

[14] Jeremy Bulow, Carmen Reinhart, Kenneth Rogoff, and Christoph Trebesch 'The Debt Pandemic: New steps are needed to improve sovereign debt workouts' September 2020 IMF p13. https://www.imf.org/external/pubs/ft/fandd/2020/09/pdf/debt-pandemic-reinhart-rogoff-bulow-trebesch.pdf

[15] Keynes, J.M., 2010. 'How to Pay for the War'. In *Essays in persuasion* (pp. 367-439). Palgrave Macmillan, London.

[16] Martin Arnold, Miles Johnson, Daniel Dombey. 'Eurozone economy: the struggle to stay afloat until a vaccine arrives', Financial Times, November 17, 2020. https://www.ft.com/content/27daf526-197f-4b48-94dc-236e49717aee

Chapter 27: The Costs of Lockdown

[1] https://www.cnbc.com/2020/03/03/who-says-coronavirus-death-rate-is-3point4percent-globally-higher-than-previously-thought.html

[2] Daniel P. Oran and Eric J. Topol, 2020. 'Prevalence of Asymptomatic SARS-CoV-2 Infection', https://www.acpjournals.org/doi/10.7326/M20-3012

[3] https://www.who.int/docs/default-source/coronaviruse/situation-reports/20200301-sitrep-41-covid-19.pdf?sfvrsn=6768306d_2

[4] https://www.reuters.com/article/us-health-coronavirus-usa-screenings-exc/exclusive-u-s-medical-testing-cancer-screenings-plunge-during-coronavirus-outbreak-data-firm-analysis-idUSKCN22A0DY

[1] Steven Woloshin, M.D., et al,' False Negative Tests for SARS-CoV-2 Infection - Challenges and Implications', *The New England Journal of Medicine*', August 26, 2020. https://www.nejm.org/doi/full/10.1056/NEJMp2015897

[2] Pilita Clark, Clive Cookson and Laura Hughes, 'How the UK got coronavirus testing wrong' *Financial Times*, March 27, 2020. https://www.ft.com/content/fa747fbd-c19e-4bac-9c37-d46afc9393fb

[3] https://www.who.int/dg/speeches/detail/who-director-general-s-opening-remarks-at-the-media-briefing-on-covid-19---16-march-2020

[4] https://www.gov.uk/government/news/government-to-monitor-impact-of-coronavirus-on-uk-medicine-supply

[5] Laura Donnelly and Tom Morgan 'UK abandoned testing because system 'could only cope with five coronavirus cases a week', *The Telegraph,* May 30, 2020. https://www.telegraph.co.uk/news/2020/05/30/revealed-test-trace-abandoned-system-could-cope-five-coronavirus/

[6] all https://www.economist.com/britain/2020/04/04/whats-gone-wrong-with-covid-19-testing-in-britain

[7] Michael D. Shear, Abby Goodnough, Sheila Kaplan, Sheri Fink, Katie Thomas, and Noah Weiland. *The New York Times*, March 28, 2020. https://www.nytimes.com/2020/03/28/us/testing-coronavirus-pandemic.html

[8] https://www.cdc.gov/about/organization/mission.htm#:~:text=As%20the%20nation's%20health%20protection,and%20responds%20when%20these%20arise

[9] Andrew Gillen, 'Lessons for Higher Education from the CDC and FDA Virus-Testing Fiasco' *National Review*, May 27, 2020.

https://www.nationalreview.com/2020/05/coronavirus-testing-fiasco-lessons-for-higher-education-accreditation-system/

Chapter 29: A Pregnancy Test for Covid

[1] https://www.prb.org/coronavirus-stress-and-fear/

[2] https://www.whitehouse.gov/briefings-statements/remarks-president-trump-vice-president-pence-members-coronavirus-task-force-press-briefing-april-17-2020/

[3] https://www.globaltimes.cn/content/1203309.shtml

[4] Lily Kuo, 'Xinjiang residents handcuffed to their homes in Covid lockdown', *The Guardian*, August 25, 2020. https://www.theguardian.com/world/2020/aug/25/xinjiang-residents-handcuffed-to-their-homes-in-covid-lockdown

[5] Nicole Kobie, 'The Complicated Truth About China's Social Credit System', *Wired*, June 7, 2019. https://www.wired.co.uk/article/china-social-credit-system-explained

[6] https://www.theguardian.com/world/2020/aug/25/xinjiang-residents-handcuffed-to-their-homes-in-covid-lockdown

[7] https://www.globaltimes.cn/content/1196804.shtml

[8] Graham Allison 'China's geopolitics are pumped up by its economic success', *Financial Times*, October 4, 2020. https://www.ft.com/content/e2902988-ca56-4d21-ab2a-b416c9006c7b

[9] https://www.theguardian.com/world/2020/oct/07/negative-views-of-china-soar-in-western-countries-poll-finds

[10] Patrick Wintour, Tobi Thomas, 'China loses trust internationally over coronavirus handling' The Guardian, October 27, 2020. https://www.theguardian.com/world/2020/oct/27/china-loses-trust-internationally-over-coronavirus-handling

Chapter 30: China Rising

[1] https://archive.nytimes.com/www.nytimes.com/library/world/asia/052500clinton-trade-text.html

[2] Prof. Paul Krugman won the Nobel Prize for Economics in 2008 for his contribution to International Trade Theory.

[3] Paul Krugman, 'Reckonings; A Symbol Issue', *New York Times*, May 10, 2000. https://www.nytimes.com/2000/05/10/opinion/reckonings-a-symbol-issue.html

[4] David H. Autor et al 2016, 'The China Shock: Learning from Labor Market Adjustment to Large Changes in Trade', National Bureau of Economic Research. https://www.nber.org/papers/w21906

[5] https://www.who.int/medicines/publications/essentialmedicines/en/

[6] Gardiner Harris, 'Heparin Contamination May Have Been Deliberate, F.D.A. Says', *New York Times*, April 30, 2008. https://www.nytimes.com/2008/04/30/health/policy/30heparin.html

[7] Qiao Lang, Wang Xiangsui, 1999. *Unrestricted Warfare*, People's Liberation Army Literature and Arts Publishing House.

[8] Quoted in Elizabeth C. Economy, 2019, 4. *The Third Revolution: Xi Jinping and the New Chinese State*, Oxford University Press.

[9] Tetsushi Takahashi, 'China's 'resist America' rallying cry resonates 70 years on', *Nikkei Asia*, October 26.2020. https://asia.nikkei.com/Spotlight/Beijing-Diary/China-s-resist-America-rallying-cry-resonates-70-years-on

[10] http://www.xinhuanet.com/politics/2020-10/29/c_1126674147.htm

[11] Brahma Chellaney, 'The Quad sharpens its edges', *The Strategist*, Australian Strategic Policy Initiative. October 19, 2020. https://www.aspistrategist.org.au/the-quad-sharpens-its-edges/

[12] Ambrose Evans-Pritchard, 'Hint of menace from China's new routemap', *The Telegraph*, November 1, 2020. https://www.telegraph.co.uk/business/2020/11/01/hint-menace-chinas-new-routemap/

[13] http://www.xinhuanet.com/politics/2020-10/29/c_1126674147.htm

[14] Elizabeth C. Economy, 2019. The Third Revolution: Xi Jinping and the new Chinese state, p124.

[15] Quoted in Elizabeth C. Economy, 2019. *The Third Revolution: Xi Jinping and the new Chinese state*, p141. From original interview with Ai Weiwei in the *Guardian*, April 12. 2012.

[16] Hung, H.F., 2015. *The China boom: Why China will not rule the world.* Columbia University Press. The title is an apparent retort to the book by the Sinophile Marxist, Martin Jacques, *When China Rules the World.*

[17] Ibid.

Index